D1001753

LONDON RECORD SOCIETY
PUBLICATIONS

VOLUME XXII
FOR THE YEAR 1985

Dedicated to William Kellaway, Hon. General
Editor of the London Record Society, 1964–1983.

A SURVEY OF DOCUMENTARY SOURCES FOR PROPERTY HOLDING IN LONDON BEFORE THE GREAT FIRE

DEREK KEENE AND VANESSA HARDING

LONDON RECORD SOCIETY
1985

The publication of this volume has been assisted by a grant from the
Twenty-Seven Foundation

Phototypeset by
Wyvern Typesetting Ltd, Bristol
Printed in Great Britain by
The Bath Press

CONTENTS

Contents

ACKNOWLEDGEMENTS

Research for this survey was undertaken as part of the work of the Social and Economic Study of Medieval London, funded by the Social Science Research Council, 1979–83 (grant number D00/23/004), attached to the Institute of Historical Research, and housed and assisted by the Museum of London.

In compiling the survey we have had help from many quarters. We would like to thank, first, the archivists and librarians of public collections for assistance on our visits and for answers to written queries. We are particularly grateful to those private persons, and to the governing bodies of those livery companies, cathedrals, Oxford and Cambridge colleges, schools, and other institutions, who keep their own records, for allowing us to see them, and to their librarians and archivists for assistance in doing so. The following have helped with advice or by providing copies and notes from records: Caroline Barron, Christopher Brooke, Martha Carlin, Chris Cooper, Tony Dyson, Judith Green, Jonathan Hunn, Jean Imray, Gillian Keir, Betty Masters, Rosalind Ransford, Carole Rawcliffe, John Schofield, Anne Sutton, and Colin Taylor. Joanna Mattingly, assistant to the Social and Economic Study of Medieval London, checked several sources and lists, and typed the whole text. Our special thanks are due to William Kellaway, without whose help and encouragement neither this survey nor the Social and Economic Study of Medieval London would have come into being.

ABBREVIATIONS

This list does not include short titles of works used within entries or groups of entries where the full title is also given.

abs.	abstract
a/c(s)	accounts(s)
bk(s).	book(s)
BL	British Library, Department of Manuscripts
BMB	baptisms, marriages, and burials; in relation to parish registers
Bodl	Oxford, Bodleian Library
B.R.A.	British Records Association
C	century; used in the form 17C, for seventeenth century, etc.
Cal. Chart. R.	*Calendar of Charter Rolls*
Cal. Docs. France	*Calendar of Documents preserved in France, illustrative of the history of Great Britain and Ireland* i, *918–1206*, ed. J. H. Round (1899)
Cal. Pat. R.	*Calendar of Patent Rolls*
Cal. Wills	*Calendar of Wills proved and enrolled in the Court of Husting, London, 1258–1688*, ed. R. R. Sharpe (1889–90)
Char. Com.	Charity Commission
CLRO	Corporation of London Records Office
comp.	compiled
cont.	contain(s), containing
Ct.	Court; as in Fire Ct.
CUL	Cambridge University Library
Davis	G. R. C. Davis, *Medieval Cartularies of Great Britain* (1958)
DB	Domesday Book
dep.	dependent
diss.	dissolved
EconHR	*Economic History Review*
EETS	Early English Text Society
EHR	*English Historical Review*
fd.	founded
GL	Guildhall Library
GLRO	Greater London Record Office
Harben	H. A. Harben, *A Dictionary of London* (1918)
HMC	Historical Manuscripts Commission; the published reports on collections are cited in the

	form HMC (8) *Ninth Report*, where the number in brackets denotes the number assigned in the list in HMSO *Sectional List* 17 (1979), 4–18
HMSO	Her Majesty's Stationery Office
HR	Husting Roll
IHR	University of London, Institute of Historical Research
incl.	include(s), including
Lambeth	Lambeth Palace Library
L&I	Public Record Office *Lists and Indexes*, listed in HMSO *Sectional List* 24 (1983), 30–7
L & P Henry VIII	*Letters and Papers of Henry VIII*
LBA, LBB, etc.	*Calendar of Letter Books A-L*, ed. R. R. Sharpe (1899–1912)
LMAS	London and Middlesex Archaeological Society
London Eyre 1244	*The London Eyre of 1244*, ed. H. M. Chew and M. Weinbaum (LRS 6, 1970)
LRS	London Record Society
LTR	*London Topographical Record*
LTS	London Topographical Society
min(s).	minutes(s); as in min. bk.
misc.	miscellaneous
Mon. Angl.	W. Dugdale, *Monasticon Anglicanum*, ed. J. Caley, H. Ellis, and B. Bandinel (6 vols., 1817–30, repr. 1846)
MS(S)	manuscript(s)
n.d.	not dated
NRA	National Register of Archives; see also HMC
par(s).	parish(es)
PCC	Prerogative Court of Canterbury
PRO	Public Record Office
PRO *Guide*	*Guide to the Contents of the Public Record Office* (2 vols., HMSO, 1963)
prop.	property
ref(s).	reference(s)
reg.	register
Regesta	*Regesta Regum Anglo-Normannorum*, 1066–1154, 3 vols. ed. H. W. C. Davis, C. Johnson, H. A. Cronne, R. H. C. Davis (1913, 1956, 1968–9)
RHS	Royal Historical Society
RO	Record Office
SSRC	Social Science Research Council (from 1984 Economic and Social Research Council)
Tax. Eccl.	*Taxatio Ecclesiastica Angliae et Walliae auctoritate Papae Nicholai IV*, circa *1291*, ed. S. Ayscough and J. Caley (Record Commission, 1802)
Trans LMAS	*Transactions of the London and Middlesex Archaeological Society*

INTRODUCTION

Records of property holding comprise one of the bulkiest, and most intractable, categories of written sources for the history of medieval and early modern towns. Few European cities, if any, are richer than London in such records. The aim of this survey is to render more readily usable the mass of documentation for property holding in the city of London up to the time of the Great Fire of 1666. The records are numerous from the twelfth century onwards,[1] and can be used to trace the histories of houses and their owners and occupiers, to map the property boundaries, to study patterns of land use and the social geography of the city, to reconstruct the physical arrangement of houses and other buildings, to follow in detail programmes of building and repair, and to chart the operation of the property market. The sources are thus of value for archaeologists and geographers, as well as for historians and all those with an interest in the city and its inhabitants before the Fire. The survey is arranged so that the records concerning particular localities in the city, defined principally according to the parishes in which they lay, may readily be identified. Much of the information was collected in the course of a detailed study of a sample group of parishes in the Cheapside area, which showed how this material can be used as evidence not only for the history of particular sites but also for elucidating the development of the city as a whole over a long period.[2]

The scope of the survey
This book surveys the documentary sources for the histories of properties and property holding in the city of London up to the Great Fire of 1666. The sources, found in record offices and collections in London and elsewhere, fall into two main groups: documents of title and records of estate management. The former, comprising original deeds and leases and copies in cartularies and registers, are numerous from the twelfth century onwards. From the thirteenth century, when they begin to survive in even greater quantities and acquire a new topographical precision, London title deeds can, in most cases, be related to particular sites on the ground. The records of property management comprise rentals, surveys, accounts, minute-books, papers, and plans. Some London rentals and accounts survive from the twelfth and thirteenth centuries, and more frequently from the fourteenth and fifteenth centuries, but they do not become numerous until after 1500, with the

1. For Pre-Conquest charters relating to London, see C. N. L. Brooke and G. Keir, *London, 800–1216: the shaping of a city* (1975), 367–70.
2. Derek Keene, 'A new study of London before the Great Fire', *Urban History Yearbook 1984*, 11–21.

increasing survival of city livery company and parish archives. They can record the names of tenants and the sums of rent paid, and, up to c. 1550, can provide extensive records of payments for building and repairs. From c. 1550 onwards the records of the deliberations of corporate bodies on the management of their holdings are increasingly informative. The great expansion of the city in the late sixteenth and early seventeenth centuries caused many landlords to have detailed surveys made of the value and structural character of their properties.

The provenance of the principal bodies of records varies over this long period. Up to the mid sixteenth century the records of property holding in the city mainly concern, on the one hand, the properties of those private individuals whose deeds and wills were enrolled in the Court of Husting (cf. 2) and, on the other, the estates belonging to religious houses or similar bodies. Records of title in the latter group can concern many transactions between private individuals. In the sixteenth and seventeenth centuries the records concern principally the holdings of corporate landlords, who by this time owned a large proportion of the land within the city. Records of property holding produced in this period for private individuals, who were in general more directly concerned with the occupation of the land, are still numerous but are less readily identifiable and provide less comprehensive coverage than formerly.

A third category of sources covered by this survey comprises administrative and judicial records of local and national government. These concern not only the estates in the possession of the City and the Crown, but also escheats, the regulation of nuisance, and disputes over ownership. Taxation- and assessment-lists of a topographical character are also described in the survey.

The Great Fire of 1666 is an obvious limit to take for a survey of sources concerning the topographical development of the city, not least on account of the records engendered by the process of rebuilding immediately afterwards (11). Other sources later than 1666 which have been covered include copies of earlier records, now lost, and plans or surveys of the seventeenth, eighteenth, or nineteenth centuries of value for identifying or understanding pre-Fire holdings. No attempt has been made to cover graphic or cartographic records of London before the Fire, other than those, essentially plans of individual holdings, produced for landlords.

In topographical extent the survey is restricted to records of properties within the liberty of the city of London, that is the walled area and the extra-mural suburbs under the city's jurisdiction. In most records of title, even in the seventeenth century when London sprawled beyond the city's limits, the distinction between the city and its suburbs on the one hand, and the county of Middlesex on the other, is scrupulously maintained; but on occasion with these records, and more frequently with other sources, it is not possible to tell whether properties in extra-mural parishes which straddled the liberty boundary lay within the city or not. In such cases, where doubt exists, references have been included in the survey. An attempt has been made to include references to areas, such as the parish of Holy Trinity Minories or the precinct of St. Katharine's Hospital, which in the earlier Middle Ages appear to have been within the city, but which later lay outside it. Records relating to Southwark are not covered. Readers should note that this necessarily restrictive policy has led to the exclusion from the survey of records concerning the important extra-mural settlement extending along the Strand towards Westminster.

The survey covers collections, public and private, in the United Kingdom, with some exceptions noted below, and includes notes on a number of collections in the United States of America (**518–28**). There are also noted, from printed sources, some collections in continental archives (**266–74**).

The survey is intended to be complete within these limits, but inevitably there will be omissions. In some cases these will be in fields which we have surveyed; where we are aware of them, they have been pointed out. This is particularly true of the Public Record Office entries (**436–53**), where several potentially interesting classes could only be sampled. Other omissions will be archives which we have not noticed. In general, we have not attempted to survey the archives of present-day property owning bodies founded after *c.* 1670, although some of these may contain records of title from the seventeenth century or earlier. The problems of identifying such holders, and of gaining access to their records, seemed too great if the survey was to be completed within the time available. The archive of British Rail, a substantial freeholder in the city, has not been consulted.

The arrangement of the survey
Each entry in the survey is identified by a number in **bold**. After an account of the Corporation of London archive, covering both judicial and estate records (**1–15**), the survey falls into two main parts. The first (**16–435**) consists of separate descriptions of the archives of individual property holders, principally institutions, arranged in several sections. The introductions to these sections describe the systematic procedures adopted in identifying the archives. Many of the institutions covered are now defunct (as most of **70–274**, religious houses and bishoprics), but their archives, and a picture of their estates in London, can be reconstructed from records surviving in the Public Record Office, the British Library, and elsewhere. Not all the surviving bodies still hold the London properties once in their possession. Many of the surviving institutions still hold their own records, but a number, including most of the city livery companies (**16–69**), have deposited their archives in record offices. A few private archives, mostly still in their owners' hands, are also noted (**420–35**).

The main Public Record Office classes relevant to the survey are described next (**436–53**), with indexes to deeds and miscellaneous accounts and a brief guide to Crown estate and administrative and judicial records.

The second main part of the survey (**454–528**) is arranged by repository (libraries and record offices in England, Wales, Scotland, Northern Ireland, and the United States of America) and covers collections of records, mostly of family origin, which do not constitute significant, separate archives in their own right. Items from institutional archives in these repositories are described in the earlier part of the survey.

Finally, there is a short section (**529–30**) noting the location of London wills and inventories.

The entries in the survey

An entry concerning the records of a property-holding institution generally begins with a brief account of the institution and the location of its archive, together with a statement on the topographical extent of its estate in the city. The records subsequently described in the entry concern that estate, unless more specific details are given. In many cases records of title will include some deeds or references concerning properties not acquired by the institution, and the coverage of such references will be indicated. Since many institutions built their estates up gradually, and at times lost parts of them, the records described in any particular group will not necessarily concern all the properties in the possession of the institution during the period covered by this survey. Major changes in an estate are covered by the statement at the beginning of an entry. For minor changes, in particular those arising from the progressive accumulation of properties, reference should be made to cartularies, registers, 'will books', or rentals, which can provide a guide to the date of acquisition of a property, after which it will be covered by records of a continuous administrative character.

Entries containing descriptions of the records of property-holding institutions are arranged by lettered (lower case **bold**) paragraphs covering topics in the following order: deeds and leases; cartularies, registers, and lease books; rentals and accounts; administrative records, principally minute books or act books; miscellaneous papers; plans. Where an archive is particularly large and complex, each of these categories is dealt with in a separately numbered entry. Not all these categories are present in every case, and different kinds of institution may have had slightly different practices of estate management and archive arrangement which dictate variations in the arrangement of entries. The descriptions of records include reference or call numbers and other means of identification, references to printed editions, approximate dates for both contents and compilation, references to any index or other searching aid, and, if necessary, a particular description of the topographical coverage of the record (generally in parentheses at the end of the description).

Sources in libraries and record offices (**454–528**) are usually listed with a separate paragraph for each large collection or deposit, with details of date and coverage. Most of these collections consist of deeds and papers only, but when there is material of other kinds it is listed in the form used in descriptions of separate archives in the earlier part of the survey.

The judicial and administrative records in the Corporation of London Records Office and the Public Record Office are described briefly, with an indication of the character and scope of the records and notes on dates, topographical coverage, and guides and indexes.

It should be noted that many of the archives of institutions covered by the survey include material of interest which does not relate to or arise from property holding, and so is not described here. Thus, no reference is made to records concerning the internal economies of religious houses, to the apprenticeship registers or quarterage books of livery companies, or to the records of poor-relief payments prominent in parochial records.

The means of topographical reference

The primary means of defining the location of a property in the city between the twelfth and late sixteenth century, in both deeds and other records, was by reference to the parish or parishes in which it lay. The practice remained common in deeds even after the Fire. The London parishes were numerous and their boundaries appear to have been constant from the twelfth century onwards; only a handful of parishes had been lost by the time of the Fire, and the boundaries of those surviving at that date are recorded on accurate modern maps. When seeking the pre-Fire records of any property it is essential to know the parish in which that property lay. Wherever possible, therefore, parish references have been adopted in this survey as the means of defining the topographical coverage of the records. In the survey entries, parishes are identified by means of a series of coded references, *1–162*, printed in *italic*. The code is explained fully on pp. xvii–xix, with a map. References to parishes are indexed on pp. 223–32, as Part ii of the Topographical Index.

In some cases the records refer only to street- or house-names, or to unspecified locations within London, and the parish or parishes within which the property lay cannot be identified. In these cases the survey entries give the street- or house-name, or 'unspec.' or 'London unspec.', according to context, and these references are indexed on pp. 233–8, in Part iii of the Topographical Index. In almost all cases of 'unspecified location in London', except where the reference derives from a record office index, it is probable that the property lay within the city and its suburbs and not outside the liberty. Part iii of the Topographical Index also includes the few references to properties outside the city which are mentioned in the survey.

In addition, reference should always be made to those entries, indexed on pp. 222–3 as Part i of the Topographical Index, describing classes of records which cover many or all parts of the city, and of which some are adequately indexed elsewhere.

Index to property- and archive-holders

The second index, on pp. 239–46, is a combined alphabetical index to the holders of property in London, and to the libraries and record offices where collections relating to London are held, as they are described in the headings to individual entries. This index does not identify all entries in which records in a particular collection may be mentioned, nor does it cover those private property holders whose present or former records are described in entries concerning libraries and record offices.

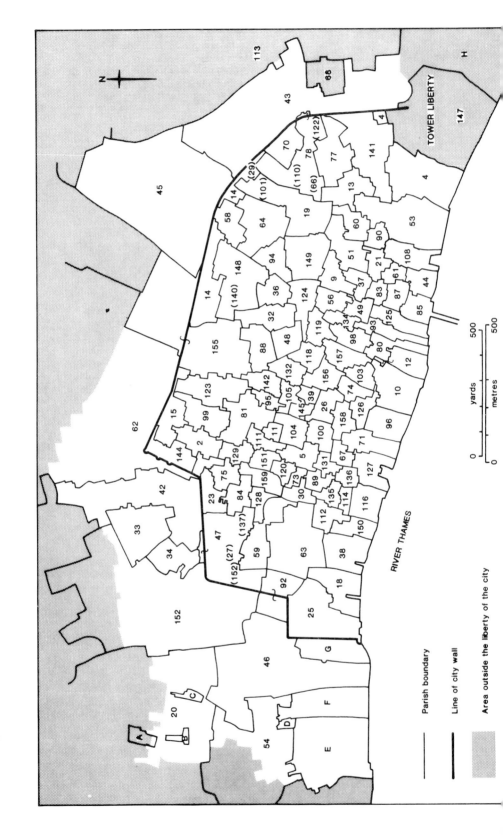

TOWER LIBERTY

RIVER THAMES

N

113
68
43
4
147
H

45
14
58
(29)
(101)
70
78
(122)
77
141
4

64
19
(110)
(66)
13
53

148
(140)
94
149
51
60
90

14
36
124
9
37
21
108
61
44

155
32
56
83
87
85

88
48
118
119
134
49
93
125
80

123
142
132
157
98
80
12

95
105
39
156
74
103
10

15
99
81
26
158
126
96

144
2
129
111
11
104
100
67
71
127

75
151
5
131
136

23
84
128
159
120
73
89
135
114
116
150

47
(137)
30
112
38

42
(152)
(27)
59
92
63
18

33
34
152
25

20
C
46
G

A
B
D
F

54
E

0   500   yards
0   500   metres

_____ Parish boundary

_____ Line of city wall

▨ Area outside the liberty of the city

KEY TO PARISH REFERENCES

The reference numbers *1–162* printed in *italic* in the text identify the parish in which the property described by the document(s) lay. A list of parish names and numbers is printed on the following two pages. The series covers the parishes of which all or a part lay in the city, and includes extra numbers for uncertainties (as when a parish is referred to only as 'All Hallows' or 'St. Mary') and for variant or successive dedications. Parish numbers marked with an asterisk * in the list are shown on the map of parish boundaries, opposite. Asterisks within parentheses denote parishes which had ceased to exist by the period depicted on the map.

The city parishes remained remarkably constant in size and number from the early medieval period. The creation, in the twelfth and thirteenth centuries, of precincts for religious houses led to the disappearance of some (*66, 110, 122, 140*) and the alteration in size of many others; two more (*29, 101*) were abolished in the fifteenth and sixteenth centuries, respectively; six new parishes were created as a result of the dissolution of the religious houses (*25, 33, 34, 47, 68*, in the sixteenth century; *70* in the seventeenth century).

Parishes are listed alphabetically by dedication (ignoring 'Saint', but observing 'All' and 'Holy') and by the 'surname' current *c.* 1350, which may not be the modern one (ignoring words such as at, de, le, etc.). The common surname variants are listed in parentheses, but do not have separate numbers; less common surnames can be found in H. A. Harben, *A Dictionary of London* (1918). Latin surnames are only noted where the English form is not an exact equivalent. Alternative dedications are listed in the form 'alias *100*'. A brief note on dates of creation and/or abolition is included if appropriate. Some unusual or erroneous parish names which occur in sources described in the survey are listed in the Topographical Index on p. 222.

MAP OF LONDON PARISHES

The map is based on the boundaries shown on the Ordnance Survey 1:2500 plan, 1878 edition, with minor adjustments. It shows the boundaries as they existed on the eve of the Great Fire. The numbers represent parishes: only those marked * in the list are shown. Numbers in parentheses represent parishes, or parts of parishes, which had been suppressed, and their approximate location. The letters represent extra-parochial precincts or liberties as follows: A, Furnival's Inn; B, Barnard's Inn; C, Thavie's Inn; D, Serjeants' Inn; E, Temple; F, Whitefriars; G, Bridewell (formerly part of *46*); H, St. Katharine's Hospital.

Key to Parish References

1 St. Agnes (alias *23, 24*)
* 2 St. Alban Wood Street
3 All Hallows (unspecified)
* 4 All Hallows Barking (by the Tower; alias *102*)
* 5 All Hallows Bread Street (Watling Street)
6 All Hallows Colemanchurch (alias *50, 77*)
7 All Hallows Cornhill (probably identical with *9*)
8 All Hallows Fenchurch (alias *60, 106, 107*)
* 9 All Hallows Gracechurch (Lombard Street; probably identical with *7*)
* 10 All Hallows the Great (*ad fenum*, at the Hay Wharf, in the Ropery; earlier *Semannescyrce*)
* 11 All Hallows Honey Lane
* 12 All Hallows the Less (on the Cellars, on the Solars)
* 13 All Hallows Staining
* 14 All Hallows on the Wall (London Wall; *29* added, 1442)
* 15 St. Alphage
16 St. Amand (alias *159, 160*)
17 St. Andrew (unspecified)
* 18 St. Andrew Castle Baynard (by the Wardrobe)
* 19 St. Andrew Cornhill (*atte Knappe*, Undershaft; *101* added, 1565)
* 20 St. Andrew Holborn
* 21 St. Andrew Hubbard (Eastcheap, towards the Tower)
22 St. Anne (unspecified)
* 23 St. Anne & St. Agnes (alias *1, 24*)
24 St. Anne Aldersgate (alias *1, 23*)
* 25 St. Anne Blackfriars (created after the Dissolution from Blackfriars precinct)
* 26 St. Antonin (later St. Antholin)
(*) 27 St. Audoen (alias St. Ewen, St. Owen; taken into *47*, 1547)
28 St. Augustine (unspecified)
(*) 29 St. Augustine Papey (on the Wall; joined to *14*, 1442)
* 30 St. Augustine by St. Paul (*parvus*, Watling Street)
31 St. Bartholomew (unspecified)
* 32 St. Bartholomew the Little (by the Exchange)
* 33 St Bartholomew the Great (created after Dissolution from precinct of St. Bartholomew's Priory)
* 34 St. Bartholomew the Less (created after Dissolution from precinct of St. Bartholomew's Hospital)
35 St. Benet (unspecified)
* 36 St. Benet Fink

* 37 St. Benet Gracechurch
* 38 St. Benet Paul's Wharf (Hithe, Woodwharf)
* 39 St. Benet Sherehog (alias *40, 153*)
40 St. Benet & St. Sithe (alias *39, 153*)
41 St. Botolph (unspecified)
* 42 St. Botolph without Aldersgate
* 43 St. Botolph without Aldgate
* 44 St. Botolph Billingsgate
* 45 St. Botolph without Bishopsgate
* 46 St. Bride (Fleet Street)
* 47 Christ Church Newgate Street (created 1547 from Grey Friars precinct, *27, 137*, intramural part of *152*)
* 48 St. Christopher (le Stocks)
* 49 St. Clement (Candlewick Street, Eastcheap)
50 Colemanchurch (alias *6, 77*)
* 51 St. Dionis Backchurch
52 St. Dunstan (unspecified)
* 53 St. Dunstan in the East (towards the Tower)
* 54 St. Dunstan in the West (Fleet Street)
55 St. Edmund (unspecified)
* 56 St. Edmund Lombard Street (King and Martyr)
57 St. Edmund without Newgate (alias *152*)
* 58 St. Ethelburga
* 59 St. Faith (by St. Paul's)
* 60 St. Gabriel (Fenchurch; alias *8, 106, 107*)
* 61 St. George (Botolph Lane, Eastcheap)
* 62 St. Giles Cripplegate
* 63 St. Gregory (by St. Paul's)
* 64 St. Helen (Bishopsgate)
65 Holy Trinity (unspecified)
(*) 66 Holy Trinity Aldgate (absorbed by *78* or precinct of Holy Trinity Priory)
* 67 Holy Trinity the Less
* 68 Holy Trinity Minories (created after the Dissolution from the Minoresses' precinct)
69 St. James (unspecified)
* 70 St. James Duke's Place (created 17C from former precinct of Holy Trinity Priory)
* 71 St. James Garlickhithe (Vintry)
72 St. John (unspecified)
* 73 St. John the Evangelist (Watling Street; earlier *162*)
* 74 St. John Walbrook
* 75 St. John Zachary
76 St. Katharine (unspecified)
* 77 St. Katharine Coleman (alias *6, 50*)
* 78 St. Katharine Cree (Christ Church)
79 St. Lawrence (unspecified)

* 80 St. Lawrence Candlewick Street (Pountney)
* 81 St. Lawrence Jewry
82 St. Leonard (unspecified)
* 83 St. Leonard Eastcheap
* 84 St. Leonard Foster Lane
* 85 St. Magnus (Bridge, the Martyr)
86 St. Margaret (unspecified)
* 87 St. Margaret Bridge Street (New Fish Street)
* 88 St. Margaret Lothbury
* 89 St. Margaret Moses (Friday Street)
* 90 St. Margaret Pattens
91 St. Martin (unspecified)
* 92 St. Martin Ludgate
* 93 St. Martin Orgar (Candlewick Street)
* 94 St. Martin Outwich
* 95 St. Martin Pomary (Ironmonger Lane)
* 96 St. Martin Vintry (Bermanchurch)
97 St. Mary (unspecified)
* 98 St. Mary Abchurch
* 99 St. Mary Aldermanbury
* 100 St. Mary Aldermary
(*)101 St. Mary Axe (joined to 19, 1565)
102 St. Mary de Berkyngcherch (alias 4)
* 103 St. Mary Bothaw
* 104 St. Mary le Bow (de Arcubus)
* 105 St. Mary Colechurch
106 St. Mary Fenchurch (alias 8, 60, 107)
107 St. Mary & St. Gabriel Fenchurch (alias 8, 60, 106)
* 108 St. Mary at Hill
109 St. Mary Magdalen (unspecified)
(*)110 St. Mary Magdalen Aldgate (absorbed by 78 or precinct of Holy Trinity Priory)
* 111 St. Mary Magdalen Milk Street
* 112 St. Mary Magdalen Old Fish Street (in (nova) piscaria, Westpiscaria; earlier 161)
* 113 St. Mary Matfellon (Whitechapel)
* 114 St. Mary Mounthaw
115 St. Mary Olaf (alias 144)
* 116 St. Mary Somerset
* 117 St. Mary Staining
* 118 St. Mary Woolchurch (Newchurch)
* 119 St. Mary Woolnoth
* 120 St. Matthew Friday Street
121 St. Michael (unspecified)
(*)122 St. Michael Aldgate (absorbed by 78 or precinct of Holy Trinity Priory)
* 123 St. Michael Bassishaw
* 124 St. Michael Cornhill

* 125 St. Michael Crooked Lane (Candlewick Street)
* 126 St. Michael Paternoster (Paternoster Royal, in the Riole)
* 127 St. Michael Queenhithe (Ripa Regine)
* 128 St. Michael le Querne (ad bladum, ubi bladum venditur, atte Corne, in foro)
* 129 St. Michael Wood Street (Huggin Lane)
130 St. Mildred (unspecified)
* 131 St. Mildred Bread Street
132 St. Mildred Poultry (Walbrook)
133 St. Nicholas (unspecified)
* 134 St. Nicholas Acon (Hakon)
* 135 St. Nicholas Cole Abbey (Old Fish Street, in piscaria, Westpiscaria)
* 136 St. Nicholas Olave (Bernard, ? in piscaria; alias 139)
(*)137 St. Nicholas in the Shambles (alias 143; taken into 47, 1547)
138 St. Olave (unspecified)
139 St. Olave Bread Street (alias 136)
(*)140 St. Olave Broad Street (absorbed by Austin Friars precinct and later 148)
* 141 St. Olave Hart Street (Crutched Friars, Mark Lane, by the Tower)
* 142 St. Olave Old Jewry
143 St. Olave in the Shambles (alias 137)
* 144 St. Olave Silver Street (Cripplegate, Monkwell Street; alias 115)
* 145 St. Pancras (Soper Lane)
146 St. Peter (unspecified)
* 147 St. Peter in the Bailey (in the Tower, ad Vincula)
* 148 St. Peter Broad Street (the Poor; incl. former Austin Friars precinct and 140 from 16C)
* 149 St. Peter Cornhill
* 150 St. Peter Paul's Wharf (the Less)
* 151 St. Peter Westcheap (Wood Street)
* 152 St. Sepulchre (without Newgate; alias 57; part taken into 47, 1547)
153 St. Sithe (alias 39, 40)
154 St. Stephen (unspecified)
* 155 St. Stephen Coleman Street
* 156 St. Stephen Walbrook
* 157 St. Swithin (Candlewick Street, London Stone)
* 158 St. Thomas the Apostle
* 159 St. Vedast (Foster Lane; alias 16, 160)
160 St. Vedast & St. Amand (alias 16, 159)
161 St. Wandrille (later 112)
162 St. Werburga (later 73)

SURVEY OF SOURCES

CORPORATION OF LONDON

The archive of the Corporation (Corporation of London Records Office, Guildhall) is the most valuable single collection of material for the topographical study of pre-Fire London. It contains a mass of administrative and judicial records with information from the mid 13C onwards relating to the properties of individual citizens, described here under the various courts or aspects of the governing body under which they were created, and also the records of 3 of the estates (Corporation, Bridge House, and Gresham) in which the Corporation had a proprietary or supervisory interest. The archives of the Royal Hospitals, of which the mayor and aldermen were governors, are located elsewhere, but see **3c** below. Records of the eyres or sessions of royal justices sitting at the Tower, some copies of which survive in CLRO, are described under PRO (**445**) as being essentially records of central government. However, all the records relating to rebuilding after the Great Fire, now in several record offices, are described in this section (**11**). The survival rate of the Corporation records has been high, and many are now calendared, indexed, or usefully described, in print or MS. See also P. E. Jones and R. Smith, *A Guide to the Records in the Corporation of London Records Office and the Guildhall Library Muniment Room* (1950). The collections in Guildhall Library are described under **459–60** and elsewhere.

1. CLRO: CHARTERS, CUSTUMALS, ETC.

Charters and custumals (listed in Jones and Smith, *Guide*, 20–4) are of more value for the history of London in general than for particular topographical studies. 'Liber Custumarum', comp. 14C, includes charters and ordinances relating to trading in various parts of the city, some memoranda relating to benefices and tithes in 1292, details of a dispute concerning the Fishwharf *c.* 1321 (*85*), and a valuable view of the lanes leading to the Thames in 1343. 'Liber Albus', comp. bef. 1419, also contains charters and ordinances, and notes on the procedure of the Husting and other courts. Both these are printed, with introductions, as *Munimenta Gildhallae Londoniensis*, vols. i–iii (in 4), ed. H. T. Riley (Rolls Ser. 1859–62); the latter is also translated and printed as *Liber Albus*, ed. H. T. Riley (1861).

Most of the other custumals etc. are derived from these or other books, of which 'Liber Horn', comp. *c.* 1311, is the earliest. However, 'Liber Lynne' is a 15C cartulary, made for John Lawneye, citizen and grocer, of 13C to 15C deeds concerning King's Lynn and London (*4, 19, 44, 51, 53, 103, 106*); the reason for its presence among the city's archives is not clear. The Lynn section is noted in *The Making of King's Lynn*, vol. 3: *A Survey of documentary sources for the Middle Ages*, ed. D. M. Owen (British Academy, Records of Social and Economic History, n.s. ix, 1984).

2. CLRO: COURT OF HUSTING

The records of this court, which existed in the 11C or earlier,[1] begin in the 13C. It was the county court of the city, and by the mid 13C met weekly to hear common pleas, pleas of land, and the probate of testaments and enrolment of private deeds. Each of these 3 functions generated a separate set of records. Admissions to the freedom and outlawries were also recorded in the pleas of land and common pleas rolls in the 13th and 14th centuries; Misc. Roll KK is a separate roll of outlawries, 1415–17.

a. Before the end of the 12C, citizens were publicising transactions concerning land in the Husting Court. From the mid 13C, deeds and wills were read at the weekly Husting Court and copied (at first in abstract and by the mid 14C verbatim) into a series of 388 rolls, 1252 to date. Enrolment of deeds was a particularly popular way of registering title (having the force of a fine in common law) between the late 13C and the early 15C. Some 30,000 deeds and wills had been enrolled by 1700, but very few enrolments were made thereafter.[2] The wills are calendared and printed, with an introduction, as *Calendar of Wills proved and enrolled in the Court of Husting, London, 1258–1688*, ed. R. R. Sharpe (1889–90); see **529a**. The deeds are briefly calendared by Sharpe in 9 MS vols., and the calendars indexed by names and places in 5 MS vols., in CLRO. Sharpe's calendar entries commonly omit second or subsequent properties recorded in deeds. For the acknowledgement of leases in Husting, see **3a**.

b. Common pleas were heard alternate weeks by the Court of Husting. Pleas of nam (unjust distraint) provide most topographical information; pleas of execution of testament and dower can be valuable, but parishes are not always named. Agreements and otherwise unrecorded deeds may be included. Pleas of error, intrusion, and nuisance were also entered but not usually heard. The 172 rolls (1272–1506) are not indexed, but much useful information can be gathered by scanning them.

c. Pleas of Land were heard alternate weeks by the Court of Husting. The sessions were distinguished by their cognizance of pleas begun under writs of right patent, which can provide much topographical and tenurial information, although parishes are not always given. Of similar value are the pleas of dower, execution of testament, and mort d'ancestor. All these may include details of otherwise unrecorded deeds. Pleas of intrusion and nuisance were also entered, but not usually heard, although the relevant parishes are usually named. From 1461 onwards the rolls

---

1. F. M. Stenton, 'Norman London' in *Preparatory to Anglo Saxon England*, ed. D. M. Stenton (1970), 30–1.
2. The rolls from 1717 to 1838 were destroyed in the fire at the Royal Exchange. Enrolments in the 19C and 20C are of a different character.

(nos. 168–216) contain only actions, presumably fictitious, under writs of right and leading to recoveries. These actions are briefly calendared by Sharpe in a MS volume, where the entries sometimes fail to list all the locations given in the original. There is a separate index to the names and places given in the calendar. There is no guide to the contents of the earlier rolls (1–167, from 1273), but much of value can be gathered by scanning them. Mayor's Court Original Bills file 5C is a bundle of writs relating to the Husting Court, Pleas of Land, 1569–71.

d. Husting Books: 10 vols. cover the periods 1448–86 and 1506–1680. These provide a record of the meetings of the Court of Husting with notices of both common pleas and pleas of land; parishes are given, but not details of pleading. They also record admissions of aliens to the liberty. Earlier notes of meetings of the court are in Journals (see **3b**) vols. 3 and 4. There is no guide to the contents.

3. CLRO: COURT OF COMMON COUNCIL AND COURT OF ALDERMEN
a. Letter Books: 50 vols., 1275–1689, so called from the letters of the alphabet by which they have been known since the fourteenth century. Books A to L, 1275–1498, are calendared by R. R. Sharpe, as *Calendar of Letter Books A–L* (1899–1912), and the series is described principally in his introduction to Letter Book A. Full translations of many extracts from Books A to I are in *Memorials of London and London Life in the XIIIth, XIVth, and XVth Centuries*, ed. H. T. Riley (1868). The books contain the earliest proceedings of the Court of Common Council and the Court of Aldermen.

The greater part of books A and B consists of sections of a register of recognizances of debts, 1275–94 and 1310–13. This has no connection with the rolls of recognizances kept by the city under the provisions of the statute of Acton Burnel (CLRO, Recognizance Rolls 1–12, 1285–1392; location 241A) which contain no references to real property. Books A and B also include sections of a register of leases of privately-owned properties acknowledged in the Court of Husting during 1281–3, 1295, and 1299–1300. Book B includes copies of the now lost coroners' rolls for 1275–8. These two books appear to have been made up during the reign of Edward II out of the fragmentary remains of series of records which no longer exist independently. Both books also contain contemporary and later memoranda of interest to the city authorities. Later books form a more uniform series in which it was intended to enter matters of general interest, sometimes described as *communia memoranda*. Up to the end of the reign of Edward III (Book G), these incl. many records of private deeds and leases entered in chronological order among ordinances, oaths, and other business. Bound in with book D is a register of apprenticeships.

The nature of the *communia memoranda* varies a good deal over the period covered by the books. From book H onwards there are few private deeds, although matters concerning the common soil and the tenements of the Bridge and the Corporation itself are regularly entered. Cases arising from the city's responsibility for orphans (cf. **7**) are frequently recorded and are sometimes informative on real property as well as chattels. From *c.* 1400 onwards the books contain little information on property holding. Much of the uncalendared series (M onwards) consists of fair copies of extracts from the Journals (**b**, below) and the Repertories (**c**, below), or orphanage matters.

Sharpe's *Calendars* provide a compressed but accurate guide to the contents of the books, but details of properties are often omitted; the indexes are in general adequate for topographical purposes. There is a 19C MS index to the whole series in 2 vols.: this is of little direct use for topographical purposes, although the headings 'streets and lanes', 'nuisances', 'buildings', and 'leases' can lead to valuable material. The 'card calendar to property references' in CLRO is a useful means of access to unpublished Letter Books before 1596, and covers private as well as corporation properties. There are, however, some valuable refs. which are not identified in either of these finding aids.

b. Journals: 46 vols. cover 1416–1669. To 1495 these contain the proceedings of both the Court of Common Council and the Court of Aldermen, and from 1495 those of the Common Council only. Vols. 3 and 4 also record meetings of the Husting Court (cf. **2d**). Two vols. of a 19C MS index cover the Journals for 1416–1694. Its design and coverage is similar to that for the Letter Books (**a**, above), and in addition the headings 'encroachments' and 'churches' can provide valuable leads; the heading 'leases' includes corporation properties, for which locations are given. Use should also be made of the 'card calendar' (see **a**, above), covering the period *c.* 1500–1596. There is, however, no complete guide to topograpical refs. in the Journals.

c. Repertories: 77 vols. cover 1495–1672. These contain the proceedings of the Court of Aldermen and are the main record of the administrative work of the city, including matters concerning the common soil and tenements. The first 5 vols. of a 19C MS index cover the period. Its design is similar to those for the Letter Books and Journals (**a** and **b**, above), but it enables a great deal of topographical material to be identified. For the period to 1596, use should also be made of the 'card calendar' (see **a**, above). Some of the 19C indexes are less adequate than others, and in order to remedy this deficiency the compiler of the 'card calendar' made a particularly thorough search of Repertories 20–3.

In the late 16C separate series of records were established for administrative decisions concerning the lands of the Corporation (**13**), the Bridge (**14**), and the royal hospitals (see **100, 102, 226, 404, 409**) but records of those decisions continued to be entered in the Repertories.

d. Remembrancia, 1579–1664. These are books of copies of correspondence, petitions, etc., principally to and from the Lord Mayor and Court of Aldermen, relating to various subjects. The *Analytical index to the series of records known as the Remembrancia. . . . A.D. 1579–1664* (1878), contains brief calendars, arranged by subject, of the contents of the series; subject headings include concealed lands, encroachments, leases, streets, walls, and ditches, Thames.

4. CLRO: Mayor's Court
This court dealt chiefly with actions relating to trade and commerce, and the topographical interest of the records is largely in the information they contain about the locations of commercial activities, and in the inventories for debt etc. of tradesmen's stock. The surviving rolls are published with introductions as *Early Mayor's Court Rolls of the City of London, 1298–1307*, ed. A. H. Thomas (1924), and *Plea and Memoranda Rolls of the City of London, 1323–1482*, 6 vols., ed. A. H. Thomas (1926–43) and P. E. Jones (1954–61).

There are also files of original bills, for the early 14C to mid 15C, and from 1560 to 1725. The medieval files (1–4) are mostly calendared on cards, with an index to the contents of some of the calendars. The 16C and later files (5–175 to *c.* 1670) have been sorted and arranged but are not indexed. Many were lost in the Royal Exchange fire of 1838. By the 16C the cases concern debt and trespass, and include cases transferred from the Sheriffs' Court, and occasional writs for the Husting Court. There is a 20C MS introduction, with examples, to the class, and a list of cases containing schedules of goods (noting date, parties, kind of goods); the list also contains notes on some other kinds of case. There is a subject-index to the list. References in cases to the parishes of *48, 64* are fictitious; other parishes referred to in the subject index are *15, 21, 34, 45, 62, 81, 83, 85, 95, 104, 155.*

5. CLRO: Mayor as Escheator

a. Escheat Rolls (Misc. Rolls EE, GG, HH), 1342–76, 1388–9: rolls of writs and inquisitions (post mortem and miscellaneous) held by the mayor as escheator, most but not all duplicated in PRO, Chancery Inquisitions files. TS calendar, indexes, and introduction by H. M. Chew (CLRO 205C); see also H. M. Chew, 'Mortmain in Medieval London', *EHR* 60 (1945), 1–15. For the mayor's a/c for escheated estates, 1416–17, see PRO, E136/108/14 (**437**).

b. Inquisitions Post Mortem (Misc. Roll LL), 1619–20: no list or index; some but probably not all duplicated in PRO.

6. CLRO: Coroners' Rolls
These contain topographical as well as biographical detail. Letter book B (see **3a**) includes copies of the now lost coroners' rolls for 1275–8.

a. Coroners' Rolls A–I, 1300–78: calendared and indexed by R. R. Sharpe, *Calendar of Coroners' Rolls of the City of London* (1913).

b. Coroner's Roll J, 1590: inquisitions held in the following parishes: *10, 15, 18, 34, 38, 43, 46, 47* (incl. Newgate gaol), *54, 62, 78, 80, 85, 96, 127, 152.*

7. CLRO: Court of Orphans
The Court of Orphans supervised the administration and distribution of the goods of freemen who died leaving children under age. It did not deal with real property, but its records include over 2000 inventories

(*c.* 1600–1760) of personal estates, including household and trade goods grouped by rooms. Many inventories give the parish in which the house lay, but the index covers freemen's names only. See C. H. Carlton, 'The administration of London's Court of Orphans', *Guildhall Miscellany* vol. 4, no. 1 (1971), 22–35; Jones and Smith, *Guide*, 68, 74–5.

8. CLRO: ASSIZE OF NUISANCE
The proceedings of the assize, held by the mayor and aldermen to settle disputes, usually between neighbours and concerning nuisances caused by buildings or occupational use, contain much useful topographical information. The records (Misc. Rolls DD, EE, II) are calendared in *London Assize of Nuisance 1301–1431*, ed. H. M. Chew and W. Kellaway (LRS 10, 1973).

9. CLRO: POSSESSORY ASSIZES
By the 14C possessory assizes in London consisted chiefly of pleas of disseisin, of rents as well as of lands and tenements, and were held by the coroner and sheriffs (later by the sheriffs alone). The surviving records ('Mort d'ancestor rolls' AA–FF, 1340–1451, and individual pleas 1317, 1380, 1470, 1583–1603) are calendared in *London Possessory Assizes, a Calendar*, ed. H. M. Chew (LRS 1, 1965).

10. CLRO: VIEWERS' REPORTS
In cases where citizens were disputing some non-tenurial matter concerning property (party walls, lights, nuisance, etc.), the mayor and aldermen could direct the city's sworn viewers (usually building craftsmen) to make a detailed view or survey of the properties or matters concerned. The CLRO Viewers' Reports are copies of these surveys, covering many parishes, kept by the city; other copies of the same may survive in the archives of the parties to a dispute.

a. Reports 1508–57 (file, envelopes, and loose certificates, in Bound File 204A and Misc. MSS Box 91): at present (1983) not indexed, but being calendared and edited in a forthcoming volume for LRS by Janet Loengard. Reports ('Presentments') 1623–36 (roll or file, Box 204A): TS list in CLRO. Reports 1659–1704 (vols. and Misc. MSS): TS index, by street or parish, in CLRO.

11. CLRO: RECORDS RELATING TO THE GREAT FIRE
Special powers were granted to cope with the problems of rebuilding the city after the Fire; the records of the bodies exercising these powers survive in CLRO, GL, and BL. See T. F. Reddaway, *The rebuilding of London after the Great Fire* (1940); Jones and Smith, *Guide*, 75–6.

a. Fire Court Decrees. The Court of Judicature appointed to determine differences between landlords and tenants as to rebuilding after the Great Fire, established by statute 18 & 19 Chas. II c. 7, met at Cliffords Inn from 1667 until 1676. Its judgments or decrees survive as BL, Add. MSS 5063–5103 (paper copies or originals, rebound as 41 vols. *c.* 1843) and CLRO, Fire Court Decrees A–I (contemp. engrossments in 9 parchment vols.). The decrees are in a slightly different order in the 2 series, and a few survive in one series and not the other. CLRO vols. A–D are calendared, with introduction and cross-references to BL vols., as *The Fire Court*, ed. P. E. Jones (2 vols., 1966, 1970). MS calendar and index of CLRO vol. E, by P. E. Jones, is available in CLRO. BL, Add. MS 14331 is a 'Tabular Analysis' or summary calendar, with index, of the contents of the BL vols. (microfilm of calendar but not index in CLRO, mf. 1967/23). CLRO, 'Alphabetical Table' is a companion vol. to the CLRO vols. of decrees, listing the contents of each alphabetically by petitioner's name. Decrees in CLRO vols. F–I for specific properties or parishes can be identified by using the 'Tabular Analysis' microfilm and the 'Alphabetical Table' in conjunction. In addition, many private archives include paper copies of decrees relating to individual properties.

b. Surveys of building plots. The Rebuilding Acts empowered the city's official surveyors (Robert Hooke, Peter Mills, and John Oliver) to determine, by survey and certification, the foundations on which individuals could rebuild their houses. Few original survey certificates survive. Transcripts of Mills's and Oliver's notebooks (or of 17C transcripts of the same), containing draft surveys and some memoranda, were made *c.* 1720: only these 18C transcripts now survive (GL, MS 84). Hooke's notebooks were not transcribed and do not survive. Payments of fees for foundation surveys were recorded chronologically in CLRO, Chamberlain's Foundation Day Book (3 vols., 1667–96), and, arranged alphabetically by street, in CLRO, Chamberlain's Foundations Posting Book (1667–76). The 18C transcripts of Mills's and Oliver's surveys are reproduced, and the Foundations Posting Book transcribed, with introduction and index, as *The Survey of Building Sites in the City of London by Peter Mills and John Oliver*, ed. P. E. Jones and T. F. Reddaway (LTS 97–9, 101, 103, 1962–6).

c. Deeds and papers, including foundation surveys, relating to properties and slips of land acquired by the City after the Fire by compulsory purchase for street improvements are described under **13**.

d. Coal Duty Accounts. An extraordinary duty on coal imports to London was granted to the City to finance public works, including the purchase of land for street widening, new markets, etc. Payments for these purposes are listed in chronological order in Coal Duty a/c bk. 1 (1669–79), ff. 94–176. Bk. 4 is an abridged copy of bk. 1, to 1672; bk. 5, f. 45 et seqq., is a rough version of bk. 1, to 1674, usually with rather less information, but occasionally including more.

12. CLRO: ASSESSMENTS
Several general, ward, and parish assessments, almost all of late 17C date, are in CLRO: see GL handlist *London Rate Assessments and Inhabitants Lists in GL and CLRO* (2nd edn. 1968). See also the assessment of ecclesiastical property in the city, 1392 (CLRO, 239A), calendared in *The Church in London 1375–92*, ed. A. K. McHardy (LRS 13, 1977).

13. CLRO: CORPORATION ESTATE

Many of the corporation's properties were associated with the walls and gates of the city or were originally waste ground in the streets and next to the defensive circuit. The value of the estate was much increased by private encroachments on to public ground during the 16C and 17C, but nevertheless included many houses and quit-rents on private ground. Many properties were acquired after the Great Fire for street improvements. For an account of the estate in the early 14C, see *LBC*, 237–9. For the 15C and 16C, see the Letter Books (**3a**), Journals (**3b**), Repertories (**3c**). In CLRO search room there is a card calendar, arranged topographically, of refs. to properties in the Repertories, Journals, and unpublished Letter Books before 1596. Comprehensive records of the management of the estate survive only from the late 16C onwards. Between then and the late 17C the corporation had holdings in: *2, 4, 10, 11, 12, 13, 14, 18, 19, 20, 21, 23, 25, 26, 30, 32, 37, 38, 42, 43, 44, 45, 46, 47, 49, 51, 53, 54, 56, 58, 59, 62, 67, 70, 74, 77, 78, 80, 81, 83, 85, 87, 88, 92, 93, 94, 95, 96, 99, 100, 101, 104, 105, 108, 111, 112, 113, 116, 117, 118, 119, 123, 124, 127, 128, 129, 132, 135, 137, 141, 144, 145, 149, 150, 151, 152, 155, 157, 158, 159,* precinct of Whitefriars.
The records are in CLRO.

a. Comptroller's (City Lands) Deeds: principally leases of city lands, but also deeds and other papers, 16C to 19C (few before 1600, most after 1666), arranged in boxes in numerical (1–1076) and alphabetical (A–W) sequences, both with gaps. A card index to the contents of this series, arranged by streets and parishes, is at present being compiled in CLRO; it covers boxes 1–171, 173–4, and A–H. The unindexed boxes in the numerical series contain principally 19C and 20C material. Several boxes contain records of a special character. The unindexed Box K contains post-Fire surveyors' certificates, none of which were entered in the later registers (**3b**). Most of these certificates concern lands bought and sold for improving the city streets and the Fleet Channel after the Great Fire, but a few concern the foundations of private houses; there is a modern topographical index in the list entitled 'City Lands Committee Papers, 1666–1704' in CLRO search room. The unindexed Box L contains 'expired' 16C–17C deeds and bonds (*4, 25, 118,* Bishopsgate Street, Leadenhall, Southwark). The unindexed Boxes M and N contain conveyances to the city of lands taken into the streets after the Fire. A guide to the contents of all the boxes which then existed, entitled 'A Numerical General Index', was compiled *c.* 1701; it contains brief records of a number of items which have since been lost.

b. City Lands Grant Books, 1–4, 1589–1672: minutes of the City Lands Committee, including brief notices of leases, encroachments, views, petitions, etc.; there is a card index of places and persons up to 1612; vol. 1 (1589–1615) also incl. self-contained lists of surrenders of leases and licences to assign. Surrenders of City Lands Leases, 1630–93 (location: 34B), 2 vols. now bound as one: abstracts of surrendered leases and of licences to assign. City Leases, *c.* 1660–90 (location: 111D), 1 vol. comp. *c.* 1690: abstract of leases (most after 1666) under topographical

8

headings. Copies of Deeds, *c.* 1650–1700 (location: 111D), 9 vols., comp. late 17C: abstracts and copies of city leases, deeds, and other papers.

c. Chamber Accounts 2: a/cs and draft rental of corporation estate, 1584–6, incomplete but rebound in reconstructed order; restored text of a/cs, but not rental, published as *Chamber Accounts of the Sixteenth Century*, ed. Betty R. Masters (LRS 20, 1984). There are also separate rentals for 1655 (Misc. MS 157.20) and 1660 (location: 37C). City Cash Accounts vols. 1–13, 1633–70: incl. detailed rental for each year (incl. receipts of quit-rents and rents for encroachments), receipts of fines on leases (incl. share of fines due to corporation as governor of the London hospitals, and, by the mid 17C, fines for Bridge House properties), and payments of quit-rents. Bodl, MS Rawl. B 385 incl. extensive repair a/cs *c.* 1630 for work at *70* and Newgate, Tower Hill, Walbrook.

d. Plans. The most useful early collections are: 'Plans of City Lands and Bridge House Properties', 2 vols. comp. *c.* 1680–1720 with a modern index; survey of the city wall and adjacent properties by William Leybourn, 1676 (Plan Drawer G. 6); survey of the public markets by William Leybourn, 1677 (Plan Drawer 92C; see Betty R. Masters, *The Public Markets of the City of London surveyed by William Leybourn in 1677* (LTS 117, 1974)); Surveyor's City Lands Plans vol. 3 (plans of corporation properties in the city *c.* 1841). From *c.* 1675 most leases of City Lands and some of Bridge House properties include plans; those relating to City Lands may be identified from the card index to the Comptroller's Deeds (see above, **a**). CLRO contains in addition several large collections of loose plans dating from the late 16C onwards (mostly late 18C and 19C); most of these, including nearly all the earlier ones, are listed under topographical headings in the card index in the search room; vols. 3–6 of the Surveyor's City Lands Plans are not covered by this index, but their contents are listed in separate files in the search room; the contents of Surveyor's Bridge House Estates Plans vol. 1 (18C London plans) are neither indexed nor listed.

14. CLRO: B<small>RIDGE</small> H<small>OUSE</small> <small>ESTATE</small>
London Bridge was maintained and repaired out of an income derived from a large estate in the city (including the houses on the Bridge) and elsewhere, from dues from the Stocks Market, and from tolls from ships and carts. The city estate was made up of properties (referred to in a/cs as 'proper rents') and quit-rents. The former changed little from the mid 14C to the 17C, but many quit-rents were lost in the 15C or 16C, and a number of new ones acquired in the mid 16C. Unless otherwise stated these estates were as follows:

A (properties): *2, 4, 11, 14, 27, ?29, ?30, 37, 47, 51, 53, 58, 59, 62, 83, 85, 89, 90, 108, 112, 118, 128, 137,* Bridge, Dowgate, Minories.

B (quit-rents): *2, 4, 9, 12, 14, 21, ?29, 32, 37, 44, 46, 49, 53, 56, 78, 80, 83, 85, 87, 92, 94, 98, 99, 101, 103, 108, 118, 119, 123, 124, 125, 126, 127, 144, 145, 155, 156, 157,* Fleet Hill, Paternoster Row.

Unless otherwise stated, the records are in CLRO. There is a TS catalogue (1933), by A. H. Thomas, and many of the records are calendared, listed, or indexed in MS.

a. Deeds. Portfolios A–K: deeds, 13C to 18C, with 20C MS calendar, cross-references to Large Register (below, **c**), and index (*11, 12, 21, 27, 29, 30, 32, 37, 43, 45, 46, 47, 49, 51, 53, 58, 59, 62, 71, 75, 80, 83, 85, 87, 89, 90, 92, 101, 108, 112, 118, 122, 124, 125, 128, 129, 132, 137, 145, 152, 156, 157*, Baynards Castle, Colechurch Street, Eastcheap, St. Paul's). Miscellaneous Deeds 1–239: deeds and leases, 14C to 18C, with 20C MS calendar and index (*11, 13, 14, 37, 43, 47, 51, 58, 62, 78, 85, 112, 118, 128, 137, 145, 147, 155*, Bridge, Cornhill, Paternoster Row).

b. Comptroller's (Bridge House) Leases: 16C to 19C (estate A). A card index to the contents of this series, arranged by modern street names, is maintained by the Comptroller and City Solicitor but is not available to the general public. Enquiries should be made at CLRO.

c. Small Register: cartulary, comp. 14C to 16C, of deeds, wills, 13C to 16C (*2, 4, 9, 10, 11, 12, 14, 21, 29, 32, 37, 44, 45, 49, 51, 53, 56, 59, 61, 72, 83, 85, 87, 89, 90, 98, 101, 108, 112, 118, 122, 124, 125, 128, 129, 137, 141, 145, 149, 157*, Bridge, Candlewick Street, Colechurch Street); also incl. rental, 1358, and 15C plan (*112*); 20C MS calendar and index to deeds etc. not incl. in Portfolio Deeds A–K, Miscellaneous Deeds, or Large Register. Large Register: cartulary, comp. early 16C and later, of deeds, wills, 13C to 17C (as Small Register, except for *72*, Candlewick Street; also *27, 43, 46, 58, 73, 74, 75, 80, 92, 123, 152, 155*, Old Change, Paternoster Row, Thames Street); 20C MS calendar and index to deeds etc. not incl. in Portfolio Deeds A–K and Miscellaneous Deeds. Grant Book, 1570–1622: memoranda of leases (estate A).

d. Small Register (not foliated): incl. rental, 1358. Bridgemasters' a/c rolls, 1382–94, 1395–8, 1405–6: annual receipts (total), details of arrears, vacancies, repairs; 20C MS transcript, index, and introduction. Bridge House Rentals, vols. 1–21, 1404–1666 (full MS translation and transcript of vol. 3): rentals and a/cs, detailed receipts and expenditure; quit-rent receipts not listed in detail from *c*. 1464 to 1557, but quit-rents in long arrears listed to *c*. 1485, then omitted. Weekly Payment Books, 1st series, vols. 1–4 (1405–45), 2nd series, vols. 1–3 (1505–38), 3rd series, vols. 1–11 (1552–5, 1575–6, 1594–1634, 1643–77): details of weekly expenditure incl. payment of wages, quit-rents, repairs to Bridge; some notes of misc. receipts; MS index to 1st series, vols. 1–2 (1404–21) with index to Bridgemasters' a/c rolls, above. Cash Books, vols. 1–7, 1602–67: weekly receipts and payments, incl. rents, but few details of properties. Bodl, MS Tanner 121, ff. 118–35: rental, 1632. For fines from Bridge House properties, see City Cash Accounts, vols. 1–13 (1633–70), described under **13c**.

e. Bridge House Grant Book, 1570–1622: memoranda of leases granted; name index. Bridge House Committee Journals, vols. 1–2, 1622–57, 1665–80: memoranda of leases granted; incomplete name index, 20C place index to vol. 1. Book of Orders, 1611–1741: reports to and orders of

Court of Aldermen concerning Bridge House property, incl. lease decisions. 'Account of Materials sold', vol. 1, 1614–30: incl. diary of repairs and views (Bridge, Paternoster Row), memoranda of sealing of leases. See also **3a**, **3c**.

f. For plans, see **13d**.

15. CLRO: GRESHAM ESTATE
The city of London shared responsibility for and revenues from Gresham College (in *64*, *148*) and the Royal Exchange (*32*, *48*, *124*) with the Mercers' Company; the majority of the records, from the 16C, are at Mercers' Hall (**47**).

a. CLRO, Gresham Estate 'Cash Books 1' (1659–70) and 'Journals 1' (from 1662): rough daily and quarterly a/cs for rents and fines (totalled) and payments, incl. salaries and workmen's wages. Ibid. 'Ledgers 1' (1665–80): first surviving vol. of full a/cs, incl. annual rentals, total receipts from fines; expenditure incl. repairs to Exchange and College; Exchange business and tenants moved to College for some years after the Fire. Ibid., 'Book of Fines for leases' (1654–61): fines for leases of shops at Royal Exchange, arranged chronologically.

LONDON LIVERY COMPANIES

Fraternities and associations of Londoners for various purposes existed in the early Middle Ages, but it was not until the later 14C that some of them became corporate bodies and began to acquire lands, in London and elsewhere, with which to support their activities. Many companies holding lands for chantry purposes lost them in 1548, or sold other lands in order to redeem rents and charges, but continued to build up their estates thereafter. Widespread acquisition of city properties, however, had virtually ceased by *c.* 1600. On the eve of the Great Fire the estates of the largest companies comprised properties in more than 40 parishes. The lesser companies, however, may have held property or rents in only one or two parishes, and some had no freehold estate at all, leasing or renting accommodation for meetings and dinners.

The records of the 83 companies which existed in or before 1666 were searched for references to property-holding up to that date; 54 archives contained such material. A few companies lost their records in the Fire but otherwise survival has been good. The records consist principally of deeds and wills, some registers and lease books, rentals and accounts, minute books, plans, and surveys; in the case of large estates acquired piecemeal the coverage changes almost from year to year. The records of the majority of the companies are in GL, although individual items may be resumed by companies from time to time, and occasionally further items, having come to light at company halls, are sent to GL. See GL, *Guide to the archives of city Livery Companies and related organisations in Guildhall Library* (pamphlet, 1982). The *Report of the Royal Commission on the City of London Livery Companies* (C. 4073; 3 vols., 1884) is a useful introduction to the companies' endowments and charitable obligations.

Descriptions of the archives, including those of the 'Great Twelve' companies, and records kept outside GL, are arranged alphabetically by company.

16. SOCIETY OF APOTHECARIES
Unless otherwise stated, the estate lay in *25*. The records are in GL.

a. MSS 8263, 8265–6, 8269: deeds and papers, 17C to 19C.

b. MS 8202/1: wardens' a/c bk., 1626–68, receipts of rent from 1633–4 onwards.

c. MSS 8200/1–2: court minute bks., 1617–80 (concern company property from 1632; also ref. to Bucklersbury in 1630). MS 8201/1: rough court minute bk., 1661–72.

17. ARMOURERS' AND BRASIERS' COMPANY
Unless otherwise stated, the estate was as follows:
A: *4, 19, 20, 45, 46, 142, 150, 152, 155* (the properties in *19, 20,* and *46*
appear to have been sold before 1600).
B (in 17C records only): *21, 43,* Frenchurch Street.
The records are in GL.

a. MSS 12114, 12119–23, 12125, 12128–31, 12136, 12139: deeds, 14C to
17C. MSS 12124, 12140: deeds and chantry certificates concerning the
company's chantries (including certificate for par. church of St. Peter
Paul's Wharf), 14C to 16C (estate A; also refs. to *9, 21, 37, 49, 53, 62, 63,
120, 138, 159*). Most locations identified in GL catalogue cards; see also
typescript calendar and index, comp. 1922 (MS 12103).

b. MS 12137: folder of wills, 1398–1636 (*4, 21, 45, 142, 152,* Fenchurch
Street; also ref. to *149*). MS 12101: abs. of title comp. 1662 (estates A and
B, except *19, 20, 46*). MS 12100: abs. of leases, *c.* 1646–*c.* 1690.

c. MS 12098: rentals 1610–1863, incl. rents and dates of leases. MSS
12065/1–4: wardens' a/cs, 1497–1707, incl. receipts and payments of rents
and expenditure on repairs.

d. MSS 12071/1–3: court bks., 1413–1675, incl. details on leases and
management of estate. MS 12072: draft court minute bk., 1643–70.

e. MS 12141: late 16C papers on lands of this and other companies
formerly held as chantry endowments (also refs. to *11, 78, 105, 144, 160*).

f. MS 12104: plan bk. 1679.

18. BAKERS' COMPANY
Unless otherwise stated, the estate lay in: *43, 53, 108,* Eastcheap, Fleet
Street, Tower Street, Warwick Lane. The records are in GL.

a. MSS 5174/1–4: audit bks., 1491–1667; individual receipts and
payments of rent are recorded, but the properties cannot always be
identified. MS 5174/1 also incl. refs. to hiring a hall in *126* (f. 1ᵛ), to
evidences concerning property in *93* (f. 30), and to the company's hall in
Basing Lane (f. 30ᵛ); MS 5174/2 incl. copies of wills (ff. 3–14ᵛ).

b. MSS 5177/1–5: court minute bks., 1537–1677, incl. records of leases
and fines.

19. BARBER-SURGEONS' COMPANY
Unless otherwise stated, the estate lay in: *43, 53, 74, 132, 144, 152.* The
records were in GL, but the earlier items have been returned to Barber-
Surgeons' Hall.

a. MS 9826: deeds 15C to 17C (no refs. to *53, 144*). MS 1108: bound
miscellanea, incl. 15C will (*53*).

b. MS 9822: expired leases, 17C (no refs. to *53, 74*).

c. MSS 5255/1–2: masters' and renter wardens' a/c bks., 1603–72; receipts of rents, fines on leases, and quit-rents (estate plus rents from Dowgate (? Swan Alley in) and Lombard Street). MS 5255A: masters' rough a/c bk., 1654–5.

d. MSS 5257/1–5: court minute bks., 1551–1651; administration of estate as in a/c bks. (some refs. to properties can be identified from marginal notes).

20. BLACKSMITHS' COMPANY
The estate lay in *18, 152*, possibly *100*; the hall in *112* was leasehold. The records are in GL.

a. MSS 8151–3: deeds, leases and 19C abs. of title, 16C to 19C (*18, 152*).

b. MS 5535: memoranda and ordinances, incl. 15C will (*100*), 15C suit for lease (*112*).

c. MSS 2883/1–5: wardens' a/cs, incl. rent receipts 1509–65 (tenements not named), 1595–1680, and fines for leases; also rent paid for hall (*112*); MS 2883/2 incl. tithe dispute (*112*).

d. MSS 2881/1–7: court minute bks. 1605–62; some information on leases. MS 2882/1: court minute bk., 1625–33; rough, similar to MS 2881.

21. BREWERS' COMPANY
Unless otherwise stated, the estate lay in: *4, 13, 38, 45, 46, 62, 71, 99*. The records are in GL.

a. MSS 5503–4, 5509, 5517, 5519, 6809, 6811–12, 6814: deeds, late 13C to 18C (pars. or streets named on GL catalogue cards; no refs. to *4*). The following contain 14C and 17C refs. to property not acquired by the company or not acquired until after 1666: MS 6809 (*78, 104*), MS 6810 (*47, 60*), MS 15175 (*124*).

b. MS 5462: benefactors' bk., comp. *c.* 1650–1750; incl. abs. of title, 14C–17C, and later rentals (topographical index). MS 5462A: register of wills etc., 1509–1714, comp. 17C–18C; incl. records of annuities from *152* and register of leases 1552–1772 (index of personal names). MS 5461: lease bk. 1668–82.

c. MS 5440: a/c and memoranda bk., 1414–40 (extracts in *A Book of London English, 1384–1425*, ed. R. W. Chambers and Marjorie Daunt (1931), 140–91; brief calendar in MS 5441); receipts of rent from hall and adjacent tenements (*49*); expenditure on repairs; many records of brewers' offences naming the places where they plied their trade. MSS 5442/1–7: wardens' a/c bks., 1502–1672; receipts of rents and fines on leases (estate, plus *152* and Houndsditch in 17C). MS 7886: renter wardens' a/c bk., 1663–75 (estate plus *152* and Houndsditch).

d. MSS 5445/1–20: court minute bks., 1531–1671; administration of estate as in wardens' a/c bks. (topographical index in MS 5446/1).

22. BRODERERS' COMPANY
The estate lay in: *2, 32, 38, 112, 144, 158, 159*. The records are in GL.

a. MSS 14679, 14686–7, 14695–6, 14792, 14804: deeds, incl. leases and abs. of title, 13C to 20C (estate plus *47*; pars. mostly named on GL catalogue cards).

b. MSS 14703, 14791: abs. of title, 18C and 19C (estate plus *126*). MS 14690: papers relating to charities, 19C, incl. abs. of title, 16C to 18C (*32*). MS 14702: schedules of deeds, 19C.

23. BUTCHERS' COMPANY
The records are in GL.

a. MSS 6464, 6467: deeds, leases, inquisitions, 16C to 18C (*21, 61, 83*; also (in MS. 6464) refs. to *85, 87, 89, 125, 136*). MS 10581: papers incl. copy deed and schedule of deeds, 17C (*61*).

b. MS 6468, leases, 16C and 17C (*47*).

c. MS 6440/1–2; wardens' a/cs, 1543–1644, rents and repairs noted but no locations.

24. CARPENTERS' COMPANY
The estate lay in: *14, 19, 45, 51, 64, 141*, Whitefriars. Some records also deal with views and works in many areas; cf. below, **e.** The records are in GL.

a. MS 8325: deeds, 16C to 17C (*141*; also refs. to *13, 25, 38, 43, 48, 53, 62, 78, 89, 118, 144, 152*). MS 8326: deeds etc., 16C to 19C (*19, 51*). MS 8327: deed, 1561 (*77*). MS 8329: deeds, 16C to 17C (*64*).

b. MS 8330: lease and papers, 17C (*14*).

c. MS 4340: abs. of title deeds, comp. *c.* 1690 and later, incl. deeds, wills, leases, 15C to 19C (estate except Whitefriars; also *77*). MS 4332: will bk., comp. *c.* 1660 and later; wills and abs. of leases (estate except *64*, Whitefriars). MS 4329A: abs. and memoranda bk., comp. *c.* 1639 and later; incl. copy or abs. wills, leases, 16C to 17C (estate).

d. MS 4326/1 (printed as *Records of the Carpenters' Company* ii, ed. B. Marsh, 1914): wardens' a/cs, 1438–1516, rents, repairs (*14*, Lime Street). MSS 4326/2–10: wardens' a/cs, 1546–1670 (a/cs for 1546–91 printed in *Records of the Carpenters' Company* iv–v, ed. B. Marsh, J. Ainsworth, 1916, 1937); rent receipts (estate). MS 4344/1: wardens' vouchers and receipts, incl. rents, 1602–4 (*14, 19, 51*).

e. MSS 4329/1–6: court minute bks., 1533–94, 1600–70 (minutes 1533–94 printed as *Records of the Carpenters' Company* iii, vi, ed. B. Marsh, J. Ainsworth, 1915, 1939); grants of leases, fines, views. MS 7784: court papers (15 files), 1600–32, incl. views of company and other properties.

25. CLOCKMAKERS' COMPANY
The records, now in GL, contain nothing on property holding before 1666. MS 3974 incl. a copy of a list of clockmakers in London and Westminster in 1662 arranged under street headings.

26. CLOTHWORKERS' COMPANY

Unless otherwise stated, the estate lay in: *2, 10, 13, 20, 32, 43, 48, 51, 53, 59, 60, 71, 74, 77, 78, 81, 89, 98, 100, 106, 118, 124, 131, 134, 141, 144, 152, 155*, precinct or parish of St. James in the Wall, Whitefriars; also (from mid 16C) Queenhithe. The records are at Clothworkers' Hall.

a. Deeds and leases, 13C to 20C: arranged by modern locations, in Boxes 1, 3–6, 9, 12, 14, 15, 19, 21, 26–30, 52, 54–62, 66, 68, 74, and misc. box file; also incl. refs. to *19* (Box 1); *127*, Bearbinder Lane (Box 5); *24, 85, 87, 116, 129* (Box 6); *4, 26* (Box 12); *46* (Boxes 19, 26, 55, 66); *18, 62* (Box 27); *132* (Box 28); *93* (Box 56); *12* (Box 59); *104* (Box 60); *5, 62, 93* (Box 68). There are TS schedules of the contents of boxes, noting only estate properties.

b. 'Wills Book': register of deeds and wills, comp. 16C to 18C, incl. copy wills 15C to 18C, copy leases 16C, memoranda of bequests. Report on the state of the company, 1653: incl. list of quit-rents payable, rent total for 1652, inventory of goods at hall. Bk. comp. 1741: lists benefactors, and abs. conveyances to company (incl. wills) from 1456. 'Register of Trusts', comp. 1837: conveyances, trusts and arrangements, 15C to 19C.

c. 'Benefactors' Book': rental *c.* 1574, arranged by donor, incl. details of current lease and net value (*2, 10, 13, 53, 74, 78, 98, 100, 118, 131, 134, 141, 152*, Fenchurch Street, Whitefriars). 'Book of Lands': rental 1605 with later additions (as Benefactors' Bk.; also Queenhithe). Bk. of particulars of leases, 1662: details of donors of and charges on tenements. 2 similar bks. of particulars, 1669, 1670: incl. details of pre-Fire leases still current. Renter and quarter-wardens' a/cs, 10 vols. 1528–1670: rents and (in early vols.) repairs in former, fines for leases and receipts from sales of property in latter.

d. Orders of courts, 1536–1683 (12 vols. incl. duplicates; courts are dated by month of master's office, not calendar month): court minutes, incl. views, grants of leases and tenancies; TS transcript of vol. 1 (1536–58); 'Summaries' (5 vols. of 20C transcripts of contemp. side-headings) for 1558–1639, often useful for identifying grants of leases, views etc.; index to orders of courts 1639–1777 (but n.b. that leases usually indexed under tenants' names); cf. two 19C bks. of extracts from court orders 17C to 19C, one arranged chronologically, one by subjects (e.g. hall, leases).

e. Ralph Treswell's plan bk., 1612 with later 17C and 18C additions: detailed ground plans of estate with memoranda of tenants and leases, also information on upper floors; some plans and accompanying information published as LTS publications nos. 72–5 (1938–41) and *LTR* 18 (1942), 51–97.

27. COOKS' COMPANY

The records are in GL (many were destroyed in 1940).

a. MS 9989, bk. of abs. of deeds comp. 1735–64 (*42*, 14C to 16C; *117*, 16C to 18C; Crooked Lane, 17C). The same material also appears in: MS 3115, register of wills, comp. *c.* 1755 (also incl. deed and a/cs for annuity in *134* and Fire Ct. decree concerning *117*); MS 5908, schedule of deeds, comp. *c.* 1750 (one deed also refers to *92*).

28. Coopers' Company
The estate lay in *56, 60, 71, 123, 125, 141*, Billiter Lane, Thames Street; also *4* or *53* to *c.* 1560. The records are in GL.

a. MSS 7531, 7533–4, 15177: deeds and leases, *c.* 1299 to 1937 (*71, 123, 125, 141*; also ref. to *13* (in MS 15177)).

b. MS 7549: wills and benefactors' bk., 1468–1844, incl. copy deeds and wills, 15C and 16C (*4* or *53, 123, 125*). MS 5618/1: list of benefactors, comp. *c.* 1718; incl. copy wills and deeds (*4, 56, 123, 125*). MS 7696: general register, comp. *c.* 1850–1950; lists title deeds, wills, 1429–1598 (*4, 60*).

c. MS 5621: annual views or rentals, 1595–1706 (estate above, except Billiter Lane). MSS 5606/1–4: wardens' a/c bks., 1529–1735, incl. rent receipts, fines for leases, and assignments (estate, but locations not always given). MSS 5607/1–5: wardens' rough a/c bks. 1621–78; contents as MSS 5606/1–4.

d. MSS 5602/1–5: court minute bks., 1567–1627, 1642–77, incl. grants of leases, assignments; MS 5602/3 incl. copy wills, 16C (*123, 125*); contemp. name index in vols. 3–5. MSS 5603/1–4: rough court minute bks., 1552–67, 1608–16, 1623–41; similar material to MS 5602.

29. Cordwainers' Company
The records are in GL. Cf. C. H. W. Mander, *History of the Guild of Cordwainers* (1931), 131–8.

a. MS 7375: deeds (*10*, 17C; *118*, 14C). MS 7371: deeds, 14C to 18C (*89*; also ref. to *92*).

b. MS 14318: charter bk. comp. 17C–18C, cont. copies of deeds, 14C–16C (*89, 108*); copies of deeds, wills, and leases, 16C–17C (*46, 54, 108, 132, 152, 155*).

c. MSS 7351/1–2: audit bks., 1595–1678, incl. receipts of rent (*10, 12, 54, 77, 89, 108, 152, 155*, Golden Lane).

d. MSS 7353/1–2: court bks., 1622–88, incl. grants and alienations of leases (locations not always given, but presumably as above in **c**; there is a ref. to George Yard in *104*).

e. MS 7528: plan 1667 (*77, 89*).

30. Curriers' Company
The estate lay in *15* and possibly elsewhere. The records are in GL.

a. MSS 14346/1–2: wardens' a/cs, 1556–94, 1627–73; rent receipts (locations not always given).

b. MS 6112/1: court minute bk., 1628–58, incl. receipts of fines for leases (locations not given).

31. CUTLERS' COMPANY

Unless otherwise stated, the estate lay in: *5, 42, 43, 46, 54, 74, 126, 152; 20, 73*, from mid 17C. The records are in GL.

a. MSS 7181, 7202, 7204: papers, 18C to 19C, incl. abs. of title and copy wills, 15C to 18C (*43, 54, 152*). MS 18879: deeds and leases, 14C to 18C (*74, 126*). MSS 18883–5: leases and papers, 15C to 19C (*73*). MSS 18889–91: deeds, leases, and papers, 14C to 18C (*42*). MSS 18895–8, 18908, 19895: deeds and leases, 15C to 18C (*46*). MSS 18894, 19894: deeds and leases, 16C to 17C (*152*). MS 18909: assignment, 17C (*54*). MS 19896: deeds and leases, 16C to 18C (*43*).

b. MS 7174: bk. incl. memoranda, *c.* 1666, of current leases and rents. MS 660/2: bk. incl. 18C memoranda of leases, 16C to 17C (*74, 126*, elsewhere unspecified).

c. MS 7164: inventories and terriers, 1586, 1624. MSS 7146/1–36: masters' and wardens' a/c rolls, incl. rentgatherers' a/cs, 1441–97, some years missing (*5, 74, 126*). MS 7147/1: wardens' a/c bk., 1586–1621, incl. renter wardens' rent receipts, fines for leases.

d. MS 7151/1: court minute bk., 1602–70, incl. grants of leases (locations not always given).

e. MS 7166: 17C memoranda bk.of rebuilding of hall 1660–66 (*126*). MSS 7180, 18878: plans and surveyors' reports, 19C (estate as above).

32. DRAPERS' COMPANY

For most purposes, the records treat the company's Corporate and Trust estates together, but the deeds relating to some of the Trust properties are catalogued separately. Unless otherwise stated, the estate was as follows:

A (Corporate and Trust, mostly acquired before 1560): *4, 11, 13, 15, 21, 26, 37, 42, 44, 48, 53, 56, 62, 74, 78, 80, 85, 87, 88, 90, 96, 98, 100, 103, 104, 108, 112, 116, 118, 119, 123, 124, 126, 128, 134, 137, 141, 148, 152, 155, 157.*

B (Trust, mostly acquired after *c.* 1550): *4, 37, 48, 54, 56, 68, 103, 152.* See W. A. Thompson, *History of the [Drapers'] Company's properties and trusts* (1939–40). The records are at Drapers' Hall.

a. Deeds and leases: Corporate catalogue, arranged by parish (5 vols. + index), late 12C to 20C (estate A; also *49, 149*; also refs. to *9, 10, 14, 36, 39, 43, 46, 51, 64, 71, 81, 83, 111, 120, 125, 136, 145, 156*, Blackfriars); Trust catalogue, arranged by trust (5 vols.), 14C to 20C (estate B; also *62, 113, 118, 127, 132, 151*, and advowson of *124*; also refs. to *21, 45, 46, 51, 108*).

b. CR1: bk. of evidences cont. copy deeds and wills, 12C to 16C, comp. 16C with additions (*11, 13, 21, 26, 44, 45, 48, 51, 53, 56, 62, 80, 90, 98, 100, 103, 104, 108, 121, 123, 124, 126, 128, 137, 141, 148, 152, 155, 157*). CR2: bk. of evidences, cont. copy and abs. deeds and wills, 14C to 17C, comp. ?17C (*4, 13, 15, 21, 37, 44, 48, 49, 54, 56, 80, 87, 88, 90, 98, 100,*

103, 112, 118, 128, 134, 137, 141, 148, 152, 155). CR5: 'Extracts from Wills', 1562–1667, comp. *c.* 1625 with additions (*21, 48, 53, 62, 90, 108*). CR6: extracts from wills, notes of trusts, *c.* 1634–1681 (*26, 37, 48, 68, 88, 152*). Vols. +419, +419a: schedule of trust estates, comp. 17C, incl. extracts from deeds, late 15C to 17C (estate A, except *21, 42, 62, 74, 85, 108, 112, 116, 119, 126, 148*; also *43, 49*). BL/A4: remembrance of charities, comp. 1625–31, incl. abs. wills, 16C to 17C (*37, 88, 112, 151*, Thames Street). BL/A3: bequests, 1563–1674, comp. *c.* 1680 (*21, 43, 53, 90, 108, 151*). BL/A1: memoranda of trusts, 16C to 18C, comp. ?18C; benefactors' names. Vol. +783: memoranda of trusts. incl. will 1655 (*62*). Vol. +379: memoranda of deeds and leases, 15C to 17C, comp. mid-17C (*62, 104*, Gutter Lane, Well Alley and Swan Alley). CR4, Record Bk. of Leases, 1538–1602: comp. 1570 and later (*56, 116*, Thames Street, Tower Street). CR3, Remembrances of Leases, 1614–59: comp. *c.* 1642 and later (*4, 11, 21, 26, 80, 87, 88, 98, 103, 118, 148, 155, 157*, Cheapside, Cornhill, Dowgate, Eastcheap, London Wall, Love Lane, Mark Lane, Tower Street). DB2, Dinner Bk.: incl. lease assignments 1617–19 (*21, 74, 88, 103, 104, 116, 118, 126, 128, 152, 155, 157*). BL3, Administration of Loans: incl. fines for leases, 1627–35 (*4, 11, 26, 37, 56, 80, 87, 88, 103, 128, 137, 157*, Cheapside, Cornhill, Dowgate, Mark Lane, Thames Street, Tower Street, and others not located).

c. RR1: rental, 1580–4 (estate A, except *42, 74, 78, 85, 96, 112, 141*). RR2: rough rentals, 1652–80 (as RR1, also *54, 74*). WA1, wardens' a/cs 1413, 1423–6, 1428–30, 1433–5, 1439–41: rents and repairs (*48, 103, 104, 157*, and places not named). RA1, renters' a/cs 1481–5: rents and repairs (*11, 48, 63, 103, 104, 157*). RA2–8, 10–12, 14, renters' a/cs, fair and rough, 1506–1674: rents, repairs to *c.* 1570. RA9, 13, renters' cashbks., 1628–31, 1657–64. WA3–20/6, wardens' a/cs 1508–1668: fines for leases, some rents. RW1–51, renter wardens' a/cs 1605–66 (rough drafts for wardens' a/cs): fines for leases, some rents. See also MB1.

d. OB1: ordinance bk., 1405, incl. copy grant (*103*). OB2: bk. of charters, ordinances, 17C, incl. charter of James I confirming lands. MB1–14: minute bks., 1515–1667, incl. lease agreements, settlements of disputes, rough wardens' a/cs to 1530 (MB2, 3: rough min. bks., 1525–6, 1531–6); no index before 1603, but MB12 (17C bk. of extracts to 1603, relating chiefly to property) is useful. Vols. +118, +119: 17C indexes to MB13, 14 from 1603, incl. refs. to leases, land. WM1: wardens' rough minutes, 1659–1701, incl. grants of leases.

e. Vol. +420: 16C bk. of precedents, incl. copy deeds, leases (*2, 20, 39, 47, 51, 60, 62, 63, 111, 123, 124, 141, 151, 156, 159*, Bishopsgate, Bread Street).

f. Individual plans: 1596, property in *103*; early 17C, hall in *148*. Plan bk., 1698 (estates A and B).

33. DYERS' COMPANY
The estate lay in: *12, 20, 74, 150*. The records are at Dyers' Hall and in GL.

a. GL, MSS 10072, 15463, 15464 (Vintners' Co.): deeds, 1439–1739 (*12*; also refs. to *71, 96*).

b. Dyers' Hall, 'Green Book', comp. 18C: abs. of deeds, leases, 16C to 18C. Dyers' Hall, 'Estate book and List of Title Deeds', comp. 1852 and later: memoranda of title, abs. of deeds, 16C to 20C.

c. Dyers' Hall, bk. of estate plans, 1721 (formerly GL, MS 8185, returned to company).

34. FISHMONGERS' COMPANY
Incorporates Stockfishmongers' Company. Unless otherwise stated, the estate was as follows:
A: *9, 19, 20, 23, 43, 44, 46, 51, 53, 62, 77, 78, 80, 85, 87, 89, 93, 108, 112, 114, 116, 125, 127, 131, 135, 152*. All properties in *20, 23, 43, 152* appear to have been sold in 1550.
B: from late 16C property also held in *42*, St. Katharine's Precinct, and Wood Street.
Unless otherwise stated, the records are in GL.

a. MSS 6687–714, 6718–19, 6742–3: deeds, late 13C to 20C (estate A; pars. mostly named on GL catalogue cards; also refs. to *13* (MS 6684), *15* (MS 6692), *56* (MS 6687), *105* (MS 6695), *156* (MS 6687)).

b. MSS 6925, 6927, 6929–31, 6934, 6936–9, 6943, 6945–6, 6948, 6950–1, 6955–7, 6959, 6961, 6973: expired leases, mid 17C to 20C (estate A and B; streets named on GL catalogue cards). See also *37*.

c. Fishmongers' Hall, bk. labelled '67': will bk. incl. some deeds, comp. early 16C to late 17C (estate A and B, except for *62*; also *158*). Fishmongers' Hall, several other vols. of 18C and 19C extracts from earlier wills: see also GL, MSS 6367, 6763.

d. MSS 5561/1,2: prime wardens' a/c bks., 1636–82, receipts of fines on leases, expenditure on hall. MS 5562/1: prime wardens' (in fact renter wardens') a/c bk., 1646–67; receipts of rent. MSS 5563/1–3: renter wardens' a/c bks. 1647–70: receipts of rent under street headings and payment of quitrents. These concern estates A and B and probably *61*.

e. Fishmongers' Hall, Bk. of Ordinances: principally ordinances written 1509, also deeds (*9, 77*). MSS 5570/1–5, Court Ledgers, 1592–1699: minute bks., incl. partics. of leases etc. (full TS calendar and index (GL, S.L37/F.537) and useful 19C indexes (MSS 5572/1–5)).

f. Papers, 16C–18C: refs. to *54* (MS 10975), *77* (MS 10013), *78* (MS 10975), *112* (MS 5835), Abchurch Lane (MS 7286). Letters and papers concerning properties destroyed in 1666 (MS 5857).

g. Fishmongers' Hall, Plan Bk., 1686: drawn surveys by William Leybourn (cf. GL, Prints and Drawings, Pr L37: plan of land in Fenchurch Street). See also plan bks. of *c.* 1740 (GL, MSS 5860/1,2) and 1772 (at Fishmongers' Hall) and uncatalogued late 17C to 19C 'Fishmongers' Plans', folio iv, in GL, Prints and Drawings.

35. FOUNDERS' COMPANY
The estate (hall and other properties) lay in *88*. The records are in GL.

a. MS 6357: deeds and leases, 1531–1700, incl. plans of hall 1700, 1767 (*88*; also ref. to *104*). MS 6356: 18C abs. of title, 1531–97 (*88*).

b. MSS 6330/1,2: wardens' a/c bks., 1497–1681, incl. rent receipts from 1540.

c. MS 6335: extracts of court orders 1603–38 (from court minutes), incl. lease 1615.

36. GIRDLERS' COMPANY
The estate lay in: *77, 98, 123, 125, 152*. The records are in GL.

a. MSS 5791–3, 5798–9: deeds and leases, 14C to 19C, incl. (MS 5793) plan 1696 (*77*); also ref. (MS 5799) to *62*.

b. MS 5817: account of benefactions, comp. 15C to 16C, incl. copy wills, lists of deeds, 15C to 16C (*77, 123, 125*).

c. MS 5814A/1: wardens' a/cs, 1654–71, incl. receipts of rent, fines for leases.

d. MS 5803: bk. of court orders 1623–1742, comp. *c.* 1750 from minute bks. now lost, arranged alphabetically by subject; a few refs. to properties (by tenants' names).

37. GLAZIERS' COMPANY
The records are in GL.

a. MS 5758, deeds and leases (severely damaged), 16C to 17C (*114*; also ref. (16C) to *96*).

38. GOLDSMITHS' COMPANY
Unless otherwise stated the estate was as follows:
   A (acquired before *c.* 1500): *2, 5, 10, 11, 13, 23, 30, 42, 45, 46, 53, 54, 60, 62, 74, 75, 85, 92, 100, 104, 105, 120, 124, 128, 129, 132, 137, 141, 144, 145, 151, 152, 159*. Properties in *10, 11, 13, 30, 53, 74, 105, 128, 141, 145*, appear to have been sold in or before 1550: cf. MS 1524, Bk. 1, p. 102.
   B (acquired after *c.* 1500): *47* (earlier *137, 152*), *48, 56* (acq. 1620), *84* (acq. 1648), *112, 135, 155* (? sold 1550).
The records are at Goldsmiths' Hall.

a. Title deeds, 16C to 20C, listed in a modern schedule arranged by property; those earlier than 1700 concern *5, 23, 42, 45, 46, 60, 62, 75, 100, 120, 132, 144, 151, 159*. The deeds also incl. grant, 1393 (= HR 121 (192)) concerning *5, 11, 75, 120, 137, 144, 145, 151, 152, 159*.

b. 'Register of Deeds': copies of deeds and wills 13C to 17C, comp. 1417–1657 (MS E/III 2 contains abs. of wills entered in this register to 1625). MS 1647: register of deeds and wills comp. 1726, incl. 17C deeds (*75, 84*). MS 1943: 19C will bk., incl. plans of company properties. MS 1913: bk.

listing all company leases in 1610 with later additions (also ref. to a leasehold property in *105*; MS 1930 cont. same information for 1638–97). MSS 1729, 1737, 1915 (part): bks. of copies of leases, *c.* 1650–70. MSS 1915 (part), 1916–18: minutes of committee of contractors for leases, recording negotiations for leases, *c.* 1650–75. MS 1924: register of assignments of company leases. MSS 1725, 1727, 1730: extracts from leases *c.* 1650–18C (incl. refs. to plans of 1692, see below, **f**).

c. MSS 1518–48: wardens' a/cs and court minutes, 1332–1659. Most of the volumes up to early 17C incl. a rough 19C schedule of contents (see also W. S. Prideaux, *Memorials of the Goldsmiths' Company*, 1896–7); later vols. incl. contemporary indexes of persons and some other matters. The vols. do not record rent receipts in detail and do not regularly incl. the total sums received. Most grants of leases appear to be recorded but are difficult to identify with specific properties; few of them are noted in the 19C schedules. MS 1518 incl. copies of deeds concerning *75*; MS 1521 incl. detailed records of the whole estate in 1494–7 (pp. 41–5, 149–225, 287–96). The 15C records of quarterage payments enumerate goldsmiths according to the streets or areas where they plied their trade; there are also 16C and 17C lists of goldsmiths holding shops in Cheapside and Lombard Street (cf. T. F. Reddaway, 'Elizabethan London: Goldsmiths' Row in Cheapside, 1558–1645', *Guildhall Miscellany* vol. 2, no. 5 (1963), 181–206).

d. MS 2524, Book of Ordinances and Statutes, 1478–83 (printed in T. F. Reddaway and Lorna E. M. Walker, *The Early History of the Goldsmiths' Company, 1327–1509* (1975), 209–74): incl. ordinances relating to estate management.

e. MS 1731: detailed description of the company's tenements, 1651, with some additions, 1670–1. Former GL, MS 8757 (now at Goldsmiths' Hall): file of draft leases and other papers, 17C–18C.

f. Loose plans of company properties, surveyed 1692 and indexed in MS 2839. See also above, **b**.

39. GROCERS' COMPANY
Unless otherwise stated, the estate was as follows:
　A: *9, 11, 26, 45, 48, 53, 62, 85, 88, 92, 103, 104, 123, 124, 128, 132, 142, 148, 149, 152, 156*, Thames Street nr. Baynards Castle.
　B (William Laxton's bequest, 1556): *157*, Abchurch Lane, Bush Lane, Candlewick Street, Eastcheap, St. Nicholas Lane, Sherborne Lane.
Unless otherwise stated, the records are in GL.

a. Grocers' Hall, deeds and copy deeds, 16C to 20C (*2, 44, 45, 124, 132*); also post-Fire deeds and leases, 17C to 20C (*98, 105, 142, 148, 157*); catalogues (1965) at Grocers' Hall.

b. MS 11616: register of evidences begun 1524, indexed 1762; wills and deeds, 15C to 17C. MS 11621: 19C transcripts of wills from MS 11616. MS 11737: list, 1786, of benefactors and estates, 15C to 18C. MS 11652: register of 17C to 18C deeds and leases, 2 vols., comp. 18C. MS 11653: list of 17C to 19C deeds, comp. 19C, similar to MS 11652. See also below, MS 11570A.

c. MS 11570A: ordinances, remembrances, and a/cs, 1463–1557, incl. summary a/cs, noting 15C repairs (*11, 26, 48, 53, 85, 95, 132*, Candlewick Street); 15C wills (*11, 26, 53*). MSS 11571/1–2: wardens' a/cs, 1454–71; rents and repairs (*11, 26, 45, 48, 53, 95, 132*, Candlewick Street, Cornhill). MSS 11571/3–15: wardens' a/cs, 1511–71: rents and fines (estates A and B). MS 11728: a/c of Middleton's charity, 1632–66 (Thames Street nr. Baynards Castle). See also below, MS 11570.

d. MS 11570, 'Black Book', comp. 1345–1463 (reproduced in *Facsimile of First Volume of MS. Archives of the Worshipful Company of Grocers*, ed. J. A. Kingdon (1886); TS index in GL, Dept. of Printed Books): ordinances, remembrances (refs. to hall, garden , *48, 156*), and rent a/cs 1448–50 (*26, 48, 53, 95*, Candlewick Street). MSS 11588/1–4: minutes of court of assistants, 1556–1668 (estates A and B); TS calendar and index in GL, Dept. of MSS.

40. GUNMAKERS' COMPANY
The estate lay in *43* and/or *45*. The records are in GL.

a. MS 5219/1: renter wardens' a/cs, 1663–1745; incl. rents paid for hall, contributions towards Proof Place.

b. MSS 5220/1, 3: court minutes 1637–71; incl. lease and rents paid for Proof Place. MS 5222/1: 18C index to court minutes.

41. HABERDASHERS' COMPANY
Unless otherwise stated, the estate lay in: *9, 20, 30, 32, 36, 38, 39, 46, 49, 53, 54, 56, 59, 62, 64, 74, 78, 83, 87, 92, 94, 117, 119, 128, 129, 132, 152, 157, 159* (properties in several parishes were not acquired until 17C). For the records, see W. Le Hardy, *The Worshipful Company of Haberdashers: the Descriptive Class List of Records* (1954). Unless otherwise stated, the records are in GL.

a. Haberdashers' Hall, deeds and leases 13C to 17C, arranged according to the charities to which they refer. Items are to be identified from the entries in the current TS calendar, filed on slips and kept in the strong room. The following files incl. relevant entries: 'Company Properties', 'Minor Charities' (Barnes, Baron, Blundell, Bodington and Boulter, Bond, Bramley, Buckland, Collins, Dowman, Essex, Gale, Hamond, Morgan, Offley, Pecok, Rainton, and Whitmore), 'Jones (Monmouth) General', 'Sundry Sales A–M' (Jeston), 'Trotman A, Trotman B, Weld' (Trotman Redundant Properties), and 'Aske General'. These cover estate as above (apart from *20, 39, 53, 54, 56, 78, 92, 94*) and also incl. refs. to *5* (Bond; from 1671 only), *10* (Aske General), *19* (Dowman), *45* (Aske, Bodington and Boulter), *96* (Pecok).

b. MS 15873: will bk. 1571–1908, comp. from 1571, incl. rental of ? c. 1571 (*26, 30, 38, 78, 117, 119, 128, 129, 152, 157, 159*). MS 15874, 'The State of the Charities, 1597', comp. early 17C: copies and abs. of deeds and leases

14C to 17C (also refs. to *155*); copies of 15C agreements concerning hall. MS 15875, 'Register of Benefactions, 1607': incl. sale of property in *152* and bonds concerning house in *39*. MS 15897, 'William Jones's Charity': translations of charters and letters patent, incl. list of company property in 1620.

c. For rental of ? *c.* 1571, see above, **b.** MS 15876: rental of company and charity property, 1657. MSS 15866/1–2: wardens' a/cs 1633–69; incl. rent receipts.

d. MSS 15842/1–2: court of assistants minute bks., 1583–1671; incl. petitions for and grants of leases (marginal notes identify many entries concerning properties).

e. MSS 15860/1–3: registers of apprentice bindings, 1583–1611; incl. bonds for debts naming place where repayment was to be made; between 1593 and 1605 private conveyances were entered in the registers (refs. to *62, 152*, Chancery Lane).

f. Haberdashers' Hall, Class XXVI no. 18, vol. 1: plan bk. of city properties, comp. 1761.

42. INNHOLDERS' COMPANY
The estate lay in Coleman Street (probably *155*). The records are in GL.

a. MS 6647/1: wardens' and renter wardens' a/cs, 1664–1705; incl. rent receipts (no locations), extracts from court minutes incl. memoranda of leases.

b. MS 6649/1; court minutes, 1642–65; incl. memoranda of rents.

c. MS 6648A: clerk's rough memoranda bk., 17C, incl. correspondence 1655 on repairs. MS 6664: vol. of inventories, late 17C to 18C, incl. note of rents 1670.

43. IRONMONGERS' COMPANY
Unless otherwise stated, the estate lay in: *13, 37, 59, 62, 83, 93, 117, 125, 132, 136, 141, 142, 151, 152*. Cf. John Nicholl, *Some account of the Worshipful Company of Ironmongers* (2nd edn. 1866), 421–6, 469–80. The records are in GL.

a. MSS 17072, 17159, 17159A, 17160, 17176, 17180, 17184, 17244, 17874: deeds, 14C to 17C (estate above, also company property in *42* (MS 17176) and *47* (MS 17180), refs. to *85, 87, 108* (MS 17159); pars. mostly named on GL catalogue cards; calendars of deeds in MSS 17158/1–3 and 17169). MS 17136: p. 257 incl. 16C deed (*37*).

b. MSS 17183, 17186, 17247–8: leases, 16C–17C (*62, 117, 136, 142, 152*). See also below, **c.**

c. MS 17003: will and charter bk., comp. 16C to early 18C, cont. wills and royal charters (estate plus refs. to *90, 108*), rentals and abstracts of leases; for 19C copies of the wills, see MS 17004. MS 17153: bk. of title deeds, comp. 18C, cont. abs. of deeds, 16C to 18C (incl. ref. to *156*). MS 17154:

vol. comp. 18C to 19C of abs. of title and leases, 16C and later (incl. refs. to Amen Corner, Water Lane).

d. MSS 16988/1–6, 'Registers' (wardens' a/cs and inventories), 1455–1670: receipts of rents, payments of quit-rents, and expenditure on repairs for 15C and 16C (details of receipts of rents omitted in 17C, but see below, MS 17161); from mid 16C the inventories list leases and other evidences (refs. to *21, 90, 108*); fines on leases recorded in 17C. MS 17170: 15C receipts for payments of quit-rents (*13*). MS 17191: list of rents due to Crown after dissolution of chantries, comp. 1650 (*83, 132, 136*). MS 17161: rentals, 1618–44; incl. ref. to St. Nicholas Lane (?*93*).

e. MSS 16967/1–6: court minute bks., 1555–1685; administration of estate, much topographical detail but no adequate index. MSS 16969/1–2: rough court minute bks., 1572–6, 1593–1613.

f. MSS 17163, 17168, 17171, 17199, 17203, 17250: papers and memoranda, 16C to 18C (also refs. to *155* (MS 17199), *156* (MS 17168), *157* (MS 17203)). MS 16966, copies of charters, 18C to 20C.

g. MS 17254: written survey of Old Street area (*62*), by William Leybourn, 1671.

44. JOINERS' COMPANY

The estate (hall and other properties) lay in *10*. The records are in GL.

a. MSS 8063–4: deeds, 1497–1830.

b. MS 8065: leases, 1574–1858; also surrender 1619 (St. Paul's churchyard).

c. MS 8060, 'Lease Book', comp. 19C: copy deeds and schedule of same, 16C to 19C.

d. MS 8041/1: renter wardens' a/cs, 1621–84; rent receipts, fines for leases (locations not given).

e. MS 8047/1: court minutes (rough), 1661–4, incl. memoranda of receipts of rent.

f. GL, Prints and Drawings, Pr 598/UPP: plan of hall and adjacent properties, 1839.

45. LEATHERSELLERS' COMPANY

The estate lay principally in: *14, 49, 64, 142*. See W. H. Black, *History and Antiquities of the Worshipful Company of Leathersellers of the City of London* (1871). The records are at Leathersellers' Hall; the company's current 'Estate Book and Schedule of title deeds' lists most of them and gives their locations.

a. Box 10, nos. 1–75: 13C to 16C deeds (*14*; also refs. to *2, 104, 128, 142, 148, 152, 155*). Box 14: 16C and 17C deeds, leases, bonds, and other papers (*64* (site of St. Helen's Priory precinct and company hall); for modern schedule see Box P). Box 'L. Co. no. 2': incl. 16C and 17C deeds

(*64*). Charter Case: incl. framed 15C and 17C deeds (*14, 64*). Box 10, separate bundle: 16C and 17C deeds and leases (*142*).

b. Box O, bk. entitled 'Wills etc.' comp. 16C and 17C: copies of 15C to 17C wills and other documents (*14, 49, 142*, Gracechurch Street; also refs. to *45, 62*). On shelf near Box P, bk. entitled 'Copies of Leases and Deeds, 1555–1660': register of leases (*14, 49, 64, 142*).

c. Boxes G and H: 3 vols. each entitled 'Liber Curtes' and cont. wardens' a/cs, rentals, and inventories, 1471–1680 (rents and fines from *14, 49, 64, 142*, Gracechurch Street, together with expenditure on the estate and copies of court minutes concerning its management; the earliest vol. also incl. refs. to *62*). Box Q: 2 vols. of wardens' a/cs (rough), 1608–80.

d. Box A, 4 vols. of court minutes, 1608–73 (fair copies) and 1608–76 (rough copies): the rough copies incl. minutes not entered in the fair copies (the box incl. a TS copy of these minutes for 1622–3): much information on leasing and the condition of properties.

e. Box P, bk. entitled 'Bonds, 1558–1646': incl. ref. to *46*.

f. In Charter Case: early 17C plan of houses in *14*. The plan bk. of 1871 is also useful for London properties.

46. MASONS' COMPANY
The estate (hall and other properties) lay in *123*. The records are in GL.

a. MS 5324: deeds, copy deeds, and leases, 1562–1707.

b. MS 5313: quarterage bk., late 17C; incl. schedule, comp. 1676, of deeds and leases, 1463–1576.

c. MS 5303/1: renter wardens' a/cs, 1620–1706; incl. rent receipts (tenements near hall), repairs to hall.

d. MS 5316: misc. file, incl. list of deeds as in MS 5324. MS 5330: misc. file, incl. bond 1569 to keep covenants of lease.

47. MERCERS' COMPANY
The London estates fall into three main groups reflected in the arrangement of the archive:

A (Company estate): *4, 5, 9, 11, 19, 26, 32, 36, 45, 53, 61, 62, 63, 71, 74, 80, 81, 83, 87, 94, 95, 100, 104, 105, 111, 119, 123, 124, 126, 129, 132, 137, 141, 142, 145, 149, 155, 156, 158*, Baynards Castle, Mark Lane. This includes the endowment of Whittington's charity (cf. Jean Imray, *The Charity of Richard Whittington*, 1968) and of Collyer's School (cf. A. N. Wilson, *A History of Collyer's School*, 1965) and of part of the former estate of the hospital of St. Thomas of Acre (cf. **85**). A number of properties in *32, 36, 45, 53, 62, 81, 83, 87, 94, 104, 105, 123, 129, 141, 142, 155*, and *156* were sold in 1550.

B (St. Paul's School estate): *26, 59, 61, 85, 145*, St. Paul's churchyard.

C (Gresham estate): Royal Exchange (*32, 48, 124*) and Gresham College (*64, 148*); see also **15**.
The records are at Mercers' Hall.

a. Deeds and leases, 13C to 20C. To be identified in two series of calendars ('Trusts' and 'Estates'), each cont. synopsis naming localities covered. London deeds before 1666 are to be found in the calendars for the following trusts: Colet (estate B, as above), Collyer (*104*), Dauntesey (*124, 149*), Lady Gresham (*26, 81, 129, 145*), Sir Thomas Gresham (Royal Exchange), Henry VIII (*81, 105, 156, 158*), Mercers' early livelihood (*81, 104*), Rich (*5, 53, 85, 98, 101, 131*), Whittington Estate (*46, 63, 80, 81, 124, 132*), Yarford (*11, 137*). Also in the calendars for the following estates: Lady Gresham (Milk Street), Chalgrave (*19, 46, 53, 104, 111, 129, 132, 142, 145, 155, 156, 158*, Tower Street), Colet (estate B, as above), Collyer (*145*).

b. Registers of Writings ii and iii (for vol. i, see **85**), comp. 16C and early 17C: copies of charters, deeds, wills, leases, rentals, inquisitions, views, legal proceedings, and parish assessments, 14C to 17C (estates A, B, and C); there is a 20C 'analysis' and calendar for each volume which organizes material under various subject headings, incl. separate properties (some categories overlap; careful use will identify all references to particular properties). Registers of Wills: Register P, comp. 16C and early 17C, incl. both views and wills with index and list of contents (estates A and C); a second vol., comp. late 17C to late 18C, incl. transcript of Register P and later material; a third vol., comp. 19C, copies the second. 'Evidence of Dr. Collett's Lands', comp. early 16C: copies of deeds, 14C to 16C (estate B). 'Registers of Leases', 3 vols., 1478–1572, 1597–1644, each with full list of contents (estates A and B; first vol. also refers to *99*). 'Gresham Estate Book of Leases' i: copies of leases 1598–1629, incl. list of lessees' names (Royal Exchange). Whittington College 'Grants' (see calendar entitled 'Whittington College & Estate'): leases of rooms in the college (*126*), 1583–1665.

c. Rental of Whittington estate in 1431 (printed in Imray, op. cit., 122–6). 'Cheke's Register': lists rents for estates A and B, as above, 1578–9. Wardens' a/cs, 1347, 1391–1464, in one vol. (for an edition, see Heather Janet Creaton, 'The Warden's Accounts of the Mercers' Company of London, 1347, 1391–1464' (University of London M.Phil. Thesis, 1976)): incl. rents for *94* and *104* and expenditure on these properties and at the hall. Renter warden's a/cs, 12 vols. 1442–1666: rents under street or parish headings, expenditure on buildings (estate A); some a/cs are in both rough and fair copies. Second wardens' a/cs, 7 vols., 1617–58: receipts from fines on leases (estate A); inventory of hall; some a/cs are in both rough and fair copies. Renter and second wardens' a/cs, first vol., 1666–71: incl. record of rearrangement of leases after the Fire (estate A). St. Paul's School surveyors' a/cs (or third wardens' a/cs), 6 vols. 1620–81: rents and fines on leases (estate B). Gresham estate a/c bk., 1596–1625: rents and expenditure on repairs (estate C). Gresham estate renter wardens' a/cs, 4 vols. 1625–75: contents as for 1596–1625 vol., except repairs; some a/cs are in both rough and fair copies. PRO, E101/522/8A: declaration, 1595–6, by master and wardens, of revenue of St. Paul's School.

d. Acts of Court. Fair series, 5 vols. 1453–1629, 1634–49; rough or 'working' series, 10 vols. 1619–75, and continuing: management of estates A, B, and C; also, in 17C vols., numerous detailed surveys of properties, with dimensions and valuations. First vol. (1453–1527) printed as *Acts of Court of the Mercers' Company, 1453–1527*, ed. L. Lyell and F. D. Watney (1936); TS transcript of second vol. (1527–60) and MS transcript and card index of third vol. (1560–95) at Mercers' Hall. There is a 19C list of marginal notes in both series (fair series to 1619 only), providing a rough guide to contents, but of little use for topographical purposes.

e. Transcript of inquisition, 1509 (*10* or *12*); see calendar of Whittington College estate. Other 16C and 17C papers concerning the Mercers' estate, including the hall, are filed with the deeds and listed in the calendars (cf. above, **a**).

f. Plan, 17C, of property in *81* (see calendar of Whittington College & Estate). Plan book of London properties, *c.* 1780 (filed under 'General Estates'). There are also 18C and 19C plans of Mercers' Hall and adjacent properties; see also BL, Prints and Drawings, Crace Collection Portfolio ix, no. 192.

48. MERCHANT TAYLORS' COMPANY
Unless otherwise stated, the estate was as follows:
A (acquired before *c.* 1580): *2, 5, 10, 12, 19, 36, 43, 45, 48, 49, 51, 53, 56, 62, 64, 67, 71, 74, 80, 90, 92, 93, 94, 96, 98, 100, 101, 105, 106, 112, 119, 120, 123, 124, 126, 136, 149, 155.*
B (acquired after *c.*1580): *30, 32, 42, 46, 68, 78, 111, 118, 141,158*, St. Swithin's Lane.
The estate is described in C. M. Clode, *Early History of the Guild of Merchant Taylors* (1888) i, 407–15. The records are at Merchant Taylors' Hall; microfilms of most of the MSS in book form are in GL (microfilms 297–364, with handlist; cited below as mf. 297, etc.).

a. Deeds and leases: Misc. Docs. A, 14C to 17C (*2, 10, 32, 36, 51, 53, 74, 80, 90, 92, 94, 96, 98, 105, 107, 111, 119, 120, 124, 149*); Misc. Docs. B, 14C to 16C (*9, 10, 98, 104, 105, 119, 126, 156*; also refs. to Blanchappleton, Stywards Inn); Ancient Title Deeds, 14C to 17C (estates A and B, also *14, 63*). Calendar, 20C, to above, 3 vols. (mf. 321). Expired leases, mid 17C onwards (in boxes by street location).

b. Ancient MS Bk. 5 (mf. 310): memorial of benefactions, comp. 1578 (estate A; also refs. to *9, 14*). Anc. MS Bk. 8 (mf. 310): evidence bk., comp. 1605; abs. of deeds, 14C to 17C, and extent, 1605 (estate A, also *42, 46, 111, 141*). Anc. MS Bk. 9 (mf. 310): wills bk., comp. before 1609; wills and grants, 14C to 17C (estate A and most of B; also refs. to *4, 14*). Anc. MS Bks. 28, 29 (mf. 311): lists of benefactors' gifts, comp. mid-17C (estate A, also *42, 46, 68*). Anc. MS Bk. 30 (mf. 312): 'benefactors' gifts', comp. *c.* 1680; abs. of grants, 14C to 17C, also noting current tenant, lease, and rent (estates A and B). Anc. MS Bk. 14 (mf. 311): abs. of leases, 1550–1660 (estates A and B); contemp. index. Anc. MS Bk. 13 (mf. 311): survey of bks., plate, etc., comp. 1689; incl. lists of muniments and pre-Fire leases (*10, 30, 36, 42, 53, 62, 71, 96, 105, 106, 132, 158,*

Elbow Lane, Knightrider Street, Moorfields, St. Swithin's Lane, Threadneedle Street).

c. Anc. MS Bk. 19: rental 1632 (estate A and most of B). Anc. MS Bk. 37, 2 vols. (mf. 312; 20C transcript and table of contents, mf. 364): records, financial and administrative, 1486–93, incl. repairs and quit-rent payments (*2, 5, 19, 67, 71, 94, 96, 98, 99, 105, 120*, Cornhill, Lombard Street, 'the Sterre'). Anc. MS Bk. 4 (mf. 310): a/c of the treasury, 1489 to late 16C; building and repairs, late 15C (*71* or *96, 105, 120*, hall). Wardens' a/cs, 22 vols. 1397–1484, 1545–1648, 1652–9, 1663–6 (mfs. 297–305, except for 1645–8, 1652–8, 1663–5, not filmed): rent receipts, fines, quit-rent payments. Draft upper renter wardens' a/cs, 1 vol. 1631, 1652, 1664–5, 1668–9: rent receipts ('west view': *2, 5, 30, 67, 71, 92, 96, 99, 100, 111, 112, 120, 123, 126, 158*, St. Swithin's Lane). Draft under renter wardens' a/cs, 3 vols. 1622, 1626, 1631–4, 1636–43, 1645–55, 1658, 1660, 1664–5, 1667–9: rent receipts, quit-rent payments ('east view': remainder of estates A and B; also part 'west view', 1660–1). Account bk. for John Hide's trust, 1604–51 (*46, 68*).

d. Court minute bks., 10 vols. 1562–1673 (mfs. 325–330): minutes of ordinary assistants' and quarterday courts, 2 series overlapping; 20C index, 1562–1748, 3 vols. (mf. 363). Anc. MS Bk. 20 (mf. 311): view bk., 1642–64 (estates A and B); damaged.

e. Anc. MS Bk. 17 (mf. 311) 'Miscellaneous, 1586–1651': precedent bk., incl. copy lease (*60*), letter to Commissioners of Building (*30*). Anc. MS Bk. 23 (mf. 311): Fire Ct. decrees, after 1666. Anc. MS Bk. 54 (2) (mf. 312): a/cs for building work, 1592–1673 (company hall, almshouses, and school; unidentified properties).

f. Anc. MS Bk. 24 (mf. 311): plan bk., 1680. Anc. MS Bk. 25 (mf. 311): plan bk., 1694–5; 19C index.

49. PAINTER-STAINERS' COMPANY
The estate (hall) lay in *67*. The records are in GL.

a. MS 5670: deeds and leases, 1423–1650.

b. MSS 5667/1, 2, 'Orders and Constitutions': court minutes, 1623–1793; incl. receipts of rent for use of hall.

c. MS 11505: terrier, 18C, with plan of hall *c.* 1766.

50. PARISH CLERKS' COMPANY
The records are in GL (many were destroyed in 1940). See R. H. Adams, *The Parish Clerks of London* (1971).

a. MSS 4896–7, 4899, 4902–3: deeds, 16C and 17C (*2, 157*). MS 4895: 17C leases of site of hall (*96*) to the company.

b. Register of deeds, comp. 1522 (destroyed in 1940, but extracts given in James Christie, *Some account of Parish Clerks, more especially of the Ancient Fraternity (Bretherne and Sisterne) of St. Nicholas now known as the Worshipful Company of Parish Clerks* (1893) and in MS 4894/1): incl. deeds 13C to 16C (*29, 58, 61, 62, 83*).

c. MS 4890: receipt bk., 1583–1657; rent paid for site of hall (*96*).

d. MS 3706: extracts from minutes 1610–1926, comp. 20C (originals destroyed in 1940); 17C refs. to hall (*96*).

e. MS 4894/1: collections for a history of the company made 1940–6, incl. notes of 12C (?) deed concerning *58* and of deeds as above, **b**; draft grant and copy of lease 16C to 17C (*2, 157*); 19C to 20C notes on site of hall (*29, 58*).

51. PAVIOURS' COMPANY
The records are in GL.

a. MSS 182/1–3: court minute bks., 1565–1670, incl. 17C records of rent paid for the hall in Worcester Place (*71*).

b. MS 183A: incl. (in larger bundle) 17C receipts for rent paid for hall and account of money spent on hall 1649; also 17C lists of faults found in paviours' work (individuals and streets named; similar lists in MS 182/25).

52. PEWTERERS' COMPANY
The records are in GL; for them and the estate, see Charles Welch, *History of the Worshipful Company of Pewterers of the City of London* (1902).

a. MSS 8703, 8707–13, 8715: deeds, leases, and abs. of title, 14C to 20C (*51, 62, 98, 157*). MS 8704: 16C will (*62*).

b. MS 7114: ordinance and record bk., comp. 15C to 16C; incl. deed (*105*). MS 7110: inventory and record bk., comp. 15C to 18C; inventories list deeds now lost (*105*); copies of 15C to 17C deeds and wills (*12, 36, 43, 141, 142, 148, 157*). MS 7109: 17C register incl. extracts from 15C to 17C deeds and wills (*51, 98, 116, 131, 157*). For 19C copies of deeds, see MS 7112.

c. MSS 7086/1–4: audit bks., 1451–1717, incl. rent receipts (*51, 62, 98, 105, 116, 131, 157*). MS 8704: 16C to 17C receipts for quit-rents (*51, 98*). MS 8714: incl. 15C receipt for rent (*105*).

d. MSS 7090/1–6: court minute bks., 1551–1675, incl. notices of tenants and leases (locations not usually given).

53. PINMAKERS' COMPANY
a. BL, MS Egerton 1142: act and a/c bk., 1464–1501; refs. to Pinners' Hall (? in *2*) and other places where the company met.

54. PLAISTERERS' COMPANY
The records are in GL.

a. MSS 6134, 6136–7, 6139–42: 16C to 18C deeds and abs. of title (site of hall and adjacent houses in *2, 15, 99*; also refs. to *92* (MS 6140) and 'le Olde Ryall' (MS 6139)). See also MS 3555/3, for 19C abstracts.

b. MSS 6122/1–2: court minutes and a/cs, 1571–63 (a vol. for 1522–39 is now lost, but there is a partial 19C transcript: MS 2192, cf. MS 3555/4); minutes for quarter days incl. details of receipts of rent, presumably from houses next to the hall.

55. PLAYING-CARD MAKERS' COMPANY
The records are in GL. There are no records of property ownership before 1666, but MS 5963/1, court minutes 1647–74, incl. refs. to courts meeting in Bishopsgate, Grub Street, Weavers' Hall.

56. PLUMBERS' COMPANY
The records are in GL.

a. MSS 2225/1, 3–4: 16C to 18C deeds (*10, 64, 134*).

b. MSS 2210/1–2: a/c bks., 1593–1721, incl. rent receipts and expenditure on hall (*10, 64*).

c. MSS 2208/1–3: court minute bks., 1621–61, incl. records of leases and rents (*10, 64*, Queen Street (in 1643; perhaps located in *62*, cf. **d**)). MS 2209/1: rough minute bk., 1659–69.

d. MS 5766: a/c bk. of gift of John Randall, 1631–9, incl. copy of will concerning properties in *45* and *62* and a/cs of rents from the same (in *45* and in Queen Street).

57. POULTERS' COMPANY
The records are in GL. See P. E. Jones, *The Worshipful Company of Poulters of the City of London* (2nd edn. 1965).

a. MS 2160: 17C deeds (*149*). MS 5081: late 17C deeds (*26*). MS 5074: 19C papers (*9*, bequeathed in 1548).

b. MS 2150/1: a/c bk., 1619–1705: incl. rent receipts (*9, 13, 149*), schedule of 16C to 17C deeds (*9, 149*).

58. SADDLERS' COMPANY
The estate lay in *2, 14, 42, 43, 54, 62, 78, 123, 141, 151, 152, 159*. Most of the records were destroyed in 1940; the remainder are in GL and at Saddlers' Hall.

a. Saddlers' Hall, 'Record Bk.' (GL MS 5385A is photographic copy), comp. 15C to 17C: incl. copy wills 1433–1568; rental, 1440–1 (? incomplete); royal charter, 1619 (estate except *2, 62, 123*). Saddlers' Hall, papers incl. copy wills, 16C and 19C (*141*, Aldgate, Fleet Street).

b. GL, MS 5384: audit bk. (audited wardens' a/cs), 1555–1822; incl. total rent receipts, memoranda of arrears of rents and outstanding fines.

c. GL, MS 5385: minute bk. 1605–65, incl. memoranda of leases, decisions on property.

59. SALTERS' COMPANY
Unless otherwise stated, the estate was as follows:

A: *5, 15, 21, 47, 61, 62, 73, 100, 111, 120, 137, 144*.

B (acquired in 17C and with no earlier records surviving): *37, 56, 157*. The records are at Salters' Hall. There is a full TS list compiled *c.* 1975, together with a check list which serves as a partial concordance between the present numbering system and that used in earlier lists. There is also a file of notes and transcripts from the records, apparently compiled by Lillian Redstone (cf. below, **a**).

a. Deeds and leases, fully described in the list: royal grants 15C to 17C (A1, A2); archiepiscopal decree 16C concerning parish church of *5* (B2); deeds and leases, 14C to 17C, also incl. refs. to *83, 131* (H1 and the former class C3), and to *106* (P1/1/1); a badly damaged 13C deed (formerly C3/6/1, calendared in Redstone's notes, f. 74ᵛ) contained refs. to *5, 37, 62, 93, 118, 120*, and St. Mildred in the street of the Lorimerie (?*132*); leases, 16C and 17C (H3).

b. Bk. of leases and wills, comp. 1611 (H2/1/1). Bk. of abs. of leases 16C–17C, comp. 17C (H2/1/2). Estate bk. comp. 1717–18, names tenants 1666 and 1668 onwards (H2/1/6).

c. Renter wardens' a/cs, 1599–1600 (J1/2 in box with D1/1/1), 1659–60 and 1661–72 (J1/1/1/1): incl. locations and names of tenants.

d. Minute bk., 1627–84, with contemp. index of personal names (D1/1/1, 2): incl. grants of leases. See also two pages of rough late 16C minutes (D3/1/1, kept in red box).

e. Detailed plan bk. of 1709 and later (no current reference number, formerly H5/1); plan of property in *62* dated 1675 (formerly H5/4).

60. SCRIVENERS' COMPANY
The records are in GL.

a. MS 8723: copy deed and fine, 1628 (*117*).

61. SKINNERS' COMPANY
Unless otherwise stated, the estate was as follows:
  A (acquired before *c.* 1500): *5, 10, 11, 15, 26, 45, 74, 93, 100, 105* (sold in 1550), *132, 156* (sold in 1550).
  B (acquired after *c.* 1500): *9, 14, 30, 53, 60, 64, 78, 80, 83, 87* (sold in 1550), *96, 101, 107, 123, 149, 158*, Lime Street.
  C (acquired after *c.* 1600): *126*, perhaps also *152*.
The records are at Skinners' Hall; they are described and numbered in the TS 'Calendar of Records of the Skinners' Company' (1965) reproduced by NRA. See also **397**.

a. 5/1–333: deeds, 13C to 17C, fully described in the 'Calendar' (also refs. to *4, 22, 32, 36, 46, 62, 63, 67, 75, 81, 94, 104, 111, 117, 120, 124, 131, 145, 155*).

b. 9/6: register bk. written 1578; incl. abs. of title and schedule of leases; some full copies of deeds were added later. 9/1: 18C bk. cont. copies of 15C to 18C wills (also refs. to *4, 49*, Petty Wales).

c. 3A/1–7: receipts and payments bks., 1491–1672; rent receipts from and expenditure on most properties can be identified.

d. 2A/1–4: court bks., 1551–1667; refs. to properties and places can be identified from the series of indexes in 2B.

e. 9/2: 15C illuminated bk. of the fraternity of Our Lady's Assumption; incl. a view concerning *132* (f. 29ᵛ).

f. 7/1 and 2: plan bks. comp. *c.* 1700 with later additions.

62. STATIONERS' COMPANY
The records are in GL.

a. MS 2571: 19C bk. of copy PCC wills, 16C (*20, 46, 59, 89, 108, 152*).

63. TALLOW CHANDLERS' COMPANY
The estate lay in: *18, 43, 45, 47, 48, 58, 62, 74, 93, 137*. See M. F. Monier-Williams, *Records of the Worshipful Company of Tallow Chandlers* (1907); annotated copy in GL, MS 6185/2. Unless otherwise stated, the records are in GL.

a. MSS 6180/1–492: deeds, 15C to 20C, catalogued in MS 6185/1, 'Inventory of deeds', *c.* 1905 (estate above, also refs. to *42* (no. 73), *118, 126* (nos. 274–5), *134* (nos. 254–5)). MS 6184: deed, 1542 (*62*).

b. MS 6165/1: 17C terrier, incl. memoranda of title, leases, tenants; copy and abs. deeds. MS 6172: 18C abs. title, incl. copy deeds, 17C–18C (*62*).

c. MSS 6152/1–3. 'Livery Accompt Bks.' 1549–1703: incl. rent and quit-rent receipts, fines for leases, in separate annual a/cs. MS 18812/1: rough renter-wardens' a/cs, 1665, 1667, 1668, 1675; rent receipts. MS 18813/1: master and warden's a/c, 1667–8, incl. fine for lease.

d. MSS 6153/1–3, 'Livery Court Bks.' 1607–68: minutes, grants of leases, etc.

e. Plans: plan bks. of 1678 and 1790 are at Tallow Chandlers' Hall.

64. TURNERS' COMPANY
The estate lay in: *19, 21*. The records are in GL.

a. MS 3804: deeds and leases, 1606–1766; also incl. schedule of deeds 1632–97 (*126*). MS 3803: papers 1697–1766, incl. abs. title 1633–1725 (*126*).

b. MS 3801: inventories of documents, plate; incl. lists of evidences, leases, 1662, 1666.

c. MS 3297/1: wardens' a/c bk., 1593–1670; incl. rent receipts, fines for leases, repairs to hall (locations not always given). MS 3298/1: upper wardens' rough a/c bk., 1638–1747; daily receipts, incl. fines for leases.

d. MSS 3295/1–2: court minute bks., 1605–88; incl. (1st vol.) audited a/cs and rent totals, and (both vols.) grants of leases, decisions on properties.

65. TYLERS' AND BRICKLAYERS' COMPANY
The estate lay in: *36, 78*, Prince's Street. The records are in GL.

a. MS 4861: deeds 1528 to 19C; abs. of title 1583–1788 (*78*); will 1614 (*118*).

b. MSS 3054/1–2: cash and audit bks. (wardens' a/cs) 1605–57; incl. rent receipts, fines for leases, payments for work on hall (properties not always located).

c. MS 3043/1: court minute bk., 1580–1667; court decisions, incl. copy will (*36*). MSS 3043/2–3: court minutes, 1620–85; incl. leases, assignments, some refs. to rents and arrears, rebuilding of hall; cf. MS 4323, 19C bk. of extracts from court minutes, 1620–1859 (incl. (pt. 3) extracts relating to properties).

d. MS 3047/1–2: search and view bks., 1605–80; incl. views of work in many places.

66. VINTNERS' COMPANY
Unless otherwise stated, the estate was as follows:
A: *12, 21, 37, 44, 46, 56, 67, 71, 77, 78, 96, 100, 120, 126, 158.*
B (from mid-16C or later): *25, 51, 84, 128, 145.*
The early records, except charters, are in GL. Full TS calendar, 2 vols., comp. before 1974: supplementary vol., comp. 1975 by HMC, using additional MSS with index to calendar (all in GL). No cross-refs. from calendars to GL MSS numbers.

a. MSS 10062–10088A, 15372, 15450, 15452, 15456, 15461–4, 15468, 15475, 15484, 15494,15498, 15500, 15504, 15506, 15508, 15511: deeds and leases, 13C to 19C (estates A and B, also *30* (MS 15464), *83* (MSS 15372, 15500, 15504), *87* (MSS 15372, 15500), *112* (MS 10065), *113* (MSS 10065, 15464); also refs. to *9, 36, 43, 47, 62, 83, 118, 141, 157*, Bishopsgate, Queenhithe (MS 15475)); pars. mostly named on GL catalogue cards. See also 5 16C deeds deposited in GL 1981, as yet uncatalogued (*21, 83, 90*).

b. MSS 15444, 15447, 15450, 15452–3, 15459, 15461–2, 15465–7, 15481, 15494, 15502, 15504–5, 15509, 15511: leases, 16C to 18C (estates A and B; also *149* in MS 15481).

c. MS 15364: will bk. comp. *c.* 1656–1800, wills, 13C to 18C (*12, 21, 25, 44, 71, 77, 78, 96, 100, 126*; also refs. to *53, 108, 119, 159*, New Fish Street, Old Fish Street, Trinity Lane); also 16C list of persons and taverns allowed to retail wine. MS 15197: ordinance bk. 1407–1646; wills 15C to 16C (as in MS 15364 except *25*, also *37, 46, 56, 120*; also refs. to *9, 18, 36, 74, 83, 93, 94, 118, 129, 134*); also conts. list of benefactors' lands, comp. 16C (*21, 37, 44, 56, 71, 78, 96, 100, 120*). MS 15443, Irish letters: cont. abs. of London leases 1687 (*51*; estates A and B post Fire).

d. BL, MS Egerton 1143 (photostat: GL MS 6594): a/cs 1507–22, of rents (not detailed), quit-rents (*37, 46, 71, 96*). MSS 15333/1–5: register of a/cs, 1522–1687, rent receipts from 1531 (properties not detailed, 1595–1612) and fines (estates A and B); MS 15333/2 conts. list 1582 of benefactors' lands (*25, 37, 44, 46, 51, 56, 71, 77, 78, 96,100, 120*, Eastcheap).

e. MSS 15201/1–4: court minute bks., 1608–59, cont. some inf. on views and leases (estates A and B); MS 15201/1 cont. assessment 1610 on taverners within 3 miles of London; MS 15201/4 cont. lists of delinquent taverns in and near London, 1639 to 1659. MSS 15202/1–2: partial indexes, 1608–10, 1629–31, to MSS 15201/1,3. See also MSS 15197, 15364, above.

f. MSS 15365–8: papers, mainly 19C, relating to charities, incl. copy wills, abs. and schedules of deeds 13C to 19C (*21, 25, 56, 71, 96*).

g. MSS 15431/1, 15432/1: plan bks. 1808 of estate ('west' and 'east' views). MSS 15431/5, 15432/3: plan bks. 1865–6, as above.

67. WAX CHANDLERS' COMPANY
The estate lay in: *18, 42, 75, 112, 127, 155*. The records are in GL. See also **323**.

a. MSS 9503, 9506, 9509–10, 9512, 9524, 9527: deeds and papers, *c.* 1240–1712 (estate above, except *18*; pars. named on GL catalogue cards).

b. MSS 9507, 9511, 9513: leases, 1477–1854 (*42, 75, 127*; pars. named on GL catalogue cards).

c. MS 9495: ordinance, oath and evidence bk., comp. 15C to 17C, incl. copy wills, 16C to 17C (*18, 112, 127, 155, 158*). MS 9514: folder of original and copy wills, 15C to 18C (*112, 155, 158*). MS 9494/1: register of leases, 1584–1744, name and place index at end (estate above, except *18*).

d. MS 9482/1, 'Treasury Book', 1618–1730: wardens' rough a/cs, incl. fines for leases, notes of rent arrears (locations not always given); rental 1660. MSS 9481/1–2: renter wardens' a/c bks., 1531–58, 1564–97, 1602–71, incl. rent receipts, fines for leases, repairs (estate above, but locations not always given).

e. MS 9485/1: court minute bk., 1584–1689, incl. table of contents noting views for repairs; memorandum of rents 1608; grants of leases (not indexed); locations not always given).

f. MS 9516: view 1565 (*75*). MS 9525: inventory of goods, 1611 (*127*).

68. WEAVERS' COMPANY
The records are in GL. See F. Consitt, *The London Weavers' Company* (1933).

a. MSS 4662–3, 4686, 4708: 14C to 17C deeds (*123*). MSS 4690, 6822: 17C deeds (*5, 20*).

b. MS 4646: bk. of a/cs, memoranda, and inventories, 1489–1741 (*123*).

c. MS 4645: ordinance, oath, and memoranda bk., 15C to 16C; 15C refs. to hall (*148*).

69. WOOLMEN'S COMPANY
The estate lay in: *141*, Eastcheap. The records are in GL.

a. MS 6907: ordinance, act, and memoranda bk., comp. 1549–1712; will and memoranda of leases, 16C (*141*).

b. MS 6901: wardens' a/c bk., 1566–1853; incl. rent receipts, 17C inventories of deeds and bonds.

c. MS 6903/1: court minutes, 1661, 1664, 1666–1700; incl. lease agreement 1664 (*141*).

RELIGIOUS HOUSES AND
BISHOPRICS

Over 170 English religious houses and bishoprics, and at least 10 continental houses, held property, in the form of land, rents, quit-rents, or advowsons, in the city of London. The houses can be identified, and their estates to some extent reconstructed, from surveys of 1291 (*Taxatio Ecclesiastica*, Record Commission, 1802), 1392 (Ecclesiastical property in the city of London in 1392, in A. K. McHardy, *The Church in London 1375–92*, LRS 13, 1977), and 1535 (*Valor Ecclesiasticus*, Record Commission 1810–34), and PRO *Supplementary Lists and Indexes* no. III, 'List of Lands of Dissolved Religious Houses.' Few of their archives, except those of surviving or successor capitular bodies, remain intact or nearly so. In general, deeds, leases, surveys, and accounts are in PRO, and cartularies and other registers in BL and other public or private collections. The aim here has been to collect, as far as possible, under the headings of individual houses, items relating to their London estate, including both archival material and accounts and surveys of the estates while in the Crown's possession up to 1547. This section also covers the estates of cathedral chapters, bishops, and some non-academic secular colleges. For the estates of ecclesiastical landlords during the Interregnum, see **462b**.

Individual houses were identified, and their locations by county, dedications, and dates of foundation and dissolution or surrender were taken principally from D. Knowles and R. N. Hadcock, *Medieval Religious Houses, England and Wales* (2nd edition, 1971). Reference to a house in the surveys of 1291, 1392, or 1535 is noted in the individual entry, and a list of the parishes mentioned in 1291 is given: several of these properties may have been lost by the date of the later surveys and accounts. The survey of 1392 is incomplete, and does not consistently identify holdings by parish, but is nevertheless a valuable source. Properties listed in the valor of 1535 are generally also covered by PRO rentals, surveys, and ministers' accounts for the 1530s and 1540s; particular returns for much of London diocese, Ely diocese, much of York diocese, and the counties of Berkshire, Rutland, and Northumberland, however, are lacking. Information from the 1392 and 1535 surveys is only included here when no other identification of the estate of a particular house exists. In a few cases these surveys provide the only known indication of a London holding. Several houses lost their London holdings before the late 13C (e.g. **117, 126, 151, 272–3**).

Deeds from the archives of dissolved religious houses were retained by the Crown when the properties to which they related were granted or sold, and now form the greater part of PRO Ancient Deeds class. In most cases, however, subsequent rearrangement of the class means that the original archive of deeds or groups of deeds cannot easily be determined; no attempt to do this has been made here, but a few instances where numbers of deeds are identifiable have been pointed out. For a general description of and index to PRO Ancient and Modern Deeds classes, see below, **441**. Some other deeds survive in BL, Additional Charters, etc. A number of *leases* from the archives of dissolved religious houses forms a separate class, PRO E303, Conventual Leases. In most cases these are leases current at the time of the dissolution, but a few are of earlier date. The leases are arranged in boxes by counties, and within counties by the religious house granting the lease. The PRO search room guide to this class is an 18C index to properties leased; it is useful for London religious houses, but London properties of non-London houses are not fully covered. As far as possible they are identified in the entries below. Monastic *cartularies* and some *registers* were located with the help of G. R. C. Davis, *Medieval Cartularies of Great Britain, a short catalogue* (1958). Deeds and cartulary entries printed in *Mon. Angl.* relating to London houses or lands in London are noted in J. M. Sims, *London and Middlesex published records, a handlist* (LRS occasional publications 1, 1970).

   Rentals and *surveys* of the estates of religious houses at or about the time of their dissolution are in PRO classes E36, E315, LR2, SC11, SC12; see PRO *Lists and Indexes* no. XXV. PRO SC6 includes occasional *accounts* for religious houses before the 16th century, and numerous accounts for the years leading up to and after the Dissolution: see *Lists and Indexes* nos. V, VIII, XXXIV and *Supplementary* no. II. The class includes some accounts for the estates of unidentified persons or bodies, some of which may relate to religious houses: these are indexed by parish in **437c**. For the reign of Henry VIII the accounts for religious houses with property in London are grouped according to the county in which the house lay; London houses are grouped together in a variety of ways. The accounts for the years immediately following the dissolution of each house provide the best guide to their holdings of property at this period, frequently giving details of current leases, and also of the Crown's alienation of individual properties. In the following descriptions accounts are only listed up to the end of the reign of Henry VIII, by which time most of the London properties had been alienated. Accounts for receipts of rent from properties not alienated until a later date, however, and of reserved rents or tenths from properties granted at fee-farm, continue in SC6/Edward VI, Philip and Mary, Elizabeth, etc.: see below, **438**. Particulars for grants and leases of former monastic or chantry lands are described under **438**, below. PRO, SC11/957 is a useful survey, 1664, of quit-rents and reserved rents of the Crown in London, under the headings of the religious houses from which they were derived.

   Parliamentary surveys of the estates of bodies abolished during the Interregnum are listed here. For other records of these estates during the same period, see **462b**.

   The entries below are as full as possible, except in the cases of some episcopal or capitular archives where time and distance prevented full investigation. Some privately-held cartularies could not be examined, for similar reasons. These omissions are indicated in the text. It should be noted that the London property of some sees was close to but just outside the liberty of the city and so is excluded from this survey.

The descriptions of the archives are arranged as follows: St. Paul's Cathedral; bishop of London; religious houses in London (following Knowles's and Hadcock's classification, which appears to be based on the archdeaconry of London); friaries in London; hospitals in London; religious houses, hospitals, chapters, and bishoprics outside London (including Holborn, Kilburn, Southwark, Westminster) arranged alphabetically by place; continental houses. All houses are given a separate paragraph number; in the cases of St. Paul's, Canterbury Cathedral, and Westminster Abbey, where the archives are large and contain much London material, the descriptions are arranged in the usual way but separate numbers have been assigned to each section. A small group of houses about whose London property there is some doubt are noted under **265**.

ST. PAUL'S CATHEDRAL

Fd. *c.* 604; not suppressed.

In 1291 the London estate lay in: *2, 4, 10, 11, 15, 18, 26, 29, 30, 32, 37, 38, 42, 45, 46, 48, 49, 59, 61, 62, 67, 71, 74, 80, 81, 85, 87, 88, 89, 92, 93, 111, 112, 118, 123, 128, 131, 135, 136, 137, 148, 149, 150, 152, 155, 159,* also pensions from the churches of *26, 30, 37, 44, 62, 74, 87, 99, 111, 112, 123, 127.* The estate was enlarged in the 14C and 15C by the endowments of numerous chantries: see below, **73b**, and also *The London and Middlesex Chantry Certificate of 1548,* ed. C. J. Kitching (LRS 16, 1980). By the 16C many early rents had been lost; a few properties were recovered or newly acquired in the later 16C and 17C. See also **462b**.

The archive at St. Pauls in the late 19C, containing deeds, registers, accounts, etc. dating from the 12C onwards, was described in H. C. Maxwell Lyte's 'Report on the Manuscripts of the Dean and Chapter of St. Paul's' in HMC (8) *Ninth Report,* part 1 (1883), Appendix, 1–72 (cited here as HMC *Report*). This remains a valuable guide to the contents of the archive, though some items were omitted and others inadequately described, and a few have since been lost. Records concerning St. Paul's acquired by the governors of Queen Anne's Bounty and since in part transferred to the St. Paul's archive are described in HMC (7) *Eighth Report,* part 1 (1881), Appendix, 632–3. A further collection of documents relating to St. Paul's, mostly of 17C date or later, was found at Shenley, Herts., in 1949, and subsequently transferred to the St. Paul's archive. In 1980 the whole of the archive at the cathedral was transferred to Guildhall Library; all items in this accession group have been, or will be, assigned MS numbers beginning with 25000 or 26000. A small number of records, evidently originally from the St. Paul's archive, came to GL before 1980; other records, or transcripts of them, are also to be found in collections at BL, Bodl, CUL, and PRO. The archive transferred to GL in 1980 included some records relating to the bishop of London's estates; those concerning London are described under **78**, below.

Unless otherwise stated, the records described below are in GL. The numbering system for deeds is described under **70**. The St. Paul's registers at the cathedral, which also include rentals, were mostly kept in press WD, and numbered accordingly; some also had descriptive names or titles from an early period. In the descriptions of these volumes below, the WD reference and any title are given in parentheses following the GL MS number.

At the time of going to press (Summer 1984) the archive transferred to GL in 1980 had not been fully catalogued, and so for the means of access to particular classes of documents readers should refer to the staff at GL.

70. St. Paul's: deeds

The following index covers all London items in the St. Paul's 'Ancient Deeds' series and similar items elsewhere in the archive and among those St. Paul's records deposited in GL before 1980. The heading 'deeds' here covers deeds, wills, leases, letters of attorney, bonds, briefs, inquisitions, receipts, extracts from plea rolls, and transcripts from these items. The 'Ancient Deeds' were numbered in the 18C 'promiscuously as they came to hand', from 1 to 3000+; MS 25616/2 lists them in that order. In the 19C the deeds were rearranged by parish and placed in boxes numbered A1–A81, and were described under that arrangement in HMC *Report*, with box and serial numbers. The present arrangement in GL reverts to the serial numbering system, and substitutes 'MS 25121' for all box numbers, although at the time of going to press (Summer 1984) deeds were still identified for production by means of the box and serial numbers. In a few cases of duplicate numbering a new serial number within MSS 25121/1–3080 has been assigned. Items from the main St. Paul's archive which were not individually numbered, or were in unnumbered boxes of various descriptions, have been given new manuscript references. Documents from the Shenley collection, already numbered 1–761, are now numbered MS 25783/1–761. St. Paul's deeds with GL MS numbers lower than 25000 were deposited in GL before 1980.

Parishes
    1: MSS 25121/578, 1252
    2: MSS 25121/632, 710, 1735, 1753; MS 25135; MS 25271/23; MS 25271/66
    4: MSS 25121/117, 527–31; MSS 25135–6; MS 25145; MSS 25271/19, 38
    5: MSS 25121/638–42; MS 25135
    9: MSS 25121/679–81
    10: MSS 25121/533–5, 710, 727–8, 740, 1195, 1206, 1282, 1426, 1734, 1753; MS 25135; MS 25271/35
    11: MSS 25121/102–3, 106–8, 539–43, 1270–2, 1649, 3046; MSS 25271/8, 30, 33
    12: MSS 25121/1171, 1829; MS 25271/63
    13: MS 25271/13
    14: MSS 25121/1766, 3077
    15: MSS 25121/167, 320–1, 544–62, 564–74, 1030, 1206, 1222, 1226, 1281–3, 1296, 1626–9, 3079–80; MS 25136; MS 25765/15
    18: MSS 25121/311–26, 575–6, 1936
    19: MSS 25121/863, 1743

20: MSS 25121/212, 603–4, 606–7, 609–18, 623–7, 1206, 1281–3, 1810, 1998–9, 3067, 3078; MS 25268
21: MSS 25121/100, 170, 239, 587–602, 1754, 1825, 3057–8; MS 25135; MS 25271/18
25: MS 25121/1778
26: MSS 25121/12, 585, 633–4
27: MS 25121/867
30: MSS 25121/157, 219, 577, 579–83, 585, 585a, 586, 635, 3038–9, 3041, 3076; MS 25135; MS 25241/22; MS 25271/61; MS 25765/5
32: MSS 25121/648–9, 651–71, 673–4, 796, 1657, 1684; MSS 25271/60, 62
35: MS 25121/1772
36: MSS 25121/650, 675, 1811–12, 1964, 3055; MS 25241/44; MS 25271/26
37: MSS 25121/677, 679–80, 682
38: MSS 25121/109, 111–13, 181, 193, 211, 224–5, 273, 407, 683–709, 711–34, 736–9, 741–68, 1767, 1790, 1838, 1952, 3055; MS 25136; MS 25241/44; MS 25267; MSS 25271/3, 15, 44; MS 25789
39: MSS 25121/769–805, 1551, 1553, 1642, 3055; MS 25135; MS 25136; MS 25241/44; MS 25264; MS 25529
41: MS 25271/30
42: MSS 25121/1–8, 143–7, 258, 306, 820, 822–5, 827–32, 1344, 1763, 1766, 1769, 1792, 3055; MS 25241/44; MSS 25271/2, 11, 44; MS 25529
43: MSS 25121/74, 306, 806–15, 819, 821, 1396, 1398–9, 1401, 1404–5, 1761; MSS 25271/13, 34; MS 25764/ 19; MS 25783/106
44: MSS 25121/159–61, 839–40, 1376; MS 25271/13
45: MSS 25121/75–89, 201, 833–8
46: MSS 25121/842–51, 853–61, 942, 1928, 2014, 3055; MS 25135; MS 25241/44; MS 25271/79; MS 25783/92
48: MSS 25121/177, 673, 869–75, 1206, 1282; MS 25271/55; MS 25816
49: MSS 25121/228, 876–86, 1235; MS 25135; MS 25271/48
51: MSS 25121/184, 234, 789, 890–936, 971–6, 1551, 1553, 1766; MS 25136; MS 25267; MSS 25271/74–5; MS 25529; MS 25783/85; MS 25789
53: MSS 25121/952, 1754; MS 25135; MS 25265; MSS 25271/8, 16, 18
54: MSS 25121/622, 937–8, 940–1, 944–51, 954–68; MSS 25271/37, 48; MS 25764/18
56: MSS 25121/969–70, 1762, 2004
58: MS 25271/75
59: MSS 25121/128–33, 210, 237, 248–50, 271, 277–81, 332–8, 340–9, 410–22, 425–9, 436–8, 440, 442–52, 454, 458, 460–2, 464–5, 467–73, 475–8, 480–4, 487–90, 492, 496–9, 503–6, 509, 511–12, 514–17, 526, 1063, 1263, 1742, 3022–3; MS 25136; MS 25240; MS 25271/45; MS 25523; MS 25529; MS 25764/15; MSS 25765/12, 22, 24, 29; MSS 25783/84, 108, 317, 356
61: MSS 25121/841, 977–9, 981–9, 991–1004, 1185, 1754, 1781, 1832–6; MSS 25135–6; MSS 25271/18, 68; MS 25442
62: MSS 25121/174–5, 544, 1008–28, 1031–48, 1054, 1283, 1754, 1763, 1770–1, 1793–4, 1806; MS 25135; MS 25240; MS 25266; MSS 25271/8, 18, 55, 62, 66, 79; MS 25529; MS 25765/13; MS 25794
63: MS 11239; MS 12190; MS 12193; MSS 12223 a–c, e; MSS 25121/206, 242–3, 360, 417, 680, 1064, 1067, 1069, 1071–2, 1075–8, 1080, 1083–4, 1086–7, 1089, 1091, 1093, 1095, 1097–1102, 1206, 1282; MS 25136; MSS 25271/4, 21; MS 25443; MS 25529; MSS 25765/8, 23, 25; MSS 25783/61–2, 81–2, 87, 109–11, 380
64: MSS 25121/1104, 1111
67: MSS 25121/796, 866, 1760
71: MSS 25121/288–91, 1113–14, 1297; MS 25271/55
73: MSS 25121/119–24, 1755, 1791, 1827–8
74: MSS 25121/240, 1115–18, 1737
75: MSS 25121/114–15, 126, 1125–34, 1136–48, 1780, 1957–9, 3055; MS 25135; MSS 25241/27, 44; MS 25271/48; MS 25765/28
77: MSS 25121/90–5, 862
78: MSS 25121/253, 268, 863; MS 25135; MS 25271/48
80: MSS 25121/15, 16, 96–8, 138, 165, 173, 221, 403, 871, 1157–70, 1172–3, 1175, 1177–8, 1180–2, 1385–7, 1780, 1830, 1957–9; MS 25135; MS 25241/27; MSS 25271/22, 55; MS 25765/9

41

81: MSS 25121/236, 264, 1149–54, 1226, 1601; MS 25271/63; MS 25783/324

83: MSS 25121/409, 678, 979, 984, 1005, 1184–90, 1195, 1264, 1754; MSS 25135–6; MS 25271/18; MS 25529

84: MS 25121/1183

85: MSS 25121/871, 1258–9

87: MSS 25121/1195, 1260–3, 1484, 1754, 1989, 3076; MS 25135; MS 25143; MSS 25271/18, 54

88: MSS 25121/1206, 1265–7, 1282

89: MSS 25121/538, 636, 1420, 1422, 1468–9, 1583–9, 3055, 3076; MS 25135; MS 25241/44; MS 25271/70; MS 25518; MS 25783/324

92: MSS 25121/18, 178, 241, 401–2, 868, 1345–59, 1361, 1364, 1369, 1375, 1774; MSS 25135–6; MS 25145; MS 25200; MS 25529

93: MSS 25121/173, 204, 209, 234, 284–5, 350–3, 403, 821, 839, 890, 936, 1155–6, 1176, 1181–2, 1376–94, 1768, 1821; MS 25271/13

95: MSS 25121/20, 58–74, 247, 1226, 1395–1409, 1766; MS 25136; MS 25241/37; MS 25765/17; MSS 25783/86, 356

96: MSS 25121/163, 191, 286, 1206, 1282, 1410–15, 1952, 1989; MS 25135; MS 25143; MSS 25271/48, 66

98: MSS 25121/592, 1178, 1191–1202, 1426, 1768, 1821; MS 25271/69

99: MSS 25121/123, 141, 171, 246, 269, 329–30, 1206, 1208–11, 1213–26, 1282, 1296, 1475, 1477, 1805, 1925–6, 3055; MS 25241/44; MSS 25271/25, 44; MSS 25764/13, 21; MSS 25765/3, 16

100: MSS 25121/205, 1203–5

104: MSS 25121/1206, 1227–32, 1282, 1754, 1989, 3076; MS 25143; MS 25271/18

105: MSS 25121/1206, 1233, 1282, 1955, 3076, 3079; MS 25271/14; MS 25816

108: MSS 25121/159–62, 251–2, 989, 1206, 1234, 1282; MS 25135; MS 25271/48

111: MSS 25121/101–8, 141, 539, 541–2, 1206, 1212, 1221, 1224–5, 1269–95, 1298–9, 1303, 1776, 1955, 1989, 1992; MSS 25135–6; MS 25143; MSS 25271/8, 61, 63, 79

112: MSS 25121/151, 166, 179–80, 182, 186–90, 208, 222–3, 229, 233, 256, 261–2, 270, 327–9, 331, 354–9, 406, 1206, 1268, 1282, 1305–8, 1311–21, 1323–43, 1934, 3036–7, 3039, 3041, 3055, 3076; MSS 25241/13, 23, 44; MSS 25271/28, 44, 46; MS 25529

113: MSS 25121/1256–7

114: MS 25121/1243

116: MSS 25121/125, 136, 306, 980, 1236–42, 1244–51, 3055; MS 25241/44

117: MSS 25121/1252, 1254–5, 1955

118: MSS 25121/1233, 1737; MS 25271/53

119: MS 25121/1766

120: MSS 25121/134, 149, 155, 164, 185, 306, 680, 1083–4, 1195, 1418, 1423–9, 1431–4, 1437–44, 1446–7, 1470–3, 1601, 1825, 1931, 1935, 1989; MS 25135; MS 25143; MS 25241/44; MSS 25271/6, 8, 9, 33, 36, 49

123: MSS 25121/141, 171, 195–6, 232, 246, 266, 329–31, 343–4, 421, 496, 1206, 1208, 1211–14, 1217–18, 1221, 1224–5, 1282, 1474–7, 2014, 3055; MS 25241/44; MSS 25271/25, 44

124: MSS 25121/367–73, 375–6

125: MSS 25121/148, 172, 176, 1259, 1479–83, 1485–9; MS 25136; MSS 25271/66–7; MSS 25765/18, 27

126: MS 25121/1526; MS 25271/40

127: MSS 25121/306, 1455, 1492, 1522–5; MS 25271/35

128: MSS 25121/139, 142, 183, 190, 207, 226, 255, 292–5, 405, 423–4, 495, 953, 1471, 1490–1, 1493–4, 1496–1521, 1917, 1936, 3055; MS 25135; MSS 25241/26, 44; MSS 25271/8, 30, 44, 46; MS 25529; MSS 25783/65, 79, 88

129: MSS 25121/118–19, 121–2, 153, 158, 192, 301–10, 789, 821, 1527–30, 1532–7, 1541–5, 1547–56, 1783–6, 2007, 3055; MS 25136; MS 25241/44; MS 25267; MSS 25271/13, 23; MS 25764/17; MS 25783/93; MS 25789

130: MS 25121/198

131: MSS 25121/17, 796, 1557–64, 1566, 1568–70, 1737, 1824–5; MS 25145; MS 25271/11

132: MSS 25121/135, 796, 1206, 1297, 1567, 1571–3; MS 25529

133: MSS 25121/199, 200, 227, 1592

134: MSS 25121/821, 1201, 1263; MSS 25271/55, 66, 69

135: MSS 25121/538, 1243, 1309–10, 1574–5, 1577–81, 1583–9, 3055; MS 25241/44; MSS 25271/44, 46, 70; MS 25518; MS 25783/324

136: MSS 25121/282–3, 861, 1538, 1576, 1591, 1593–1605, 3076
137: MSS 25121/57, 377–400, 459, 498, 514, 589, 1606–9, 1756; MS 25135; MSS 25271/45, 48, 57, 62
138: MS 25121/1823; MS 25262
140: MS 25121/1590
141: MSS 25271/16, 22
144: MSS 25121/1531, 1546, 1610–11, 1614–23, 1775, 1955; MS 25271/66
145: MSS 25121/9–11, 14, 19, 572, 1624–6, 1630–41, 1643–50, 2014, 3036–7, 3039, 3041, 3046; MSS 25241/13, 23; MSS 25271/33, 79; MS 25816
148: MSS 25121/1652–6, 3077
149: MSS 25121/362–4, 1659, 1662
150: MSS 25121/287, 1651, 1663; MS 25135
151: MSS 25121/149, 213, 215–16, 218, 1206, 1282, 1546, 1658, 1660, 3046; MS 25271/33
152: MSS 25121/127, 168, 202–3, 238, 244–5, 267, 298–300, 404, 620, 631, 1283, 1601, 1649, 1664–76, 1678–84, 1782, 1955, 1989, 3046; MS 25135; MS 25143; MSS 25241/12, 25; MSS 25271/32, 33, 60–1
153: MS 25121/1717
155: MSS 25121/140, 1775
156: MSS 25121/214, 1224–5; MSS 25271/41, 53
157: MS 25121/1716
158: MSS 25121/1206, 1718–23
159: MSS 25121/21–30, 33–43, 45–9, 53–4, 259, 265, 301, 680, 1300–1, 1322, 1661, 1724, 1726–9, 1732, 1753, 1779, 3055; MS 25136; MSS 25271/8, 30; MS 25529; MS 25783/90; MS 25816
160: MS 25135; MS 25241/44; MS 25264
161: MS 25121/2066
162: MSS 25121/152, 1738–41A, 1819, 1825; MS 25271/6

Other localities
London: MSS 25121/11, 110, 408, 510, 654, 819, 1070, 1174, 1179, 1297, 1705, 1748–50, 1764–5, 1777, 1798–9, 1801, 1808–9, 1813–16, 1820, 1860, 1927, 1929, 1966, 2006, 2038, 3074; MS 25139; MSS 25241/14–17, 20–1, 24; MSS 25271/1, 5, 22, 35–6, 67, 73; MS 25434; MS 25819
Abchurch Lane: MS 25783/356
Aldersgate Street: MS 25240
Aldgate, outside: MS 25136
Aldgate ward: MSS 25121/154, 816–18, 825
Alsies Lane (? Ivy Lane): MSS 25121/456, 1744
Atheling Street: MS 25121/57; MS 25271/57
Baynards Castle, precinct of, near: MS 25121/1756; MS 25136
Botolph Lane: MS 25265
Bread Street: MSS 25121/57, 637, 672, 1565
Bridge ward: MS 25121/871
Broad Street: MSS 25121/537, 676, 1758
Broad Street ward: MS 25121/871
Bucklersbury: MS 25121/2004; MS 25783/723
Candlewick ward: MS 25121/871
Carter Lane: MS 25121/1804; MS 25443
Cateaton Street: MSS 25121/990, 1745
Cecile Lane (probably identical with Diceres Lane, q.v.): MSS 25121/474, 485, 507–8, 1061
Cheap ward: MS 25121/871
Cheapside: MSS 25121/137, 231, 263, 1430, 1464, 1725, 1730–1,1733, 1754, 1818, 1952, 1989, 3055; MS 25135; MS 25143; MS 25200; MS 25241/44; MSS 25271/8, 11, 18, 79; MS 25783/356
Cornhill: MSS 25121/365–6, 374, 1478
Creed Lane: MS 25529; MS 25765/19
Diceres Lane (probably identical with Cecile Lane, q.v.): MS 25121/486
Distaff Lane: MS 25121/1650; MS 25135; MS 25518
Do Little Lane: MS 25121/1082
Dowgate ward: MS 25121/871

43

Eastcheap: MSS 25121/1007, 1500, 1936; MS 25135
Elsing Spital: MS 25121/1207
Fenchurch Street: MS 25783/356
Fish Market (*piscaria*; uncertain whether in Cheapside or Old Fish Street): MSS 25121/343–
   4, 421, 496; MS 25271/79; see also Old Fish Market, Old Fish Street
Fleet Street: MSS 25121/852, 939, 943, 1822, 1995; MS 25271/79; MS 25783/356
Friday Street: MSS 25121/1416–17, 1419, 1421, 1435–6, 1445, 1465, 1920–1, 3076
Gutter Lane: MSS 25121/535, 710, 1734–6; MS 25271/79
Holborn: MSS 25121/1787, 1789; MS 25240
Holy Trinity Priory, Aldgate: MS 25121/864
Ivy Lane (see also Alsies Lane): MSS 25121/412, 453, 493, 1913–15
Lime Street: MS 25271/79
Ludgate, outside: MSS 25121/296–7
Ludgate Hill: MS 25240; MS 25795
Ludgate Street: MS 25121/1360
Madlane (? not London): MS 25121/116
Mincing Lane: MS 25121/1766
Munfitchet Castle, land near: MS 25121/1746
Old Change: MSS 25121/31–2, 44, 50–2, 55–7; MS 25443; MS 25783/356
Old Dean's Lane (now Warwick Lane, q.v.): MSS 25121/124, 150, 169, 272, 430–5, 439,
   479, 502
Old Fish Market (probably Cheapside): MSS 25121/1302, 1304; see also Fish Market
Old Fish Market (probably Old Fish Street): MSS 25121/214, 260, 1195, 1650; see also Fish
   Market
Old Fish Street: MS 25121/1582; MS 25135; MS 25271/8, 11
Paternoster Row: MSS 25121/463, 500–1, 2014, 3018–19, 3054; MS 25136; MS 25529; MS
   25765/30
Philip Lane: MS 25121/563; MS 25271/51
Physicians, College of: MS 25783/404
Poultry: MS 25136
Pudding Lane: MS 25783/356
Raton Lane: MS 25121/735
St Bartholomew's Hospital: MSS 25121/643–7
St. Bartholomew's Priory: MS 25121/647
St. Helens Priory: MSS 25121/1105–10, 1112
St. Lawrence Lane: MS 25271/70; MS 25518
St. Martin le Grand precinct: MS 25271/1344
St. Paul's precinct: MS 12223d; MSS 25121/254, 257, 339, 441, 466, 491, 494, 513, 518–20,
   522–5, 537, 713–14, 865, 1059–60, 1062, 1065–6, 1068, 1073–4, 1079, 1081, 1085, 1088,
   1090, 1092, 1094, 1096, 1367, 1495, 1756–7, 1773, 1788, 1796–7, 1800, 1802–3, 1807,
   1831, 1837, 1842–4, 1847, 1855, 1858–9, 1902, 1918, 1922–3, 1933, 1937–41, 1948–51,
   1955–6, 1960, 1962–3, 2000, 3015–17, 3021, 3026–7, 3061–2; MS 25240; MS 25442; MS
   25529; MSS 25764/14, 16; MSS 25765/6, 7, 14, 26; MSS 25783/316, 336, 339, 356, 380,
   382, 429, 705–11, 713–14, 717, 719, 721, 725–6
Sermon Lane: MSS 25121/361, 621; MS 25529
Silver Street: MSS 25121/1612–13
Sporones Lane: MS 25121/3065
Staining Lane: MS 25121/1253
Thames, land towards or near: MSS 25121/10, 521
Thames Street: MSS 25121/112–13, 861
Timberhithe: MS 25121/735
Vintry: MS 25121/3065
Warwick Lane (see also Old Dean's Lane): MS 25240
Wood Street: MSS 25121/120, 156, 217, 220, 1539–40, 1549A, 1783–6; MS 25783/356

71. ST. PAUL'S: REGISTERS

a. MS 25504 (Davis, no. 596: WD4, 'Liber L'; extensive extracts printed
in HMC *Report*): register, comp. 12C, of deeds (*20, 26, 30, 38, 44, 56, 62,*

64, 72, 74, 75, 86, 93, 99, 109, 127, 128, 158, near Billingsgate, Cheapside, Cornhill, St. Paul's precinct, London unspec.); also rentals (see below, **73**).

b. MS 25501 (Davis, no. 597: WD1, 'Liber A sive Pilosus'; ff. 1–37ᵛ printed and collated with surviving originals in *Early Charters of the Cathedral Church of St. Paul, London,* ed. Marion Gibbs, Camden Soc. 3rd ser. 58, 1939): register, comp. 13C and later, of 12C and 13C deeds (*4, 11, 15, 18, 19, 20, 27, 30, 36, 38, 44, 45, 46, 56, 59, 62, 64, 67, 74, 81, 89, 92, 93, 96, 98, 99, 108, 111, 112, 120, 123, 128, 132, 135, 136, 137, 140, 142, 144, 145, 148, 149, 150, 151, 155, 161,* Bread Street, Cheapside, Eastcheap, Gutter Lane, Holborn, *Huettawiereslane,* St. Paul's precinct, London unspec.).

c. Bodl, MS Ashmole 801, ff. 50–73ᵛ (Davis, no. 599): abs. of deeds, comp. late 14C (*21, 26, 27, 36, 37, 38, 39, 62, 63, 117, 135, 144, 149,* Cateaton Street, *Whittawyereslane*).

d. MS 25502 (WD2, 'Liber C'): register comp. 14C to 15C, incl. copies of rentals (see below, **73**); pleas; ordinances for chantries (*38, 39, 59, 75, 80, 160,* St. Paul's precinct).

e. MSS 25511, 25511A (Davis, nos. 600–1: WD11, 11a, 'Dean Lyseux's Inventory, 1440', two texts): table of abs. of evidences (parishes covered in **70**, above, except for *2, 12, 13, 14, 25, 28, 35, 41, 48, 51, 58, 64, 77, 113, 114, 119, 130, 133, 134, 140, 141, 158, 160*; also refs. to *16, 24, 142*); also lists contents of several lost registers (*38, 42, 59, 63, 99, 125, 148,* St. Paul's precinct, Sermon lane, London unspec.).

f. CUL, MS Ee. 5. 21 (Davis, no. 605): 15C register incl. (f. 121) list of London churches belonging to St. Paul's (*20, 26, 30, 37, 38, 44, 54, 56, 59, 62, 63, 64, 74, 75, 93, 99, 111, 112, 123, 127, 128, 144, 148, 150, 158*).

g. BL, MS Harl. 4080 (Davis, no. 602; *Registrum Eleemosynariae D. Pauli Londinensis,* ed. Maria Hackett, 1827): 17C to 18C transcript of lost 14C(?) register of almoner (*5, 21, 38, 42, 59, 62, 63, 92, 112, 120, 128, 131, 162*); also rental (see below, **73**).

72. St. Paul's: lease registers

a. MSS 25630/1–11: 'Deans' Registers', each identified by dean's name, cont. chapter acts, business, copy leases of dean and chapter estate, 1536–1642, 1660–70 (*15, 18, 20, 21, 30, 36, 37, 38, 39, 42, 43, 44, 45, 46, 48, 51, 53, 54, 59, 60, 61, 62, 63, 73, 74, 75, 77, 80, 81, 83, 84, 87, 89, 92, 93, 95, 98, 99, 103, 111, 112, 113, 116, 119, 120, 125, 126, 128, 129, 131, 132, 134, 136, 141, 149, 150, 158, 159,* precincts of St. Paul, St. Martin le Grand); the vols. were bound up in their present form in the 18C and some leaves have been lost.

b. MS 19331/1: lease bk., dean's estate, 1664–1736 (*62, 63,* churchyard).

c. MS 19859/1: lease bk., petty canons' estate, 1609–1787, incl. copy leases *c.* 1609–27, memoranda of leases 1627–41, 1661–1787 (*47, 59, 63, 75, 80, 112*).

73. ST. PAUL'S: RENTALS AND ACCOUNTS BEFORE *c.* 1550

Rentals and/or accounts survive for the estates listed below, **a–g**. The following vols. contain material for more than one category: MS 25512 (WD 12, mid 13C); MS 25509 (Davis, no. 603: WD 9, 'Statuta majora', 13C to 14C); MS 25516 (WD 16, 'Liber I', *c.* 1299); MS 25505 (WD 5, 15C); MS 25508 (WD 8, 'Liber statutorum', 15C); MS 25520 (Davis, no. 604, wrongly identified as WD 10: WD 20, 'Statuta minora', 15C); CUL, MS Ee. 5. 21 (Davis, no. 605: 'Liber statutorum', 15C); MSS 25534/1–2 (WD 49, WD 50, 16C); MS 25634 (WA 57, 16C); PRO, E315/397 (16C). See also MS 25504 (WD 4); MS 25502 (WD 2); Bodl, MS Ashmole 801; BL, MS Harl. 4080, described under **71**. MS 25508 (WD 8), f. 38, lists all a/cs rendered at St. Paul's, with the terms at which they were due.

a. Estate of dean and chapter.
Rentals. MS 25504 (WD 4), ff. 47–50^v: rental, mid 12C, properties described by tenant or ward; subheadings printed in HMC *Report*, p. 66; rental printed in full in H. W. C. Davis, 'London lands and liberties of St. Paul's, 1066–1139', *Essays in Medieval History presented to T. F. Tout*, ed. A. G. Little and F. M. Powicke (1925), 45–59. MS 25504 (WD 4), ff. 114^v–117^v: rental, early 13C (*4, 5, 9, 10, 15, 20, 26, 27, 28, 32, 36, 38, 45, 46, 49, 54, 59, 62,67, 71, 74, 80, 81, 87, 88, 89, 90, 92, 93, 95, 99, 101, 108, 111, 112, 119, 123, 128, 131, 133, 136, 145, 149, 151, 152, 155, 159*). MS 25512 (WD 12), ff. 1–7^v: rental, mid 13C (estate above, except for *5, 46, 50, 128, 131, 152*; also *30, 37, 63, 65, 66, 130, 135, 137*, 'St. Andrew *apud Turrim*', 'St. Nicholas *de Wdestrate*' (? error for *129*)); also incl. (ff. 8^v–9) details of socage rents due from unspec. London properties. MS 25509 (WD 9), ff. 1–9: rental, later 13C (as MS 25504, ff. 114^v–117^v, except for *5, 46*; also *30, 63, 65, 129, 130, 135, 137*); also incl. (ff. 1–9, 37) lists of socage rents. MS 25502 (WD 2), f. 99^v: list of socage rents, 14C or 15C.
Accounts. MS 19563; MS 19930; MSS 25125/1–99; MSS 25126–9; MS 25132: incomplete series of a/c rolls, 1315–1488, and some undated 14C or 15C a/cs (rents and repairs in *2, 4, 5, 10, 15, 20, 21, 26, 28, 32, 38, 42, 45, 46, 54, 59, 63, 71, 73, 80, 81, 87, 88, 92, 98, 99, 111, 112, 119, 123, 125, 126, 128, 131, 132, 135, 136, 137, 148, 150, 151, 158, 159, 162*; incl. also a/cs, 14C only, for *29, 37, 49, 62, 67, 74, 85, 90, 93, 95, 96, 108, 149*, Billingsgate, Coleman Street, Gracechurch); the later 14C and 15C rolls also incl. a/cs for an increasing number of chantry estates, originally recorded separately (see **b**, below) but by *c.* 1500 mostly incorporated with dean and chapter estate. See also MS 25204, late 15C list of quit-rents due as part of estate above but not recoverable without court proceedings. MSS 25166/1–9: a/cs of Dean Worsley (1479–99), incl. deanery and personal estates (London totals). MSS 25534/1–2: summary a/c of receipts, 1509–11. MS 25634: a/c bk., 1525–6 (rents and repairs for estate listed above, except for *28, 87, 158, 162*; also receipts from chantry props. in *30, 39, 43, 48, 51, 61, 62, 77, 93, 95, 104, 116, 118, 129*). Bodl, MS Ashmole 801, ff. 30–8: a/c, 1531–2 (rents in *4, 5, 10, 15, 21, 30, 38, 39, 42, 43, 45, 46, 48, 51, 59, 61, 62, 63, 71, 77, 80, 83, 89, 92, 93, 95, 98, 99, 111, 112, 116, 125, 126, 128, 129, 131, 132, 136, 150, 159*); ibid. ff. 28–9^v lists vacancies. PRO, E315/397, f. 135: rental, 1536–7 (estate as in

preceding, also *2, 20, 26, 28, 32, 52, 73, 81, 88, 104, 118, 119, 123, 135, 137, 148, 151, 152, 158,* 'St. Margaret Bread Street'). MS 25206: a/c, 1541–2, for rents and pensions formerly due from religious houses and now from the Crown (*54, 71, 112, 113, 120, 128,* Aldgate Street, Bow Lane, Bread Street, Carter Lane, Fleet Street, Friday Street, Gracechurch parish, Ivy Lane, the Minories, Old Fish Street, Sherborne Lane, Tower Hill). MSS 25205/1–3: a/cs of receiver-general, 1502–3, early 16C, 1536–7 (incl. dean and chapter estate, totals from chantry estate, pensions from churches (listed under **f**, below); rents recorded in *20, 29, 30, 36, 38, 54, 59, 62, 63, 92, 99, 111, 112, 129, 149, 152,* Ivy Lane, Sporyer Row).

b. Chantry estates.
Pre-Reformation: MS 25504 (WD 4), ff. 91, 114: list, early 13C, of chantry property (*38, 44, 108, 130,* Ludgate). MS 25509 (WD 9), ff. 9–15: calendar of obits, mid 13C, few details of locations. MS 25502 (WD 2), ff. 100–101ᵛ: list of chantries, 14C (*5, 35, 38, 39, 44, 63, 75, 80, 89, 92, 105, 108, 112, 117, 123, 130, 135, 137, 152, 155, 159, 160, 162,* Cheapside, Dowgate, Eastcheap, Gutter Lane, Ivy Lane, Milk Street, Old Dean's Lane, Silver Street); ibid., ff. 102–108ᵛ, calendar of obits, 14C, incl. rents (*2, 4, 5, 10, 30, 38, 42, 59, 61, 63, 92, 98, 108, 112, 118, 123, 125, 126, 136, 137, 150, 159,* bishop's palace, St. Paul's churchyard, Broad Street, Cheapside, Fleet Street, Jewry, Milk Street, Old Fish Market, Paternoster Row, Silver Street). MS 25134: calendar of obits, 14C or 15C (as MS 25502, ff. 102–108ᵛ, except for *4, 98, 108, 112, 123,* St. Paul's churchyard, Fleet Street, Silver Street; also *20, 80, 81, 114, 144, 152,* near brewhouse, Aldermanbury, Friday Street, Poultry, Seething Lane). MSS 25121/1826, 3045; MS 25137; MS 25140; MS 25144; MSS 25150–1; MSS 25158–61; MS 25163: a/cs for rents and repairs and associated items for individual chantries, 14C to 16C (*4, 9, 10, 21, 30, 37, 38, 39, 42, 43, 45, 48, 51, 53, 61, 62, 63, 73, 77, 83, 87, 92, 93, 95, 96, 98, 104, 111, 112, 116, 120, 125, 126, 131, 138, 145, 152, 159, 160,* near bakehouse). From the late 14C some, and by the late 15C almost all, of these chantry estates were incorporated with the dean and chapter's estate, and appear in those a/cs (see above, **a**). MS 25121/1998: a/c of cantarist, 1484–5, small payments to chantries.
Reformation and later. MS 25526: vol. of chantry certificates, *c.* 1548, arranged by chantry (*4, 10, 21, 30, 36, 37, 38, 39, 42, 46, 48, 51, 61, 62, 63, 73, 75, 77, 81, 83, 89, 92, 93, 94, 98, 99, 111, 112, 118, 120, 126, 127, 128, 129, 131, 136, 137, 145, 149, 159,* Gutter Lane, Old Dean's Lane, Paternoster Row, Philip Lane, Warwick Lane). MS 25136: incl. fragments of articles on chantries, 1546, and answers of dean and chapter; rentals of chantry and obit lands, mid 16C and later (*4, 18, 20, 30, 38, 43, 46, 51, 59, 61, 63, 74, 80, 83, 92, 98, 99, 103, 111, 112, 116, 128, 129, 131, 136,* St. Paul's churchyard, Broad Street, Friday Street); valor of tenths from late chantry lands, *temp.* Elizabeth (*38,* Philip Lane). MS 25121/ 1999: rental, 1565–6, of former chantry lands (*38, 111,* Philip Lane). PRO, SC12/11/46: schedule of payments for performance of chantries, mid 16C (Aldgate, Paternoster Row).

c. New Work accounts.
The fabric of the cathedral was divided into 'old work' and 'new work', in theory those parts built or rebuilt before and after 1240. The Old Work was the responsibility of the bishop, who appointed its keeper, and its endowment probably derived from the bishop's estates (see below, **78**); the New Work was the responsibility of the canons: K. Edwards, *English Secular Cathedrals in the Middle Ages* (1967), 230–3.

MS 25121/1911: fragment of a/c, 1323 (Aldermanbury, Philip Lane). MS 25634: incl. a/c for New Work rents, 1525–6 (*18, 20, 38, 54, 59, 63, 92, 99, 149*; also ref. to *15*). PRO, E315/397, f. 143: summary a/c, 1536–7, total receipts plus arrears or repayments (*18, 54, 59, 63, 99*).

d. Almoner's rents.
MS 25504 (WD 4), f. 92: note of rents, 13C, no London locations. MS 25516, f. 58: rental, end 13C (*38, 42, 59, 63, 92, 112, 128, 137*). BL, MS Harl. 4080 (see above, **71g**; *Registrum Eleemosynariae D. Pauli Londinensis*, ed. Maria Hackett, 1827), f. 1: rental, 1345 (*5, 38, 42, 59, 62, 63, 112, 128*). MS 25505, f. 52; MS 25508, f. 18; MS 25520, f. 56; CUL, MS Ee. 5. 21, f. 76ᵛ: lists of rents, 15C (*5, 38, 42, 59, 112, 128*; also (MS 25508 only) St. Paul's brewhouse). MS 25173: list of rents, 1526 (*5, 42, 59, 63, 112, 128, 135*). See also MS 25161, chantry a/cs, 14C to 15C: incl. memorandum on dorse of a/c for 1383–4 of almoner's rents (*38, 112*).

e. Pittancer's rents.
MS 25504 (WD 4), ff. 92ᵛ–103ᵛ: calendar of pittances, early 13C (*20, 30, 38, 46, 59, 63, 81, 92, 111, 112, 123, 136, 150, 152, 160*, St. Paul's churchyard, Old Fish Market). MS 25509, ff. 2ᵛ–3: similar calendar, later 13C (as preceding, except for *63, 150*). CUL, MS Ee. 5. 21, ff. 79ᵛ–90: calendar of pittances, ?14C, with 16C notes (*2, 4, 30, 38, 39, 42, 59, 61, 63, 81, 92, 98, 108, 118, 125, 126, 128, 136, 144, 150, 152, 155, 159*, churchyard, Broad Street (? Bread Street), Cock's Lane, Friday Street, Holborn, Jewry, Milk Street, outside Newgate, Old Fish Market, Sermon Lane, Vintry). MS 25505, ff. 56–60: list of pittances, 15C (*2, 20, 38, 59, 63, 92, 111, 112, 137, 144, 150, 160*, churchyard, Bread Street, Friday Street, Vintry). MS 25508, ff. 20–3: list of pittances, 15C (as preceding, except for churchyard; also near brewhouse, Paternoster Row). MS 25520, ff. 59ᵛ–64: calendar of pittances, 15C (*38, 59, 63, 92, 111, 137, 150*, Bread Street parish, near brewhouse).

f. Pensions from churches.
Pensions were due to the chamber from the following London churches: *20, 26, 30, 37, 38, 44, 56, 59, 62, 64, 74, 75, 93, 99, 111, 112, 127, 128, 142, 148, 150, 155, 158*. For deeds, see MS 25504 (WD 4), ff. 27–31ᵛ (printed in HMC *Report*, pp. 62–5).

MS 25504 (WD 4): ff. 82–6, inquisition *c.* 1181 (as above, except for *20, 56*); ff. 88–9ᵛ, 104–112, list, early 13C? (as above, except for *56*; also *49, 63, 136*). MS 25512, ff. 1–5: list of pensions or rents, mid 13C (as above, also *63*, St. Peter *Reineri*). MS 25509, f. 3ᵛ: list, later 13C (as above). MS 25502, f. 97: list, 14C (as above, except for *59*). MS 25205/1: incl. a/c of receipts, 1502–3 (as above, except for *99, 142, 148, 155*; also *13, 36, 42,*

54). MSS 25534/1–2: rough a/cs, 1509–11, incl. total receipts from pensions. MS 25634, f. 27: chamberlain's a/c, 1525–6 (pensions from *62, 136,* 'divers churches'). MS 25516, f. 5: a/c, *c.* 1299, of taxation on pensions (*26, 30, 37, 44, 62, 74, 87, 99, 111, 112, 127*). MS 25505, ff. 52ᵛ, 61ᵛ; MS 25508, ff. 18ᵛ, 24; MS 25520, ff. 57, 66ʳ⁻ᵛ, 68ᵛ: a/cs, 15C, of taxation on pensions (as MS 25516, f. 5; MS 25508 omits *87,* adds *142, 155*). CUL, MS Ee. 5. 21, f. 92: a/c, 15C but copied from earlier register, of taxation on pensions (as MS 25516, f. 5; also *142, 155*). MS 25206: a/c, 1541–2, of rents and pensions formerly due from religious houses and now from the Crown (incl. pensions from *13, 44, 46, 54, 56, 64*).

g. Other accounts.
MS 25504 (WD 4), f. 97ᵛ: memorandum, early 13C, of rents to chamberlain from Ivy Lane. MS 25121/3047: a/c, 1371–2, of receipts from tallages levied in repayment of loan on St. Paul's properties (*39, 42, 89, 99, 120, 129, 150, 159*). MS 25516: f. 1, a/c, 1283–6, of keeper of brewhouse; f. 58ᵛ, list, *c.* 1299, of rents due to altar of St. Mary for wax (*42, 54, 62, 67, 92, 123, 150*). MS 25520, ff. 88ᵛ–9: rental, 14C or 15C, of prebend of Holborn. CUL, MS Ee. 5. 21, ff. 111ᵛ–112: 'old' and 'new' rentals, 15C, of prebend of Holborn. PRO, E101/473/15: chamberlain's a/c, 1407–8 (Knightrider Street). PRO, SC6/1108/19: view of a/c, lands late of John Bernyngham, prebendary of Mapesbury, 1451–2 (Paternoster Row, *Sporones Lane*). PRO, E101/474/5, 10: a/cs of repairs 1507–8, 1524–5, possibly relate to St. Paul's (Trinity Lane, unspec.). PRO, SC12/18/68: arrears of rent due to St. Paul's from dissolved monasteries, 1541–2.

74. St. Paul's: rentals and accounts *c.* 1550–1666

a. Estates of dean and chapter, canons etc.
Rentals. MS 25178: rental of chamber, 1582, rents and pensions (*10, 28, 30, 36, 37, 38, 44, 46, 54, 59, 62, 74, 75, 93, 99, 111, 112, 127, 128, 136, 148, 150, 158,* 'St. Michael Olive' (probably *136*), churchyard near St. Paul's library, Ivy Lane, Paternoster Row, Sermon Lane, Warwick Lane). MS 25783/427: memorandum bk. of rents and pensions, ?17C (as in MS 25178, except for *28, 46;* also from *20, 26, 39, 43, 63, 80, 92, 131, 141, 149, 152, 159*). MS 25431: (?partial) rental, 17C (*20, 38, 53, 63, 149,* churchyard, Ivy Lane, Paternoster Row, Warwick Lane). MS 25783/434: 'Mr Winterborn's rental', *c.* 1650, lists tenants, terms, and rents (no locations). MS 25783/433: memoranda of rents of minor canons, 17C (*63,* churchyard, Aldersgate Street, Thames Street, Warwick Lane, Watling Street). See also MS 25207, valor of rents due to Crown, 1572 (*5, 18, 30, 38, 59, 63, 92, 95, 112, 118, 150,* Abchurch Lane, Candlewick Street, Fleet Street, Ivy Lane, Milk Street, Old Dean's Lane, Old Fish Street, Warwick Lane); MS 25182, memorandum, 1570, about tithes (*15, 38, 111*).
Accounts. MS 25636; MSS 25637/1–2; MS 25497; MSS 25638–9; MS 25499; MS 25640; MS 25678; MSS 25643/2–3: a/cs, incomplete series 1548–57, 1570–84, 1592–4, 1608–9, 1622–36, 1662–70, for estates of dean and major canons, New Work, chamberlain, bakehouse, receiver-general, entered consecutively, rearranged alphabetically by place after

1666 (*5, 10, 15, 18, 20, 21, 26, 30, 36, 37, 38, 39, 42, 43, 44, 46, 47, 51, 54, 59, 61, 62, 63, 74, 75, 80, 83, 92, 93, 95, 98, 99, 111, 112, 125, 127, 128, 129, 131, 132, 134, 136, 141, 148, 149, 150, 152, 158, 159*; unpaid rents from some of the above parishes and from *2, 4, 13, 32, 56, 71, 73, 81, 87, 88, 89, 104, 116, 118, 119, 123, 126, 135, 137, 151* were recorded *c*. 1550 and for some years but omitted from later a/cs). MS 25532: notebk. of subchamberlain, with rough a/cs 1554, 1566–72, 1582 (estate as preceding). PRO, SC12/37/42: list of arrears of rent, 1649 (*18, 38, 43, 51, 59, 83, 95, 98, 99, 128, 129, 132*, St. Paul's bakehouse, Bucklersbury, Carter Lane, Fleet Street, Holborn, Paul's Wharf, Philip Lane, Sermon Lane, Warwick Lane). MS 25130: a/c of New Work rents, 1559–60 (*18, 20, 38, 59, 63, 92, 99, 112, 149*). MS 25637A; MS 10303; MS 25639 (part); MS 25677; MSS 25641–2: a/cs of receiver-general, 1555–7, 1574–5, 1609–10, 1641–2, 1663–4 (totals from other a/cs, some details).

b. Other a/cs.
MS 25618: workmen's wages at cathedral, 1561–4. MS 25619: estimates for repairs to cathedral, 1608. MS 25490: view and estimate for repairs, 1620. MS 25486: a/cs for works at cathedral, 1633–9. MS 25488: payments bk. (? workmen's wages), 1637–40. MS 25783/419: folder of documents about building works at cathedral, 1622–99. MSS 25575/1–5: a/cs and papers for post-Fire rebuilding of cathedral.

75. St. Paul's: ADMINISTRATION
a. MS 25513 (WD 13, 'Liber Goodman'): chapter acts, 1411–62, incl. presentations to and appropriations of London churches and chantries, appointments of officers, admissions to prebends, elections of deans, etc., together with leases of some London properties (*123*, Fleet Street, St. Paul's precinct (incl. the old palace); not all the leases known to have been granted in this period are entered).

b. MS 25515: visitations of churches, 1458 (*62, 63*).

c. MSS 25630/1–11: Deans' Registers, cont. principally copy leases (see above, **72a**), also chapter acts and business, 1536–1642, 1660–70.

d. MSS 25738/1–2: dean and chapter minute bks., 1660–85; mostly brief records of leases as above in **c**.

e. MSS 25660/1, 25661: seal bks., 1660–98; memoranda on use of chapter seal, incl. for leases as above in **c**. See also MS 25590 for a/c of leases sealed 1642, 1668 (no topographical detail).

f. MS 11770: minute bk. of committee for repair of St. Paul's, from 1664 onwards, cont. topographical information on precinct.

76. St. Paul's: PARLIAMENTARY SURVEYS ETC.
a. MSS 11816, 11816A, 11816B (18C copy), 25631–2: parliamentary surveys of the dean and chapter estate, 1649–57, incl. pensions from churches (*15, 18, 20, 26, 30, 37, 38, 39, 42, 43, 44, 46, 47, 51, 54, 59, 61, 62, 63, 74, 75, 80, 83, 92, 93, 95, 98, 99, 111, 112, 113, 125, 128, 129, 134, 135, 136, 139, 148, 150, 158, 160*).

b. MSS 25633/1–2: contracts for the sale of dean and chapter lands, 1649–58 (pars. as listed above in **a**, except for *15, 26, 37, 44, 74, 93, 111, 113, 136, 148, 150, 158, 160*; and with the addition of *36, 132, 144*). For original leases and sales by the parliamentary commissioners, see MSS 25240 and 25783; individual items are indexed above in **70**.

77. ST. PAUL'S: PLANS
GL, Prints and Maps Section (from St. Paul's 1980 deposit): 2 rolls of rough plans, probably mostly 17C, with few locations given (incl. plans of plots in Botolph Lane; Bread Street; Wood Street; large houses in or nr. St. Benet's Hill; Paternoster Row, 1674; unidentified waterfront property, ? Paul's Wharf; parts of St. Paul's churchyard); rough plans of St. Paul's churchyard, possibly pre-Fire; plan of tenements nr. Dean Street, n.d. Bodl, MS Tanner 145, ff. 125–6: rough plans and descriptions of houses (Carter Lane, Old Change).

78. LONDON, BISHOP
The estate lay chiefly outside London, but included property near the cathedral (*59, 63, ?112*) and in Cornhill (*149*). In 1550 the new see of Westminster was abolished and some properties (*53, ?75, 84, 128*) transferred to the bishop of London (see **254**, below). In the later 17C the bishop occupied 'London House' in *42*. The bishop of London was responsible for the Old Work of St. Paul's: this was originally endowed with rents in *59, 63*, and quit-rents in numerous parishes, most of which appear to have been lost by the 16C. The distinction between the 2 estates is not always clear. See Pamela J. Taylor, 'Estates of the bishopric of London from the 7th century to the early 16th century' (London Ph.D. thesis, 1976), especially pp. 73–80, 83. See also **462b**.
Unless otherwise stated the records are in GL.

a. Some early deeds of the bishop's medieval estate may be included in St. Paul's (dean and chapter archive) deeds, MSS 25121/1–3080 (see **70**). Early deeds of the properties acquired in 1550 are probably at Westminster Abbey (see **247**). MS 12041: deeds, 1648–1745 (*42*). MSS 12235, 12207: deeds, 1587, 1649 (*53*). MSS 1588–90, 12042–4, 12195–12201, 12203–4, 12208–9, 12211–16, 12218–23, 12225, 12227–34, 12644, 12657, 12662, 19972: deeds, leases, *c.* 1582–18C (*59, 63*, St. Paul's churchyard). MSS 12677–8, 12681–2, 12210, 12234, 12677–8, 12681–2, 19970–1: leases, 1577–81 (*75, 84*, St. Martin le Grand). MS 12673: leases, 1628–1805 (*112*). MSS 12039, 12206, 12217, 12234: leases, 1587–1808 (*128*). MS 12683 (leases, 1660–1895, concerning *149*) was returned from GL to the Church Commissioners in 1971.

b. MS 10234/1: register of leases, 1660–1710, indexed by tenant (*53, 59, 63, 84, 112, 128, 149*, St. Martin le Grand). MS 10237: estate bk., 18C, with memoranda of leases, arranged by place, from 16C or 17C (*42, ?53, 63*, Ave Maria Lane, churchyard, Cock Alley, Paternoster Row, St. Martin le Grand).

c. Rentals and Accounts.
In the followng descriptions, 'precinct' includes properties in or near the

churchyard, crypt, gates, Greenhaw, and palace, and nearby in *59, 63*.
Bishop's estate, to c. 1550. CUL, MS Ee. 1.3: precedent bk., 15C, incl.
rental of bishop's lands, 1447–8 (tenants named, no locations). MS 25423/
3: 'general' a/c or rental, late 14C (precinct). MS 25411: a/c of collector of
rents at palace, 1401–2. MSS 25424/5, 8, 17: summary a/cs, 1394–5, 1401–
2, 1460–1 (palace, no details). MSS 25425/2–3: summary a/cs, 16C. MSS
10123/1–3: bailiff's a/cs, 1518–19, 1527–8 (precinct; unleviable rents
(probably Old Work) in *30, 38, 42, 48, 92, 112, 125, 152*).
Old Work accounts, to c. 1550. MS 25423/1: rental, 1350 (*20, 30, 38, 42,
48, 59, 62, 63, 83, 89, 92, 112, 113, 114, 118, 125, 135, 137, 145, 150, 151,
152, 157, 162*). PRO, SC6/917/11; PRO, E101/473/1, 9; MSS 25413/3–4;
MS 25423/2; MS 10311; PRO, SC6/917/18; MS 25413/5; PRO, SC6/Hen
8/2109; MS 25612; PRO, E101/474/11: a/cs for Old Work (sometimes
incorporated in bishop's receiver's a/cs), 1382, 1394–5, 1405–6, 1409–10,
1421–3, 1453–4, 1509–10, 1521–2, 1529–39 (*30, 38, 42, 48, 59, 63, 92, 112,
125, 148, 149, 152*, precinct; ref. to *73* in MS 25413/3). PRO, SC6/1140/25:
a/c of bishop's receiver, 1464–5, incl. Old Work total.
Bishop's estate, incl. Old Work, from 1550. PRO, SC6/Edw 6/306–7: a/cs,
1550–1 (*53, 84, 128*; Old Work total). PRO, SC6/Phil & Mary/193–4: a/cs,
1555–6 (*53, 84, 128*, precinct, Cornhill). PRO, SC6/Eliz/1458–71: a/cs,
some summary only, 1559–67, 1573–4 (as preceding). MSS 25424/19–31;
MSS 10123/4–18: a/cs, incomplete series 1558–1606 (as preceding). MS
11927: memorandum of rents, *c.* 1590 (*53, 84, 128*, St. Martin le Grand).
MS 25428: part of rental, 17C (*53*, precinct, St. Martin le Grand). MSS
10128/1–2: rough rentals, 1660 (*84*, precinct, Billingsgate, Cornhill). MS
19586: notebk. incl. daily rent receipts, 1660 (precinct and nearby). MSS
10124/1–2: receiver-general's a/cs, 1662–3 (totals only).

d. MS 12191: survey of London House (?*63*), 1660. PRO, SC12/23/55:
survey of bishop's property, 1666 (*53, 59, 63, 128, 149*, precinct, St.
Martin le Grand). MS 12192: Fire Ct. decrees, 1668–71 (*59, 63, ?128*).

79. LONDON, HOLY TRINITY PRIORY, ALDGATE
Fd. 1107–8; diss. 1532. London prop. 1291, 1392. See E. Jeffries Davis,
'The beginning of the Dissolution: Christ Church, Aldgate, 1532', *TRHS*
4th ser. 8 (1925), 127–50, and M. C. Rosenfield, 'Holy Trinity, Aldgate,
on the eve of the Dissolution', *Guildhall Miscellany*, vol. 3, no. 3 (1970),
159–173.
In 1291 the estate lay in: *2, 4, 6, 8, 9, 10, 11, 13, 14, 15, 19, 21, 30, 36, 37,
38, 39, 43, 44, 45, 48, 49, 51, 53, 56, 58, 59, 61, 62, 67, 71, 74, 75, 78, 81,
83, 87, 90, 92, 93, 94, 95, 96, 98, 99, 100, 101, 103, 104, 105, 108, 112, 116,
118, 119, 122, 123, 124, 126, 127, 131, 135, 136, 141, 145, 149, 151, 152,
155, 156, 157, 158, 159*. At other dates it also included *5, 29, 32, 63, 66, 77,
80, 88, 117, 120, 125, 129, 132, 140*.

a. PRO, E303/8/4–5: leases, 16C (*123*).

b. Glasgow U. L., Hunter MS U.2.6 (Davis, no. 610; *The Cartulary of
Holy Trinity Aldgate*, ed. G. A. J. Hodgett, LRS 7, 1971): cartulary,
comp. 1425–7, of deeds 12C to 15C, chronicle material, and memoranda

of rent-payers (most of estate above (indexed), also *27*, ?*57*, *85*, *110*, *137*, *139*, ?*148*, St. Katharine's Hospital). BL, MS Lansd. 448 (Davis, no. 611): 15C cartulary (16 ff.), partly reproducing preceding (churches of *8*, *14*, *29*, *43*, *56*, soke of Aldgate). BL, Cotton Ch. xiii 18: 14C–15C roll of charters, mostly 12C (churches of *43*, *56*, *78*, *122*).

c. PRO, E164/18: rental, later 14C (estate above). PRO, SC11/437: valor, *c.* 1537–8 (most of estate above). PRO, E36/162: rental *c.* 1540 (estate above; includes unpaid and unleviable rents). PRO, SC12/11/16: rental, *c.* 1540, damaged (most of estate above). PRO, SC12/3/12: rental, *c.* 1540 (*123*).

d. PRO, E315/279, ff. 1–13: a/c, 1532–6 (total receipt, details of properties sold). PRO, SC6/Hen 8/2356: a/cs, 1536–41 (totals only). PRO, SC6/Hen 8/ 2363–6: a/cs, 1541–5 (most of estate above).

e. Hatfield House, Cecil MSS: plan of priory site, *c.* 1592 (HMC (9) *Salisbury (Cecil) MSS* xiv, 48; reproduced in W. R. Lethaby, 'The priory of Holy Trinity or Christ Church, Aldgate', *The Home Counties Magazine* ii (1900), 45–53).

f. PRO, E135/22/49: fragment of legal proceedings, mid 15C (soke of Aldgate).

80. LONDON, ST. BARTHOLOMEW'S PRIORY
Fd. 1123; diss. 1539. London prop. 1291, 1392, 1536. See also St. Bartholomew's Hospital, below, **100**. See E. A. Webb, *Records of St. Bartholomew's Priory, Smithfield* (1921).
In 1291 the estate lay in: *1*, *2*, *5*, *9*, *11*, *14*, *15*, *18*, *20*, *26*, *30*, *33*, *38*, *42*, *46*, *53*, *54*, *62*, *63*, *67*, *75*, *81*, *84*, *88*, *92*, *94*, *95*, *100*, *104*, *112*, *117*, *119*, *120*, *124*, *125*, *126*, *128*, *129*, *132*, *135*, *137*, *138*, *150*, *151*, *152*, *155*, *158*, *159*; also pension from the church of *123*. At other dates it also included *8*, *10*, *21*, *27*, *58*, *71*, *77*, *83*, *89*, *99*, *111*, *116*, *118*, *123*, *127*, *140*, *142*, *145*, *156*. The site became *33* after the Dissolution. For the precinct after 1547, see **451**.

a. Oxford, Queen's Coll., Deed no. 2508: 13C deed (*81*). PRO, E303/9/ 214–291: leases, mostly 16C (*5*, *11*, *20*, *42*, *71*, *83*, *84*, *94*, *95*, *104*, *129*, *142*, *152*, *159*).

b. Bodl, Middlesex Roll I (printed in Webb, *Records*, 428–77): rental, 1306 (estate above, except for *9*, *11*, *21*, *24*, *119*, *142*, *150*, *151*). PRO, E326/10609: memorandum of rents, 15C (probably *11*). PRO, SC12/27/ 18: rental 1538 (estate above, except for *8*, *10*, *58*, *71*, *75*, *77*, *89*, *116*, *118*, *120*, *123*, *125*, *126*, *127*, *140*, *145*, *151*, *155*, *156*). PRO, SC12/28/4: rental, 1545 (as preceding but incl. *71*, *151*).

c. PRO, DL29/287/4714: view of a/c, 1516–17 (site). PRO, SC6/Hen 8/ 2125: a/c 1535–6, noting totals received, specifying vacancies and arrears (*15*, *18*, *30*, *38*, *42*, *62*, *67*, *81*, *92*, *94*, *95*, *99*, *128*, *135*, *137*, *150*, *152*). PRO, DL28/33/8–10: summary a/cs 1540–2 (rectory of *152*, precinct, St. Bartholomew's Fair). PRO, DL43/7/13: valor, 1541–2 (rectory of *152*). PRO, DL43/7/14: rental, 1543–4 (*33*, *152*; 'Petywales', prob. in or near *33*).

81. London, St. Helen's Priory
Fd. bef. 1216; diss. 1538. London prop. 1392, 1536.
The estate lay in: *10, 11, 19, 32, 45, 58, 59, 60, 64, 74, 85, 94, 96, 99, 100, 101, ?104, 112, 113, 119, 120, 124, 128, 129, 141, 144, 145, 148, 149, 153, 155, 157*, Bread Street, Cheapside.
Unless otherwise stated the records are in PRO.

a. E303/8/6–26: leases, 16C (*2, 19, 58, 64, 101, 120, 124*).

b. SC12/30/19: rental, 1538 (estate above, except for *104, 145*; also refs. to *46, 118*). SC11/452: valor of quit-rents, 1543–4 (*11, 58, 81, 99, 128, 129, 149*, Bread Street). SC11/985: valor, rents only, *c.* 1540 (*19, 45, 58, 59, 64, 80, 96, 99, 101, 112, 113, 120, 124, 141, 144, 148, 155, 157*). LR2/262, ff. 5ᵛ–6ᵛ: rental, 1546 (*11, 32, 45, 58, 64, 94, 100, 101, 112, 113, 120, 124, 128, 129*, Bread Street, Cheapside).

c. SC6/1258/2: a/c 1350–2 (tenants named, not located). SC6/Addenda/3479: a/c 1509–12 (most of estate above, by street; quit-rents totalled; also refs. to *83, 90*). Bodl, MS Rawl. D. 809: a/c of rent arrears, 1518–31 (*19, 58, 60, 64, 74, 94, 99, 101, 112, 113, 119, 124, 144, 148, 155*, Cripplegate). SC6/Hen 8/2396–2401: a/cs, 1539–46 (estate above, also Watling Street). SC6/Hen 8/2377: detailed a/c, 1539–40 (*64*).

82. London, chapel of St. James by Cripplegate
Fd. bef. 1216; dependency of Garendon Abbey, Leics., from 1341; diss. 1536. London prop. (under heading of Garendon) 1392, 1535.
The precinct of St. James on the Wall was in the 16C alleged to be a parish, but afterwards regarded as lying within *144*. It was acquired by the Clothworkers' Company (see **26**, above).

a. Clothworkers' Hall, Company Deeds Box 19: incl. bundle of general documents 1–9, with memoranda of history, 15C papers concerning free chapel, 16C note of rents (*46, 53, 98, 134*, precinct); also, bundle of leases etc., 14C to 18C (*144*, precinct).

b. PRO, E315/403, ff. 132ʳ⁻ᵛ, 134ᵛ, 139: rental, *c.* 1540, of Garendon Abbey (Abchurch Lane, Fleet Street, Sherborne Lane, precinct). PRO, E315/397, f. 122: rental, *c.* 1540, of Garendon Abbey (London unspec.). PRO, LR2/262, f. 22: rental, 1546 (chapel).

c. PRO, SC6/Hen 8/1825–31: a/cs, 1536–42 (*46, 54, 98*, near Tower, precinct).

d. Clothworkers' Hall, Plan Book of 1612, incl. plan of precinct.

83. London, college of St. Martin le Grand
Fd. ?7C, conf. 1068; appropriated to Westminster Abbey, 1503. London prop. 1291, 1392, 1535.
In 1291 the estate lay in: *1, 6, 21, 42, 46, 54, 128, 137, 144, 149, 159*; also pensions from churches of *6, 15, 42, 135*. In 1392, in addition to the lands listed for the canons of St. Martin's, the prebendary of Chrishall (one of the college prebends) had property in Cripplegate Ward within.

The estate records are at Westminster Abbey and are described under the headings for that house: see **247–53**, below.

84. LONDON, ABBEY OF ST. MARY GRACES BY THE TOWER
Fd. 1350; diss. 1538. London prop. 1392, 1535.
The estate lay in: *10, 13, 19, 20, 21, 26, 32, 36, 42, 43, 44, 46, 53, 60* or *106, 88, 89, 96, 125, 127, 128, 141, 152.*
The records are in PRO.

a. E303/10/292–354: leases, mostly 16C (estate above, except for *19, 20, 42, 53*); see PRO class list to identify individual leases. E135/22/48: copy lease, 1533–4 (East Smithfield).

b. SC12/11/43: rentals, 1523–9 (estate above, except for *20, 42*; also *24, 149*). SC11/985: rental, *c.* 1540 (estate above, except for *20, 53, 88, 125*). SC12/11/13: valor, *c.* 1540 (*43, 44, 46*). SC12/29/22: valor, *c.* 1540 (total receipts, charges noted in *13, 20, 24, 26, 36, 43, 44, 45, 46, 96,125*). SC11/452: valor, 1543–4 (*36, 96*). LR2/262, f. 8^{r-v}: rental, 1546 (*13, 20, 21, 36, 43, 44, 46, 53, 60, 89, 127, 152*).

c. SC6/1258/1: bursar's a/c, 1391–2 (total receipt; charges, incl. repairs, noted in Holborn, Tower Hill). SC6/917/16: rent collector's a/c, 1402–3, with summary receipts, detailed exp. and vacations (*10, 26, 53, 88, 89, 96,* Bridge Street, East Smithfield, *le Stonehall,* Tower Street). SC6/Hen 8/2385, 2396–2401: a/cs 1540–6 (estate above, except for *88*).

85. LONDON, HOUSE OR HOSPITAL OF ST. THOMAS OF ACRE
Fd. early 13C; diss. 1538. London prop. 1291, 1392, 1535.
In 1291 the estate lay in: *39, 43, 45, 62, 74, 95, 105, 141, 155, 157.*
In the early 16C the estate lay in: *5, 12, 32, 39, 46, 62, 74, 83, 88, 92, 95, 98, 100, 104, 105, 111, 117, 123, 124, 128, 131, 142, 144, 145, 155, 156, 157, 158,* Basing Lane, Bishopsgate Street, Distaff Lane, Foster Lane, Knightrider Street. The site of the hospital and adjacent properties (*95, 105, 142*) were acquired after the Dissolution by the Mercers' Company (see **47a**, above). Records at Mercers' Hall are referred to below as MC.

a. A few 13C deeds concerning the site of the hospital may be identified in the Mercers' Company archive (see **47a**).

b. MC, Reg. of Writings i (Davis, no. 621; London material calendared by R. R. Sharpe in J. Watney, *Some Account of the Hospital of St. Thomas of Acon* (1st edn. 1892), 237–97): cartulary, comp. late 15C (*12, 26, 39, 62, 74, 95, 98, 100, 105, 123, 142, 156, 157, 158*; also ref. to *80*). PRO, E135/2/57 (Davis, no. 623): 16C cartulary of deeds and wills, 15C to 16C (*83, 95, 105, 142, 145, 155*; also refs. to *71, 81*). PRO, E135/20/2 (Davis, no. 624): part of register of leases, 1510–19 (*95, 105, 142, 145, 155*). Some leases of hospital property are entered at end of MC, Register of Leases i (see **47b**).

c. PRO, SC11/433, SC11/452, SC11/985, SC12/11/11, SC12/18/77, LR2/262; rentals and valors, *c.* 1540. PRO, SC6/1258/3, SC6/917/23–4: rent a/cs, 1442–3, 1449–50, 1482–9. GL, MS 25466 (probably to be transferred to MC): a/c, 1532–3, totals only. PRO, E315/269: bk. of a/cs, 1517–37 (estate above). PRO, SC6/Hen 8/2373–5, 2396–2400: a/cs and views of a/c, 1538–46.

86. LONDON, HOUSE OF KNIGHTS TEMPLARS
Fd. *c.* 1128, in Holborn; moved to New Temple, Fleet Street, 1161; order suppressed 1312.

a. Records of the Templars' London estate, which passed to the Knights Hospitallers, are included in BL, MS Cotton Nero E vi (Davis, no. 852): see **88**, below.

b. PRO, E142/107: inquisition, *temp.* Edward II, concerning pension (?London).

87. LONDON, CHARTERHOUSE, CARTHUSIAN PRIORY OF THE SALUTATION
Fd. 1371; diss. 1537. London prop. 1392, 1535. See *VCH Middlesex* i, 159–169.
The estate lay in: *2, 4, 5, 9, 18, 19, 20, 37, 38, 42, 44, 45, 48, 53, 59, 60* or *106, 61, 62, 63, 80, 85, 87, 88, 94, 98, 100, 112, 116, 118, 123, 124, 127, 135, 137, 141, 142, 144, 150, 152, 155, 159*, Candlewick Street; the site lay outside the city. Many Charterhouse deeds are identifiable among the Ancient Deeds in PRO. For the school and hospital founded on the site in 1611, see below, **403**.
The records are in PRO.

a. E303/8/29–159: leases, mostly 16C (*5, 9, 18, 20, 42, 44, 45, 48, 53, 61, 62, 85, 87, 88, 94, 98, 116, 118, 124, 127, 135, 137, 142, 150, 152,* Candlewick Street); see PRO search room guide to the class to identify individual leases.

b. LR2/61 (Davis, no. 607): cartulary, late 15C; ff. 18–28ᵛ, foundation charters; ff. 28ᵛ–42, deeds and extent (site, *152*); ff. 45ᵛ–98, London deeds (estate above, except for *18, 100, 123, 127*; also refs. to *21, 83, 90*).

c. SC12/22/77: rental, 1404–5 (apparently estate above, identified by streets). SC11/451: similar rental, mid 15C. SC12/11/14: valor, mid to late 15C (*118, 124*). SC12/25/55: rentals, 1516–17, 1524–5 (estate above, identified by streets). SC11/950: rental, after 1531–2 (*9, 18, 20, 42, 53, 61, 62, 63, 85, 94, 98, 100, 112, 118, 123, 124, 127, 141, 144, 155*). SC12/26/60: rental 1538–9 (estate above, identified by streets). SC11/985: valor, *c.* 1540 (precinct, *9, 19, 20, 42, 45, 53, 62, 63, 85, 98, 118, 124, 141, 144, 152, 155*). SC12/32/31: valor, *c.* 1540 (*37, 45, 60, 118, 137*). SC12/3/14: valor, *c.* 1540 (*116,135*). SC11/452: valor, 1543–4 (*20, 41, 62, 127,* Gracechurch Street; also 'St. Margaret Bread Street'. LR2/262, ff. 6ᵛ–7ᵛ: rental, 1546 (precinct, *5, 19, 20, 38, 45, 53, 62, 88, 112, 124, 135, 150, 159,* 'St. Margaret Bread Street').

d. E315/384: incl. a/cs for chantry, 1481–2 (*18, 123, 127*). SC6/Hen 7/397: a/c, 1493–5 (most of estate above, identified by streets). SC6/Hen 8/1700: view of a/c, 1506–7 (totals only). SC6/Hen 8/2112–15: views of a/c, 1514–26 (totals only, vacancies specified). LR12/20/627: rough memorandum bk. of arrears, 1538–9 (unspecified). SC6/Hen 8/2379: view of a/c, 1539–41 (most of estate above). SC6/Hen 8/2396–2401: a/cs 1539–46 (estate above, except for *2, 4, 37, 44, 48, 59, 80, 116, 142*, Candlewick Street; also ref. to 'St. Margaret Bread Street').

e. SC12/36/26: survey 1544–5 of site of Charterhouse. MP1/68, rough 16C plan, house nr. Stocks (*?48*).

88. LONDON, CLERKENWELL, PRIORY OF ST. JOHN OF JERUSALEM (KNIGHTS HOSPITALLERS)
Fd. *c.* 1144; diss. 1540. London prop. 1392, 1535.
The estate (including lands formerly belonging to the Knights Templars) lay in: *1* or *24, 18, 20, 38, 46, 54, 71, 73* or *162, 74, 75, 80, 88, 92, 111, 116, 124, 127, 131, 136, 151, 152*, New Temple.

a. BL, MS Cotton Nero E vi (Davis, no. 852; *The Cartulary of the Knights of St. John of Jerusalem in England, Secunda Camera, Essex*, ed. M. Gervers (1982), comprises only the second part, with no London entries): cartulary, begun 1442, of deeds and wills, 12C to 15C; *prima camera*, arranged by *tituli* for Clerkenwell, New Temple, London (estate above, except for *71, 88, 124*). BL, MS Cotton Nero C ix (Davis, no. 853): cartulary, detached from preceding (country props. except for f. 156ᵛ, ref. 1543–4 to parsonage of *129*).

b. BL, MS Lansd. 200 (Davis, no. 854): lease bk. 1492–1500, contemp. index and marginal heads (*54, 80, 152*). BL, MS Cotton Claud. E vi (Davis, no. 855): lease bk. 1503–26, similar to preceding (*46, 54, 62, 127, 152*); also (ff. 129ᵛ, 193ᵛ) refs. to advowson of *27*. PRO, LR2/62 (Davis, no. 856): lease bk. 1528–39, no index but marginal heads (*54, 71, 127, 152*). PRO, LR2/63 (Davis, no. 857): bk. of confirmations of priory's leases, copy leases and grants made in Ct. of Augmentations or by archbishop of York, 1537–47; no index but marginal heads (various properties).

c. PRO, LR2/262, f. 22: rental, 1546 (Chancery Lane, Fleet Street).

d. PRO, SC6/Hen 8/2402–13: a/cs, 1539–46 (estate above, except for *18, 38, 73* or *162, 92*; possibly also refs to *26, 148*).

89. LONDON, CLERKENWELL, PRIORY OF ST. MARY
Fd. *c.* 1145; diss. 1539. London prop. 1392, 1535.
The estate was as follows:
    A (held in mid to late 13C): *4, 5, 8, 11, 12, 15, 20, 21, 27, 36, 38, 42, 46, 49, 51, 54, 62, 71, 80, 85, 92, 93, 94, 96, 99, 100, 104, 105, 111, 116, 117, 119, 120, 123, 125, 127, 128, 129, 132, 135, 137, 145, 148, 149, 150, 151, 152, 156, 158, 159*, St. Martin le Grand.
    B (held in mid 16C): *2, 5, 10, 11, 15, 20, 21, 24, 26, 30, 32, 36, 37, 38, 42, 44, 46, 51, 56, 59, 62, 71, 74, 75, 77, 80, 81, 84, 85, 87, 88, 92, 93, 96, 98, 99, 100, 103, 104, 105, 112, 118, 119, 120, 123, 124, 125, 127, 129, 135, 137, 145, 148, 149, 151, 152, 155, 156, 157, 158, 159*.
Unless otherwise stated, the records are in PRO.

a. Lambeth, Reg. Warham, f. 122 (printed in W. O. Hassall, 'Two papal bulls for St. Mary, Clerkenwell', *EHR* 57 (1942), 97–101): bull, 1186, confirming properties (Ludgate, Philip Lane, church of *Stanengah*', unspec.). BL, MS Cotton Faust. B ii (Davis, no. 263; *The Cartulary of St. Mary Clerkenwell*, ed. W. O. Hassall, Camden 3rd ser. 71, 1949): cartulary, comp. mid 13C and later, of deeds, etc., 12C–14C (estate A; also ref. to *75*).

b. SC11/985: valor of rents, *c.* 1540 (*20, 37, 75, 84, 88, 98, 118, 119, 123, 152, 155*, Old Fish Street). SC12/19/4: valor, *c.* 1540 (total only, charges noted in *88, 119, 152*). SC11/452: valor of quit-rents, 1543–4 (*10, 11, 30, 46, 71, 84, 85, 92, 93, 96, 98, 105, 118, 119, 120, 124, 127, 132, 149, 152,* 'Horssebrygge'). LR2/262, ff. 12ᵛ–14: rental, 1546–7 (*10, 11, 30, 46, 71, 84, 85, 92, 93, 96, 104, 105, 117, 118, 119, 120, 127, 132, 149, 152, 157,* Cornhill, Foster Lane).

c. SC6/Hen 7/396: bailiff's a/c, 1489–90, rents, quit-rents (estate B, except for *10*). SC6/Hen 8/2116–20, 2380, 2396–2401: a/cs, 1524–7, 1532–5, 1539–46, rents and/or quit-rents (estate B).

90. LONDON, HALIWELL, PRIORY OF ST. JOHN THE BAPTIST
Fd. bef. 1127; diss. 1539. London prop. 1392, 1535.
The estate lay in: *9, 10, 11, 12, 14, 15, 19, 26, 32, 36, 43, 45, 56, 60* or *106, 62, 81, 83, 85, 87, 99, 104, 105, 112, 118, 119, 120, 123, 124, 125, 127, 129, 134, 141, 145, 148, 151, 152, 155, 156, 159,* 'St. Christopher in Fenchurch Street' (probably *48*), Cutler Lane, Seacoal Lane.
Unless otherwise stated the records are in PRO.

a. E303/11/Middlesex, Haliwell, nos. 1, 10, 16, 17, 19, 20, 23, 24, 25, 32, 35, 39, 41, 43: leases, 16C (*9, 11, 14, 60, 62, 83, 104, 112, 145*).

b. BL, Add. MS 5937, ff. 74–5 (Davis, no. 609): 16C–17C extracts from lost cartulary or register, of abbreviated deeds and charters, mostly 12C and 13C (*10, 26, 62, 92, 105, 116, 123, 152, super Walbroc*).

c. SC12/11/35: valor 1534–5, fragment lost (estate above, except for *26, 43, 105, 118, 145,* St. Christopher). SC11/985: valor of rents, *c.* 1540 (*14, 19, 32, 45, 60, 62, 99, 112, 123, 145, 151*). SC12/27/13: valor, *c.* 1540 (London rents totalled, charges noted in *19, 26, 60, 62, 105, 112, 145, 156*). SC11/452: valor of quit-rents, 1543–4 (estate above, except for *11, 19, 62, 83, 99, 123, 127, 148, 151, 155, 156*). LR2/262, ff. 14ᵛ–15ᵛ: rental, 1546 (*11, 60, 62, 81, 104, 112, 129, 145, 152, 156,* 'St. Christopher in Fenchurch Street').

d. SC6/Hen 8/2396–2401: a/cs, 1539–46.

91. LONDON, AUSTIN FRIARS
Fd. 1253; diss. 1538. London prop. 1392.
The estate lay in: *10, 21, 36, 48, 81, 148* (formerly *140*), 'St. Martin Queenhithe'.
The records are in PRO.

a. SC11/985: valor of rents, *c.* 1540. LR2/262, f. 10ᵛ: rental, 1546 (*148*). SC6/Hen 8/2385, 2396–2401: a/cs, 1539–46.

92. LONDON, CARMELITE (WHITE) FRIARS
Fd. 1247; diss. 1538. London prop. 1392.
The estate consisted of the site and property in Whitefriars precinct and
54; possibly also *141* (*VCH London* i, 510).
The records are in PRO.

a. E303/9/175: lease, 16C (precinct).

b. SC11/985, SC12/11/17: valors, *c.* 1540 (precinct, *54*). SC11/452: valor,
1543–4, no rents detailed. LR2/262, ff. 9ᵛ–10; rental, 1546 (precinct, *54*).

c. SC6/Hen 8/2385, 2396–2401: a/cs, 1539–46 (precinct, *54*).

93. LONDON, CRUTCHED FRIARS
Fd. bef. 1269; diss. 1538. London prop. 1392.
The estate lay in: *4, 10, 43, 45, 53, 137, 141*, Old Change.
The records are in PRO. For deeds, see **473**.

a. SC12/11/13, valor, *c.* 1540 (*10*). SC11/985, valor, *c.* 1540. LR2/262, f.
10ᵛ: rental, 1546 (*141*, Tower Street).

b. SC6/Hen 8/2385, 2396–2401: a/cs, 1539–46.

94. LONDON, DOMINICAN (BLACK) FRIARS
Fd. 1221 in Holborn; moved to Ludgate 1275/86; diss. 1538. London
prop. 1392.
The estate lay in the precinct (subsequently *25*) and nearby in *18*. The
precinct was enlarged in 1352 by the acquisition of land formerly belonging to Ogbourne Priory, Wilts. (*Cal. Pat. R. 1350–54*, p. 323; see **193**,
below).
The records are in PRO.

a. E303/9/180: lease, 16C (precinct).

b. LR2/262, f. 9ʳ⁻ᵛ, SC11/985, SC12/11/13, 17, 18: rentals, *c.* 1540.

c. SC6/Hen 8/2385, 2396–2401: a/cs, 1539–46.

95. LONDON, FRANCISCAN (GREY) FRIARS
Fd. 1224; diss. 1538. London prop. 1392.
The estate comprised the site and precinct, formerly in the parishes of *24,
27, 137*, and *152*, from which *47* was formed after the Dissolution.

a. BL, MS Cotton Vit. F xii, 'Register', comp. *c.* 1536 (ed. with other
documents in C. L. Kingsford, *The Grey Friars of London*, 1915,
republished 1965): summary of deeds, gifts, history from 13C (precinct as
above; ref. to rent in *120*, house in Thames Street).

b. PRO, E101/507/5: a/c of expenses relating to chapel, early 14C. PRO,
LR2/262, f. 10ᵛ, SC11/985, SC12/11/17: rentals and valors, *c.* 1540
(precinct). PRO, SC6/Hen 8/2385, 2396–2401: a/cs, 1539–46.

95A. LONDON, FRIARS OF THE SACK (OF THE PENANCE OF JESUS)
Fd. *c.* 1257; order closed 1274.

The friars occupied a site in *42* until *c.* 1270 and then one in *88* and *142* until *c.* 1305, and held property in *98*, but no independent archive concerning their holdings survives: see *VCH London* i, 513–14.

96. LONDON, MINORESSES (NUNS OF THE ORDER OF ST. CLARE), ABBEY OF B.V.M. AND ST. FRANCIS WITHOUT ALDGATE
Fd. *c.* 1293–4; diss. 1539. London prop. 1291, 1392, 1535.
The estate lay in: *4, 10, 19, 32, 42, 43, 45, 74, 81, 85, 88, 96, 98, 104, 105, 113, 119, 128, 129, 132, 135, 137*, Bow Lane, Fleet Street, Old Fish Street; the precinct subsequently became *68*.
The records are in PRO.

a. E303/9/181, 183, 187–9, 195–7, 199–200: leases, mostly 16C (*43, 104, 113, 119, 137*).

b. SC11/955: rental, 1539–40 (estate above, mostly identified by street). SC11/985: valor, *c.* 1540 (estate above). SC12/11/12: valor, ?*c.* 1540 (*98, 119*). SC11/452: valor, 1543–4 (*85, 88*, Fleet Street). LR2/262, f. 5: rental, 1546 (*42, 85, 88*, Fleet Street). SC12/11/38, list, mid 16C, tenements in precinct.

c. SC6/Hen 7/395: a/c of rents, 1487–8 (most of estate above, identified by street). SC6/Hen 8/2122–3: a/cs, 1515–16, rents and repairs (tenants named, properties not identified). SC6/Hen 8/2121, 2427–8, 2396–2401: a/cs, 1531–2, 1538–46. LR12/20/627, memorandum of arrears, 1538–9 (*129*).

97. LONDON, DOMUS CONVERSORUM
Fd. 1232; ceased 17C. London prop. 1392. The site was in *54* outside the city but there were rents and properties in the city, including: *11, 54, 85, 105, 111, 112, 117, 119, 134, 137, 152*, Friday Street.

a. For grants of lands in London, see *Cal. Chart. R.* i, 199, 290, 292, 309, 351.

b. For a full list of a/cs, see PRO *Lists and Indexes*, no. XXXV, pp. 160–4. Many of these a/cs have no details of income, only of expenditure.

98. LONDON, HOSPITAL OF ST. ANTHONY OF VIENNE
Fd. *c.* 1254; appropriated to college of St. George, Windsor, 1475; not suppressed but ceased by 1565. London prop. 1291.
In 1291 the estate lay in *36*; *14* was added at a later date.
The records are at The Aerary, St. George's Chapel, Windsor Castle. See J. N. Dalton, *The Manuscripts of St. George's Chapel, Windsor Castle* (1957), 275–88, for a descriptive list.

a. I. G. 10: will 1449 (*14*). XV. 37. 5–7, 9, 11, 35, 49: deeds, leases, 15C to 16C, (*14, 36*). XVI. 2. 2–5, 10, 11, 16–18, 24–6, 31–3, 36, 37, 42–5, 53, 54, 59, 64–73: leases, agreements, etc., later 16C to late 17C (*36*). XV. 37. 42: memoranda of leases, 15C to 16C (*36*).

b. For registers, lease bks., etc. see St. George's Chapel (**258**), below.

c. XV. 37. 4, 15, 22, 24, 27, 29, 31, 32, 37, 39, 72–6, 86, 89, 90, 99, 100, 106–111: a/cs, incl. rentals, 15C to 17C (*14* (to mid-16C), *36*). XV. 37. 26, 28: a/cs of arrears, 1506–10 (*14, 36*).

d. IV. A. 3: parliamentary surveys, 1649, of lands of St. George's Chapel, incl. *36*.

99. LONDON, HOSPITAL OR FRATERNITY OF ST. AUGUSTINE PAPEY
Fd. 1430; diss. 1547.

a. BL, MS Cotton Vit. F xvi, ff. 113ᵛ–23, fragments of register, 15C–16C (Davis, no. 616; extracts in T. Hugo, 'The hospital of le Papey in the city of London', *Trans LMAS* 5 (1881), 183–221): incl. refs. to *14, 29*, tenements at Baynards Castle).

100. LONDON, ST. BARTHOLOMEW'S HOSPITAL
Fd. 1123; re-fd. 1544. London prop. 1392, 1535.
The estate was as follows:
    A (held in 1547): *5, 12, 14, 15, 18, 20, 30, 38, 42, 45, 46, 58, 62, 63, 75, 92, 96, 98, 104, 112, 132, 135, 137, 144, 145, 149, 151, 152, 157*. Other properties may have been held at an earlier date, and lost or disposed of by 1547: see **a** and **b**, below.
    B (acquired 1547–1666, in addition to A): *14, 27, 32, 47, 53, 56, 62, 88, 112, 141, 148, 152, 155*, Foster Lane.
Unless otherwise stated the records are at the hospital. See HMC 'Report on the records of Hospitals in the City of London and Borough of Hackney Health District, 1137–1974' (1977).

a. Deeds, 12C to 17C (estate A, also *2, 4, 27, 29, 32, 48, 53, 54, 67, 87, 88, 89, 116, 117, 118, 120, 125, 126, 127, 129, 136, 150, 159*); modern card-calendar.

b. 'Great Cartulary' (Davis, no. 617; *The Cartulary of St. Bartholomew's Hospital*, ed. N. J. M. Kerling, 1973): cartulary in 2 vols., comp. 15C (estate as in **a** (Deeds), above; also *10, 13, 80, 81, 85, 100, 105, 108, 111, 156*; also refs. to *21, 51, 74, 99, 119*). 'Little Cartulary' (Davis, no. 618); 15C cartulary relating to quit-rents, also incl. extracts from rentals (estate A, except for *30, 38*; also incl. *4, 10, 13, 27, 32, 48, 53, 54, 67, 81, 87, 88, 89, 100, 105, 108, 116, 118, 120, 125, 126, 127, 129, 134, 148, 150, 156*, Milk Street). 'Repertory Book' (Davis, no. 619): register of deeds, 14C to 17C (estate B). Hb 5: copies of 17C wills (*20, 32, 62*).

c. Hc 3/1, 'Inventory of lands 1546': rental of estate A, acquired from Crown 1547. Hb 1, General Accounts: a/cs incl. detailed annual rentals, fines, building expenditure, 1547–1671. Hb 3, Treasurers' General Accounts: files of rough a/cs of expenditure, 1620–62, some years missing. Hb 8, Treasurers' Cash Bks.: receipts and payments, 1642–58. Hb 15, Renters' Cash Bks.: daily receipts, incl. rents, 1651–6. Hb 6, Balance Bk.: annual state of a/c in December, incl. arrears of rent, 1652–74. Bodl, MS Rawl. B 362, ff. 1–9: rent receiver's a/c, 1600–1.

d. Ha 1, Minutes of Board of Governors, 1549–1675: incl. lease decisions, orders to view and repair; vols. 1–3 (1549–1607) have full modern index, subsequent vols. have contemp. name indexes; vol. 1 also incl. church-wardens' a/cs, St. Nicholas Shambles and Christ Church parishes (see **305** and **367**, below). Ha 2/1, 'Old Records': vol. cont. minutes of board of governors, 1552–7; details of fines for leases from 1610; lists of rent arrears, 17C.

e. Hc 9/1, Book of Surveys: written surveys of state of repair of properties, 1587–1664. Hb 7: bks. of rent arrears and losses caused by Great Fire; vol. 1 incl. lists of houses destroyed, rent arrears from 1673. Papers concerning property burned in Fire, incl. views, notes on leases, title, plans, 1666–72.

f. Plans and Maps: full list of early plans in archivist's office, but not all plans have been identified. Hc 19/1/1, vol. of 16C and 17C plans; Hc 19/1/2, vol. of 17C and 18C plans; Hc 19/2–6, vol. of 18C and 19C plans.

101. LONDON, HOSPITAL OF ST. KATHARINE BY THE TOWER
Fd. 1148; not suppressed. London prop. 1392, 1535.
The estate lay in East Smithfield (?*43*), also in *4* (rents), and *4, 20, 53, 60, 90, 95, 98, 99, 104, 111* (quit-rents).
See C. Jamison, *History of the Royal Hospital of St. Katharine by the Tower* (1952).
Unless otherwise stated the records are in GL.

a. MSS 9860–1, 9866, 9871, 9873, 9879: royal charters and confirmations, 1292–1498 (precinct, East Smithfield). MSS 9864, 9868: licence and confirmation, 1370, 1378 (*4, 80*). MS 9753/1: deeds, leases, 1539–1668 (*4*, precinct). MS 9754: leases, 1508, 1542 (precinct). MS 9703: incl. 16C bonds to perform covenants of leases, etc. MSS 9874, 9877: exemplifications of pleas, 1440–55 (*37, 43*).

b. PRO, E315/406, ff. 31–2, SC12/19/29: valors, *c.* 1540 (total only). PRO, E315/408, ff. 69–71: rental, 1546 (rents in precinct, *4, 43, 126*, Thames Street; quit-rents as above). PRO, SC12/27/5: inspeximus, 1599–1600, of rental 1546.

c. MS 9680: precinct constable's a/cs, *c.* 1598–1706, incl. refs. to lease and repair of minister's house, church.

d. MS 9774 (Prints and Drawings, Map Case 290): plan of precinct, 1687.

102. LONDON, HOSPITAL OF ST. MARY OF BETHLEHEM (BETHLEM HOSPITAL)
Fd. 1247; not suppressed. London prop. 1392.
The original hospital lay in *45*. It was rebuilt in Moorfields in 1674, moved to Southwark in 1815, and to Beckenham, Kent, in 1930. It came under the City's jurisdiction by 1346, and was administered with Bridewell Hospital (**409**, below) from the later 16C until 1948. Some records concerning both foundations are at King Edward's School, Witley, Surrey, the successor to Bridewell Hospital. Records relating solely to Bethlem are in the Archives Dept., Bethlem Royal Hospital, Beckenham, Kent. See NRA Report, 1959, by A. E. B. and D. M. Owen.

The estate lay in *45*; the archive includes material of 17C date relating to property acquired later.

a. There appear to be no early deeds, but see **b**, below. Bethlem, Box 41: deeds, leases, *c.* 1622–1805, and plan, 1677 (*45*). Ibid., Box 64: deeds, papers, 1613–1806 (*54*). Ibid., Box 20: deeds, leases, 1626–1937 (*62*).

b. Witley, Muniment Book 1554–1732: incl. material relating to other royal hospitals; also, f. 30, schedule, *c.* 1550, of tenements in Bethlem; ff. 47ᵛ–170, leases, incl. Bethlem properties, 16C to 18C; f. 175 et seqq., copy foundation charter, 1247, incl. bounds, and memoranda of later inquisitions etc.; ff. 205–8, schedule of leases, 1632; ff. 229ᵛ–232, Fire Ct. decree (*75*).

c. PRO, C270/22: visitation, 1403, incl. refs. to properties, leases. GL, MS 12815/1, Christ's Hospital Register Book, 1552–1702: incl. (f. 56ʳ⁻ᵛ) rental of Bethlem properties, *c.* 1553. PRO, SP16/224, no. 21 (*Cal. S. P. Dom. 1631–3*, p. 424): report on hospital, 1632, incl. valuation of estate, discussion of rents and fines.

d. Witley, Box 67: rent rolls, 1605–6, 1621–2, 1665–6, and later (Bethlem and Bridewell). Bethlem, Rent Rolls: a/cs, 1631–9, 1647–8, and later (Bethlem).

e. CLRO, Repertories, mid to late 16C, incl. decisions relating to Bethlem properties. Witley, Court Minute Books, 1559–62, 1574–9, 1597–1610, 1617–59, 1666 to date (microfilms at Bethlem: also GL, microfilms 510–515, 1559–1659 only): minutes, incl. leasing business (Bethlem and Bridewell; contemp. indexes to personal names only).

103. LONDON, [NEW] HOSPITAL OF ST. MARY WITHOUT BISHOPSGATE (ST. MARY SPITAL)
Fd. 1197; diss. 1538–40. London prop. 1392, 1535.
The estate lay in: *2, 4, 5, 8* or *106, 9, 11, 13, 14, 20, 21, 24, 26, 27, 30, 37, 39, 42, 43, 45, 49, 51, 53, 58, 61, 62, 71, 74, 78, 80, 81, 83, 84, 85, 87, 89, 90, 92, 93, 94, 96, 98, 99, 100, 103, 104, 108, 116, 119, 123, 124, 125, 128, 129, 136, 141, 144, 145, 148, 149, 151, 152, 156, 159.*
Unless otherwise stated the records are in PRO.

a. E303/8/27: lease, 16C (*93*).

b. BL, MS Cotton Nero C iii, ff. 198, 219–26: 16C copy of letters patent, 1318, confirming properties (estate above, except for *5, 14, 20, 21, 24, 27, 37, 51, 74, 80, 84, 85, 87, 89, 99, 106, 108, 125, 144, 149*; also incl. *65, 95, 111, 118*, parish of St. Paul, *in merceria, Waremansacre*). E36/265 (Davis, no. 620): late 14C cartulary, now barely legible, many pages missing (list of contents refers to estate above (except for *5, 24, 37, 51, 81, 84, 125, 136, 144*) and also to *10, 15, 29, 32, 38, 75, 101, 105*).

c. SC11/972–6: rentals, 1454, 1468, 1472, 1496, 1504, 1514 (refs. to *45, 113*, Bishopsgate Street, alleys). SC11/977: rental 1516 (estate above). SC11/978: rental 1519, some entries incomplete (estate above, except for *45, 51, 84*). SC11/979: rental 1523 (estate above, except for *45, 51, 84*).

SC11/980: rental, Michaelmas term 1539 (part of estate above). SC11/985: rental, *c.* 1540 (*2, 14, 20, 43, 45, 62, 74, 83, 89, 93, 98, 103, 104, 116, 128, 136, 144, 149, 151, 152, 159*). SC11/452: rental 1543–4 (*10, 11, 14, 21, 24, 26, 45, 49, 51, 74, 80, 85, 89, 92, 93, 104, 118, 125, 151, 152, 159,* St. Albertus (probably *2*)). LR2/262, ff. 11–12: rental 1546 (as preceding, also *96, 98, 138*).

d. SC6/Hen 8/2378, 2395–2401: a/cs, 1539–46 (estate above, except for *4, 5, 13, 27, 37, 39, 53, 58, 81, 84, 94, 99, 106, 108, 119, 123, 124, 129, 145*; also incl. *118*).

104. London, hospital of St. Mary within Cripplegate (Elsing Spital)
Fd. 1331; diss. 1536. London prop. 1392, 1535.
The estate lay in: *4, 9, 10, 11, 15, 30, 38, 45, 53, 62, 81, 95, 99, 104, 123, 126, 132, 152, 159,* Friday Street.
Unless otherwise stated, the records are in PRO. See also **265k, 476**.

a. E303/10/355–384: leases, 16C (estate above, except for *30, 38, 45, 81, 123, 132, 152*); see PRO, search room class list to identify individual leases.

b. BL, Cotton Ch. xiii. 10: rental, 1448 (estate above, identified by street). BL, Cotton Ch. xi. 68: valor, 1461 (total rents, repairs, quit-rents). PRO, E315/397, f. 131: survey, *c.* 1540 (total receipt, refs. to some payments out). SC11/440: valor, *c.* 1540 (estate above except for *4, 9, 53, 104, 123, 132,* Friday Street). SC12/34/18, rental, *c.* 1540 (estate above, mostly identified by street; also ref. to *78*). SC11/452: rental, 1543–4 (*81, 95, 123, 132, 152, 159,* Friday Street). LR2/262, f. 1: rental, 1546, partly damaged (most of estate above).

c. SC6/1304/8: renter's a/c, 1403–4 (estate above, except for *4, 9, 30, 45, 53, 126*). SC6/1257/3: kitchener's a/c, 1408–9, incl. some payments out; repairs (*30*). SC6/915/25: a/c, total only, details of some payments out. SC6/Hen 8/2424–8, 2342–55: a/cs 1535–46.

d. E135/21/7: inquisition 1330 into possible losses to parishes of *15* and *99* through the building of the hospital.

105. London, hospital of the Savoy
Fd. 1505–17; diss. 1553, and estate granted to St. Thomas's Hospital, Southwark; Savoy Hospital re-fd. 1556, but with no lands in London. London prop. 1535.
The estate lay in: *11, 19, 26, 30, 36, 39, 128, 152, 153, 159.*
Unless otherwise stated, the records are in GLRO, St. Thomas's Hospital archive (see **226**).

a. H1/ST/E65/17/7: lease 1547 (*11*). H1/ST/E67/1/12, 29, 32–4, 39, 43: leases, 1542–50 (*26, 128, 152, 159*). H1/ST/E68/1/4: lease, 1550 (*152*)

b. H1/ST/E15, St. Thomas's Hospital Lease Bk.: incl. Savoy Hospital leases, 1536–53. See also H1/ST/E14, 'Foundation Book', incl. surrender, grant, and rental of Savoy Hospital lands, 1553; GL, MS 12815/1, Christ's Hospital Register, incl. (ff. 26–7) rental of former Savoy lands, *c.* 1553.

106. ALNWICK, NORTHUMB., ABBEY OF B.V.M.
Fd. 1147–8; diss. 1539. Owned rectory of *54.*

a. PRO, LR2/262, f. 20: rental, 1546. PRO, SC6/Hen 8/7364–70: a/cs, 1539–46.

107. ANKERWYKE, BUCKS., PRIORY OF ST. MARY MAGDALENE
Fd. *c.* 1160; diss. 1536. London prop. 1392, 1536. The property in Candlewick Street was granted to the refounded Bisham Priory in 1537–8: see **118.**

a. PRO, E315/397, f. 3: survey, *c.* 1540 (London unspec.). PRO, SC6/Hen 8/234–5: a/cs 1535–8 (*46,* Candlewick Street).

108. BARKING, ESSEX, ABBEY OF ST. MARY AND ST. ETHELBURGA
Fd. *c.* 666, *c.* 965; diss. 1539. London prop. 1291, 1392. In 1086 the abbey held half a church and 28 houses in London: DB ii, ff. 17ᵛ–18.
In 1291 the estate lay in: *42, 104,* with a pension from the church of *4.*

a. PRO, SC11/985: rental, *c.* 1540 (*2, 35, 38, 49, 54, 81, 91, 108, 117, 142, 148*). PRO, LR2/262, f. 16ᵛ: rental, 1546 (*4* (vicarage of), *81,* unspec.). PRO, SC6/Hen 8/964–70: a/cs, 1539–46 (*5, 42, 81, 117, 137, 142*).

109. BARLINGS, LINCS., ABBEY OF B.V.M.
Fd. 1154–5; diss. 1537. London prop. 1392.

a. BL, MS Cotton Faust. B i (Davis, no. 19): cartulary, 13C to 14C; f. 133ᵛ, writ (*18*).

110. BARNWELL, CAMBS., PRIORY OF ST. GILES AND ST. ANDREW
Fd. *c.* 1092, 1112; diss. 1538. London prop. 1291, 1392.
In 1291 the estate lay in *19.*
The records are in PRO.

a. LR2/262, f. 16: rental, *c.* 1540 (*42*). SC6/Hen 8/7286–93, 7295: a/cs, 1538–46 (*42*).

111. BATH AND WELLS, BISHOP
In 1291 and 1331 the bishop had temporalities in *8, 46,* and *129,* but may have lost them soon after the latter date: *The Register of Ralph of Shrewsbury, bishop of Bath and Wells, 1329–1363,* ed. T. S. Holmes (Somerset Rec. Soc. 9–10, 1896), 82. In 1217×19 the bishop acquired a property in Bishopsgate and Broad Street (probably in *64* and *148*), but no later record of this has been found, unless the property was associated with that in *32* disposed of by the bishop in 1539. In 1539 the bishop exchanged his residence in the Strand for property in *68* (C. L. Kingsford, 'Bath Inn or Arundel House', *Archaeologia* 72 (1921–2), 243–77).

Records of some of the bishop's properties are preserved among the manuscripts of the dean and chapter of Wells: not seen, but calendared in *Calendar* [*of the Manuscripts of the Dean and Chapter of Wells* (2 vols., HMC, 1907–14)]. The Somerset Record Office reports (November, 1983) that the diocesan records in its care contain nothing relating to property or estate management in London. See also **246, 462b**.

a. Registers at Wells. 'Liber Albus i' (Davis no. 1003): 13C register; f. 17, copy deed concerning Bishopsgate and Broad Street (*Calendar* i, 16). Ledger Book D, etc., is a series of dean and chapter registers of leases beginning in 1535 and incl. confirmations of episcopal leases of property in *68* and the grant of 1539 concerning *32* (eg. *Calendar* ii, 251–3, 255).

112. BAYHAM, SUSSEX, ABBEY OF B.V.M.
Fd. 1199–1208; diss. 1525. London prop. 1291 (*62*).

a. BL, MS Stowe 924 (Davis, no. 38): 17C transcript of BL, MS Cotton Otho A ii (cartulary *c*. 1245, subsequently damaged and pages missing); f. 134, grant, 13C, *in vico Germani* (*?10*).

113. BEDDGELERT, CARNARVON, PRIORY OF ST. MARY
Fd. 6C, 1200×40; diss. 1536 and property granted to Bisham Priory (**118**).

a. PRO, SC6/Hen 8/109: a/c for Bisham Priory, 1537–8, incl. property late of Beddgelert (nr. Paul's Wharf).

114. BEELEIGH, ESSEX, ABBEY OF B.V.M. AND ST. NICHOLAS
Fd. 1180; diss. 1536. London prop. 1291, 1392.
In 1291 the estate lay in: *19, 53*.

a. BL, Add. MS 19051, f. 3^{r-v}: list of possessions, *c*. 1536 (*19*). PRO, LR2/262, f. 16: rental, 1546 (*19*). PRO, SC6/Hen 8/952–61: a/cs 1536–46 (*19*).

115. BERMONDSEY, SURREY, ABBEY OF ST. SAVIOUR
Fd. 1082; diss. 1538. London prop. 1291, 1392, 1535.
In 1291 the estate lay in: *1, 4, 6, 8, 9, 10, 12, 13, 19, 21, 35, 39, 42, 44, 48, 49, 51, 53, 54, 56, 61, 67, 71, 74, 75, 80, 83, 87, 89, 90, 93, 94, 96, 98, 103, 104, 108, 112, 114, 118, 120, 123, 124, 125, 126, 127, 128, 129, 131, 134, 135, 136, 137, 144, 145, 151, 152, 156, 157, 158, 159*; there were also pensions from the churches of *20, 85*.

a. BL, MS Harl. 231 (Davis, no. 46; *Annales Monastici* iii, ed. H. R. Luard (Rolls Ser. 1866), 423–87): annals, 1042–1432; incl. some refs. to properties (*10, 20, 104, 111*).

b. PRO, SC12/37/7, LR2/262: rentals, 1546 (properties not specified). PRO, SC6/1107/11: a/c during vacancy, 1418, rents and arrears (*1, 4, 10, 14, 21, 39, 44, 48, 49, 51, 53, 56, 67, 71, 74, 80, 83, 85, 87, 90, 93, 98, 103, 104, 108, 112, 118, 124, 125, 126, 127, 128, 131, 135, 136, 137, 145, 151, 152, 156, 159*). PRO, SC6/Hen 8/3464–8: a/cs, 1539–46 (*20, 83, 85*, London unspec.).

Religious Houses and Bishoprics

116. Biddlesden, Bucks., abbey of B.V.M.
Fd. 1147; diss. 1538. London prop. 1291, 1392, 1535.
In 1291 and later the estate lay in *135*.

a. BL, MS Harl. 4714 (Davis, no. 54): cartulary, early 16C; London refs. on ff. 344–7.

b. PRO, E315/397, f. 8: survey, *c.* 1540. PRO, SC12/37/7: rental, 1546. PRO, SC6/Hen 8/237–42; a/cs, 1538–46.

117. Bindon, Dorset, abbey of B.V.M.
Fd. 1172; diss. 1539. In early 13C the abbey granted land in *148* to St. Albans Abbey (Chatsworth Library, Derbyshire, cartulary, f. 176; see below, **213**).

118. Bisham, Berks., priory of Jesus Christ and B.V.M.
Fd. 1337; diss. 1536; reoccupied 1537–8 by monks from Chertsey. London prop. 1392.
The original priory had property in *18*; the re-foundation also had property in Candlewick Street (late of Ankerwyke Priory) and near Paul's Wharf (late of Beddgelert Priory). The records are in PRO.

a. LR2/262, f. 21^v; SC12/37/7: rentals, 1546 (Candlewick Street). SC6/Hen 8/107–14: a/cs, 1536–46 (*18*). SC6/Hen 8/109: a/c, 1537–8 (*18*, Candlewick Street, Paul's Wharf).

119. Blackmore, Essex, priory of St. Laurence
Fd. 1152–62; diss. 1525.
The priory acquired a property in *105* in 1291: HR 20(70), 47(41), 56(125). Rents from this and from *60* were transferred to Waltham Abbey in 1532: *L & P Henry VIII* v, no. 766 (2); grant recited in PRO, E135/3/44, bishop of London's confirmation of the same. See **241**, below.

120. Boxley, Kent, abbey of St. Mary V.
Fd. 1143×6; diss. 1538. London prop. 1291, 1535.
In 1291 the estate lay in: *101, 124*.

a. Lambeth MS 1212 (Davis, no. 159): cartulary, 13C–14C, of see of Canterbury (**133**); ff. 107^v–108, copy grants, bef. 1193 to Boxley, 1193×9 Boxley to Canterbury (land on Thames, probably *116*; see *Cal. Chart. R. 1257–1300*, pp. 8, 354).

b. PRO, SC11/334: rental, 1317 (*124*, unspec.). PRO, SC6/Hen 8/1762–8: a/cs, 1538–46 (*101, 124*).

121. Bridgwater, Som., hospital of St. John the Baptist
Fd. bef. 1213; diss. 1539. London prop. 1392, 1535.

a. PRO, LR2/262, f. 24: rental, 1546 (*159*). PRO, SC6/Hen 8/3137–43, 3151–4: a/cs, 1538–46 (*54, 159*).

67

122. BURNHAM, BUCKS., ABBEY OF ST. MARY
Fd. 1266; diss. 1539. London prop. 1392, 1535.

a. PRO, E315/397, f. 18: rental, *c.* 1540 (London unspec.). PRO, LR2/262, f. 21ᵛ; SC12/37/7: rentals, 1546 (nr. Baynards Castle).

BURTON LAZARS, LEICS., LEPER HOSPITAL, see **165.**

123. BURTON UPON TRENT, STAFFS., ABBEY OF ST. MARY V. AND ST. MODWEN
Fd. 1002–4; diss. 1539, and re-fd. as college; diss. 1545. London prop. 1392.
The estate lay in *152*; for some early deeds relating to this, see **500b.**

a. BL, MS Loans 30 (Davis, no. 91): 13C cartulary, with later additions; f. 147, copy plea, 14C. Burton Library, Burton upon Trent, deposited by Marquess of Anglesey (Davis, no. 92): fragment (42 ff.) of 13C cartulary; not examined, but probably contains no London material.

b. PRO, SC6/1107/14: a/c, 1455. PRO, SC6/Hen 8/3356–60: a/cs, 1541–6. BL, Add. MS 6674, ff. 268–9: 19C copy of minister's a/c, 1542–3.

124. BURY ST. EDMUNDS, SUFF., ABBEY OF ST. EDMUND
Fd. 1020–2; diss. 1539. London prop. 1392.
See R. M. Thomson, *The Archives of the Abbey of Bury St. Edmunds* (Suffolk Rec. Soc. 21, 1980) and also D. C. Douglas, *Feudal Documents from the Abbey of Bury St. Edmunds* (1932).
The London estate lay in: *66* or *78, 100*, and *125*.

a. CUL, MS Mm. 4. 19, 'Nigrum Registrum de Vestiario' (Davis, no. 118): cartulary, comp. late 12C to 14C; London refs. on ff. 45, 113, 142, 154, 169, 228 (estate above). PRO, DL42/5 (Davis, no. 108): cartulary of cellarer's lands, comp. 13C to 14C; see f. 113ʳ⁻ᵛ (*100*). BL, MS Harl. 638, 'Registrum Werketone' (Davis, no. 106): cartulary, comp. 13C to 15C; London refs. on ff. 124–138 (*125*, Cornhill, London unspec.). BL, MS Harl. 645, 'Registrum Kempe' (Davis, no. 124): register, comp. 13C to 15C; ff. 200ᵛ–201, 240ᵛ, 249ᵛ, rentals, *temp.* Edw. I (London unspec.). BL, Add. MS 14847, 'Registrum Album' (Davis, no. 96): cartulary, late 13C; London refs. on ff. 22, 28ᵛ, 47, 65ᵛ (*66* or *78, 100*). BL, MS Harl. 743, 'Registrum J. de Lakynghethe' (Davis, no. 97): collection of evidences, comp. after 1327; London refs. on ff. 29, 37, 151–2, 260 (*66* or *78, 100*). CUL, MS Ee. 3. 60, 'Registrum W. Pynchebek' (Davis, no. 119; *The Pinchbeck Register*, ed. Lord Francis Hervey, 1925): 14C register of pleas etc., incl. (f. 191ᵛ) ref. to *78*. BL, MS Harl. 3977 (Davis, no. 126): register of custumaries, 14C; f. 50ᵛ, rental of sacrist (London unspec.). CUL, MS Ff. 2. 33 (Davis, no. 117): register of sacrist, comp. 14C to 15C; London refs. on ff. 34ʳ⁻ᵛ, 54ʳ⁻ᵛ, 81ᵛ (estate above). BL, MS Lansd. 416, 'Registrum T. Ikworthe' (Davis, no. 115): register of infirmarer, comp. *c.* 1425; f. 63, ref. to church of St. Mary and St. Bartholomew in London (? *100, 31*). BL, Add. MS 7096, 'Registrum Curteys' (Davis, no. 130): once contained London material (see f. 219ᵛ) but pages now missing.

CUL, Add. MS 4220 (Davis, no. 110): cellarer's register (part), comp. later 15C: London refs. on ff. 95ᵛ–97 (estate above). CUL, MS Ff. 2. 29, 'Registrum Rubeum Vestiarii' (Davis, no. 120): 15C register incl. (f. 5) plea, as in CUL, MS Ee. 3. 60 (*78*). BL, MS Harl. 308, 'Registrum Reeve' (Davis, no. 134): 16C lease bk.; see f. 85ᵛ (*66* or *78*).

b. Accounts: for a full list, see R. M. Thomson, *op. cit.*

125. BUTLEY, SUFF., PRIORY OF B.V.M.
Fd. 1171; diss. 1538. London prop. 1291, 1535.
In 1291 the London estate was the church of St. Stephen and St. Olave, later identified as *155*.

a. Bodl, MS Tanner 90, ff. 24–67 (Davis, no. 140; *The Register or Chronicle of Butley Priory, Suffolk, 1510–35*, ed. A. G. Dickens, 1951): 18C transcript of lost 16C register; p. 67, ref. to pension from *155*.

b. PRO, LR2/262, f. 17: rental, 1546. PRO, SC6/Hen 8/3420–6, 7439: a/cs, 1538–45.

126. CAMPSEY ASH, SUFF., PRIORY OF B.V.M.
Fd. *c.* 1195; diss. 1536.
The priory had property in London (*104, 135* or *136*) which it alienated *c.* 1230: *The Cartulary of St. Mary Clerkenwell*, ed. W. O. Hassall (Camden 3rd Ser. 71, 1949), nos. 331, 343, 344.

CANTERBURY, KENT, CATHEDRAL PRIORY (CHRIST CHURCH), subsequently DEAN AND CHAPTER

Fd. 598, 997; refd. for dean and chapter 1540. London prop. 1392, 1535. Unless otherwise stated the records are in Canterbury Cathedral Archives. There are significant collections at Lambeth (Jane Sayers, *Estate Documents at Lambeth Palace Library* (1965); M. R. James, *A Descriptive Catalogue of the Manuscripts in the Library of Lambeth Palace* (3 vols. 1930–2), for MSS. 242–3) and in BL, and other items in Bodl and CUL. See also **462b**.
    Many of the surviving records were damaged in 1670 by the fire in the cathedral Audit House. Some records were destroyed and the order of others disturbed by an air raid in 1942. The best overall guide to the records at Canterbury is provided by the three MS 'Schedules' compiled at the beginning of the 19C by C. R. Bunce. Bunce's schedules contain many valuable later additions and annotations. A substantial body of the records takes the form of a series of volumes known as 'Registers' (referred to here as Reg A, etc.). Registers A–R (formerly identified as Regs A–Q and as Regs 1–18) are an artificial series including cartularies, letter books, rentals, accounts, custumals, and other records (for subsequent registers in the series, see below, **128** and **131**). For a guide to the

contents of Regs A–V, see the MS 'Index' in 3 vols. compiled by J. B. Sheppard and summarized in HMC (7) *Eighth Report* part I (1881) Appendix, 315–55 and HMC (8) *Ninth Report* part I (1883), 72–129; see also HMC (55) *Report on Manuscripts in Various Collections* I (1901), 208–13. There are numerous more recent MS and TS lists in the Cathedral Archives, most of them numbered in the 'MS Cat' series. For other printed guides of value, see: HMC (4) *Fifth Report* part I (1876), 427–62 (deeds, cf. below, **127**); C. E. Woodruff, *A catalogue of manuscript books in the library of Christ Church, Canterbury* (1911); R. A. L Smith, 'The Central Financial System of Christ Church, Canterbury, 1186–1512', *EHR* 55 (1940), 353–69; idem, *Canterbury Cathedral Priory* (1943).

The London estate varied in extent at different times and included:

A (rents and tenements): *5, 9, 19, 32, 49, 51, 53, 56, 58, 80, 81, 83, 85, 87, 92, 100, 103, 104, 105, 111, 116, 120, 123, 124, 125, 126, 127, 152.*

B (pensions from churches up to the early 16C): *4, 5, 9, 51, 53, 73, 83, 100, 103, 111, 125, 126, 145, 159, 162* (not all of these appear in all the rentals and accounts for pensions).

C (pensions from churches in the late 16C): *5, 9, 39, 51, 53, 67, 73, 83, 100, 111, 125, 126, 131, 132, 145, 159.*

The approximate extent of the estate at different times can be judged from the rentals listed in **129**.

127. CANTERBURY CATHEDRAL: DEEDS

Most London deeds and some leases, dating from the 12C to the 17C, are to be found in the Chartae Antiquae series and may be identified from the MS calendar in Bunce's Schedule 1 (in 3 vols.; the London deeds are described in vol. 2: *5, 9, 19, 32, 53, 73, 80, 81, 83, 87, 92, 100, 103, 104, 105, 111, 120, 124, 125, 126, 159, 162*; for *125*, see Chartae Antiquae L 119, where there are also refs. to *29, 96*); see also 'Conveyances made during Commonwealth' (listed in MS Cat 73: Eastcheap only).

Leases of cathedral tenements (Bunce's Schedule 3 lists the leases that survived in early19C): 14C to 17C leases (*32, 83, 87, 104, 124*; these were transferred to the Ecclesiastical Commissioners and some of them have since been returned to Canterbury, where they are in the Church Com Dep series); 15C to 17C leases (*32, 87, 104*; the typescript list provided by the Church Commissioners covers more leases than were actually returned). See also the London leases in 'Box in Basement 100' (listed in MS Cat 70: one lease earlier than 1700 concerns *104*).

128. CANTERBURY CATHEDRAL: CARTULARIES AND REGISTERS

For rentals contained in the registers, see **129**.

a. Cartularies etc. Reg I incl. a late 13C cartulary (Davis, no. 165) with deeds concerning *53* and *120*, and other matter concerning *73, 100, 104, 124, 126, 159*. Reg E is a late 13C cartulary (Davis, no. 168) cont. London deeds as in Reg B, below. Regs A–D form a late 13C to 15C cartulary (Davis, nos. 169–72), where London deeds are to be found in Reg A (*9, 19, 53, 83, 103, 128*) and in Reg B (*5, 9, 32, 44, 49, 53, 85, 87, 100, 103,*

104, 111, 120, 124, 125, 126, 127, 159). BL, MS Cotton Galba E iv (Davis, no. 182): early 14C memoranda book incl. list of new building work in London 1286–1318 (also in Reg K). Reg J: incl. 15C copies of enrolled deeds and pleas (*36, 104, 105, 123, 145*). Reg K: incl. copies of pleas and memoranda (*103, 104*). Cambridge, Corpus Christi College, MS 298 (Davis, no. 189): incl. 16C memoranda (*32, 83, 87, 142*; estate B).

b. Registers of priory acts and letters. CUL, MS Ee. 5. 31 (Davis, no. 181): incl. presentations to London churches (as in estate B) and grants concerning property (*9, 104, 105*), 1285–1331. Bodl, MS Ashmole 794, ff. 207–22, parts of Reg H, and Reg L: fragments of the same mid 14C register, incl. presentations to London churches and letters concerning the London estate in general (specific reference to property in *104*); some letters from Reg L are printed in *Literae Cantuarienses*, ed. J. B. Sheppard (Rolls Ser. 1887–9). The intact series of priory registers, covering the period 1390–1540, comprises Regs S, T1, and T2 (Regs S and T1 incl. valuable 18C indexes: London refs. are to be found under parishes, names of properties, and the heading 'Quit-Rents') and incl. presentations to London churches, leases, bonds, etc. concerning quit-rents, appointments of officials and some *sede vacante* business (cf. **d**, below); cover much of estates A and B.

c. Registers of dean and chapter acts. Regs U, V, V1, V3–7, W–Z, and 27, covering the period 1541–1667, with gaps (especially 1607–60): many of these registers are damaged by fire and there are many disordered loose leaves from damaged registers of this period still surviving (not examined); the more complete vols. incl. 18C indexes similar to those for Regs S and T1. For the contents of Regs V1 and V3, see MS Cat 60; the contents of these vols. are similar to those of Regs S, T1, and T2, above, and in addition incl. confirmations by the dean and chapter of archiepiscopal confirmations of leases by parish churches of which the archbishop was patron.

d. Records of the priory's *sede vacante* jurisdiction. These cover all matters normally the concern of the archbishop, incl. London churches and wills, late 13C to mid 16C. The principal registers of acts are to be found in Regs F, G, N, Q, R, and V2, in CUL, MS Ee. 5. 31, and in Bodl, MS Ashmole 794 (for details, see David M. Smith, *Guide to Bishops' Registers of England and Wales* (RHS, 1981)), but some acts *sede vacante* are recorded in the priory's registers of its own business (e.g. Reg S); see also '*Sede Vacante* Scrapbooks', 3 vols. (vol. 2 contains index to vols. 1 and 2 and to detached items in Chartae Antiquae series; an index to vol. 3 is in MS Cat 64). For London institutions, see *Calendar of Institutions by the Chapter of Canterbury Sede Vacante*, ed. C. E. Woodruff and I. J. Churchill (Kent Arch. Soc. Records Branch 8, 1923); for wills, see **529**.

129. CANTERBURY CATHEDRAL: RENTALS OF THE LONDON ESTATE
BL, MS Cotton Faust. B vi, f. 101^{r-v} (also in Reg B, f. 263^{r-v}): list of London possessions 1098×1108 (see B. W. Kissan, 'An early list of London properties', *Trans LMAS* n.s. 8 (1938–40), 57–69). Literary MS

14, ff. 15ᵛ–18, and Literary MS 15, ff. 14ᵛ–17: almost identical copies of a London rental of *c.* 1200 or earlier (the Canterbury portion of the same rental has been dated *c.* 1180: W. Urry, *Canterbury under the Angevin Kings* (1967), 2, 15–17). Literary MS 16, ff. 2–6, is a copy of a rental containing virtually the same list of tenants as MSS 14 and 15, but, since the total of rent is higher, perhaps of a slightly later date; these 3 rentals are arranged by the terms at which the rent was due and contain hardly any topographical information, but the estate appears to have been identical with that covered by the rental in Reg K, below. Reg K, ff. 66ᵛ–9: rental of *c.* 1220 arranged topographically and referring to the tenants in the rentals of *c.* 1200 (*5, 9, 49, 51, 53, 56, 58, 73, 80, 81, 83, 85, 87, 100, 103, 104, 105, 111, 116, 120, 125, 126, 127, 145, 152, 159, 162*). Reg J, pp. 330–9: 14C copy of composite mid 13C and later rental which refers to tenants in rentals of *c.* 1200 (*9, 49, 56, 58, 80, 81, 83, 85, 87, 92, 100, 103, 104, 105, 116, 120, 125, 126, 127, 152*; also ref. to *37*). Extracts from a rental similar to the mid 13C exemplar on which the rental in Reg J is based were copied into a 13C London municipal collection (BL, Add. MS 14252, ff. 88ᵛ–9: printed in *EHR* 17 (1902), 483–4). The rentals in Regs K and J are conflated in Reg B, ff. 248–61. BL, MS Cotton Galba E iv (Davis, no. 182), f. 34: early 14C list of pensions (estate B). Reg B, ff. 264–5: extracts from assessment by wards of 3*s.* in the pound rent, 1321–2, apparently incl. full details of all the assessments on rents for tenements in which the priory had an interest (no other record of this assessment appears to survive, but for a similar assessment of 1324–5,see WAM 12339: **249**). Reg B. ff. 261ᵛ–3: late 14C rental of quit-rents (*9, 49, 53, 81, 83, 85, 100, 104, 105, 116, 120, 125, 127*). Reg H, f. 152ᵛ: rental of 1420 (estate B, *104*, and totals for other properties). Church Com Dep 70445 incl. rentals of 1539 (*32, 87*), 1582 (estate C; *9, 19, 81, 83, 92, 100, 104, 120, 126*), 1614 (estate as for 1582 rental, plus *67, 85, 123*), and a damaged mid 16C rental. Church Com Dep 70446 incl. rentals of 1541 (*9, 19, 32, 80, 83, 85, 87, 92, 100, 104, 105, 120, 123, 124, 125, 127*), rentals of 1560 and 1561 (estate as for 1541 rental), and a damaged mid 16C rental.

130. CANTERBURY CATHEDRAL: ACCOUNTS
For the a/cs at Canterbury, see the file of MS and TS lists in the Cathedral Library. The a/cs are best discussed in two groups: those of the Old Foundation (to 1540) and those of the New Foundation (from 1540).

a. Old Foundation.
Accounts of rent collectors in London. Box of 45 uncatalogued 'Bedels' Rolls, London' for 1274–1513; Chartae Antiquae, L 108ᵃ, a/c for 1495–6; Lambeth, ED 608, a/c for 1510–11: these vary widely in coverage and amount of detail and many provide only totals for quit-rents; tenements let at farm were in *104* up to *c.* 1400 and thereafter in *32, 83, 87, 104, 124*. *Treasurers' accounts.* Miscellaneous Accounts 1 and 2, for 1207–1336 and 1371–84, and part of BL, MS Harl. 1006, for 14C: a/cs of receipt and expenditure in book form incl. total receipts from London and some expenditure there. Rolls 8–22 in the uncatalogued box 'Treasurers' Accounts', for 1407–84 and undated; Lambeth, ED 80–90, ED 2013, and

MS 951/1, nos. 30–1, for 1406–1519 and undated; and 15C fragments in Miscellaneous Accounts and box of 'Uncatalogued Accounts': a/cs of receipt and expenditure in roll form incl. totals of quit-rents and details of pensions and farms with expenditure on building as in rent collectors' a/cs, above. The box of 'Uncatalogued Accounts' also incl. similar a/cs in book form, 1511–12, 1520–1. Miscellaneous Accounts 21–5, possibly the damaged ibid. 26, but not subsequent vols. in the same series, incl. annual lists of rents (totals for quit-rents, details of pensions and farms) subordinate to the main series of treasurers' a/cs, 1374–1433 and possibly later. Lambeth, MSS 242–3, for 1257–1391, expenditure a/cs in book form incl. building in London (*104*).

Sacrists' accounts (pensions from *53, 100*). BL, Add. MS 6160 (Davis, no. 184), ff. 90–1: copy of a/c, 1299. 70 annual rolls in the 'Accounts of Priory' series, 1361–1501 (see C. E. Woodruff, 'The Sacrist's rolls of Christ Church, Canterbury', *Archaeologia Cantiana* 48 (1936), 38–80). Lambeth, ED 75–9, 1442, 1458, 2059–61: a/cs and rentals, 1430–1534. Miscellaneous Accounts 5, 9–16, 30: incl. a/cs in book form 1462–1534.

Assisae Scaccarii. 21 annual rolls in 'Accounts of Priory' series (1224–1340 and 13C undated) and Reg H, ff. 172–217 (copies of late 13C a/cs): summaries of a/cs of monastic officials incl. treasurer and sacrist, and occasionally the London rent collector, sometimes preserving evidence which does not survive elsewhere.

Minor accounts. Miscellaneous Accounts 70; Scrapbooks A, p. 69 and B, pp. 63, 131, 146, 220: a/cs concerning quit-rents and repairs, 15C and early 16C.

b. New Foundation.
The treasurers' a/cs contain no information on the London estate and the receivers' a/cs contain only the total received from the collector.
Accounts of London rent collectors. Miscellaneous Accounts 17: details of rents and farms, 1541–4. Ibid. 18: tabular a/c, 1551–5. Ibid. 19: registers of a/cs, 1599–1624, 1630–3, incl. totals and allowances.

131. CANTERBURY CATHEDRAL: ADMINISTRATION
Chapter Act Books, 4 vols. 1561–1628, each with a later index: records of chapter meetings incl. decisions concerning grants of leases and livings, confirmation of leases granted by incumbents of chapter livings, and management of estate. For the extent of the estate in this period, see **129**.

132. CANTERBURY CATHEDRAL: MISCELLANEOUS
Collections of letters concerning the affairs of the priory and the Dean and Chapter (the London references concern presentation to livings): 'Eastry Correspondence', mostly late 13C and early 14C, calendar and index in Schedule 1, pp. 186–218; 'Christchurch Letters', 3 vols. (for some letters from vol. 1, see *Christ Church Letters*, ed. J. B. Sheppard (Camden Soc. n.s. 19, 1877); the letters in vol. 2 are calendared in MS Cat 67; vol. 3 contains no London material); 'Canterbury Letters', 2 vols., 15C to 18C. 'Inventories' no. 23 is a London inventory of 1313. 'Surveys

of Estates', vol. 23, f. 92, is a parliamentary survey of London quit-rents, 1654 (*9, 19, 100, 120*).

133. CANTERBURY, ARCHBISHOP
In the late 9C the archbishop probably acquired land which later lay in *114, 116, 127* and *136* (T. Dyson, 'Two Saxon land grants for Queenhithe' in *Collectanea Londiniensia . . .*, ed. J. Bird, H. Chapman and J. Clark (LMAS special paper 2, 1978), 200–15), and his soke on what seems to be part of the same site is mentioned *c*. 1200 and in the 13C (*Cal. Ancient Deeds*, A1803; *London Eyre 1244*, no. 262). Properties in the city formed part of the archbishop's manor of Mortlake in or before 1086 (DB i, f. 30ᵛ) and his soke in London is mentioned *c*. 1120 (*EHR* 14 (1899), p. 428). At the end of the 12C, the archbishop acquired land in London beside the Thames, probably in *116* (see **120**) or possibly in *53*, where his soke is recorded shortly afterwards (*The Cartulary of Holy Trinity Aldgate*, ed. G. A. J. Hodgett (LRS 7, 1971), no. 223); see also **155**. In the early 13C he also had a substantial holding in *120*. By 1291 his estate appears to have been reduced to holdings in *5* and *125*. During the 13C–14C he acquired the advowsons of a number of churches (incl. *53*), which had previously belonged to Canterbury Cathedral Priory (cf. **127–32**). By the 16C he appears to have possessed no more in the city than these churches, for which see the archiepiscopal registers and the records of *sede vacante* jurisdiction (**128d**). See also **462b**.

a. Cartularies. Lambeth Palace, MS 1212 (Davis, no. 159): 13C–14C cartulary incl. copies of ? 9C grant (see above) and 12C–13C deeds concerning London (*120*, and probably *116*). Bodl, MS Tanner 223 (Davis, no. 160): 16C register incl. copies of some material from Lambeth, MS 1212, and 17C memoranda on the archbishop's London churches (taken from 'the Great Register that is now unbound').

134. CANTERBURY, KENT, ABBEY OF ST. AUGUSTINE
Fd. 598–605; diss. 1538. London prop. 1291, 1392, 1535.
In 1291 the estate lay in: *53, 58, 105, 132*.

a. BL, MS Cotton Faust. A i, 'Black Book' (Davis, no. 194; *The Register of St. Augustine's Abbey, Canterbury*, ed. G. J. Turner and H. E. Salter, 1915, 1924): register, late 13C, incl. rentals (*53, 85, 90, 132*) and copy deeds (*53, 132*). BL, MS Cotton Claud. D x, ff. 9–319, 'Red Book' (Davis, no. 193): cartulary, 13C to 14C; London refs. on ff. 238–243ᵛ, 318 (*51, 53, 85, 132*; also rubrics ref. to *14, 149*). BL, MS Cotton Julius D ii (Davis, no. 192): register, 13C to 14C; ff. 107, 128, deeds (*53, 132*); f. 143, rental, 13C (London unspec.). Canterbury, Lit MS E 23 (Davis, no. 206): reg. of leases, 1521–2 (*51*).

b. BL, MS Arundel 310 (Davis, no. 202): register, *c*. 1330, incl. (f. 146) rental (London, total only). Lambeth, ED 299: valor, 1523–4 (London unspec.). PRO, LR2/262, f. 21; SC12/37/7: rentals, 1546 (*132*).

c. BL, Harl. Roll 2.19: a/c, 1406–8 (London unspec.). Lambeth, ED

2058, 298: treasurers' a/cs, 1446–7, 1459–60 (London totals). PRO, SC6/ Hen 8/1755–61: a/cs, 1537–45 (*51, 53, 118, 132*).

135. CANTERBURY, KENT, PRIORY OF ST. GREGORY
Fd. by 1086; diss. 1536. London prop. 1392 (*120*).

136. CHADDESDEN, DERBYS., COLLEGE OR CHANTRY
Fd. *temp.* Edward III (see Knowles and Hadcock, *Medieval Religious Houses*, 457). London prop. 1392 (*85*, Farringdon ward within).

137. CHERTSEY, SURREY, ABBEY OF ST. PETER
Fd. 666; diss. 1537, when monks moved briefly to Bisham Priory, Berks. (**118**). London prop. 1291, 1392, 1535.
In 1291 the estate lay in: *10, 38, 44, 62, 98, 136, 157*.

a. Calendars/extracts from several of the cartularies are printed in *Chertsey Abbey Cartularies*, ed. M. S. Giuseppi, C. A. F. Meekings, P. M. Barnes (Surrey Rec. Soc. 12 (2 vols. in 5 parts), 1915, 1928, 1933, 1958, 1963). BL, MS Cotton Vit. A xiii (Davis, no. 222; see *Mon. Angl.* i, 425–34): cartulary, comp. 13C; London material (unspec.), incl. charters from 10C, on ff. 30ᵛ–31, 50ᵛ, 55, 58ᵛ, 78. BL, MS Lansd. 435 (Davis, no. 223; extracts in *Chertsey Abbey Cartularies*, vol. 2, pt. 1): register, comp. mid 14C; London refs. on ff. 14, 43ᵛ, 63ᵛ–64, 70–72, 77, 109–10 (*10, 150*); f. 108, note of abbot's revenues (*10, 38, 44, 62, 98, 136, 157*). Cartulary *penes* Lord Clifford of Chudleigh (Davis, no. 224; extracts in *Chertsey Abbey Cartularies*, vol. 2, pt. 2): similar material to preceding. PRO, E164/25 (Davis, no. 225; *Chertsey Abbey Cartularies*, vol. 1, pts. 1–3): 15C cartulary (*10, 38, 44, 62, 89, 92, 136*).

b. BL, Harl. Chs. 44. B. 49–56, 59–66, and 44. C. 1: 15C–16C acquittances for rent received (*136* or *139*).

138. CHESHUNT, HERTS., PRIORY OF ST. MARY
Fd. bef. 1183; diss. 1536. London prop. 1392 (*30, 94, 98, 104*, wards of Billingsgate, Cheap, Farringdon within, Vintry, Walbrook).

139. CHICHESTER, SUSSEX, DEAN AND CHAPTER
See fd. 1075 (from Selsey). London prop. 1291 (canons), 1392 (dean). In 1291 and later the estate lay in *152*. Some of the records listed below also concern properties of the bishop (see **140**). See also **462b**. The records are at the West Sussex Record Office: see F. W. Steer and I. M. Kirby, *Diocese of Chichester: a catalogue of the records of the Dean and Chapter, Vicars Choral, St. Mary's Hospital, Colleges and Schools* (1967).

a. For 13C cartulary concerning the chapter estate, see **140a**. Cap. I/27/1–4: registers of leases (incl. confirmations of bishopric leases), 1555–1677; vols. 2–4 contain contemporary indexes, and there is an index to vol. 1 in Cap. I/51/8.

b. Rentals. Cap. I/12/2, f. 392ᵛ: 17C copy of pre-Reformation rental. Cap. I/23/1, ff. 119, 172. Cap. I/23/4, and Cap. I/26/3–11 incl. 16C and 17C rentals, usually in tabular form.

c. Act Books. Cap. I/3/0, 1, 1a, and 2 incl. leases and confirmations of bishopric leases 1472–1710; these are calendared in *The Acts of the Dean and Chapter of the Cathedral Church of Chichester, 1472–1544* and *1545– 1642*, ed. W. D. Peckham (Sussex Rec. Soc. 52, 1951–2, and 58, 1959), and in a TS calendar for 1660–1710 in Cap. I/51/11.

d. Parliamentary surveys etc. Cap. I/30/1, ff. 8–50: very detailed survey, 1649. Cap. I/30/4, ff. 7–9: contract for sale, 1654.

140. CHICHESTER, SUSSEX, BISHOP
London prop. 1291, 1392.
In 1291 and later the estate lay in *20, 54.* See also **462b**.
The records are at the West Sussex Record Office: see F. W. Steer and I. M. Kirby, *Diocese of Chichester: a catalogue of the records of the bishop, archdeacons and former exempt jurisdictions* (1966).

a. Cartularies etc: for 13C deeds concerning the London estates of the bishop and the dean and chapter (cf. **139**) in the 13C cartulary 'Liber Y' (Ep. V/1/6) and in the 14C register 'Liber E' (Ep. VI/1/4), see *The Chartulary of the High Church of Chichester*, ed. W. D. Peckham (Sussex Rec. Soc. 46, 1942–3). Ep. VI/55/1: register of leases 1661–1733, with contemp. index. For earlier episcopal leases, see **139a, c**; for a single 16C lease, see Cap. I/16/1, ff. 139ᵛ–40.

b. For 14C–17C rentals and a/cs mentioning the London estate, see Ep. VI/1/3, ff. 9ᵛ, 165ᵛ and Ep. VI/4/1, 4.

c. Ep. VI/54/1: 17C copies of papers concerning land leased to guild in church of St. Dunstan West, 1548–57; see **310f**.

141. CHICKSANDS, BEDS., PRIORY OF ST. MARY
Fd. *c.* 1150; diss. 1538. London prop. 1291, 1392, 1535.
In 1291 the estate lay in: *105, 132, 155.*

a. PRO, LR2/262, f. 23ᵛ; SC12/37/7: rentals, 1546 (*105, 132*). PRO, SC6/ Hen 8/11–13: a/cs, 1539–40, 1541–2, 1545–6 (*105, 132*).

142. CIRENCESTER, GLOS., ABBEY OF ST. MARY
Re-fd. 1117–31; diss. 1539. London prop. 1291, 1392, 1535.
In 1291 the estate lay in: *46, 92.*

a. 'Registrum A', 'Registrum B', *penes* Lady Vestey (Davis, nos. 255–6; *The Cartulary of Cirencester Abbey*, 2 vols., ed. C. D. Ross, 1964 (Reg. A and part Reg. B), and *The Cartulary of Cirencester Abbey*, ed. M. Devine, 1977 (rest of Reg. B)): 2 cartularies, 13C and 14C, partly duplicate, of deeds, pleas, etc. (*46, 92*).

b. PRO, SC6/Hen 8/1240–6: a/cs 1539–46 (*46*).

143. CLEEVE, SOM., ABBEY OF B.V.M.
Fd. 1186×1191; diss. 1537.

a. PRO, SC6/Hen 8/3127: a/c, 1536–7 (London unspec.).

144. Coggeshall, Essex, abbey of B.V.M.
Fd. 1140; diss. 1538. London prop. 1392, 1535.

a. BL, Add. MS 19051, f. 9: 18C list of possessions of former Essex houses, incl. Coggeshall (*10*).

b. PRO, E315/397, f. 111: survey, *c.* 1540 (Tower Hill).

145. Colchester, Essex, abbey of St. John the Baptist
Fd. 1096; diss. 1539. London prop. 1291, 1535.
In 1291 the estate lay in *53*.

a. Colchester, Borough Muniments (Davis, no. 267; *Cartularium Monasterii . . . de Colecestria*, ed. S. A. Moore, Roxburghe Club, 1897): cartulary, later 13C (*53, 80, 118, 156*, Ebbgate, *Stanenetha* (prob. *53*)).

b. BL, Add. MS 19051, f. 6: 18C note of possessions, *c.* 1539 (*53*).

c. PRO, SC6/1107/15–17: a/cs, 1421–3, 1432–3 (inn in London). PRO, SC6/Hen 8/976–8: a/cs, 1538–44 (*53, 118*). PRO, E315/279, f. 45: a/c, 1543–4 (*53*).

146. Coventry and Lichfield, bishop
In the late 12C the bishop of Coventry acquired land in London near Newgate (probably *152*). No London land is noted for 1291, and this property may have been lost before then. The property (*mansum de Ly Stronde*) recorded for the bishop of Coventry and Lichfield in 1535 is evidently different, and lay outside the city. The archives at Lichfield have not been visited, but may contain more than the material noted below. See J. C. Cox, 'Catalogue of the Muniments and MS. Books of the Dean and Chapter of Lichfield', *Collections for a History of Staffordshire* (William Salt Archaeological Society 6 pt. 2, 1886); HMC (37) *Fourteenth Report* Appendix VIII, pp. 205–236.

a. Lichfield, Dean and Chapter, 'Magnum Registrum Album' (Davis, no. 563; *Magnum Registrum Album*, ed. H. E. Savage, in *Coll. Hist. Staffs*, William Salt Arch. Soc., 1924): 14C cartulary, incl. 12C deeds (probably *152*).

147. Croxden, Staffs., abbey of B.V.M.
Fd. 1176–8; diss. 1538. London prop. 1535 (unspec.).

a. PRO, LR2/183, f. 166ᵛ: rental, temp. Henry VIII (London unspec.).

148. Croxton, Leics., abbey of St. John the Evangelist
Fd. bef. 1160 or 1162; diss. 1538. London prop. 1392.

a. PRO, LR2/262, f. 22ᵛ: rental, 1546 (*150*).

149. Dartford, Kent, priory of St. Mary and St. Margaret
Fd. 1346; diss. 1539. London prop. 1392, 1535.

a. PRO, SC6/Hen 8/1757–60: a/cs, 1540–45 (*2, 12, 78, 92, 93, 104, 148*).

150. Dunmow, Little, Essex, priory of St. Mary V.
Fd. 1106; diss. 1536. London prop. 1291, 1392.
In 1291 the estate lay in: *18, 45, 120, 159*.

a. BL, MS Harl. 662 (Davis, no. 318): cartulary, 13C to 14C, incl. copy
deeds, rentals; London refs. on ff. 3ᵛ, 74–79ᵛ, 125ᵛ (*18, 45, 85, 98, 120,
137, 159*).

151. Durham, cathedral priory
Fd. 1083; diss. 1539. The records are extensive but yielded no further
London refs. than those noted below, and it is probable that the priory
had no city property after the mid 13C. By 1267 it held a manor in the
Strand (? later Durham House): Misc. Ch. 6856, 5477, 5566. The MSS are
dean and chapter muniments, in the Department of Palaeography and
Diplomatic, The Prior's Kitchen, The College, Durham.

a. Deeds. 1. 4 Ebor. 27: deed, 1109×38 (London unspec.; transcribed in
Proc. Soc. Ant. 2nd ser. 32 (1919–20), 145); possibly connected with the
bishop of Durham's Domesday holding of the manor of Waltham, Essex,
with a gate (Aldgate) and 12 houses in London (DB ii, f. 15ᵛ). 3. 13 Pont.
5, 1. 4 Ebor. 28: deed and copy deed, *c.* 1227 (*56*, also copy of 1. 4 Ebor.
27). 1. 7 Pont. 11: lease, 1403 (*120*); no apparent connection with priory.

b. Cartuarium III (Davis, no. 329): cartulary, *c.* 1400, concerning lands
outside Durham; f. 126ʳ⁻ᵛ, copies of deeds noted above (*56*, unspec.), but
not 1. 7 Pont 11.

c. 'Repertorium Magnum' (Davis, no. 342); mid 15C inventory of
muniments, incl. refs. to deeds and cartulary entries above.

152. Ely, Cambs., cathedral priory of St. Etheldreda, subsequently
dean and chapter
Fd. 673, 970, as abbey; cathedral priory from 1108; Spinney Priory united
with Ely 1449; diss. 1539; re-fd. as cathedral chapter 1541. London prop.
(Ely) 1291, 1392.
Unless otherwise stated, the records (EDC, EDR) are in CUL. A
catalogue is being compiled by Mrs. D. M. Owen (draft available for
consultation in CUL), but listing is not yet complete and some records are
not yet available. See also D. M. Owen, 'The Muniments of Ely
Cathedral Priory', *Church and Government in the Middle Ages*, ed. C. N.
L. Brooke, D. E. Luscombe, G. H. Martin, and D. M. Owen (1976); 'Ely
Chapter Ordinances and Visitation Records, 1241–1515', ed. S. J. A.
Evans, *Camden Miscellany* 17 (Camden Soc. 3rd Ser. 64, 1940); E.
Miller, *The abbey and bishopric of Ely* (1951). See also **462b**.
The priory's estate lay in: *9, 20, 27, 116, 129*. This became the endowment
of the cathedral chapter from 1541 (*27* became part of *47* in 1547). The
priory also held property in *12* for a short time. Property in *104*, formerly
of Spinney, was held until 1539.

a. EDC 1B, Boxes 9–10: deeds, 13C to 15C (*9, 12, 20, 27, 54, 104, 116,
152, 159*). EDC 6/3: 2 boxes of papers relating to Holborn estate (*20*), not
listed or available in 1983.

b. EDR G/3/28, 'Liber M' (Davis, no. 369): cartulary, comp. *c.* 1290–1300; ff. 19, 31, 119 (London unspec.). BL, Add. MS 41612 (Davis, no. 375): register of deeds, pleas, etc. 13C to 14C; ff. 22, 66ᵛ–67ᵛ, 82ᵛ, 98 (*12, 20*). BL, Add. MS 9822, 'Liber A' (Davis, no. 378): register of deeds, extracts etc., 14C to 15C; f. 75ᵛ (*20*). BL, MS Egerton 3047 (Davis, no. 371): part of cartulary, 15C; ff. 6, 114ʳ⁻ᵛ, 115, 249ᵛ–253 (*9, 12, 20, 27, 116, 119*, unspec.). Bodl, MS Ashmole 801, ff. 74–143 (Davis, no. 372): second part of same cartulary as preceding; ff. 77–91ᵛ (*9, 12, 20, 27, 54, 116, 129, 152, 159*).

c. EDC 2/4/1, 2, 'Leiger Books': lease bks., 1537–1639, indexed. EDC 2/6/1, 'Patent Book': capitular confirmations of episcopal leases, 1540–1640.

d. Rentals and surveys. PRO, E315/397, f. 29: survey, *c.* 1540 (*9, 20, 27, 116, 129*). EDC 1/C/3: valor, 1540–1 (as preceding). PRO, LR2/262, f. 17ᵛ: valor, 1546, of possessions of late priory still held by the Crown (*104*). EDC 1/C/6: valor, *temp.* Elizabeth (*9, 20, 47, 116, 129*). EDC 6/2/20, 21: parliamentary surveys, 1649–50 (*9, 47*). EDC 6/2/50: abstract, *c.* 1660, from survey and rental, *c.* 1649–50 (*9, 20, 47, 116, 129*). EDC 6/2/51: rental or memorandum of leases, 1660 (as preceding). EDC 1/C/5: rental, early 18C, with notes and extracts from medieval records.

e. Accounts. EDC 5: obedientiaries' rolls (listed in catalogue); not examined (many fragile or decayed, but some transcripts available) but London rent receipts probably in 5/13/1–18, treasurers' a/cs, 14C to 16C. PRO, SC6/1257/4–9: treasurers' a/cs, 1428–9, 1434–40, 1466–7 (*116, 129*, probably *27*). PRO, SC6/Hen 8/258–63, 7288–93, 7295: a/cs, 1540–46, of lands granted to dean and chapter (*9, 20, 27, 116, 129*). PRO, SC6/Phil & Mary/489: a/c, 1554–5, of lands of late priory (*104*). EDC 3/3/1–58: views of receivers' a/cs, 1542–1667, of rents and expenditure (*9, 20, 27, 116, 129*). EDC 3/4/1–20, EDC 3/3/69: receivers' rough a/cs, 1590–1624, 1633–42 (as preceding). EDC 3/14: 2 boxes of 'receivers' rentals', 1628–67 and later, noting arrears, rents by term; tenants not always named.

f. EDC 2/1/1, 2, 'Order books', 1550–1643: incl. memoranda of grants of leases.

153. ELY, BISHOP
See fd. 1108. London prop. 1392.
The London estate lay in: *20* (Ely Place, outside the Liberty), *54*.
See E. Miller, *The abbey and bishopric of Ely* (1951); HMC (27) *Twelfth Report, Appendix 9*, pp. 375–88; D. M. Owen, *Handlist of the Records of the Bishop and Archdeacon of Ely* (1971). Unless otherwise stated, the records (EDR, EDC, CC) are in CUL. See also **462b**.

a. BL, MS Cotton Tib. ii (Davis, no. 358): 13C register incl. survey and miscellanea; ff. 257ᵛ–258, copy agreement 1272 (*54*). BL, MS Cotton Claud. C xi (Davis, no. 359): register, incl. survey and miscellanea; ff. 348ᵛ, 351ᵛ, 352ᵛ–353, inquisitions, deeds, pleas, 14C (*20, ?54*). BL, Add. MS 41612 (Davis, no. 375): cartulary, comp. *c.* 1273–1366, incl. inquisitions, pleas; ff. 22, 66ᵛ–67ᵛ, 98 (*20*); f. 82ᵛ (*12*). BL, Add. MS 9822, 'Liber

A' (Davis, no. 378): cartulary, 14C to 15C, incl., f. 75^v, list of charters handed over to new bishop, 1359 (*20, 54*). EDR G/3/27, 'Liber R' (Davis, no. 362): register incl. survey, 15C miscellanea; ff. 215–218, 225^v, deeds, pleas, 13C to 14C (*20, 54*); f. 233^v, plea concerning hosting in New Temple, 1257–8. EDR G/2/3, 'Liber B' (Davis, no. 377; W. A. Pantin, 'English Monastic Letter-books', *Historical Essays presented to James Tait*, ed. J. G. Edwards, V. H. Galbraith, and E. F. Jacob, 1933): register, 15C to 16C, incl. leases, etc. (*20, 54*).

b. CC 95550–1, 95553–4: lease bks., incl. grants by bishops, 1516–62; not all indexed, but most grants clearly headed. EDC 2/6/1, 'Patent Book': capitular confirmations of episcopal leases, 1540–1640; not indexed.

c. PRO, SC11/821: valor of temporalities, 1453–4 (*20*). EDC 1/C/4: valor, 1538–9 (*20, 54*). PRO, SC6/1132/10–13: a/cs, 1298–1300, 1302, 1311, 1316, some summary (unspec., but arrears and charges specified). EDR D/6/2: a/cs, 1372–3, 1378–9, 1396–7, 1409–18, 1434–6. PRO, SC6/1137/10: a/cs, 1423–4, 1430–53, 1469–83, several years missing. PRO, SC6/Hen 7/2108: a/cs, 1484–1528. EDR D/5/9: rough bk. of receipts, 1541–2 (*20*). BL, Add. Roll 34274: (?bishop's) bailiff's a/c, 1549 (*20*). PRO, SC6/Eliz/280–7: a/cs, 1581–3, 1586–7, 1590–9, some years missing; London totals only.

d. Bodl, MS Rawl. D 809: f. 62, survey of dilapidations, Ely House (*20*), 1684–5; ff. 90–1, abs. title to Ely House, 1594–1655.

154. EVESHAM, WORCS., ABBEY OF ST. MARY AND ST. EGWIN
Fd. *c.* 995; diss. 1539–40. London prop. 1291, 1392, 1535.
In 1291 the abbey held the church of *124*. At a later date it also held land in *53, 78*.

a. PRO, E303/20/100, 109, 114, 116; leases, 15C to 16C (*53, 78*). PRO, E303/21/198: lease, 16C (*124*).

b. BL, MS Cotton Vesp. B xxiv (Davis, no. 381): misc. register, 12C to 13C; ff. 12^v, 56, memoranda of gifts (*124*). BL, MS Harl. 3763 (Davis, no. 382): register, 13C to 14C, partly duplicating preceding; London refs. on ff. 57^v, 60, 92^v, 98, 106, 134 (*53, 78, 124*; also ref. to Cheap). BL, MS Cotton Titus C ix, ff. 1–38 (Davis, no. 385): register, 15C; London refs. on ff. 4^v, 37 (*53, 66, 124*).

c. PRO, LR2/262, f. 22^v: rental, 1546 (*78, 124*). PRO, LR2/184, f. 370: rental, n.d. (London unspec.). PRO, SC6/Hen 8/4047–56: a/cs, 1540–6 (*124*, London unspec.).

155. EYNSHAM, OXON., ABBEY OF ST. MARY V.
Fd. 1005: diss. 1539.

a. Oxford, Christ Church, Chapter Library (Davis, no. 399; *Cartulary of Eynsham Abbey*, ed. H. E. Salter, Oxf. Hist. Soc. 49 and 51, 1906–8): general cartulary, late 12C; nos. 140–1 (in printed text) refer to grant of house in soke of archbishop of Canterbury, *c.* 1193.

156. FAVERSHAM, KENT, ABBEY OF ST. SAVIOUR
Fd. 1148; diss. 1538. London prop. 1291, 1392.
Land in London was granted at the foundation: *Mon. Angl.* iv, 573–4. In the mid 13C the abbey held property near the Fleet: *London Eyre 1244*, no. 353; C. J. A. Armstrong 'Thirteenth-century notes on the rights of the abbey of Faversham in London, from a MS. of Grenoble', *EHR* 54 (1939), 677–85. In 1291 the estate lay in: *93, 98, 125, 134.*

a. Cdr. L. M. M. Saunders Watson, Rockingham Castle: cartulary or register, 15C to 16C (Davis, no. 401). Not examined; possibly contains material relating to London estate. A transcript, probably now lost, was made in 1920 for Kent Archaeological Society by Miss Joan Wake.

157. FOTHERINGHAY, NORTHANTS., COLLEGE OF B.V.M.
Fd. 1411; diss. 1548. London prop. 1535.

a. PRO, E315/398; SC12/4/34: valors, *c.* 1540 (*20*). PRO, SC12/37/13: survey, *c.* 1548 (*20*).

GARENDON ABBEY, see **82.**

158. GLASTONBURY, SOM., ABBEY OF ST. MARY V.
Fd. 6C, 940; diss. 1539. London prop. 1291, 1535.
In 1291 the estate lay in *39.*

a. Marquess of Bath, Longleat Muniments MS 39 (Davis, no. 434; *The Great Chartulary of Glastonbury*, ed. Dom A. Watkin, Soms. Rec. Soc. 59, 63, 64, 1944–50): cartulary, *c.* 1338–40; pp. 128–9, bull, 1168, ref. to house in London. BL, MS Arundel 2 (Davis, no. 445): register, 1352–66; London refs. on ff. 14ᵛ, 29–31 (*39*).

b. BL, Add. MS 17450 (Davis, no. 448; *Rentalia et Custumaria Glastoniae,* ed. C. J. Elton, Soms. Rec. Soc. 5, 1891): 13C rentals, etc.; f. 5, London rent (prob. *39*). PRO, LR2/262, f. 23ᵛ: rental, 1546 (unspec.). PRO, SC6/Hen 8/3148–9, 7406: rent a/cs, 1538–45 (*39, 152,* Warwick Lane).

159. GLOUCESTER, ABBEY OF ST. PETER, subsequently DEAN AND CHAPTER
Fd. *c.* 1022; diss. 1540; re-fd. as cathedral chapter 1541. London prop. 1291, 1535. See I. M. Kirby, *Diocese of Gloucester: a catalogue of the records of the Dean and Chapter, including the former St. Peter's Abbey (in Glos. R.O. and Cathedral Library)* (1967). The cathedral library was not visited, and the references below are taken from guides and other sources. There may be further material there not noted here. See also **462b.**
In 1291 the estate was the church of *96.*

a. Cathedral Library, D 1609/x. 7: deed, 1370 (*20*).

b. PRO, C150/1 (Davis, no. 454; *Historia et Cartularium . . . Monasterii Gloucestriae,* ed. W. H. Hart, Rolls Ser. 1863–7): cartulary, 13C to 16C, incl. copy deeds, pleas (*20, 96*). See also Cathedral Library, dean and chapter registers A–E (Davis, nos. 455–6, 458–9): not examined, but *Regesta* ii, Addenda no. 379a and p. 410, notes charter, 1096, probably from Register A (*96*).

c. PRO, SC6/Hen 8/1248–59: a/cs, 1540–6 (*20*). Glos. RO, D 936/A/1/1–2: dean and chapter's treasurer's a/cs, 1609–34, 1634–64 (pension from *96*, lost by 1664).

160. Godstow, Oxon., abbey of St. Mary and St. John the Baptist
Fd. 1133; diss. 1539. London prop. 1291, 1392.
In 1291 the estate lay in *45*.

a. PRO, E164/20 (Davis, no. 462): cartulary, comp. *c.* 1404, of deeds etc., 12C–15C, in Latin. Bodl, MS Rawl. B 408 (Davis, no. 463; *The English Register of Godstow Nunnery*, ed. A. Clark, EETS orig. series 129, 130, 142, 1906–11): later 15C English version of preceding (Bishopsgate, Cornhill, Eastcheap, Fleet Street, Westcheap, nr. West gate of St. Paul's).

b. PRO, SC6/1108/3: a/c, 1446 (*46*). PRO, SC6/Hen 8/2927: a/c, 1539–40 (*46*).

161. Hastings, Sussex, priory of Holy Trinity
Fd. 1189–99; moved to Warbleton, Sussex, 1413. London prop. 1291 (*38*).

162. Hatfield Peverel, Essex, priory of St. Mary V.
Fd. after 1087; diss. 1536. London prop. 1291 (*85, 129*).

163. Higham Ferrers, Northants., college of B.V.M., St. Thomas the Martyr, and St. Edward the Confessor
Fd. 1422; diss. 1542. London prop. 1535 (Friday Street, Soper Lane).

164. Hitchin, Herts., priory of St. Saviour
Fd. 1361–2; diss. 1538. London prop. 1392 (?*80, 98*).

165. Holborn, Middx., hospital of St. Giles
Fd. bef. 1118; transferred to jurisdiction of Burton Lazars (Leics.) 1299; diss. 1539. London prop. 1291, 1392; 1535 (under heading of Burton Lazars).
In 1291 the estate lay in *93*.

a. BL, MS Harl. 4015 (Davis, no. 491): cartulary, comp. 1402, of deeds, 12C to 15C; pars. listed on ff. 2ᵛ–3 (*4, 5, 10, 15, 20, 21, 24, 26, 27, 29, 30, 32, 37, 38, 39, 42, 45, 46, 48, 51, 53, 54, 62, 63, 71, 74, 75, 81, 83, 85, 87, 88, 89, 92, 93, 94, 95, 99, 100, 104, 116, 127, 128, 131, 132, 135, 136, 137, 141, 144, 150, 151, 152, 156, 158, 159*, St. Mary Coneyhope); also refs. to *101* (f. 50ᵛ), *120* (f. 62).

166. Hornchurch, Essex, priory of St. Nicholas and St. Bernard
Fd. 1159, dep. on St. Bernard, Montjoux; suppressed 1391, and granted

to New College, Oxford (**401**). The principal London property ('Mount Joys Inn') lay in *77* and *78*; in the 13C the priory seems also to have had an interest in *157*.

a. Deeds and leases, 13C and 14C, preserved in the archives of New College, inaccurately calendared in H. F. Westlake, *Hornchurch Priory: a kalendar of documents in the possession of the warden and fellows of New College, Oxford* (1923); these incl. 13C deeds concerning property in *53* which seems not to have come into the possession of the priory. This collection is covered by the numbers under the heading 'Early Deeds: Essex, Hornchurch' (no ref. to London) in F. W. Steer, *The Archives of New College, Oxford* (1974), 517; the best form of reference is still the 18C numbers cited by Westlake. In addition, 14C deeds concerning *78* (New College Archives, 11905–11910) are listed in Steer, op. cit., 520; there are copies in New College Archives 9791 ('Registrum Evidenciarum', vol. 5), pp. 333–7.

167. HORSHAM ST. FAITH, NORF., PRIORY OF ST. MARY V.
Fd. *c.* 1105; diss. 1536. London prop. 1291, 1535.
In 1291 the estate lay in: *89, 92, 131*.

a. PRO, LR2/262, f. 17ᵛ: rental, 1546 (rectory of *89*). PRO, SC6/Hen 8/ 2621–3: a/cs, 1535–7 (*89, 92*).

168. HOUNSLOW, MIDDX., PRIORY OF HOLY TRINITY
Fd. early 13C; diss. 1538. London prop. 1392, 1535.

a. PRO, SC11/985: valor, *c.* 1540 (*42*). PRO, SC6/Hen 8/2396–2401, 2427–8: a/cs, 1538–46 (*42*).

169. IRTHLINGBOROUGH, NORTHANTS., COLLEGE OF ST. PETER
Fd. 1388; diss. 1547. London prop. 1535.

a. PRO, SC12/37/13: survey, *temp.* Edw. VI (*31, 46, 49*).

170. KENILWORTH, WARWICKS., ABBEY OF B.V.M.
Fd. (as priory) 1125; diss. 1539. London prop. 1291 (*152*).

a. BL, Add. MS 47677 (Davis, no. 502): cartulary, comp. after 1514; ff. 277–9, 13C–14C deeds (*152*).

171. KILBURN, MIDDX., PRIORY OF ST. MARY AND ST. JOHN THE BAPTIST
Fd. 1139; diss. 1536. London prop. 1392, 1535.
The estate lay in: *5, 10, 45, 46, 49, 53, 54, 74* or *75, 83, 84, 85, 98, 104, 105, 112, 125, 128, 144, 145, 149, 152, 158, 159*.
The records are in PRO.

a. E315/397, f. 134: survey, *c.* 1540 (total only). SC11/452: valor, 1543–4. LR2/262, f. 2ᵛ: rental, 1546. SC6/Hen 8/2343–55, 2427–8: a/cs, 1537–46. LR12/20/627: bk. of memoranda of arrears, 1538–9 (*10* only).

172. KINGSTON UPON THAMES, SURREY, COLLEGE OF ST. MARY MAGDALENE
Fd. *c.* 1355; diss. 1540. London prop. 1392.

a. BL, Add. Ch. 22665: licence to alienate, 1353 (*125*).

173. KIRKSTEAD, LINCS., ABBEY OF B.V.M.
Fd. 1139; diss. 1537. London prop. 1291, 1392.
In 1291 the estate lay in: *20, 42, 137.*

a. BL, MS Cotton Vesp. E xviii (Davis, no. 519): cartulary, 13C; f. 214ᵛ, list of *carte Lundon'* (outside Aldersgate, unspec.).

b. PRO, SC12/23/14: valor, *c.* 1544–5 (*42*). PRO, SC6/Hen 8/2062–71: a/cs, 1536–46 (*42*). PRO, E315/279, f. 40: a/c, 1540–2 (*42*).

LAUNCESTON PRIORY, see **533**

174. LEEDS, KENT, PRIORY OF ST. MARY AND ST. NICHOLAS
Fd. 1119; diss. *c.* 1540. London prop. 1392, 1535.
The estate was granted to the dean and chapter of Rochester, *c.* 1541 (see **211**).

a. Kent County Archives Office, DRc/T478/1–10: deeds, 1325–1504 (*74*).

b. PRO, SC6/Hen 8/1757–61: a/cs, 1540–44 (*74*).

175. LEICESTER, ABBEY OF ST. MARY DE PRÉ OR B.V.M.
Fd. 1143; diss. 1538. London prop. 1291, 1392, 1535.
In 1291 and later the estate lay in *152*.

a. Bodl, MS Laud Misc. 625 (Davis, no. 548): cartulary, early 16C, incl. copy deeds, rentals; London refs. on ff. 105–6, 147ᵛ, 152, 156, 177.

b. PRO, LR2/181, f. 264ᵛ: rental, *c.* 1540. PRO, E315/279, f. 20: a/c, 1535–6 (probably *152*). PRO, SC6/Hen 8/1827: a/c, 1537–8.

176. LEICESTER, NEWARK COLLEGE (OF THE ANNUNCIATION OR ST. MARY THE GREAT)
Fd. 1353–4: diss. 1548. London prop. 1535. For the later history of the property, see **440**.

a. PRO, DL 29/224/3567–71: a/cs, 1528–30, 1532–3, 1539–43 (London unspec.).

177. LESNES, KENT, ABBEY OF ST. THOMAS THE MARTYR
Fd. 1178; diss. 1525. London prop. 1291, 1392.
In 1291 the estate lay in *126*.
The records are in PRO.

a. SC12/9/36: valor, 1362 (London total only). SC12/9/37: valor, 1403 (London total only). SC12/11/32: rental, ? mid 15C (*116*, outside Cripplegate, Wood Street). SC11/357: valor, 1472 (*78, 116, 127*, nr. Cripplegate). LR2/262, f. 23: rental, 1546 (*2, 42, 78*). SC6/1108/11: rent a/c, possibly of Lesnes, 1431–2 (London total only).

178. LEWES, SUSSEX, PRIORY OF ST. PANCRAS
Fd. 1077: diss. 1537. London prop. 1291, 1535.
In 1291 the estate lay in: *104, 111, 158*. In 1324 Lewes (counted as an alien religious house) had rents in Walbrook ward: PRO, E106/7/18, m. 4, also in King's College, Cambridge, Muniments, 'Oak Cartulary' (Davis, no. 146), f. 68.

a. For a copy of a confirmation charter, 1135×54, of lands in London (Bishopsgate, Smithfield, unspec.) in Paris, Bibliothèque Nationale, see *Cal. Docs. France*, no. 391, also noted in *Regesta* iii, no. 168.

b. BL, MS Cotton Vesp. F xv (Davis, no. 557; *Chartulary of St. Pancras Priory, Lewes*, ed. L. F. Salzman, Sussex Rec. Soc., vols. 38, 40, 1932–4, and supplementary vol., 1943): 15C cartulary of deeds etc. from 11C (*64, 104, 111, 158*, London unspec.).

c. PRO, SC11/662: valor, *c.* 1540 (*111*, nr. Guildhall). PRO, SC11/850: valor, *c.* 1540 (London total only).

179. LEWISHAM, KENT, PRIORY
Fd. 918, 1044, dep. on St. Peter, Ghent (see **266**); diss. 1414, and lands transferred to Sheen (**220**).

a. BL, MS Cotton Otho B xiv, ff. 5–149ᵛ (Davis, no. 891): 15C inventory of muniments of Sheen, incl. (f. 83) properties formerly bel. to Lewisham (*156*).

180. LILLESHALL, SHROPSHIRE, ABBEY OF B.V.M.
Fd. bef. 1148; diss. 1538. London prop. 1291 (*141*).

a. PRO, SC6/1108/16, 17: a/cs of vacancy, 1431, with ref. to land in London.

181. LINCOLN, BISHOP
London prop. 1392, 1535. This was in *20* outside the city limits, acquired *c.* 1161–2: see *The 'Registrum Antiquissimum' of the Cathedral Church of Lincoln*, ed. C. W. Foster (Linc. Rec. Soc. 27–8, 1931–3); *The Register of Bishop Repingdon, 1405–19*, ed. M. Archer (Linc. Rec. Soc. 74, 1982).

182. MALMESBURY, WILTS., ABBEY OF ST. MARY V.
Fd. 10C; diss. 1539. London prop. 1291, 1392, 1535.
In 1291 the estate lay in *134* (property and pension from church).

a. Bodl, MS Wood empt. 5 (Davis, no. 641): 13C cartulary; f. 55, grant of church of *134*. BL, Add. MS 38009 (Davis, no. 642): 13C cartulary, 16 ff. (*134*). PRO, E164/24 (Davis, no. 644; *Registrum Malmesburiense . . .*, ed. J. S. Brewer and C. T. Martin (Rolls Ser. 1879–80), with notes on other cartularies): 13C cartulary (*46, 134*). BL, MS Cotton Faust. B viii, ff. 128–265 (Davis, no. 647): 14C cartulary and rental; London refs. on ff. 155–169, 239–255ᵛ (*20*). BL, MS Lansd. 417 (Davis, no. 645): cartulary, late 14C to 15C; London refs. on ff. 30, 85ᵛ–86, 216ᵛ–219 (*20, 46, 134*).

b. PRO, LR2/262, f. 22ᵛ: rental, 1546 (*54, 134*). PRO, SC6/Hen 8/3986–92: a/cs, 1539–46 (*20, 134*, London unspec.).

183. MARKYATE, HERTS., PRIORY OF HOLY TRINITY
Fd. 1145; diss. 1537. London prop. ?1291 (entry cancelled), 1392 (*93*).

184. MARLOW, LITTLE, BUCKS., PRIORY OF ST. MARY
Fd. ? later 12C; diss. 1536.

a. BL, MS Harl. 391, ff. 103ᵛ–104ᵛ (cartulary of Waltham Abbey): prioress assigns house in *Garcherche* (*37*) to Waltham *c.* 1200; see **241**.

185. MATTERSEY, NOTTS., PRIORY OF ST. HELEN
In 1535 the prior of Mattersey or Mersey was said to have property in *Lond'*, identified by the editors of the *Valor Ecclesiasticus* as London, but it seems more likely that this is a reference to Lound, Notts., near Mattersey.

186. MERTON, SURREY, PRIORY OF ST. MARY V.
Fd. 1114–17; diss. 1538. London prop. 1291, 1392, 1535.
In 1291 the estate lay in: *5, 11, 26, 37, 38, 51, 56, 62, 75, 80, 85, 88, 92, 93, 95, 96, 98, 100, 101, 103, 104, 112, 123, 128, 135, 137, 145, 150, 151, 152, 158*.
See A. Heales, *The Records of Merton Priory* (1898).

a. Leases, 1491, 1502 (*62*), noted in Heales, *Records*, and then in his possession. Oxford, Magdalen Coll., Macray Deeds, misc. no. 161: rent receipt (*128*).

b. BL, MS Cotton Cleop. C vii (Davis, no. 662; contents noted in Heales, *Records*): cartulary, 13C and later (*62, 88, 95, 137, 142, 145, 152*, London unspec.).

c. Bodl, MS Laud Misc. 723 (Davis, no. 663): 14C register of court rolls and rentals, incl. (f. 65), valor (*37*). PRO, SC12/37/7; LR2/262, f. 20ᵛ: rentals, 1546 (*37, 67*). PRO, SC6/Hen 8/3463–7: a/cs, 1537–46 (*11, 26, 27, 37, 38, 51, 62, 67, 80, 85, 88, 92, 93, 95, 96, 100, 104, 123, 128, 137, 145, 150, 151, 152*, Broad Street).

187. MISSENDEN, BUCKS., ABBEY OF ST. MARY V.
Fd. 1133; diss. 1538. London prop. 1291, 1535.
In 1291 the estate lay in: *20, 41, 119, 152*.

a. BL, MS Harl. 3688 (Davis, no. 670; *The Cartulary of Missenden Abbey*, vol. iii, ed. G. Jenkins, HMC with Bucks. Rec. Soc., 1962): cartulary, comp. *c.* 1330 (*20, 30, 111, 116, 119, 142*). BL, MS Sloane 747 (Davis, no. 672): register, 15C to 16C, of grants and leases; ff. 13ᵛ–14 (*20*).

b. PRO, SC12/37/7; LR2/262, f. 21ᵛ: rentals, 1546 (*20*). PRO, SC6/Hen 8/238–42: a/cs, 1539–46 (*20*).

188. NEWARK (*Novus Locus*), GUILDFORD, SURREY, PRIORY OF ST. MARY
Fd. 1189–99; diss. 1538. London prop. 1291, 1392, 1535.
In 1291 the estate lay in: *2, 28, 62, 83, 99, 104, 112, 131, 137, 151*.

a. PRO, SC12/37/7: rental, 1546 (*104, 111*, Cheap, Cornhill, Shambles). PRO, SC6/Hen 8/3464–8: a/cs, 1539–46 (*62, 67, 104, 111, 116, 135, 156*, London unspec.).

NEWARK COLLEGE, LEICESTER, see **176**.

189. NEWNHAM, BEDS., PRIORY OF ST. PAUL
Fd. 1165, 1180; diss. 1540. London prop. 1291 (*74*).

a. BL, MS Harl. 3656 (Davis, no. 692): 15C cartulary; (ff. 8, 19ᵛ) grants, probably 12C, of *Achisburia* in London.

190. NOCTON, LINCS., PRIORY OF ST. MARY MAGDALENE
Fd. temp. Stephen; diss. 1536. London prop. 1535.

a. PRO, SC11/431: valor, *c*. 1540 (*54*). PRO, SC6/Hen 8/2006–16: a/cs, 1535–46 (*54*).

191. NOTLEY, BUCKS., ABBEY OF ST. MARY V. AND ST. JOHN THE BAPTIST
Fd. 1162; diss. 1538. London prop. 1392, 1535.

a. BL, Harl. Roll 0 26, m. 4: copy grant, 1298 (*59, 89, 131*). Oxford, Christ Church, college archives, M. 76: lease, 1538 (Friday Street).

b. PRO, SC12/37/7, LR2/262, f. 22: rentals, 1546 (Wood Street). PRO, SC6/Hen 8/237–42: a/cs, 1538–46 (*131*, Friday Street, Wood Street).

192. NUNEATON, WARWICKS., PRIORY OF ST. MARY V.
Fd. *c*. 1155; diss. 1539. London prop. 1535; prob. also 1392 (as *Novo Eton*).

a. PRO, LR2/182, ff. 242ᵛ, 272; LR2/181, f. 47: rentals, *c*. 1540 (Old Fish Street). PRO, SC6/Hen 8/3739–45: a/cs, 1538–46 (*112*).

193. OGBOURNE, WILTS., PRIORY
Fd. bef. 1147; dependent on abbey of Bec, Normandy (**267**). London prop. 1291, 1392.
In 1291 the estate lay in: *42, 108*. In 1324 the prior had an inn in Castle Baynard ward (? *18*), in which he stayed when in London, and 16*s*. 8*d*. rent in Billingsgate ward: King's College, Cambridge, Muniments, 'Oak Cartulary' (Davis, no. 146), f. 68; PRO, E106/7/18, m. 4. See M. Morgan (Chibnall), *The English lands of the abbey of Bec* (1946); see also **94**.

194. OSNEY, OXON., ABBEY OF ST. MARY V.
Fd. (as priory) 1129; diss. 1539. London prop. 1291, 1392, 1535.
In 1291 the estate lay in: *99, 152*.

a. For the records, comprising 3 cartularies (BL, MS Cotton Vitell. E xv; Oxford, Christ Church, Chapter Libr.; PRO, E164/26), and Osney charters in Bodl and Christ Church, see *The Cartulary of Oseney Abbey*, ed. H. E. Salter (Oxf. Hist. Soc. nos. 89–91, 97–8,100, 1929–31, 1934–5, 1936): London refs. in vols. v and vi (*38, 57, 75, 103, 129, 152*).

195. OSPRINGE, KENT, HOSPITAL OF ST. MARY
Fd. bef. 1234; approp. to St. John's Coll., Cambridge, 1516 (**392**).
The estate lay in *105*.
The records are at St. John's College.

a. D54. 1–4: deeds, 13C to 15C.

b. D110. 290: rental, 1470–1. D2/1/1–3: a/cs, late 13C.

196. OTTERY ST. MARY, DEVON, COLLEGE
Fd. 1337; diss. 1545. London prop. 1535 (Blossoms Inn in *11, 81*), subsequently granted to St. George's College, Windsor (see **258**, below).

197. OXFORD, BISHOP
See fd. at Osney 1542; moved to Oxford 1545. Between 1547 and 1589, when the see was re-endowed, the bishop had a house in *152* (cf. **480**).

a. Bodl, MS Oxf. Dioc. Papers c. 2088: register, incl. lists of the endowments (p. 92) and copies of letters patent of 1547 and 1589.

b. Bodl, MS Oxf. Dioc. Papers c. 2148: box of papers incl. valor, mid 16C, with ref. to London property.

c. PRO, SC6/Eliz/1827–61: a/cs during vacancies 1563–89.

198. OXFORD, HOSPITAL OF ST. JOHN THE BAPTIST
Fd. bef. *c.* 1180; granted to Magdalen College, Oxford, 1457. In 1277 the hospital acquired a tenement in *18*. The records are at Magdalen College (see **399**).

a. Macray Deeds, Kent, London, and Somerset, nos. 140–3: 13C deeds.

199. PANFIELD, ESSEX, PRIORY
Fd. 1070–7, dep. on abbey of St. Stephen, Caen; diss. 1413.
Panfield's London property, in *151*, recorded in 1291, was probably that granted to Caen 1069×79; see **269**.

200. PETERBOROUGH, NORTHANTS., ABBEY OF ST. PETER
Fd. 655–6, *c.* 966; diss. 1539. London prop. 1291, 1392, 1535. In 1291 the estate lay in *63*; by *c.* 1400 also in *46*. On the foundation of the see of Peterborough in 1541, the abbey's former estate was divided between the bishop and the dean and chapter, the London properties going to the bishop; see below, **201**.
The registers belonging to the dean and chapter are in CUL; accounts etc. are in Northants. RO and elsewhere. See J. D. Martin, *The Cartularies and Registers of Peterborough Abbey* (Northants. Rec. Soc., 28, 1978), and *The Court and Account Rolls of Peterborough Abbey: a handlist* (Univ. of Leicester History Dept., Occasional Publication no. 2).

a. London, Soc. of Antiquaries MS 60, 'Liber Niger' (Davis, no. 754), and BL, Add. MS 39758 (Davis, no. 758): both incl. chronicle and mid 12C list of benefactors, incl. ref. to grant by Earl Harold of land in London *iuxta Paulesbiri et prope portum Headredi*: see *The Chronicle of Hugh Candidus, a monk of Peterborough*, ed. W. T. Mellows (1949), 70, 128. CUL, Peterborough 5 (Davis, no. 756): cartulary, mid 13C; ff. 66–7, 12C–13C deeds (*63, 152*). CUL, Peterborough 1 (Davis, no. 757): cartulary, mid 13C; ff. 186, 196–7, 284ᵛ, 13C deeds (*63*). BL, MS Cotton Vesp. E xxii (Davis, no. 766): register, late 13C to early 14C; f. 89ᵛ, grant 1308 (probably *63*). London, Soc. of Antiquaries MS 38 (Davis, no. 759): cartulary, comp. *c*. 1370: ff. 211–13, 13C–14C deeds (*63*). CUL, Peterborough 6 (Davis, no. 760), formerly contained London material, listed in table, but pages now missing. BL, Add. MS 25288 (Davis, no. 768): register, early 15C; f. 91ᵛ, note of taxation on abbey's lands (*63*); f. 139, grant, 15C (*46*). CUL, Peterborough 2 (Davis, no. 769): register, mid 15C; f. 29ᵛ, note of taxation on abbey's lands (*63*). BL, MS Cotton Vesp. A xxiv (Davis, no. 773; *The Book of William Morton*, ed. W. T. Mellows, P. I. King, and C. N. L. Brooke, Northants. Rec. Soc. 16, 1954): a/c and memorandum bk., *c*. 1448–67; incl. refs. to Fleet Street (*46*).

b. BL, Add. MS 40629: valor, 1539–40 (London tenants named, locations not given). PRO, SC11/842: valor, 1541–2, of abbey lands given to bishop. Northants. RO, PDC AR/I/15: a/c of abbot's receiver, 1404–5. Ibid., PDC AR/III/11–12: a/cs of same, 1503–5. PRO, SC6/Hen 8/2787–91: a/cs, 1541–6, incl. ref. to lands granted to bishop.

201. PETERBOROUGH, BISHOP
See fd. 1541. The London endowment of the former Peterborough Abbey in *46, 63* was granted to the bishop. The diocesan records, at Northants. RO, have not been examined but may contain 16C–17C leases, accounts, surveys, minutes, etc. See also PRO, SC11/842, valor of endowment of bishopric, 1541; PRO, SC6/Eliz/1656, a/c during vacancy, 1559–60. See also **462b**.

202. PIPEWELL, NORTHANTS., ABBEY OF B.V.M.
Fd. 1143; diss. 1538.

a. BL, MS Cotton Otho B xiv, ff. 150–204 (Davis, no. 778): 14C notes and extracts, apparently from cartularies; ff. 193ᵛ–194 (*54*). The other surviving cartularies (Davis, nos. 774–7, 779) contain no London refs.

203. PONTEFRACT, YORKS., COLLEGE OF HOLY TRINITY AND B.V.M. (KNOLLES ALMSHOUSE)
Fd. 1385; not suppressed. London prop. 1535.

a. Bodl, MS Barlow 49, ff. 115–65 (Davis, no. 783): cartulary, 14C to 15C (*2, 4, 9, 51, 104, 108, 141, 151, 159*). The later history of the property in *51* may be recorded in Duchy of Lancaster records (**440**).

204. PRITTLEWELL, ESSEX, PRIORY OF ST. MARY
Fd. 1121, dep. on Lewes; diss. 1536. London prop. 1291 (*101*).

In 1324 Prittlewell (counted as an alien religious house) had a void plot in Aldgate ward, worth nothing: PRO, E106/7/18, m. 4.

205. QUENINGTON, GLOS., HOUSE OF KNIGHTS HOSPITALLERS
Fd. 1144–62; diss. 1540. In 1392 the abbot (*sic*) of *Quenyndon* held property in Farringdon ward without; this presumably refers to Quenington, despite the inconsistency, but no other references are known.

206. RAMSEY, HUNTS., ABBEY OF ST. MARY AND ST. BENEDICT
Fd. *c.* 969; diss. 1539. London prop. 1291, 1392, 1535.
In 1291 the estate lay in: *11, 19, 62, 104, 128, 148*.

a. BL, MS Cotton Vesp. E ii (Davis, no. 787): cartulary, mid 13C; London refs. (unspec.) on ff. 17–18, 25ᵛ–26, 28–29ᵛ. PRO, E164/28, and Bodl, MS Rawl. B 333 (Davis, nos. 788, 790; *Chronicon Abbatiae Ramesiensis*, ed. W. D. Macray, Rolls Ser. 1886): 14C register and 14C cartulary (London unspec., 11C to 14C).

b. PRO, SC11/314; SC11/318; SC12/8/58; SC12/11/36: valors and rentals, *c.* 1540 (*62*). PRO, SC11/452; LR2/262, f. 16: rentals, 1543–4, 1546 (*11*).

c. PRO, SC6/1258/12: a/c, 13C (London rents, unspec.). BL, Add. MS 34758: a/c or rental, mid to late 13C (London rent total). PRO, SC6/1259/7: a/c of expenses, 1341, incl. repairs. BL, Add. MS 33446: rent bk., 1361–2 (London, no details). BL, Add. Ch. 34644: receiver's a/c, 1425–6 (*11, 62*, Austin Friars). PRO, SC6/Hen 8/2124: London rentgatherer's a/c, 1523–4, incl. detailed repairs. PRO, SC6/Hen 8/7287–93: a/cs, 1539–46 (*11, 62*, Broad Street).

207. READING, BERKS., ABBEY OF TRINITY, ST. MARY V., AND ST. JOHN THE EVANGELIST
Re-fd. 1121; diss. 1539. London prop. 1291, 1392.
In 1291 the estate lay in: *10, 37, 39, 80, 83, 93, 94, 118, 125, 148, 156*.

a. BL, MS Egerton 3031 (Davis, no. 801): cartulary, late 12C; London refs. on ff. 19, 40, 48ᵛ, 49ᵛ, 100ᵛ, 104 (*80, 83*, unspec.). BL, MS Harl. 1708 (Davis, no. 802): cartulary, mid 13C; London refs. on ff. 29, 111–114 (estate as in 1291). BL, Add. Roll 19617 lists charters (incl. London) from which MS Harl. 1708 was probably compiled. BL, MS Cotton Vesp. E xxv (Davis, no. 803): cartulary, 14C; London refs. on ff. 59–61, 136ᵛ–137ᵛ, 228 (*10, 39, 80, 83*, unspec., probably *18*).

b. PRO, SC6/Hen 8/115–23: a/cs, 1538–46 (*18*).

208. REIGATE, SURREY, PRIORY AND HOSPITAL OF B.V.M. AND HOLY CROSS
Fd. *c.* 1217; diss. 1536. In 1392 *Reygate* held a small rent in Langbourn ward.

209. REWLEY (*Locus Regalis*), OXFORD, ABBEY OF B.V.M.
Fd. 1281; diss. 1536. London prop. 1291, 1392, 1535.
In 1291 the estate lay in *158*.

a. PRO, E303/14 (Oxon)/1: lease, 16C (*155*).

b. PRO, SC12/37/7; LR2/262, f. 21ᵛ: rentals, 1546 (*155, 158*). PRO, SC6/ Hen 8/ 2924–6: a/cs, 1536–40 (*155, 158*).

---

210. ROCHESTER, KENT, CATHEDRAL PRIORY OF ST. ANDREW
Fd. 7C, 1080; diss. 1540; reconstituted for dean and 6 prebendaries, 1541 (see **211**). London prop. 1291, 1392, 1535.
In 1291 the estate lay in *61*, with a pension from the church of *4*.
Unless otherwise stated, the records are in Kent County Archives Office, with full catalogue.

a. DRc/T63, T368–9, T370/1–3, T371/1–2, T372/1–2: deeds and leases, 12C to 16C (*9, 46, 51, 53, 75*).

b. DRc/R1, 'Textus Roffensis' (Davis, no. 817; *Textus Roffensis*, ed. T. Hearne, 1720): cartulary, 12C; London refs. (unspec.) in caps. 43, 155, 201; cap. 43 (charter of Æthelbald, 733) also transl. in D. Whitelock, *English Historical Documents* i, *c. 500–1042* (2nd edition 1979). DRc/R3, 'Registrum Temporalium' (Davis, no. 820): 14C register; f. 7, charter of Æthelbald, 733, as above. BL, MS Cotton Domit. A x, ff. 90–208 (Davis, no. 818): cartulary, 13C; ff. 191ᵛ, 201ᵛ (*157*). BL, MS Cotton Faust. C v (Davis, no. 822): register of *acta*, 1379–1417; London refs. on ff. 7ᵛ–8, 17, 46ᵛ, 78ᵛ–9, 108–109ᵛ (*61, 75*, Fleet Street, Gutter Lane). DRc/Elb 1A, part 2: register, *c.* 1478–1504; f. 8ᵛ, will 1449 (*46*); ff. 10ᵛ–13ᵛ, rental, late 15C (*Berkyngchurch*, unspec.). See also **211b**, below.

c. BL, MS Cotton Vesp. A xxii, ff. 56ᵛ–129 (Davis, no. 821): 13C register, incl. (ff. 92–94ᵛ) rental of sacrist (*Berkingechirche*).

d. DRc/F12: cellarer's a/c, 1383–4 (London unspec.). DRc/F17: treasurer's receipts, 1511–12, of rents, repairs (Fleet Street, unspec.).

e. DRc/L12, 13: records of legal proceedings, 1373, 1378 (*46*, unspec.).

---

211. ROCHESTER, KENT, DEAN AND CHAPTER
Fd. 1541, and endowed with lands of Rochester Cathedral Priory (*46*; quit-rent from *61*) and Leeds Priory (*74*); see **174, 210**; see also **462b**.
Unless otherwise stated, the records are in Kent County Archives Office.

a. For pre-Reformation deeds, see **174** and **210**. DRc/Ele 243–4: leases, 1552–1610 (*46*).

b. DRc/Els 1: composite vol. comp. ? 18C; incl. abstracts of leases, *c.* 1340–16C (*46, 74, 75*); memoranda of 16C–17C leases from registers; rentals 1632, 1640, 1707. PRO, E135/3/7: memorandum of leases, 1543–1605 (*46, 74*). DRc/Elb 1–4: registers of leases, 1575–1640, contents listed. DRc/Arb 1: register of leases, 1660–72, no contents list. DRc/Els 3: abs. of leases, comp. *c.* 1667. DRc/Elr 15, 'The Dean's Old Book': memoranda of lease renewals, 1627–1718. DRc/Elr 19: similar to preceding, with additional notes on fines. CCRc/E1/1, 2: 19C copy of estate bk., listing leases and details from 1661.

c. PRO, E315/389, f. 42: valor of lands for bishopric of Rochester, mid 16C (*74*). DRc/Els 2, 4: rentals, *c.* 1635, 1667 (*46, 74*). DRc/FRb 1–15: incomplete series of a/c bks., 1550–1668 (*46, 61, 74*). BL, Cotton Ch. v. 25: memorandum of rents, 17C (*46*).

d. DRc/ESp 1/2, ff. 1–40; ESp 1/4, ff. 1–28: parliamentary surveys, 1649 (*46, 74*). CCRc/E 4/2: (duplicate) parliamentary surveys, 1649 (*46, 74*).

e. DRc/LP 19/1/29: plan, probably 1670s (Fleet Ditch). DRc/EP 26: plan, 1689 (*46*).

212. Royston, Herts., priory of St. John the Baptist and St. Thomas the Martyr
Fd. 1173–9; diss. 1537. London prop. 1291, 1392.
In 1291 the estate lay in *54*.

a. PRO, SC6/Hen 8/1606–15, 1632–3: a/cs, 1536–46 (*54*).

213. St. Albans, Herts., Abbey
Fd. *c.* 793, *c.* 970; diss. 1539. London prop. 1291, 1392.
In 1291 the estate lay in: *1, 2, 15, 36, 38, 75, 105, 124, 129, 132, 135, 148, 152, 156, 162*.

a. Chatsworth Library, Derbyshire (Davis, no. 832): late 14C cartulary; London refs. on ff. 160–71, 176–93ᵛ (*1, 2, 10, 32, 36, 38, 42, 45, 48, 67, 88, 92, 101, 124, 129, 132, 135, 138, 148, 151, 152, 156*). BL, MS Cotton Nero D vii (Davis, no. 844): catalogue of benefactors, 14C and 15C ; London refs. on ff. 29ᵛ, 34ʳ⁻ᵛ, 39ᵛ, 93, 95ᵛ, 96ᵛ (*2, 42, 129, 148*, unspec.). BL, MS Harl. 602 (Davis, no. 839): register incl. rentals, acquittances, 14C and 15C; London refs. on ff. 55, 58, 60, 61 (*2, 38*, Old Fish Street). College of Arms, MS Arundel 3 (Davis, no. 841): 15C *acta*; ff. 96ᵛ–97ᵛ (*10, 132*, unspec.). BL, MS Arundel 34 (Davis, no. 835): 16C register, incl. deeds and rentals; London refs. on ff. 17–19, 63, 73ᵛ (*42, 148*).

b. PRO, LR2/262, f. 24; SC11/1027: rentals, *c.* 1540 (London unspec.). PRO, SC11/452: rental of quit-rents, 1543–4 (*2, 24, 38, 148*, Lothbury, Shepe Alley).

c. PRO, E315/272, f. 23: a/cs, 1525–6 (London total only). PRO, E315/274, f. 23: a/cs, 1529–31 (London total, repairs to *148*). PRO, SC6/Hen 8/1619–24, 1626–31: a/cs, 1540–6 (*2, 36, 38, 42, 92, 129, 148, 151*).

214. St. Davids, bishop
In 1392 the bishop of St. Davids had shops in the ward of Farringdon without.

215. St. Osyth (Chich), Essex, abbey of St. Peter, St. Paul, and St. Osyth
Fd. (as priory) 1121; diss. 1537. London prop. 1291 (*32*).

a. PRO, SC11/200: valor, 1491–2 (Coleman Street). PRO, SC11/984; SC12/23/25: valors, *c.* 1540 (*113*). PRO, LR2/262, f. 16ᵛ: rental, 1546

(*113*). PRO, SC12/37/11: part valor, n.d., of possessions of unknown monastery, possibly St. Osyth (*113*).

216. SALISBURY, BISHOP
London prop. 1291, 1392.
In 1291 the estate lay in *46* and *54*, but the records noted below apparently refer only to *46*. The property was lost in 1564. The principal records are in Wilts. RO.

a. Wilts. RO, Bishoprick 109: letters patent of 1564 concerning surrender of the London property.

b. Copies of 12C and 13C deeds concerning the London estate are to be found in Salisbury Chapter Records, 'Liber Evidentiarum C' (late 13C; Davis, no. 869), ff. 61ᵛ, 67, 96ᵛ; Wilts. RO, D1/1/2 ('Liber Evidentiarum B', early 14C; Davis, no. 864), ff. 54, 59, 75; Wilts. RO, D1/1/3 ('Registrum Rubrum', early 14C; Davis, no. 865), ff. 45ᵛ, 50ʳ⁻ᵛ, 65, 73ᵛ. Texts of some, but not all, of these deeds are printed in *Charters and documents illustrating the history of the cathedral, city and diocese of Salisbury*, ed. W. R. Jones and W. D. Macray (Rolls Ser. 1890). Wilts. RO, D1/1/5 ('Liber Niger', 15C; Davis, no. 866) incl. 14C and 15C deeds (ff. 51–57ᵛ), 15C leases (ff. 9, 37), 15C and 16C rentals (ff. 57ᵛ, 230ᵛ). Copies of 16C episcopal leases confirmed by the dean and chapter are in the first surviving Chapter Lease Book: Wilts. RO, Bishoprick 460 (*c.* 1502 to 1561). The bishops' registers (see D. M. Smith, *Guide to Bishops' Registers* (RHS, 1981), 188–99) contain numerous incidental refs. to the bishop's house and chapel in *46*.

c. Rentals: see above, **b**.

217. SALISBURY, WILTS., TRINITY HOSPITAL
Fd. *c.* 1350; not suppressed.
The archive incl. 14C deeds concerning *123*: Wilts. RO, 1446/82–94 (see W. Smith, 'A medieval archive from Trinity Hospital, Salisbury', *Archives* 16 (1983), 39–46). The 15C and later a/cs and rentals of the hospital (Wilts. RO, 1446/unsorted boxes) do not record income from London property.

218. SAWTRY, HUNTS., ABBEY OF B.V.M.
Fd. 1147; diss. 1536. London prop. 1291, 1391, 1535.
In 1291 the estate lay in: *127, 136*. See also **500**.

a. PRO, SC11/313: valor, n.d. (Bread Street). PRO, SC6/Hen 8/1666–74: a/cs, 1535–45 (Bread Street).

219. SEMPRINGHAM, LINCS., PRIORY OF ST. MARY
Fd. *c.* 1139; diss. 1538. London prop. 1291, 1392.
In 1291 the estate lay in *152*.

a. PRO, SC6/Hen 8/2018–26, 2029: a/cs, 1537–46 (*152*).

220. SHEEN, SURREY, PRIORY OF JESUS OF BETHLEHEM
Fd. 1414; diss. 1539. London prop. 1535.

a. BL, MS Cotton Otho B xiv, ff. 5–149 (Davis, no. 891): 15C inventory of muniments, mostly from suppressed alien priories; f. 83, Lewisham Priory, dep. of Ghent (*156*); ff. 122, 125, Ware Priory, dep. of St. Évroul (*51*). See **179, 243**.

b. PRO, SC12/18/54: rental, ? late 15C (*Brok Key*, London unspec.). PRO, SC6/Hen 8/3464–8: a/cs, 1539–46 (*51*).

221. SHOTTESBROOK, BERKS., COLLEGE OF ST. JOHN THE BAPTIST
Fd. 1337; diss. 1547. London prop. 1392.

a. Berks. RO, D/Eos T.1: charter, 15C (*56*).

b. BL, MS Egerton 3029 (Davis, no. 894): late 14C cartulary; ff. 57ᵛ–66 (*56*).

222. SHOULDHAM, NORF., PRIORY OF HOLY CROSS AND B.V.M.
Fd. after 1183; diss. 1538. London prop. 1291, 1392, 1535.
In 1291 the estate lay in: *105, 132*.

a. Deed, *c.* 1200 (*105, 132*), printed in F. Blomefield (and C. Parkin), *An essay towards a topographical history of the County of Norfolk* vii (1807), 418–19.

b. PRO, SC11/985: valor, *c.* 1540 (*105, 132*). PRO, LR2/262, f. 17: rental, 1546 (*105*). PRO, SC6/Hen 8/2632–8: a/cs, 1539–46 (*105, 132*).

223. SHREWSBURY, SHROPSHIRE, ABBEY OF ST. PETER AND ST. PAUL
Fd. 1083×6; diss. 1540.
The abbey acquired a house in *58 c.* 1275: National Library of Wales, MS 7851 (Davis, no. 895; *The Cartulary of Shrewsbury Abbey*, ed. Una Rees (Aberystwyth, 1975), no. 381).

224. SOPWELL, HERTS., PRIORY OF ST. MARY
Fd. 1140; diss. 1537. London prop. 1291; possibly also 1392 (as 'Stapwell Abbey').
In 1291 the estate lay in *156*.

a. PRO, LR2/262, f. 17ᵛ: rental, 1546 (Walbrook).

225. SOUTHWARK, SURREY, PRIORY OF ST. MARY OVERY
Fd. 1106; diss. 1539. London prop. 1291, 1392, 1535. See *VCH London* i, 480–4.
In 1291 the estate lay in: *6, 10, 11, 12, 20, 42, 44, 45, 48, 49, 53, 61, 71, 74, 80, 83, 85, 87, 89, 90, 92, 93, 94, 96, 98, 99, 100, 103, 104, 108, 111, 112, 116, 118, 120, 123, 126, 127, 128, 135, 138, 144, 145, 151, 152, 159, 162*: also churches of *32, 132*. At other dates it also incl.: *2, 9, 37, 39, 54, 67, 124, 131, 132, ?148*, 'St. Margaret Broad Street'.

a. BL, Add. MS 6040 (Davis, no. 908): fragments of cartulary, 13C to

?14C (*44, 93, 96, 116, 118*). BL, MS Cotton Faust. A viii, ff. 151–78 (Davis, no. 909): part of 14C register of deeds, pleas, etc. (*9, 37, 80, 83, 108, 112, 127, 151*, Candlewick Street).

b. PRO, SC12/37/7, rental 1546 (Southwark, illegible). PRO, LR2/262, f. 21: rental, 1546–7 (unspec.).

c. PRO, SC6/Hen 8/3464–8: a/cs, 1539–46 (most of estate above).

226. SOUTHWARK, SURREY, HOSPITAL OF ST. THOMAS THE MARTYR
A. The medieval hospital. Fd. 1173, 1215; diss. 1540. London prop. 1392, 1535.

a. Bodl, MS Rawl. D 763, ff. 1–31 (Davis, no. 910): part cartulary, 15C (*4, 29, 43, 45, 96, 127, 137, Stanyngchurch* (probably *13*), unspec.). BL, MS Stowe 942 (Davis, no. 911; *Chartulary of the Hospital of St. Thomas the Martyr, Southwark*, ed. L. Drucker, 1932): 16C cartulary (*4, 13, 37, 43, 45, 53, 59, 63, 80, 82, 85, 87, 90, 93, 96, 103, 114, 124, 125, 127, 128, 129, 134, 135, 137, 141, 151, 152, 157*). PRO, E315/400, f. 114: survey, 1540 (as in MS Stowe 942, except for *37, 59, 82, 87, 93, 96, 103, 135, 157*).

B. The Royal Hospital. Fd. 1553.
The estate (incl. that of former Savoy Hospital; see **105**, above) lay in: *11, 12, 19, 21, 26, 36, 39, 44, 47, 61, 78, 80, 112, 126, 128, 135, 141, 152, 159*. The records are in GLRO.

a. H1/ST/E65: deeds and leases, 15C to 20C (*4, 12, 26, 43, 44, 59, 61, 78, 98, 112, 135*; also refs. to *75, 89*). H1/ST/E67/1–6, E68/1–4: leases, 16C and 17C (*12, 19, 21, 26, 36, 39, 44, 47, 74, 126, 128, 152, 153, 159*).

b. H1/ST/E14, 'Foundation Book': register, comp. 16C to 18C, incl. surrender, grant, and rental of Savoy Hospital lands, 1553 (*11, 19, 26, 30, 36, 46, 128, 152, 153, 159*); memoranda of gifts, 16C (*21, 47, 85, 120,* Aldersgate Street, Bucklersbury, Distaff Lane, Holborn). H1/ST/E65/89/1: bk. of copy deeds, 16C and 17C (*12, 61, 135, 141*). H1/ST/E16: 19C memorandum bk. of deeds and leases, 16C to 19C (estate above, except for *12, 21, 47, 112, 126, 135*; also incl. *59, 74, 153*). H1/ST/E15: lease bk., 1536–66 (estate above, except for *12, 21, 39, 61, 78, 80, 112, 126, 141*; also incl. *153*). H1/ST/E33: abstract of leases, 1638 (estate above).

c. H1/ST/A24/1, 'Book of Government of the Hospital': bk. comp. 1556–82, incl. statutes, treasurers' a/cs (incl. fines for leases), renters' a/cs and rentals, 1562–82. H1/ST/E29/2–5, 'Rentals': treasurers', rent-collectors', and stewards' a/cs, 1582–1694. H1/ST/E35/1, 2: rough a/cs, 1615–21, 1629–35, with memoranda of arrears. H1/ST/D3/1: treasurers' daily receipt bk., 1613–21, incl. fines for leases. H1/ST/D7/1, 'Hospital cash book': treasurers' daily receipts and payments, 1649–55, incl. rents. H1/ST/E26/1, 'Debt book': incl. memoranda of payments of fines for leases, *c.* 1572–1750. H1/ST/D33/1: building a/cs for hospital, also incl. repairs to city properties, 1565–86.

d. H1/ST/A1/1–5: min. bks. of governors, 1556–1608, 1619–77, incl. grants of leases; index to A1/5.

e. H1/ST/E102: view bk., 1622–71, with detailed views and measured surveys.

227. SPINNEY, CAMBS., PRIORY OF ST. MARY AND HOLY CROSS
Fd. bef. 1227–8; united with Ely, 1449. Its property in *104* passed to Ely; above, **152**.

228. STANLEY, WILTS., ABBEY OF B.V.M.
Fd. 1154; diss. 1536. London prop. 1291 (*54*). BL, MS Harl. 6716 (Davis, no. 929) contains no London material.

229. STRATFORD-AT-BOW, MIDDX., PRIORY OF ST. LEONARD
Fd. bef. 1122; diss. 1536. London prop. 1291, 1392, 1535.
In 1291 the estate lay in: *135, 150*.
The records are in PRO.

a. E315/397, f. 133: survey, *c.* 1540 (London total; ref. to Ivy Lane). LR2/262, f. 23ᵛ: rental, 1546 (Bucklersbury). SC6/Hen 8/2343–55, 2424–8: a/cs, 1535–46 (*19, 83, 94, 157*, Broad Street, Bucklersbury, Budge Row, Candlewick Street, Eastcheap, Friday Street, Gutter Lane, Ivy Lane, Knightrider Street, Kyrone Lane, St. Lawrence Lane).

230. STRATFORD LANGTHORNE (HAM), ESSEX, ABBEY OF B.V.M.
Fd. 1135; diss. 1538. London prop. 1392. Property in *2* for a short period in 13C: HR 2 (74).

a. PRO, LR2/262, f. 16: rental, 1546 (*19, 49, 119*). PRO, SC6/Hen 8/962–71: a/cs, 1537–46 (*19, 49, 119*).

231. SUDBURY, SUFF., COLLEGE OF ST. GREGORY
Fd. 1375; diss. 1544. London prop. 1392, 1535.

a. BL, Add. Ch. 26693: rental, 1538 (Cornhill).

232. SYON, MIDDX., ABBEY OF ST. SAVIOUR, ST. MARY, AND ST. BRIDGET
Fd. (at Twickenham) 1415; moved 1431; diss. 1539. London prop. 1535.
The estate lay in *38*.
The records are in PRO.

a. E303/11 Middx.)/53, 77: leases, 16C.

b. SC12/19/31, E36/152: valors, *c.* 1540. SC6/1100/1, 8, 9, 14, 17; SC6/1101/13, 14, 20; SC6/Hen 7/383, 390, 1296–1304; SC6/Hen 8/2126–31: a/cs, series nearly complete, 1467–1536.

233. TAKELEY, ESSEX, PRIORY
Fd. 1066×86; cell of abbey of St. Valéry, Picardy (**274**); suppressed 1391.
The London property, formerly held by St. Valéry, lay in *144*; transferred subsequently to New College, Oxford (**401**).

a. Deeds, late 12C–14C: Oxford, New College Archives, 11911–15. Copies of these and of a lost deed of *c.* 1200 are in New College Archives:

9745 ('Registrum Secundum'), f. 2^{r-v}; 9791 ('Registrum Evidenciarum', vol. 5), pp. 343–6; 11916.

234. TEWKESBURY, GLOS., ABBEY OF ST. MARY
Fd. *c.* 980 (as priory); diss. 1540. London prop. 1291 (church of *10*).

a. BL, MS Cotton Cleop. A vii (Davis, no. 953; printed in *Mon. Angl.* ii, 67–83): calendar of charters, 13C; f. 78, note of grant of *Semannescirce* (*10*), 12C. For a confirmation of this grant, see *Earldom of Gloucester Charters: the charters and scribes of the earls and countesses of Gloucester to A.D. 1217*, ed. R. B. Patterson (1973), no. 179.

235. THAME, OXON., ABBEY OF B.V.M.
Fd. *c.* 1140; diss. 1539. London prop. 1291, 1392.
In 1291 the estate lay in *126*.

a. Marquess of Bath, Longleat MS 44 (Davis, no. 957; *The Thame Cartulary*, ed. H. E. Salter, Oxf. Rec. Soc. 25–6, 1943): cartulary, 13C (*152*).

b. Bodl, MS Christ Church MM R. 3: receipt bk., 1544–8, of Christ Church, Oxford (see **398**, below); notes rent in *152* as former property of Thame.

236. TILTY, ESSEX, ABBEY OF B.V.M.
Fd. 1153; diss. 1536. London prop. 1291, 1392.
In 1291 the estate lay in *124*.

a. See W. C. Waller, 'Records of Tiltey Abbey . . . preserved at Easton Lodge', *Trans. Essex Arch. Soc.* n.s. 8 (1903), pp. 353–62, for description of lost 15C registers (Davis, no. 971; translation in Essex RO, T/B3): incl. deeds, rentals (Milk Street, Wood Street).

b. PRO, LR2/262, f. 16: rental, 1546 (*129*). PRO, SC6/Hen 8/952–61: a/c, 1536–46 (Milk Street, Wood Street).

237. TONBRIDGE, KENT, PRIORY OF ST. MARY MAGDALENE
Fd. late 12C; diss. 1525. In 1392 the prior of *Troubrigge* had a rent of 1*d.* in Walbrook ward. There was no house at Trowbridge, Wilts., at this date, and possibly Tonbridge is meant; no further references known.

238. TORTINGTON, SUSSEX, PRIORY OF ST. MARY MAGDALENE
Fd. *c.* 1180; diss. 1536. London prop. 1291, 1392, 1535.
In 1291 the estate lay in: *29, 85, 156, 157*.

a. PRO, SC6/Hen 8/3674–81, 7442: a/cs, 1536–46 (*85, 157*, Bearbinder Lane, Candlewick Street).

'TROWBRIDGE PRIORY', see **237**.

239. VALE ROYAL, CHESHIRE, ABBEY OF ST. MARY V., ST. NICHOLAS, AND ST. NICASIUS
Fd. 1281; diss. 1539. London prop. 1535.

a. BL, MS Harl. 2064, ff. 4–64 (Davis, no. 983; *The Ledger-Book of Vale Royal Abbey*, ed. J. Brownbill, Lancs. and Cheshire Rec. Soc. 68, 1914): 17C transcript of lost register, 13C to 15C, incl. valor 1336 (London unspec.). BL, MS Harl. 2060, ff. 110ᵛ–111: extract from preceding.

b. PRO, E315/397, f. 51: survey, *c.* 1540 (*62*, but possibly *recte 46*). PRO SC6/Hen 8/7384–9, 7392–7405: a/cs, 1539–46 (*46*).

240. WALDEN, ESSEX, ABBEY OF ST. MARY AND ST. JAMES
Fd. (as priory) 1136–44; diss. 1538. London prop. 1291, 1392, 1535.
In 1291 the estate lay in: *42, 75*.

a. BL, MS Harl. 3697 (Davis, no. 984): cartulary, late 14C; London refs. on ff. 212ᵛ–221, 298 (*39, 42, 74, 85, 103, 134*).

b. PRO, SC11/202: valor, *c.* 1540 (London unspec.).

241. WALTHAM, ESSEX, ABBEY OF HOLY CROSS
Fd. (as church) bef. 1060; diss. 1540. London prop. 1392. See R. W. Ransford, 'The Early Charters of Waltham Abbey, Essex, 1062–1230', London Ph.D. thesis, 1983; incl. transcripts from cartularies and PRO Ancient Deeds.

a. BL, MS Harl. 391 (Davis, no. 989): cartulary, *c.* 1220, with additions; London refs. on ff. 17ᵛ, 23, 25ᵛ, 80–104ᵛ, 120ᵛ (*21, 37, 108*, London unspec.). BL, MS Cotton Tib. C ix, ff. 48–260 (Davis, no. 990): cartulary, 13C with additions, of deeds (*21, 37, 53, 108, 142, Kattenelane*, London unspec.); f. 229ʳ⁻ᵛ, rental, 13C (as deeds, also *19, 48, 58*, Baynards Castle). BL, MS Harl. 3739 (Davis, no. 992): cartulary, 16C, incl. transfer of lands late of Blackmore Priory (diss. 1525) to Waltham (*60, 105*); see **119**, above.

b. PRO, SC12/6/64: valor, *c.* 1540 (*108*, London unspec.). PRO, SC11/452: valor, 1543–4 (*4, 90, 108*). PRO, LR2/262, f. 17: rental, 1546 (*4, 90, 108*). PRO, SC6/Hen 8/964–70, 972–3: a/cs, 1539–46 (*4, 90, 108*).

242. WARDEN, BEDS., ABBEY OF B.V.M.
Fd. 1136; diss. 1537. London prop. 1291, 1392, 1535.
In 1291 the estate lay in *75*.

a. Manchester, John Rylands Library, Lat. MS 223 (Davis, no. 998; *Cartulary of the Abbey of Old Wardon*, ed. G. H. Fowler, Beds. Hist. Rec. Soc. 13, 1930): part of 13C cartulary (St. Martin le Grand, Gutter Lane).

b. PRO, SC6/Hen 8/14–29: a/cs, 1537–46 (*75*).

243. WARE, HERTS., PRIORY OF ST. MARY
Fd. bef. 1081, dep. on abbey of St. Évroul, Normandy; diss. 1414, and lands transferred to Sheen (**220**). London prop. 1291, 1392.
In 1291 the estate lay in *51*. In 1324 Ware (counted as an alien religious house) had a house in Aldgate ward: PRO, E106/7/18, m. 4.

a. BL, MS Cotton Otho B xiv, ff. 5–149ᵛ (Davis, no. 891): 15C inventory of muniments of Sheen, incl. (f. 125) properties formerly bel. to Ware (*51*).

244. WARWICK, HOSPITAL
The brothers of the hospital of Warwick (*Warr'*) held land in *54* in 1291; it is not clear which of the 2 or 3 hospitals there was meant.

245. WAVERLEY, SURREY, ABBEY OF B.V.M.
Fd. 1128; diss. 1536. London prop. 1291, 1535.
In 1291 the estate lay in *20*.

a. PRO, E315/406, f. 50: valor, prob. *c.* 1540 (London unspec.).

246. WELLS, DEAN AND CHAPTER
Did not own property in London, but the muniments (not seen) incl. records of the bishop's estates (see **111**) and some additional material: see *Calendar* [*of the Manuscripts of the Dean and Chapter of Wells* (2 vols., HMC, 1907–14)].

a. Wells, Charters 377, 500 (*Calendar* ii, 628–9, 652): 14C and 15C deeds (*149*, London unspec.).

WESTMINSTER, ABBEY OF ST. PETER

Fd. 7C, *c.* 959; diss. 1540; re-fd. for dean and chapter. London prop. 1291, 1392, 1535. In 1291 the estate lay in: *1, 2, 4, 5, 10, 20, 28, 42, 46, 49, 51, 53, 54, 67, 71, 74, 75, 80, 81, 83, 85, 87, 88, 92, 94, 96, 99, 103, 105, 108, 111, 117, 119, 120, 123, 124, 125, 131, 132, 135, 137, 144, 145, 151, 152, 155, 156, 158, 159, 162*; also pensions from the churches of *46, 85, 87, 92, 120*.

The abbey's London estate was greatly enlarged in 1503 when the college of St. Martin le Grand, with all its London properties (see **83**, above), was appropriated to the abbey for Henry VII's chantry. The estate records of the two bodies were also largely amalgamated. After the dissolution of the abbey in 1540 much of the estate was assigned to the new see of Westminster, founded later that year. A few of the properties so assigned were transferred in 1550 on the abolition of the see to the bishop of London (see below, **254**, and above, **78**), but the rest of the estate remained with the dean and chapter. The abbey was re-founded in 1556 and dissolved again in 1560; the estates held by the dean and chapter after that date seem to have been substantially those held by the abbey before 1540. Few financial records survive for the period 1540–60; PRO ministers' accounts for former abbey properties up to 1547 are described in **249**, below, and for revenues remaining with the Crown after that date under **438**, below. Accounts for the dean and chapter, and for the abbey 1556–60, are described together under **250**, those specifically relating to the bishopric under **254**. During the Interregnum the estates of the dissolved dean and chapter were assigned to the school or college and almshouse of Westminster; the surviving records for this period are included under **248c** and **250c**, below, but see also **462b**.

Unless otherwise stated, the records are at Westminster Abbey. The archive there, which includes that of St. Martin le Grand, comprises early and royal deeds and charters, numbered I–LXXXIX, other loose items (deeds, accounts, etc.) numbered WAM 1–66959, and several series of books. Items I–LXXXIX and WAM 1–66959 are described (and in the case of deeds, calendared) on slips arranged numerically in boxes labelled 'Descriptions'. There is a slip-index to the 'Descriptions' slips, identifying most of the references in deeds and similar material but not the uncalendared references in accounts, etc. A series of notebooks compiled by the former librarian L. E. Tanner gives some idea of the arrangement of material within the numerical sequence (with special notes of seals). Notebook 1 also includes a list of Muniment Books 1–14; there are transcripts and indexes to several of these and other volumes.

247. WESTMINSTER ABBEY: DEEDS

Deeds, leases, acquittances, etc., 12C to 17C, for both Westminster Abbey and St. Martin le Grand estates are mostly noted in the index to the WAM series under 'London: churches and parishes' (*1, 2, 3, 4, 6, 11, 14, 15, 18, 20, 21, 23, 24, 26, 32, 33, ?34, 35, 36, 42, 45, 46, 47, 49, 51, 53, 54, 59, 61, 62, 66, 67, 71, 73, 74, 75, 77, 80, 81, 84, 85, 87, 89, 90, 92, 95, 96, 98, 104, 105, 108, 111, 112, 113, 114, 116, 119, 120, 124, 126, 127, 128, 131, 135, 137, 144, 145, 152, 157, 158, 159*, St. Martin le Grand). See also 'London: wards' (Aldermanbury, Aldersgate, Broad Street, Cornhill), and 'London: streets, houses, etc.' (Adelstreet Lane, Aldersgate, Billingsgate, Blowbladder Street, Bread Street (*Bradestrate*: certainly in some cases Broad Street), Broken Wharf, Candlewick Street, Castle Baynard, Cheap, Coleman Street, Cornhill, Cripplegate, Ebbgate, Fetter Lane, Fleet Bridge, Fleet Street, Friday Street, Gracechurch, Gunpowder Alley, Gutter Alley alias King's Alley, Holborn, Lombard Street, Ludgate, St. Martin le Grand Lane, Milk Street, Newgate Market, Old Fish Market, Old Fish Street, Silver Street, Temple Bar, Temple Gate, near Tower, West Smithfield, Wood Street; streets fully covered under parish-name index are not noted here). Early charters, 11C and 12C (Dowgate, *Stæningahaga*) and references to unspecified properties in London are indexed under 'London'. Further references not indexed by parish or street incl. WAM 13431 (*4*), 13484 (*42*), 28537 (*47*), 13782 (*50*), 13755 (*54*), 36714 (*62*), 16006 (*65*), 9270 (*81*), 36730 and 66495 (*84*), 1224 and 5811B (*105*), 37030 (*119*), 13912 (*128*), 13701–2 (*137*), 320 (*159*), 13765 (Eastcheap), 13732–3B and 28390 (Newgate Market), 13802 and 13805 (St. Vedast's Alley), 4871 (Silver Street).

A calendar of some 300 early charters (1066–1216) of the abbey, from originals and cartulary copies, is being prepared for publication by LRS by Dr. Emma Mason.

248. WESTMINSTER ABBEY: REGISTERS

a. Westminster Abbey, registers of deeds.

See J. Armitage Robinson and M. R. James, *The Manuscripts of*

Westminster Abbey (1909) for descriptions of some of the following Muniment Books. BL, MS Cotton Faust. A iii (Davis, no. 1011): cartulary comp. end 13C to 14C; ff. 4–143, royal charters, 11C to end 13C, with table of grants (*85*, St. Mary 'Niwekirke' (*118*), *Stæningahaga*, numerous London unspecified); ff. 149–217, papal bulls incl. 12C confirmation of *118* and other churches; ff. 218–355, episcopal, abbatial, and private charters, from 12C, with table of contents (churches of *71, 85, 87, 92, 120*; unspecified London lands). BL, MS Cotton Titus A viii, ff. 2–64 (Davis, no. 1012): cartulary comp. 14C; incl. narrative, and some charter material as in preceding; also (f. 40), confirmation, ?12C, of churches and pensions (*1, 2, 46, 49, 53, 71, 80, 85, 87, 92, 120*). WAM 9309: 14C roll of abstracts of memoranda or charters, *c.* 1275–1360 (*20, 26, 30, 42, 54, 74, 75, 80, 81, 83, 85, 87, 92, 94, 103, 108, 117*, ? *118, 119, 120, 135, 137, 144, 150, 151, 152, 157, 158, 159*). Muniment Bk. 11, 'Westminster Domesday' (Davis, no. 1013): cartulary comp. 14C and 15C; royal and papal charters from 11C, also private charters from ?12C arranged by obedientary (many London properties: vol. fully indexed on slips in boxes). Muniment Bk. 1, 'Liber Niger' (Davis, no. 1015): late 15C register of deeds, pleas, rentals, etc., 14C and 15C, with full 20C typescript calendar and index; refs. to pensions from churches (see below, **249a**), valuations etc. of obedientaries' rents (*2, 3, 38, 46, 49, 71, 79, 80, 87, 90, 92, 99, 120, 132*, Silver Street, Wood Street and Gutter Lane; further ref. to Wood Street, f. 79). College of Arms, Young MS 72 (Davis, no. 1016; detailed abstract in S. Bentley, *Abstract of charters . . . in a cartulary of the abbey of St. Peter, Westminster*, 1836): late 15C version of preceding, incl. refs. (ff. 82, 116) to Wood Street and Gutter Lane. Muniment Bk. 2: 16C vol. of transcripts of royal charters and inspeximuses, 11C to 16C (*80, 85, 133*, Bermannecirce, Cheapside, Dowgate, unspecified); charter 1556 refounding abbey lists parishes wherein properties lay (*2, 4, 5, 15, 20, 24, 42, 46,* ?*48, 49, 51, 53, 54, 62, 67, 71, 73, 74, 77, 80, 81, 83, 84, 85, 88, 94, 96, 103, 105, 108, 111, 114, 116, 117, 119, 120, 124, 131, 135, 137, 144, 151, 158, 159*, St. Martin le Grand).

b. St. Martin le Grand, registers of deeds.
WAM 13167: late 13C cartulary roll, part lost (extracts printed in *Regesta* iii, nos. 521–61); deeds, letters, etc., 12C and 13C (*1, 15, 42, 51*, St. Andrew *versus Turrim* (?*21*), close, Aldersgate, land near and soke of Cripplegate, ward of Ralph Sperling, unspec.); misc. 14C entries on dorse (refs. to *1, 15, 42, 114, 135*). WAM 13286: leaf from ?14C cartulary, incl. part of one 13C London deed, details lost. Muniment Bk. 5 (Davis, no. 615): register, comp. mid 15C and later, of royal, papal, and episcopal charters from 11C (*1, 15, 42, 77, 84, 135, 137*, Aldersgate, Cripplegate), records of disputes over privileges, sanctuary, common lanes; ff. 92–5, presentations, late 15C (*24, 84*). BL, MS Lansd. 170: 16C collection incl. (ff. 52–118) copies of royal and papal charters, probably from Muniment Bk. 5.

c. Registers of leases.
Register bks. 1–18: registers of grants (leases, presentations, etc.) 1485–1504, 1509–36, 1542–1642, 1660–9; incl. copy leases and bonds to perform

covenants, fine or consideration not usually noted (London estate, incl. St. Martin le Grand from 1509, and elsewhere); contemp. index in most vols.; 20C TS calendar (omits some details) and slip index to all vols., also TS indexes to vols. 1–4 (in boxes with calendars). WAM 42189: bk. of memoranda of Westminster College leases, mid 17C (Interregnum), noting tenant, date, rent, and term (estate of dean and chapter).

249. WESTMINSTER ABBEY: RENTALS AND ACCOUNTS TO 1547
a. Westminster Abbey.
General. The bulk of the abbey's London estate was assigned to the chamberlain (see below) but the following sources contain material for the whole estate. WAM 28931–2, 28999: taxation assessments 1293–6 (*1, 2, 4, 5, 10, 20, 28, 42, 46, 49, 51, 53, 54, 67, 71, 74, 75, 80, 81, 83, 85, 87, 88, 92, 94, 96, 99, 103, 105, 108, 111, 117, 119, 120, 123, 124, 125, 131, 135, ?137, 144, 145, 151, 152, 155, 156, 158, 159, 162*). WAM 12339: assessment of rents, 1324–5, arranged by wards; tenants named but properties not located (cf. **129**). WAM 12355: taxation assessment *temp.* Richard II; pensions from churches, temporalities (estate as in WAM 28931 above, also *132*). Muniment Bk. 1 (see above, **248a**), ff. 140–3ᵛ: late 14C taxation assessment, totals of obedientiaries' rents. PRO, SC12/ 37/21: rental, apparently Westminster Abbey, 15C (estate as WAM 28931 above, except for *1, 54, 144, 145, 152, 156, 162*; also incl. *15, 39, 48, 62, 73, 79* (crossed out), *114, 116, 127, 132, 142*, Fleet Key, Silver Street). WAM 33090: rental 1507–8, incl. 'desperate rents' and pensions, arranged quarterly (*2, 3, 10, 26, 39, 42, 49, 67, 71, 73, 74, 75, 78, 80, 83, 85, 87, 92, 94, 96, 99, 103, 105, 108, 111, 117, 119, 120, 124, 127, 128, 131, 132, 135, 137, 142, 145, ?149, 151, 156, 158*). PRO, SC12/12/8: 16C list of possessions (*46, 91*). WAM 32197: fragment of a/c for tenants' repairs *temp.* Henry VIII (Newgate Market, unspecified). PRO, SC12/19/30: valuation *c.* 1540, incl. totals of obedientiaries' rents.
Chamberlain. Unless otherwise stated, this estate lay in: *2, 4, 5, 10, 15, 26, 32, 39, 42, 46, 48, 49, 51, 53, 54, 62, 67, 71, 73, 74, 75, 78, 80, 81, 83, 85, 87, 88, 92, 94, 96, 99, 103, 105, 108, 111, 116, 117, 119, 120, 124, 125, 127, 131, 132, 135, 137, 142, 144, 145, 151, 156, 157, 158, 159*; also pensions from churches of *2, 46, 49, 71, 80, 85, 87, 92, 120*.

Rentals. WAM 12331: late 13C memorandum incl. chamberlain's pensions from churches. WAM 9306: rental, probably chamberlain's, 1344–5, incl. notes of socage payments. Muniment Bk. 1 (see above, **248a**), ff. 140–3ᵛ: late 14C taxation assessment, incl. pensions from churches (as above, also *90*, possibly in error). WAM 12335: memorandum, ?14C, of tenths from pensions from churches. Muniment Bk. 11 (see above, **248a**), f. 651: 15C list of pensions from churches. Bodl, MS Top. Lond. e. 6, c. 4 ff. 1, 2: leaves from detailed rental, 1429, probably of chamberlain (*2, 32, 42, 75, 88, 105, 117, 124, 132, 145, 151*, Bishopsgate Street, Fleet Street). PRO, SC12/12/5 rental, *c.* 1540, incl. arrears and unleviable rents (estate above, also Crooked Lane, Philip Lane). WAM 18818: abbreviated rental, 1528; tenants named, most properties not located. PRO, SC12/19/30: valuation *c.* 1540, incl. pensions from churches.

Accounts. WAM 18717: a/c of expenses 1291–2, incl. socage payments at Cornhill, Guildhall, Queenhithe. WAM 18718–34: a/cs, 14C (individual years) of pensions, totals for other receipts, socage payments specified. WAM 18736–817, 18819, 18821–7, 18828*: a/cs and views, 1418–1536 (some duplicates, odd years missing), details of rents, pensions, repairs, and socage and quit-rent payments. PRO, SC6/Hen 7/398: a/c 1495–6, details of rents, pensions. WAM 18820: extracts from a/c 1527–9, incl. arrears and charges. PRO, SC6/Hen 8/2414: incl. chamberlain's a/c, 1542–3, details of rents and pensions. WAM 37050: views of a/cs, incl. chamberlain's, 1542–4, details of rents and pensions. See also WAM 33292: two leaves from a/c of chamberlain (?), 15C, incl. repairs (Grub Street), legal expenses (Dowgate, Poultry; money spent at the Mitre in Cheapside).

Cellarer. WAM 18829–18881: a/cs, 1281–5, 1299–1300, 1331–99 (odd years missing); few references to London rents, except for 18842, 18880 (Holborn). WAM 18882–18958: a/cs 15C and 16C to 1536 (series not continuous, some a/cs only partial); full a/cs incl. 'foreign rents' (*20*); WAM 18889 mentions former rent (*10*). WAM 32043: rental (?partial), 1535–6 (Holborn).

Refectorer. WAM 19503–19617: a/cs, 1373–1537 (odd years missing, some duplicates), incl. rent receipts (*111, 117*, Silver Street).

Sacrist. The estate lay in Cheapside (probably *159*), Fetter Lane (probably *20*), Fleet Bridge (probably *46*).

WAM 19184: valuation, *c*. 1540 (Cheapside, Fleet Bridge). WAM 19618–59: a/cs, 14C (individual years), mostly partial and/or summarised; London rents specified in WAM 19621, 19629. WAM 19660–807: a/cs, 1407–1532 (odd years missing); most a/cs incl. rent receipts, allowances, repairs. WAM 31909: fragment of rental or a/c, 1527–8 (Fetter Lane). PRO, SC6/Hen 8/2414: incl. sacrist's a/c, 1542–3 (Fetter Lane). WAM 37050: views of a/cs, incl. sacrist's, 1542–4 (Fetter Lane).

Treasurer. WAM 19838–20000, 23001–23073: a/cs, 13C to 16C (individual years); most a/cs do not incl. city rents, but see WAM 19868–73, rent receipts 1378–86 (Cornhill, Silver Street); also WAM 19874–9, rent receipts 1386–94 (Silver Street). WAM 24562–621, 23074–178: a/cs of collector of rents or treasurer 'intrinsecus', 1352–71, 1390–1537 (odd years missing); rent receipts, repairs, quit-rent and socage payments (Wood Street). PRO, SC6/Hen 8/2414: incl. treasurer's a/c, 1542–3 (Wood Street). WAM 37050: views of a/cs incl. of treasurer 'intrinsecus', 1542–3 (Wood Street).

Warden of St. Mary's (Lady) Chapel. WAM 23179–98: a/cs, late 13C and 14C, rents and farms (summaries or totals only; no London details). WAM 23199–317: a/cs 1400–1529 (odd years missing); rents (detailed in most years) and repairs (*30, 92, 108, 135, 137*). WAM 31832: memoranda of rents, 1515–16, 1526–7 (Billingsgate, Old Fish Market). PRO, SC6/Hen 8/2414: incl. a/c for Lady Chapel, 1542–3 (*108, 135*). WAM 37050: views of a/cs. incl. totals for Lady Chapel, 1542–4.

Miscellaneous. WAM 6019: rental of lands of Thomas Purveys, *temp*. Edward IV (*87, 94*). WAM 6629–30: inventories of goods of Sir Thomas Charleton, *temp*. Edward IV (Aldermanbury).

b. St. Martin le Grand to 1547.

The estate incl. rents, quit-rents, and pensions from churches, lay in: *1* or *24, 15, 42, 53, 77, 81, 84, 111, 114, 116, 128, 135, 137, 145* (lost by *c.* 1500), *159, 160*, Barbican, Distaff Lane, Fleet Street. Rents were also received from properties in the precinct (extraparochial, later *23* and *84*), including the sanctuary, Dean's Court, Cock Alley, Four Dove Alley, St. Martin's Lane. After 1503 the accounts were made in the abbot of Westminster's name.

Rentals. WAM 13324: rental and valuation, *?temp.* Henry VII; rents, pensions, payments, estimates of repairs needed. WAM 13325: rental *?temp.* Henry VIII. PRO, E 315/317, ff. 146–53: rental 1539–40. PRO, SC 12/36/27: similar rental, heading and date lost. PRO, SC11/452: valor of obit rents 1543–4 (*93, 114, 135, 137*, Cornhill). WAM 13309: fragment of 16C rental (precinct).

Accounts. WAM 13310–11: rent-collectors' a/cs 1385–6, 1391–2; total receipts, detailed payments. WAM 13321: a/c, late 14C (damaged); rent and quit-rent receipts (estate above, also *155*). WAM 13312: a/cs of overseer of works, 1444–8, incl. repairs (*114*, Close, Distaff Lane, Foster Lane, 'le George', Old Fish Street, Smithfield). WAM 13313, 13315–17: a/cs 1503–4, 1514–15, 1517–20; quit-rent and pension receipts and payments totalled, rents totalled by street or par. WAM 13318–20: detailed a/cs, 1525–7 and undated; receipts (incl. notes of leases), arrears, vacations, repairs. PRO, SC6/Hen 8/2414: incl. a/c for St. Martin le Grand, 1542–3. WAM 37050: incl. views of a/cs for St. Martin le Grand, 1542–4. WAM 33212: a/c 1546–7, receipts totalled, vacations and unleviable rents detailed.

250. WESTMINSTER ABBEY: RENTALS AND ACCOUNTS AFTER 1547
a. Accounts of rent-collector.

Rents and quit-rents from abbey and St. Martin le Grand estates: *1, 2, 4, 5, 15, 20, 42, 48, 49, 51, 53, 54, 62, 67, 71, 73, 74, 75, 77, 80, 81, 83, 84, 85, 87, 88, 94, 96, 103, 105, 108, 111, 114, 116, 117, 119, 120, 124, 125, 131, 135, 137, 138, 142, 151, 158, 159*, precinct of St. Martin le Grand. WAM 33214, 33185, 33207, 33025, 33217–18, 34160: a/cs 1549, 1553–78; details of receipts, arrears, rents respited. WAM 13322–3: a/cs for St. Martin le Grand, 1548–9, 1551–2; total receipts, details of vacations and allowances. WAM 37950: a/c of arrears, 1559 (*2, 49*, Wood Street). WAM 34159: incomplete draft rental *temp.* Elizabeth, naming pars. but omitting rents. WAM 38568: rent-collector's memorandum of certain quit-rents, 1566. WAM 41502, 41516–17, 41531–2, 41537, 41586–7, 42107: rent-collectors' and receivers-general's a/cs, 1604, 1616–19, 1622–4; total receipts, details of arrears. WAM 41746*: a/c 1635–6, details of receipts, arrears, table of tenants' names. WAM 34161: particular of arrears, 1660 (*2, 15, 46, 53, 83, 84, 85, 87, 120, 135, 152*). WAM 33889*A–C: a/cs 1670, details of rents, pensions from churches, 'dead and desperate' rents. WAM 33889*D: a/c of abbey estates, *c.* 1670; London properties described, with measurements, details of current and past leases, rents (part of estate above, omitting quit-rents; also *46*). Cf. also WAM 18828, remembrance of decayed rents, 1556–8 (*5, 67, 80,*

120); WAM 41467, memorandum of rents increased, 1610 (*46*, Broken Wharf, Newgate Market, St. Martin le Grand). Bodl, MS Jones 16, ff. 1–41: rental of all rents naming pars. and streets, mid 17C.

b. Accounts of receivers-general.
Receipts from rectory and rectory-house of *46*, tenement in Newgate Market, totals from rent-collectors.
   WAM 33192–8K, 33205, 33219–36, 33354–420, 33237, 33240, 33242–63, 34290: a/cs 1548–75, 1584–1643, some duplicates, odd years missing; receipts as above, also (WAM 33371–412, 33243–57) some details of pensions from churches, arrears on collectors' a/cs (*2, 15, 49, 83, 85, 87, 120, 124, 135, 137*, Aldersgate Street). WAM 33421: a/cs 1647–8, totals only. WAM 33265, 33423–8: a/cs 1662–7, receipts for *46*, totals.

c. Accounts of deputy-receiver for school and almshouse of Westminster (during Interregnum).
Rents from estate as in **a**, above.
   WAM 33422, 33422*: a/cs. 1654–8, total receipts, details of arrears. WAM 43669: schedule of rent arrears, 1658, totals only. PRO, E101/668/45: warrants, orders, and a/cs of governors, 1658–60. See also **248c**, above.

d. Miscellaneous accounts.
WAM 37175: a/c of repairs, 1548 (Bell Alley, Lambards Hill, St. Leonard's Corner). WAM 37177–240: memoranda of payments to workmen, ?1548 (few indications where work done, but incl. St. Martin le Grand).

251. WESTMINSTER ABBEY: ADMINISTRATION
Chapter Act Bks. 1–4 (1542–56, 1560–1642, 1660–85): minutes of chapter decisions incl. grants of leases (terms and rents usually noted), presentations, building works, leasing policy; vol. 4 (1662–85) also incl. agreements for rebuilding burnt properties in *46*, Fetter Lane, Gutter Lane, St. Martin le Grand, Tower Street. Vols. 1 and 2 are originals with signatures, vols. 3 and 4 copies. There is a bound MS transcript, 1904, of vol. 1 (1542–56, 1560–1609).

252. WESTMINSTER ABBEY: PLANS
WAM 13344: plan, 1713, of former precinct of St. Martin le Grand.

253. WESTMINSTER ABBEY: MISCELLANEOUS
WAM 38440: 16C memorandum of inquisition, 1279, listing churches in abbey's patronage (*46, 49, 54, 71, 80, 85, 87, 92, 120*). WAM 5811B: list of religious houses and others excommunicated for nonpayment of tenth on properties within archdeaconry of London, 1302.

254. WESTMINSTER, BISHOP (1540–50)
The endowment of the see was mainly made up of former lands of Westminster Abbey (incl. St. Martin le Grand). Certain rents (*53, 84, 128*) passed on the dissolution of the see to the bishop of London (see **78**, above).

PRO, E315/426: valor of estates assigned to bishopric of Westminster (1540–50); rents and farms (*2, 4, 10, 15, 20, 24, 27, 39, 42, 53, 62, 67, 71, 74, 77, 81, 84, 85, 96, 99, 103, 105, 111, 114, 116, 119, 125, 127, 128, 131, 132, 135, 137, 151, 158, 159,* St. Martin le Grand). PRO, SC11/845: valor of the same, 1542–3 (*53, 84, 128*). GL, MS 25457/1: a/c 1544–5, bishop of Westminster (*53, 84, 128*). See also WAM 6484C, 6489: 16C copies of Edward VI's letters patent dissolving the see and transferring its jurisdictions to the see of London.

255. Westminster, hospital of St. James
Fd. 12C; assigned to Eton College 1449; diss. 1531. London prop. 1392. The records are at Eton College (see **406**, below).

a. Title deeds from the hospital's property in London are incorporated in the Eton College Archive. Cf. ECR 16/St. James/7, 10: copies of royal charters (*5, 111*).

b. ECR 16/St. James/2: a/c of repairs, 1454–5 (*5, 111*). Ibid. 3: rent a/c, 1485–1500 (*5, 14, 111, 123,* unspec.). ECR 61/VR/E/1: a/c, 1497–1500, total only, detailed arrears and charges (*5, 111,* Paul's Wharf).

255A. Westminster, college of St. Stephen
Fd. 1348; diss. 1547. London prop. 1535.

a. BL, MS Cotton Faust. B viii (Davis, no. 1023): 15C register incl. deeds and assignments of income (*13, 26, 45, 54,* Warwick Lane). For royal grants of London property in 14C, see *Mon. Angl.* vi, 1349–50.

256. Winchcombe, Glos., abbey of St. Mary V and St. Kenelm
Fd. 8C, 10C; diss. 1539. London prop. 1392, 1535.

a. 'Liber B' or 'Landboc', 'Liber A', *penes* Lord Sherborne, formerly deposited at Glos. RO, D. 678 (Davis, nos. 1037, 1038; *Landboc . . . de Winchelcumba,* ed. D. Royce, 2 vols., 1892, 1903): 2 cartularies, 13C and 15C (London unspec., 12C).

b. PRO, LR2/262, f. 23: rental, 1546 (*46*). PRO, SC6/Hen 8/1240–6: a/cs, 1539–46 (*46*).

257. Winchester, bishop
London prop. 1392 (*12, 80,* Queenhithe ward). The bishop's principal estate in or near London was in Southwark. See also **462b**.

a. Hants. RO, Eccles 155648: valor, 1503, incl. total receipts, allowance for payments out (*10, 12,* unspec.). Ibid., Eccles 159272 et seqq.: pipe roll a/cs, 13C to 15C, usually incl. rent totals, details of arrears, expenditure, etc. (in 13C, from Old Fish Street; 14C, 15C, from *10, 12*; in 1415–16, from Vintry).

b. Hants. RO, Eccles 249406: parliamentary survey 1647; incl. rents in city (*10,* unspec.).

258. WINDSOR, BERKS., ST. GEORGE'S CHAPEL
Fd. 1348; not suppressed.
The estate lay in: *30, 116*; also *11* and *81*, formerly bel. to college of
Ottery St. Mary, Devon, from *c.* 1550. The hospital of St. Anthony of
Vienne, London (estate in *36*) was appropriated to the college in 1475,
but the archives remained distinct for the most part (see **98**, above). See
also **462b**.
The records are in The Aerary, St. George's Chapel, Windsor Castle. See
J. N. Dalton, *The Manuscripts of St. George's Chapel, Windsor Castle*
(1957).

a. II. B. 1–17: deeds, 15C to 17C (*30, 71, 116, 128*, Knightrider Street).
XV. 50. 46–53: deeds, leases, 16C to 18C (*30, 116*). II. B. 18, XI. A. 24,
XV. 8. 6: papers, etc., 16C (*11, 81*). XVI. 6. 1: deeds, leases, 16C to 19C
(*11, 81*). An agreement, 1423, between the duke of Exeter and the dean
of Windsor, concerning rent from *116*, is in the archives of the dean and
chapter of Exeter: HMC (55) *Various Collections* IV, p. 82.

b. VII. B. 1: register of leases (1), 1660–71.

c. IV. B. 19, 'Dr. Stokes' Book': memorandum and rental of lands, *c.*
1639 (*11, 30, 36, 81, 116*). IV. B. 6, 'Howel's transcript': compilation,
1636–60, of memoranda of properties and leases (as preceding). XIII. B.
4, 'Rental Book': tabular rental, *c.* 1660 (as preceding). IV. B. 7–8, 'Dr.
Derham's Book': survey, comp. 1718, of lands incl. memoranda from *c.*
1660 (as preceding).

d. Accounts: rent receipts, payments, etc. in stewards' and receiver-
generals' rolls; see Dalton, *Manuscripts*, 98–129.

e. IV. A. 3: parliamentary surveys, 1649 (*11* and *81, 30, 36, 116*).

259. WINTNEY, HANTS., PRIORY OF B.V.M. AND ST. MARY MAGDALENE
Fd. bef. 1200; diss. 1536.
In 1223–4 the prioress was party to a fine concerning land in London: W.
J. Hardy and W. Page, *Calendar to Feet of Fines, London and Middlesex* i
(1892), p. 215, no. 7.

260. WOBURN, BEDS., ABBEY OF B.V.M.
Fd. 1145; diss. 1538. London prop. 1291, 1392, 1535.
In 1291 the estate lay in *75*; in 1392 apparently in *38, 75*.
No records remain at Woburn Abbey: see G. S. Thomson, 'Woburn
Abbey and the Dissolution of the Monasteries', *TRHS* 4th Ser. 16 (1933),
129–60.

a. PRO, LR2/262, f. 24: rental, 1546 (Thames Street). PRO, SC6/Hen 8/
30–5: a/cs, 1537–46 (unspec.).

261. WORCESTER, BISHOP
In 1291 the bishop had property in *67, 127*. There was also an inn outside
the city in the parish of St. Mary le Strand: Worcester, dean and chapter,

Reg. I or A.4 (Davis, no. 1070; *The Cartulary of Worcester Cathedral Priory*, ed. R. R. Darlington (1968), nos. 53, 72, 548).

The unpublished records at Worcester have not been examined for this survey, but Susan Brock, 'Report on the Muniments of Worcester Cathedral, 8th–19th century, Class B' (HMC, 1981), indicates no further records relating to property in the city of London.

a. BL, Harl. Ch. 43. I. 35 (printed in M. G. Cheney, *Roger, bishop of Worcester 1164–79* (1980), pp. 297–8): grant by bishop, 1164×79, of land in his soke in London.

b. BL, MS Cotton Tib. A xiii (Davis, no. 1068; printed from 18C transcript as *Hemingi Chartularium Ecclesiae Wigorniensis*, ed. T. Hearne, 1723): 11C cartulary, incl. (f. 18ᵛ) copy grant *c*. 889, of *Hwætmundes stan*. An associated grant of *c*. 898 (Cambridge, Corpus Christi College, MS 189, f. 199ᵛ) refers to *Ætheredes hyd*; T. Dyson, 'Two Saxon land grants for Queenhithe', in *Collectanea Londiniensia*, ed. J. Bird, H. Chapman, and J. Clark (1978), argues that both grants relate to the same property, and prints the text of the latter grant.

c. PRO, SC6/1143/18 (printed in *The Red Book of Worcester*, ed. M. Hollings (1934–50), p. 543): a/c, 1302–3, during vacancy, incl. socage rents in London.

262. WROXTON, OXON., PRIORY OF ST. MARY V.
Fd. *c*. 1217; diss. 1536. London prop. 1291 (*159*).

263. YORK MINSTER (ST. PETER'S)
Fd. bef. 314, 625; not suppressed.
The minster's London property was Serjeants' Inn (*54* or extraparochial; see **413**), acquired 1409. See H. C. King, *Records and Documents concerning Serjeants' Inn, Fleet Street* (1922), for history and numerous extracts from HR, PCC wills, and records listed below.
Unless otherwise stated, the records are in the Minster Library, York. There are 3 files of 'calendars' listing them by class in some detail. See also **462b**.

a. BL, MS Cotton Vit. A ii (Davis, no. 1089): late 14C register, with additions; f. 131, grant 1409 (*54*). MS L2 (2)a (Davis, no. 1088: 'Liber Domesday'): 14C to 15C register; ff. 129–131, case concerning rent payable by St. Bartholomew's Priory, 1426. MS M2 (2)a: 'Index cartarum', late 15C–16C; ff. 41–4, list of charters, 13C to 16C (London unspec., probably *54*; f. 43ᵛ, charter *c*. 1400 relating to *46, 54, 74, 104*). MS M2 (2)b: similar to preceding, London refs. on ff. 11–13.

b. MSS Wa–We: lease registers, 1508–1703, indexed (under S). MS S1 (1)a: terrier, 18C, giving history, noting leases 1570–1757.

c. MS S1 (2)f: rental, mid to late 17C, and list of land sales during Interregnum; London refs. on ff. 22, 32. MS E (39–136): incomplete series of chamberlains' a/c rolls, 1426–1634, incl. rents; extracts printed in

The Fabric Rolls of York Minster, ed. J. Raine, Surtees Soc. 35 (1859). MS E2 (2–4): a/c bks., 1599–1631, 1667–81, incl. rents.

d. MS U1: papers, mostly 18C–19C, relating to legal proceedings and sale of Serjeants' Inn; incl. memoranda on title from 1409, copy deed and plan of 1650s, negotiation of rebuilding terms in 1669, plan and elevation of late 17C–18C.

264. YORK, ABBEY OF ST. MARY
Fd. 1088–9; diss. 1539. London prop. 1535.

a. BL, Add. MS 38816, ff. 21–39 (Davis, no. 1097): fragment of 12C cartulary; f. 28ᵛ, confirmation charter (ref. to land in London, unspec.). BL, MS Harl. 236 (Davis, no. 1100), f. 10: copy of same charter in 14C cartulary. St. Albans Abbey cartulary at Chatsworth (Davis, no. 832), f. 176, incl. agreement concerning London property (*38, 101*), late 12C.

b. A list of a/c rolls is being compiled (1983) at the Borthwick Institute by David Smith; no London material noted so far.

265. OTHER ENGLISH RELIGIOUS HOUSES
The following religious houses may have held property in London, but no references have been found other than those cited below.

a. Ashridge (Herts., formerly Bucks.), monastery or college of Bonhommes. Fd. 1283; diss. 1539. Tenement in Fleet Street, 1349: *Cal. Wills* i, 574.

b. Beauvale (Notts.), priory of Holy Trinity, St. Mary V., and All Saints. Fd. 1343; diss. 1539. A rent in *92* was left to the priory in 1456 (*Cal. Wills* ii, 542–3; also GL, MS 1311/1, ff. 36ᵛ–39), charged with a rent to the church of Finedon, Northants. (**384a**).

c. Cobham (Kent), college of St. Mary Magdalene. Fd. 1362; diss. 1539. Rents in *48*, 1407/9: *Cal. Wills* ii, 382.

d. Dorchester (Oxon.), abbey of St. Peter, St. Paul, and St. Birinus. Fd. 634, 1140; diss. 1536. Rent in *12*, 1359/61: *Cal. Wills* ii, 20.

e. Flaxley (Glos.), abbey of B.V.M. Fd. 1151; diss. 1536–7. Tenements in *38*, 1292: HR 21(17); *Cal. Pat. R. 1281–92*, p. 479.

f. Hurley (Berks.), priory of St. Mary. Fd. bef. 1087; diss. 1536. Rent, unspec., 1381: *Cal. Wills* ii, 275.

g. Latton (Essex), priory of St. John the Baptist. Fd. bef. 1200; diss. 1534. Tenements in *62*, 14C: HR 69(8), 91(63).

h. 'Moreton' priory: identity uncertain. Land in *119*, 13C: HR 2(95).

i. Poulton (Glos., formerly Wilts.), priory of St. Mary. Fd. 1348–50; diss. 1539. Hostel in *148*, 1357: *Cal. Wills* ii, 6, but will disputed.

j. Sibton (Suff.), abbey of B.V.M. Fd. 1150; diss. 1536. Tenement in Aldgate ward, 1305: *Calendar of Early Mayor's Court Rolls*, ed. A. H. Thomas (1924), 218.

k. Thele, or Stanstead St. Margaret's (Herts.), college. Fd. 1316; granted to Elsing Spital, London (**104**), 1431. Property in *32*, 1349: *Cal. Wills* i, 618.

l. Vaudey (Lincs.), abbey of B.V.M. Fd. 1147–9; diss. 1536. Ref. to houses of abbot in *152*, c. 1308: *Cal. Wills* i, 204.

OVERSEAS RELIGIOUS HOUSES

At least 10 overseas religious houses, including at least 6 in Normandy, held property in London at an early date (mid 11C to mid 12C). In several cases this was subsequently transferred to, or regarded as held by, a dependent priory or cell in England. Thus for the property of the priory of St. Bernard, Montjoux, see Hornchurch (**166**); for St. Évroul, Normandy, see Ware (**243**); see also Ghent, Bec, St. Stephen, Caen, and St. Valéry, below. By the mid 15C no London property remained in alien hands: the dependent priories had either been 'naturalized' or suppressed, or the parent house had lost or disposed of the property in some other way. Much of the property so lost went to new 14C or 15C religious or collegiate foundations. See D. Knowles, *The Religious Orders in England* (3 vols., 1948–59), esp. ii, 157–66; M. Morgan, 'The suppression of the alien priories', *History* 26 (1941–2), 204–12. An inquisition of 1324 into lands of religious houses *de potestate regis Francie* is recorded, with textual variations, in PRO, E106/7/18, mm. 4, 9, and King's College, Cambridge, Muniments, 'Oak Cartulary' (Davis, no. 146), f. 68; details under individual houses. PRO, E106, extents of alien priories, was not fully searched; none of the items relating to specific houses contains any London material, but some of the general extents or 'states' may.

The aim here has been to identify overseas religious houses with London property, and where possible to indicate where these properties lay and what became of them, but not to undertake a full search for all records relating to those properties. The references given below derive largely from a search of *Regesta, Cal. Docs. France*, and *Tax. Eccl.*, and any printed records and other works relating to the houses in question. Dates of foundation, etc., are taken from L. H. Cottineau, *Répertoire topo-bibliographique des abbayes et prieurés* (Macon, 1935–70), which includes extensive bibliographies for each house. The uncertainties noted below as to the location or fate of the estates can probably be resolved by further research. It is also possible that further religious houses with interests in London might be discovered.

266. BELGIUM: GHENT, ABBEY OF ST. PETER (MONT BLANDIN)
Fd. 610×35; Benedictine.
Many of the Ghent charters are suspect or spurious, but by the early 12th century, and probably in the 11th, the abbey held a property called

Wareman acre (probably in *53*, and neighbouring parishes). See A. van Lokeren, *Chartes et documents de l'abbaye de Saint Pierre au Mont Blandin à Gand* (Ghent, 1868); P. H. Sawyer, *Anglo-Saxon Charters, an annotated list and bibliography* (RHS, 1968), no. 1002; *Regesta* ii, nos. 730, 1148; ibid. iii, no. 340; J. Dhondt, 'La donation d'Elftrude à St. Pierre de Gand', *Académie Royale de Belgique, Bulletin de la Commission Royale d'Histoire* 105 (1940), pp. 117–164. See also O. Oppermann, *Die älteren Urkunden des Klosters Blandinium und die Anfänge der Stadt Gent* (Utrecht, 1928), reviewed in *EHR* 43 (1928), 615–17. A rental or survey of the abbey's property in 1281 (printed in van Lokeren, *Chartes*, no. 896, p. 420) incl. references to *53*, and Walbrook. In 1291 the abbey had property in: *53, 90, 108, 156*. The dependent priory of Lewisham (**179**) later held a property in *156*, possibly the same.

267. FRANCE: BEC, NORMANDY, ABBEY OF B.V.M.
Fd. 1034; Benedictine.
In the late 11C the abbey acquired a property in London (*Regesta* ii, no. 1013); *c.* 1181 the abbey had an interest in a property, possibly the same, called *Musterlinbur'* (Windsor, St. George's Chapel Muniments XI G II (early 13C roll of Bec charters), printed in *Select documents of the English lands of the abbey of Bec*, ed. M. Chibnall, Camden 3rd ser. 73 (1951) no. 8). For other references, see also *Early charters of St. Paul's*, ed. M. Gibbs, Camden 3rd ser. 58 (1939), no. 165; *Cal. Wills* i, 62. The location of this property or properties is uncertain; it or they probably passed to the dependent priory of Ogbourne, Wilts. (**193**). See M. Morgan (Chibnall), *The English lands of the abbey of Bec* (1946); A. A. Porée, *Histoire de l'abbaye du Bec* (Évreux, 1901).

268. FRANCE: CAEN, NORMANDY, ABBEY OF HOLY TRINITY
Fd. *c.* 1066; Benedictine nuns.
In the late 12C the abbey acquired property in *92: Charters and custumals of the abbey of Holy Trinity, Caen*, ed. M. Chibnall (British Academy, Records of Social and Economic History n.s. 5, 1982).

269. FRANCE: CAEN, NORMANDY, ABBEY OF ST. STEPHEN
Fd. 1064; Benedictine.
The abbey acquired a house in *151* in 1069×79: *Placita Anglo-Normannica, Law cases from William I to Richard I, preserved in historical records*, ed. M. M. Bigelow (1879, reprinted 1974), pp. 261–3; *Regesta* i, no. 105; ibid. ii, no. 1575; *Cal. Docs. France*, nos. 452–3, 459, 1409. By 1291 the property was held by the dependent priory of Panfield, Essex (**199**).

270. FRANCE: FÉCAMP, NORMANDY, ABBEY OF HOLY TRINITY
Fd. 658, 952; Benedictine.
In 1291 and 1392 the abbey had property in *38*. In 1324 the abbot had an inn in Castle Baynard ward, in which his bailiff stayed when in London, and 18*s.* rent: King's College, Cambridge, Muniments, 'Oak Cartulary' (Davis, no. 146), f. 68; PRO, E106/7/18, m. 4.

271. France: Grestain, Normandy, abbey of B.V.M.
Fd. *c.* 1050; Benedictine.
In 1189 Richard I confirmed the abbey's English possessions, including a house in London, the gift of Maud, wife of Robert, count of Mortain, the founder (d. ? 1091): C. Breard, *L'abbaye de Notre Dame de Grestain* (Rouen, 1904), 29, 206–8. In 1291 the abbey held property in *1*.

272. France: Montreuil-sur-Mer, Picardy, abbey of St. Saviour and St. Winwaloe
Fd. *c.* 600, 878; Benedictine.
The abbey had property in Westcheap (apparently *81*) in the 12C: *Cartulary of St. Mary Clerkenwell*, ed. W. O. Hassall (Camden Soc. 3rd ser. 71, 1949), no. 273. The abbey had lost the property by the mid 13C. Deeds relating to the same property are in the archive of Balliol College, Oxford (**396**).

273. France: Paris, priory of St. Martin des Champs
Fd. 1060, 1079; Cluniac.
In 1107–8 William Giffard, bishop of Winchester, gave land *in foro* or *in magno vico*, formerly belonging to Odo, bishop of Bayeux (d. 1097), to the priory of St. Martin *de campis*: J. Depoin, *Recueil des chartes et documents de St. Martin des Champs, monastère parisien* (Ligugé and Paris, 1912–21); *Regesta* ii, no. 646. The archives of St. Martin des Champs, in Archives Nationales, Paris, are noted in *Inventaire, sommaire, et tableau méthodique des fonds conservés aux Archives Nationales*, I, *Régime antérieur à 1789* (Paris, 1871), pp. 499–501. To judge from papal confirmations, the priory ceased to lay claim to the London land between 1143 and 1147 (Archives Nationales, LL 1351, ff. 5, 6^v, 9^v), and no London rents are noted in the later 13C rentals (ibid., LL 1375, *passim*). The land may have passed to the English dependent priory of Barnstaple (fd. *c.* 1107), but no London land is recorded for either house in 1291.

274. France: St. Valéry-sur-Somme, Picardy, Abbey
Fd. 611, 10C; Benedictine.
In 1291 the abbey had property in *144*. In 1324 the renter of St. Valéry had an inn in Cripplegate ward in which he stayed when in London, and 6 shops, rendering 50*s.*: King's College, Cambridge, Muniments, 'Oak Cartulary' (Davis, no. 146), f. 68; PRO, E106/7/18, m. 4. The property subsequently passed to the dependent priory of Takeley, Essex (**233**).

PARISHES AND CHAPELS

LONDON PARISHES

Before the Reformation most London parishes had numerous endowments of lands or quit-rents for chantries, obits, and other purposes. These 'superstitious' endowments were transferred to the Crown on the suppression of the chantries in 1548. Only a few parishes have accounts or minutes dating from before 1548, but the endowments of most parishes were listed in 1546 (PRO, LR2/241–3) and 1548 (PRO, E301/34: *London and Middlesex Chantry Certificate, 1548*, ed. C. J. Kitching, LRS 16, 1980). Accounts for the lands of suppressed chantries in the Crown's hands from 1548 begin in PRO, SC6/Edw 6/293, mm. 40–106, and continue in subsequent accounts; see also PRO, LR2/244. Further surveys of former chantry lands still held by the Crown, and of rents reserved in grants of such lands, were made in 1550 (PRO, SC12/38/57–9), 1619 (PRO, SP14/106), and 1664 (PRO, SC11/957). In the following descriptions of parish records, the heading 'Estate before 1548' identifies the estate as recorded in the first 3 sources listed above (PRO, LR2/241–3, E301/34, and SC6/Edw 6/293). Kitching, *Chantry Certificate*, prints abstracts from E301/34 with cross-references to LR2/241–3. Not all the estates listed were forfeited to the Crown: endowments for church upkeep, education, and other non-superstitious uses were retained by the parish concerned. For records concerning the estates of suppressed chantries, see **438**.

After 1548, most parishes held, in addition to any non-superstitious endowments they had retained, some property associated with the church or churchyard. These holdings were soon augmented by new bequests and donations. Churchwardens' accounts and vestry minutes of the later 16th and 17th centuries are often not specific as to the location of parish properties; in some cases deeds and churchwardens' remembrancers provide a guide. Parish records contain much material not strictly relevant to this survey, and as a general rule only those containing information relating to parish properties, or lists of inhabitants, are listed below. The 'business relating to parish houses' noted for vestry minutes consists of decisions to let, buy or sell, view, or repair parish property. A few parishes have no surviving records of this kind before 1670.

Unless otherwise stated, all parish records listed below are in GL, described in the subject catalogue under L 92. Parts of some archives (*21, 38, 42, 103, 156, 157*) were catalogued on deposit as GL Additional MSS: for a general description of this class, see **460**. See also GL handlists *Churchwardens' accounts of parishes within the City of London* (2nd edn. 1969), *Vestry Minutes of parishes within the City of London* (2nd edn.

1964), *London rate assessments and inhabitants' lists in GL and CLRO* (2nd edn. 1968), and *Parish registers*, pt. 1 (4th edn. 1969).

Parishes are listed here in the order in which they appear in the key (pp. xviii–xix, above); modern surnames are given in parentheses, as are the parish code numbers.

275. St. Alban Wood Street (*2*)
Estate before 1548: *2, 62, 100, 131, 155*.

a. MS 7673/1, churchwardens' a/cs 1584–1639: rents (*2*, Holborn Bridge); at end, copy grant 1584 of land in par. to build shops, and a/c for cost of building. MS 7673/2, churchwardens' a/cs 1637–75: rents as in preceding vol. MS 7674, overseers' a/cs 1627–75, incl. (at end) assessment arranged by street, 1628.

b. MS 1264/1, vestry min. bk. 1583–1676: mostly par. business, incl. memorandum 1610 of dispute over par. lands; (at end), assessment 1649.

276. All Hallows Barking (*4*)
Estate before 1548: *4, 34, 48, 62, 126, 127, ?141*. See also GL, MS 10008: extract from certificate, late 16C.
The registers are at the church.

277. All Hallows Bread Street (*5*)
Estate before 1548: *5, 62*.

278. All Hallows Gracechurch (Lombard Street) (*9*)
Estate before 1548: *9*, Bell Alley, Lyon Alley.

a. MS 1853: deed 1576 (*43*); MS 18994, copy of same 1694.

b. MS 18486: vol. comp. 1813 of copy wills and deeds from 1548, copied from 'Old Book' (*9, 43, 68, 118, 149*). MS 19003: vol. similar to MS. 18486, comp. *c.* 1723, incl. abs. of leases from 1669, description of par. lands.

c. MS 4051/1, churchwardens' a/cs 1614–84: rents (unidentified), annuities (*9, 43*, probably *118*).

d. MS 4049/1, vestry min. bk. 1618–53: incl. business relating to par. houses; memorandum 1664 of par. bounds; assessments; (inverted at end) extracts from wills (as in MS 18486); copy of foundation survey 1669; abs. leases 1639–64 (*9, 43*). MS 4049/2, vestry min. bk., 1667–1702; incl. business relating to par. houses and rebuilding.

e. MS 19273, 19C legal papers: incl. draft abs. title, copy deeds, etc., from 1670 (*9, 118*).

279. All Hallows the Great (*10*)
Estate before 1548: *10, 96*.

a. MS 2142: copy leases etc. incl. lease 1669 (*96*).

b. MS 5170: vol. comp. *c.* 1780–1825, incl. copy wills and deeds from 1433, also disputes and decrees concerning par. land; view of par. houses 1614 (*10, 96*).

c. MS 818/1, churchwardens' a/cs, 1616–1708: receipts from rents, repairs to church and other buildings.

d. MS 819/1, vestry min. bk. 1574–1684: business relating to par. houses; assessments arranged by street; (pp. 148–50) inventories, incl. lists of leases; (p. 215 et seqq.) copies of bequests and gifts to par.; (p. 242) a/c of rents of par., 1666.

280. ALL HALLOWS HONEY LANE (*11*)
Estate before 1548: *11, 62, 71, 151*, Milk Street.

a. MS 5026/1, churchwardens' a/cs 1618–1743: rents (*111*); repairs to church; contributions lists, 1642; assessment *c.* 1672, houses named.

b. MS 5022: register of BMB 1538–1697; assessments.

281. ALL HALLOWS THE LESS (*12*)
Estate before 1548: *12*.

a. MSS 823/1, 2, churchwardens' a/cs 1630–51, 1651–86: rents (unidentified, *12*); assessments.

b. MS 824/1, vestry min. bk. 1644–1830: incl. (flyleaf) note of leases (cellar under church); assessment.

282. ALL HALLOWS STAINING (*13*)
Estate before 1548: unspec., but see **b**, below.

a. MS 7616: deeds and copies, 1597–1642 (*13, 46, 141*).

b. MS 4956/1, churchwardens' a/cs 1491–1550: rents, repairs; f. 185^v, copy will 1350 (probably *60*). MS 4956/2, churchwardens' a/cs 1533–1628 (partly duplicating MS 4956/1): rents, repairs; also copy wills and leases, from 1350 (*13, 60, 71*, St. Katharine by the Tower); f. 261, extract from bishop's register concerning church enlargement. MS 4956/3, churchwardens' a/cs 1645–1706: rents. MS 4958/1, churchwardens' rough a/cs 1558–73: rents, repairs; also clerks' wage rate assessments *c.* 1539–75, arranged by street. MS 4958/2: incl. rough a/cs 1574–8; rate assessments 1574–1605, arranged by street.

c. MS 4957/1, vestry min. bk. 1574–1655: business relating to par. houses; assessment 1652, arranged by street.

d. MS 90/2: 19C vol. of misc. extracts, incl. copy will 1577 (*13, 141*).

283. ALL HALLOWS ON THE WALL (LONDON WALL) (*14*)
Estate before 1548: *14*.
The parish of St. Augustine Papey (*29*) was united with this in 1442.

a. MS 3720: deed 1672 relating to gift of 1611 (*19*).

b. MS 5084: register of BMB 1583–1604; incl. at end, copy will, deeds, leases, 1611–72 (*14, 19, 101*).

c. MS 5090/1, churchwardens' a/cs 1455–1536 (not complete): apparently no rent income; repairs to church; printed in C. Welch, *Churchwardens' Accounts of the parish of Allhallows, London Wall, 1455–1536* (1912). MS 5090/2, churchwardens' a/cs 1566–1681: rents (unspecified), repairs (church and almshouse); assessments.

284. St. Alphage (*15*)
Estate before 1548: *2, 15, 62*.

a. MS 5752: vol. begun 1704 of abs. of wills, leases etc. from 1504 (*15*). MS 4854: 19C copy of preceding.

b. MS 1432/1, churchwardens' a/cs 1527–1553: rents, quit-rents, repairs (properties mostly unspecified; Wood St. mentioned 1530, Grub Street (*62*) 1536). MSS 1432/2–4, churchwardens' a/cs 1553–1677: rents; some memoranda about leases and fines; assessments.

c. MSS 1431/1, 2, vestry min. bks. 1593–1711: incl. business relating to par. houses; assessment 1596 arranged by street.

285. St. Andrew Castle Baynard (by the Wardrobe) (*18*)
Estate before 1548: *18, 71, 100*.

a. MS 1339: copy lease 1613 to this and other pars. of Puddle Dock (*18*). MS 14399: copy agreement to buy rent-charge, 1638 (*18*).

b. MS 2088/1, churchwardens' a/cs 1570–1668: rent receipts, quit-rent payments (probably all *18*); also incl. inquisition and evidence relating to patronage dispute, 1582–3; inventory of writings 1502–1656.

286. St. Andrew Cornhill (Undershaft) (*19*)
Estate before 1548: *19*.
The parish of St. Mary Axe (*101*) was united with this in 1562 and the archive contains records relating to both parishes.

a. MS 4142: deeds, etc., 1364–1782 (*19, 45, 101*). MS 4143: deeds and copies, 1593–1832 (*19*). MS 4139: deeds, etc., 1634–1805 (*19*, formerly *101*). MS 4149: 19C papers incl. extracts from wills, 16C–17C (*19, 68, 148*) and schedule of writings 1550–1662 (*19*). MS 1853: deed 1576 (*43*).

b. MS 4115: churchwardens' remembrancer, comp. *c.* 1620–5: incl. inventory of writings relating to par. properties from 14C; memoranda of rents due, and form of a/c 1625–6; memoranda of par. estates with dates of benefaction (*19, 43, 101, 148*). MS 4116: register of par. writings, comp. *c.* 1777–1850, probably taken from MS 4115. MS 4135: Benefactions Bk., comp. 1830, listing gifts to par. chronologically (pars. as in MS 4115, additional refs. to rents in Leadenhall Street, Lime Street, Pope's Head Alley). MS 4129: 'Trust Committee Remembrancer' of par. charities, 1840, incl. brief notes on origins.

c. MS 4147: arbitration 1522 in dispute over fraternity in church (*101*). MSS 4148, 4138: bishop's licence and letters patent for union of pars. 1561–2 (*19, 101*).

287. St. Andrew Holborn (*20*)
Estate before 1548: *20*.

a. MSS 9613, 10598, 10599A/1: documents relating to John Thavie's estate, incl. copy will 1350, deeds and papers 1524–1784 (*20*); MS 10599A/1 also incl. lease 1653 (*152*). MS 10597: deeds etc. relating to Lady Hatton's Charity, 1588–1662 (*62, 152*). MS 4260/1: deeds relating to Stafford Charity, 1604–88 (*20, 131*). MS 4257: Stafford Charity documents incl. Fire Ct. decree 1670 (*131*).

b. MS 4525: 'Particular of legacies' comp. 1655, listing rents in Shoe Lane, Holborn, Fetter Lane; (at end) copy purchase of rent 1647 (*20*). MS 4523A: list of benefactions, comp. 1775–6, noting properties (*20, 152*) and date of benefaction. MS 14150 is copy taken from preceding *c.* 1818.

c. BL, Harl. Roll H 28: lightwardens' a/cs, 1477–8, incl. rent receipts, arrears; printed in C.M. Barron and J. Roscoe, 'The medieval parish church of St. Andrew Holborn', *LTR* 24 (1980). GL, MS 19592: churchwardens' a/cs, 1666–79: rent receipts, costs of rebuilding par. houses.

d. MS 4251/1, vestry min. bk. 1624–1714: business relating to par. houses (*20*, unspecified).

e. MS 4249, 'Bentley's Register 1584': collection of memoranda relating to par. incl. vestry mins. *c.* 1584–1614, with lease decisions etc.; notes of par. feoffees; notes on history of par., based on records no longer surviving. Printed in E. Griffith, *Cases of Supposed Exemption from Poor Rates . . . with a Sketch of the history of the par. of St. Andrew Holborn* (1831), and discussed in Barron and Roscoe, *LTR* 24 (1980).

288. St. Andrew Hubbard (*21*)
Estate before 1548: *21*.

a. GL, Add. MSS 143–7: deeds and leases 1608–1627 (*21*). GL, MS 5068: 19C abs. of deeds and leases, 17C to 19C (*21*); also 19C schedule of par. bks. and papers incl. memoranda of properties.

b. MS 1279/1, churchwardens' a/cs 1454–1524: rents, repairs and quit-rent payments (unidentified, probably in par.). MSS 1279/2, 3, churchwardens' a/cs 1524–1712: incl. rents from 1574.

c. MS 1278/1: vol. cont. register of BMB 1538–1600 and vestry mins. 1600–68, intermixed; mins. incl. business relating to par. houses, bonds, memoranda of gifts to poor and par. (*21*).

289. St. Anne and St. Agnes (*23*)
Extracts relating to the parish from the following and other records are printed in W. McMurray, *The Records of Two City Parishes . . . SS. Anne*

and Agnes, Aldersgate, and St. John Zachary, London (1925).
Estate before 1548: *10, 23.*

a. MS 6775A: papers incl. copy will 1463 (*23*), rough list of documents,
16C. MSS 9886/1, 2: deeds and leases, 1546–1675 (*23*).

b. BL, MS Stowe 861: register incl. copy will, deeds, statutes, for William
Gregory's chantry, 15C to 16C (*23*). MS 9885: single folio 'Kalendar of
Wylles', 1461–1523, probably comp. 16C (*10*, unspec.). MS 1605: bk.
comp. late 16C of wills, deeds, leases, etc. from 1461 (*10, 23, 62*); also
incl. a/cs for Gregory's lands (rents, repairs, quit-rents) 1553–1564 (*23*).
MS 2294: schedule 1864 of title deeds from 15C (*23*), also list of gifts or
annuities, no dates (*62*).

c. MS 9883, churchwardens' a/cs for Gregory's lands, 1564–5, par.
revenues 1569–70: rents, quit-rent payments, repairs (probably *23*). MS
9884, churchwardens' a/cs, payments only, *c.* 1571: repairs to church and
par. houses. MSS 587/1, 1A, churchwardens' a/cs 1636–87: rents, fines,
quit-rent payments, repairs.

d. MS 9882, churchwardens' vouchers 1560–1682: acquittances received
for payments, incl. rents to Crown, repair works.

290. Sᴛ. Aɴɴᴇ Bʟᴀᴄᴋꜰʀɪᴀʀꜱ (*25*)
Created *c.* 1544.

a. MS 9331: abstracts incl. abs. title to rectory estate, 1577–1694. MS
9201a: 18C case papers incl. copy grant, 1607 (*25*). MS 10518: documents
1611–1734 relating to charity school (*18*). MS 9297: papers incl. copy will
1659 (*25*).

b. MS 9266: 'Gift Bk.' or churchwardens' remembrancer comp. 1743–
1821; lists annuities, incl. rent charge given 1659 (*25*). MS 9289: 'Benefaction Bk.', comp. 1838; memoranda of par. estates, incl. abs. deeds, and
gifts (*25*); notes on glebe (*18*).

c. MS 4511/1, vestry min. bk. 1669–1701: early years incl. information on
rebuilding, church foundations, etc.

d. MS 3839: 18C translation of royal charter to par. 1608.

291. Sᴛ. Aɴᴛoɴɪɴ (Aɴᴛʜoʟɪɴ) (*26*)
Estate before 1548: *10, 26, 95, 96, 145.*

a. MS 7615: 18C and 19C papers incl. schedules of deeds from 1616 (*26*).

b. MS 1046/1, churchwardens' a/cs 1574–1708: rents, fines (*20, 26*);
payments incl. a/c for building house by church, 1654.

c. MS 1045/1, vestry min. bk. 1648–1700: business relating to par. houses
(*26*); at end, rent a/cs 1666–8 (*20, 26*, Shoreditch, Whitechapel); undated
plans of houses in Field Lane (*20*), Whitechapel.

292. Sᴛ. Aᴜɢᴜꜱᴛɪɴᴇ Pᴀᴘᴇʏ (*29*)
The parish was united with All Hallows on the Wall (*14*) in 1442 and the

fraternity of the Papey was then founded in the former parish church: see
99.

293. St. Augustine by St. Paul (Watling Street) (*30*)
Estate before 1548: *30, 53, 111*.

a. MS 635/1, vestry min. bk.: incl. copy vestry orders 1601–1685, relating
to par. houses (*30, 73*, Abchurch Lane); assessments 1626, 1644, 1654.
MS 8901: 19C bk. of extracts from preceding (indexed); also cont. notes
on charities, with abs. wills from 1503, notes of leases 17C and later (*30,
73*, Abchurch Lane). MS 10553: description of charities from Char. Com.
report 1822, mentions old par. bks. and deeds no longer surviving.

294. St. Bartholomew by the Exchange (*32*)
Estate before 1548: *32, 48, 125*.

a. MS 4390: deeds incl. covenant to levy fine 1654 (*9*).

b. MS 9920: 19C notes on par. endowments, 16C and later (*9, 32*).

c. MS 4383/1, churchwardens' a/cs 1598–1698: rents, fines, with annual
inventory of evidences (*9, 32*, Southwark).

d. MS 4384/1, vestry min. bk. 1567–1643: business relating to par. houses
(not usually identified); also copy wills from 1526, indexed (*32*); p. 302,
inventory of goods in parsonage house 1619; p. 459, particular of gifts and
legacies. MS 4384/2, vestry min. bk. 1643–76: business relating to par.
houses; also (p. 19) copy will 1643 (*32*); assessments.

e. MS 8864: 19C case papers concerning lectureship endowment, citing
will 1631 and other 17C deeds (*9*).

295. St. Bartholomew the Great (*33*)
Created 1544.

a. MS 4029: papers incl. copy wills 1563, 1632 (*33, 42*). MS 4009, leases
1622–1738 (*33*).

b. MS 6489/1: 19C 'Register of documents', extracts and copies from
charters etc. relating to priory and parish from 12C. MS 6489/2: 19C
register of deeds, wills, leases from 1563 (*33, 42*).

c. MS 3989/1, incomplete series of churchwardens' a/cs 1625–1699, in 1
vol.: rents (unspecified). MS 9165, churchwardens' rough a/c 1662–3:
rent received and paid (*33*).

d. MS 3990/1, vestry min. bk. 1662–1710: memorandum of rents *c.* 1666;
business relating to assessments and rebuilding.

e. MS 4047/1: assessment 1652. MS 6677/2: register of BMB 1647–1716,
incl. list of contributors to steeple repair *c.* 1647.

296. St. Benet Fink (*36*)
Estate before 1548: *36, 116*.

a. MS 1303/1, churchwardens' a/cs, 1610–99: receipts from annuities and assessments; fine for lease 1665; dispute 1661 over houses (St. Swithin's Alley); assessments.

297. St. Benet Gracechurch (*37*)
Estate before 1548: *37*.

a. MS 4057: churchwardens' remembrancer comp. 1610–96; memoranda of benefactions from *c.* 1380, leases, rentals 1627–30 and 1653 (*37*); (p. 21) note of rent 1579 (*9*).

b. MS 1568, churchwardens' a/cs 1548–1723: rents, fines, quit-rent payments (*37*, unspecified).

c. MS 4214/1, vestry min. bk. 1631-1758: business relating to par. houses; 18C abstract of par. gifts and rents (*37*); assessment 1631, with much topographical detail; 'copy' assessment, ?*c.* 1631, houses named, possibly incomplete.

298. St. Benet Paul's Wharf (*38*)
Estate before 1548: *38, 141*.

a. GL, Add. MSS 198, 239: lease and copy, 1533 (*38*). GL, MS 1339: copy lease 1613 to this and other pars. (*18*).

b. MS 887, 'Register of Bequests', begun late 17C or 18C: extracts from MSS 877/1, 878/1; (pp. 31, 54) Fire Ct. Decrees (*38*); (p. 73), list of writings relating to tens. in par., 1626–71.

c. MS 878/1: vol. cont. churchwardens' a/cs 1605–48, incl. rents; vestry mins., 17C, incl. memoranda of leases, purchases, bequests (*18, 38, 116, 150*); assessments 1608–9, arranged by street.

d. MS 877/1, vestry min. bk. 1579–1674: incl. business relating to par. houses from 1640s; (p. 353) memoranda 1585, 1596, of tenants of shed belonging to par.

299. St. Benet Sherehog (*39*)
Estate before 1548: *39, 112*.

300. St. Botolph without Aldersgate (*42*)
The records described below include those for the fraternity of the Trinity, St. Fabian, and St. Sebastian in the parish church.
Estate before 1548: *42, 60, 149*.

a. GL, Add. MSS 57–80, 82–9, 92–8, 100–11, 118–127, 129, 132, 192–3: wills, deeds etc., 14C to 17C, par. and fraternity property (*42*). GL, MSS 5141, 10905, 10905A, 10907, 10907A, 10909, 10912, 10912A, 10913: deeds, etc. 15C to 17C (*42*). MS 10912B/1: deeds, 16C to 18C (*42, 75*). MS 10911: documents relating to John Morley's charity, 1589 (*75*). MS 10911A: deeds, 1592 (*99*). MS 10908: deeds and copies, 16C to 19C (*112*). Oxford, New College Archives, 9583: 18C abs. title, 14C to 16C, to par. property (*42*).

b. BL, Add. MS 37664 (Davis, no. 625; *Register of the fraternity of the Holy Trinity and SS. Fabian and Sebastian in St. Botolph without Aldersgate*, ed. P. Basing, LRS 18, 1982): cartulary of parish fraternity, comp. 14C and 15C, of wills, deeds, leases, 13C to 15C (*8, 42*); incl. a/cs for rents, repairs, quit-rent payments, *c.* 1432–56.

c. GL, MS 1473/1: bk. of 'parish rents and gifts', comp. 1667 and later: abs. deeds and memoranda, 14C to 17C (*33, 42, 62, 74, 75, 99, 112, 131*); rental *c.* 1667, noting leases, quit-rents; memoranda of leases granted, 1654–1744. MS 1473/2: similar bk., comp. end 18C. MS 6641: bk. of 'copies of records', comp. 18C or 19C, probably mostly from MSS 1473/1, 1453/1; also incl. parliamentary survey 1650 (rectory); table of benefactors and gifts, 1559–1694. MS 1461: schedule comp. *c.* 1840 of deeds and documents: lists surviving deeds from 1307, deeds noted in MS 6641, and 'deeds not previously listed', 14C to 18C (*42*; one deed for *149*).

d. MSS 1454/1–105: churchwardens' a/c rolls 1466–1636, incomplete series: rents, repairs, quit-rent payments (*42, 149*, some uncertain). MS 1455/1, churchwardens' a/cs 1638–79: rents, fines, quit-rent payments (*42, 112*, uncertain); assessments.

e. MSS 1453/1, 2: vestry min. bks. 1601–78: business relating to par. houses; MS 1453/1 begins with list of benefactors.

301. St. Botolph without Aldgate (*43*)
Estate before 1548: *43, 47*.

a. MSS 3485–6: will, leases, etc. 1557–1863 (*43*). MSS 3606/1, 2: deeds etc. 1574–1857 (*43, 113*). MSS 9961, 9964–7, 9969: deeds etc., 13C to 18C (*43*). MSS 4482, 9962–3: deeds etc., 16C to 19C (*78*). MS 9970: deeds etc., 1597–1623 (St. Katharine's precinct).

b. BL, MS Cotton App. xix (Davis no. 626): cartulary. 15C–16C (*43, 77, 78, 123*). GL, MS 9236: bk of vestry mins. and memoranda, comp. 1583–1640 and later, 3 vols. bound in 1; part 1, begun 1583, incl. copy wills, deeds, memoranda and vestry mins. to *c.* 1614 (*43*, St. Katharine's precinct); part 2, begun *c.* 1605, register of vestry orders, incl. business relating to par. houses, and (p. 51) inventory of writings (*43, 78*); part 3, later 17C, is particular of deeds, 1397–*c.* 1687 (*43, 78*). MS 2636: 17C vol. relating to John Webster's gift, incl. copy grant (*43*). MS 2630. 'Trust Money' bk., 19C: list of annuities from 1468 (*43, 46, 78*, Billiter Lane, Blackfriars); abs. of title deeds from 1562, with later plans (*43*). MS 2633: 19C vol. relating to Robert Dow's gift, 1605–1704 (*43*).

c. MS 9235/1, churchwardens' a/cs 1547–99, 2 parts bound in 1: part 1, fair a/cs 1547–85, some rents, repairs; part 2, rental 1559 of poor's lands (*43*) and rent a/cs, with fines, repairs, 1559–99. MS 9235/2, churchwardens' a/cs 1586–1691: rents, fines (in many years not itemized). MS 9237, churchwardens' poor a/cs, Portsoken ward, 1622–78: rental, rent receipts and mins. relating to same properties (*43*). PRO, SC11/32: rent rolls of poor's lands, 1653, 1665, 1678–9 (*43, 78*, Holborn, East Smithfield, Whitechapel).

d. Bodl, MS Rawl. D 796B (GL microfilm 427): vol. comp. *c.* 1633 by par. clerk, incl. a/cs of wardmotes 1622–37; list of Portsoken ward's evidences and bonds; extracts from par. vestry min. bks. 1605–24, incl. material relating to par. houses (*43*); abs. of deeds and writings, 16C to 17C (*43, 78*); copy deeds etc. from vestry min. bk. *c.* 1468–1601 (*43*); material relating to Portsoken; some a/cs 1614–22, incl. rents.

e. MSS 9234/1–7: vols. of par. clerks' memoranda, 1583–1600, incl. vestry mins. relating to par. houses (tables of contents in most vols. indicating subjects); extensive BMB information. MS 9223: register of BMB 1594–1607; also incl. rental, par. clerks' memoranda, and vestry mins. relating to par. estate, 1614–16 (*43*; partly illegible). MS 9234/8: vol. of par. clerks' memoranda 1617–25, 1640s–1672, incl. vestry mins. relating to par. houses; BMB information. T. R. Forbes, *Chronicle from Aldgate* (New Haven, Conn., 1971) uses information from MSS 9234/1–8 and 9223, also BMB Registers MSS 9220, 9221, 9222/1.

302. ST. BOTOLPH BILLINGSGATE (*44*)
Estate before 1548: *44, 56, 83, 108, 134, 148.*

a. MS 59 (Davis, no. 627): register, comp. 1418–1530, of deeds and wills 13C to 16C (*10, 19, 44, 56, 83, 85, 108, 134, 148, 152*, Lombard Street).

b. MS 942/1, churchwardens' a/cs 1603–74: incl. rents, fines (*44*).

c. MS 943/1, vestry min. bk. 1592–1673: incl. few mins. relating to par. houses; assessments 1592, 1593, 1606, arranged by street and wharf.

303. ST. BOTOLPH WITHOUT BISHOPSGATE (*45*)
Some of the parish's endowment was transferred to the Bishopsgate Institute at its foundation in 1894, and its title deeds (16C to 19C) probably form part of the uncatalogued collections there; see **454**, below. Estate before 1548: *45, 48, 58.*

a. MS 4524/1, churchwardens' a/cs 1567–1632: rents (probably *45*). MS 4524/2, churchwardens' a/cs 1632–62: rents, fines (probably *45*); (ff. 123, 139) agreement and a/c for building almshouses in churchyard, 1649; occasional inventories and valuations of paupers' goods. MSS 4525/1–4, churchwardens' rough a/cs, annual bklets. 1627–65, bound as 4 vols.: running receipts, incl. rents and payments, as in MSS 4524/1–2; binding of MS 4525/1, 1621 bklet., is 17C plan of 'A Watte Courte'. MS 1517, churchwardens' a/cs 1664–6: rents.

b. MS 4526/1, vestry min. bk. 1619–90: business relating to par. houses; at end, copies of gift deeds (*45*).

304. ST. BRIDE (*46*)
Estate before 1548: *46.*

a. MSS 6617/1–9: copy wills, deeds etc. (*46, 78, 92, 152*). MSS 3595, 6630, 14834: leases etc. 1623–1893 (*46*). MS 9341: Fire Ct. decree 1668 (*46*).

b. MS 14822: benefactors' bk. comp. late 17C; abs. and copy wills and deeds, 1635–75 (*46, 78, 92, 152*). MS 14824: similar bk. comp. 18C; lists benefactions (mostly money, one house). MS 6618: rough par. terrier, 19C; lists benefactions from 1432 (*46, 78, 92, 152*).

c. MS 6557/1, lease bk. 1647–1731: leases, Fire Ct. decrees; (pp. 59–63) rental 1666 (*46*).

d. MS 6652/1, churchwardens' a/cs 1639–78: rents, fines, quit-rent receipts and payments (*46*). MS 6553, churchwardens' rough a/cs 1665–6 (few details). MS 6626: rent rolls 1669, 1732 (*46*). MS 6567: bk. of churchwardens' receipts for Sandbach charity, 1606–1714 (*78, 92, 152*), rent 1610–30 (Fleet Street).

e. MS 6654/1, vestry min. bk. 1645–65: incl. business relating to par. houses (*46*), lease of rectory *c.* 1645.

f. MS 14819: list 1666 of householders of *46, 54, 92*, with claims for burnt properties. MSS 6570/1–3: 3 vols. of par. papers 1665–1757 (contents listed in vol. 1), incl. claims, petitions, vestry orders, settlements relating to post-Fire rebuilding; list of new houses 1677. MS 6570A: 19C calendar of MS 6570, also abs. wills relating to par. and church, 1307–1732, from HR, PCC, etc. MS 6539: list comp. 1638 of wills requesting burial in par., 1274–1587.

305. CHRIST CHURCH NEWGATE STREET (*47*)
This parish was created in 1547 from the former parishes of St. Audoen or Ewen (*27*) and St. Nicholas Shambles (*137*), the intramural part of the parish of St. Sepulchre (*152*), and the former precinct of the Greyfriars; the Greyfriars church became the parish church.

a. MS 9264: bk. (much damaged), cont. register of BMB 1538–68; copy and transl. letters patent 1547 (sites of Greyfriars and St. Bartholomew's Hospital; churches and lands of *27, 137*; tenements in *5, 12, 14, 15, 18, 20, 30, 38, 42, 45, 46, 54, 58, 63, 75, 92, 96, 98, 104, 112, 132, 135, 137, 144, 145, 149, 151, 152, 157*, St. Sexburga); memoranda of vestry mins; valuation of goods of *27* and *137*; view of church *c.* 1605.

b. St. Bartholomew's Hospital, Minutes of Board of Governors, vol 1: churchwardens' a/cs 1546–8, incl. rents (*47*).

c. MS 9163, 'Poor Rate Ledger', 1634–1704: assessments from 1634, arranged by street; at end, memoranda relating to par. houses.

306. ST. CHRISTOPHER (*48*)
Estate before 1548: *46, 48, 105*.

a. MS 4424, 'Record Bk.' comp. 1483 to end 17C: incl. copy wills 1357–1631 (*9, 11, 32, 36, 48, 80, 81, 94, 105, 118, 124, 149*); leases, 15C to 17C (*48, 54, 105, 148*); (f. 35) memorandum of par. lands, not dated; (ff. 139ᵛ–140) extract from chantry certificate and grant (*48, 54*); some vestry mins. relating to par. houses; assessments, 16C; inventories of church goods, various dates. Partly printed (chiefly vestry mins., inventories) in *Minutes of the Vestry Meetings and other records of the parish of St. Christopher le Stocks* . . . , ed. E. Freshfield (1886).

b. MS 4423/1, churchwardens' a/cs 1575–1661 (*Accomptes of the church- wardens of the Paryshe of St. Christofer's in London 1575–1685*, ed. E. Freshfield, 1885–95): rents, quit-rent payments (*48, 54*); annual assess- ments *c.* 1575–96, some arranged by street; inventories of goods, incl. writings relating to *54*. MS 4423/2, churchwardens' a/cs 1661–1735: rents, quit-rent payments (*54*); partly printed in Freshfield, *Accomptes*.

c. MS 4425/1, vestry min. bk. 1593–1731: business relating to par. houses (*48, 54*); assessments; partly printed in Freshfield, *Minutes of the Vestry Meetings*.

307. St. Clement Eastcheap (*49*)
Estate before 1548: *4, 36, 49, 56, 83, 125*.

a. MS 10963: deeds etc. 1620–1912 (*36, 49, 83*).

b. MS 977/1, churchwardens' a/cs 1636–1740: rents, fines, quit-rents; (f.1) list of yearly annuities and rents (Bishopsgate Street, unidentified); (ff. 50ᵛ–56ᵛ, 371–2) memoranda of benefactions with abs. wills, deeds, leases, 15C and 17C (*45, 49, 83, 94, 108, 112, 125*, Finch Lane, unidentified).

c. MS 978/1, vestry min. bk. 1640–1759: business relating to par. houses; at front, memorandum of par. houses 1641 (*49*, Eastcheap, Finch Lane, unidentified).

308. St. Dionis Backchurch (*51*)
Estate before 1548: *45, 51, 88, 155*, Fenchurch Street.

a. MS 11280A/1: par. papers incl. copy wills from 1581 (*51*, unidentified); Fire Ct. decree 1668 (*51*).

b. MS 17602: register of BMB 1538–1736; incl. on flyleaves view of houses, 1568 (*51*), charges of building cellar under parsonage house. MS 20213: list of par. benefactors, 1439–1726, comp. 18C (*51*). MS 1267/1: 19C vol. of abs. from par. records 1504–1854, incl. list of yearly gifts or annuities (*51*, unidentified).

c. MS 4215/1, churchwardens' a/cs, 1624–1729: incl. rents, quit-rent payments (*51*); assessment 1631; at end, plan of churchyard 1669.

d. MS 4216/1, vestry min. bk. 1647–73: business relating to par. houses.

309. St. Dunstan in the East (*53*)
Estate before 1548: *4, 10, 53, 83, 108, 141, 145*.

a. MS 7883: bk. of benefactions, comp. 1761 and later; incl. abs.wills and deeds from 1444 (*13, 53, 106, 149*, Mark Lane, Water Lane); rental and plans of par. lands, 1761.

b. MS 4887: 'Ancient Record Bk', begun *c.* 1494, much stained; incl. copy wills and leases, 1433–1556 (*4, 13, 53, 83, 116*, Mincing Lane);

churchwardens' a/cs 1494–1509, with rents, repairs, quit-rent payments (*4, 53, 83, 108, 145,* Crutched Friars); vestry mins. 1537–1651, incl. business relating to par. houses (*53, 116,* Old Fish Street).

c. MSS 7882/1, 2, churchwardens' a/cs 1635–84: incl. rents, fines, quit-rent payments (*53, 90, 116,* Mincing Lane, Old Fish Street, Thames Street, Tower Street; also rent from Chamber for Leadenhall in *149*); (p. 202) list of leases 1668–70.

310. ST. DUNSTAN IN THE WEST (*54*)
Estate before 1548: *20, 46, 54.*

a. MS 3784: wills and copy wills, 15C to 18C (*46, 54,* Holborn). MS 3757: deeds of John Land's charity, 1550–1847 (*54*).

b. MS 2983: register of deeds, agreements, etc., 1562–1648, relating to par. lands and annuities (*54, 98,* Fleet Street, Whitefriars); also relating to vicarage and tithes. MS 2984: similar register, principally leases, 1648–1738 (*54*). MS 2979: bk. of benefactions and memoranda, comp. 1734; incl. table of benefactions from 16C, copy will 1623 (*54*); memoranda relating to par. boundaries 1536 and foundation of Sion College 1623; quit-rents payable by par. 1634; conveyance of advowson to par. trustees 1647; list of yearly rents *c.* 1650 (*43, 54,* Fetter Lane, Whitefriars). MS 18720: incl. extracts from Char. Com. Report, 1819–25, noting benefactions (*43, 54, 98,* Fleet Street).

c. MS 2968/1, churchwardens' a/cs 1516–1608: rents, fines, repairs (*54,* Fleet Street, Shoe Lane, unidentified); (ff. 125–6, 288–9, 323) copy wills (*54, 98*); (f. 301) list of pews and rents 1561; 1593–4, list of contributors to new churchyard, arranged by street. MS 2968/2, churchwardens' a/cs 1608–1628: incl. rents, fines, repairs (*54,* Fetter Lane, Fleet Street), quit-rents received (*54, 98*); 1614, collection for church repair, arranged by street; MSS 2968/3–5, churchwardens' a/cs 1628–1681, similar to preceding vol.

d. MSS 3016/1, 2, vestry min. bks. 1588–1701: incl. business relating to par. houses.

e. MS 3783: assessments for scavengers' wages, 1628–30, arranged by street. MSS 2969/1–2: 2 vols. of assessments 1658–1671, arranged by street.

f. MS 3780: bk. of depositions about par. boundaries, 1600. MS 18717: papers relating to Dr. White's estate, incl. case papers and depositions about tithe and vicarage income 1620–1. MS 3781: bk. of depositions about title for case *c.* 1624. MS 18691: 19C papers about tithes, incl. copy licence, Chancery proceedings, ministers' a/cs, etc. from 1386. For papers concerning lands in *54* leased by the bishop of Chichester to the guild in the church of St. Dunstan 1548–57, see West Sussex RO, Ep. VI/54/1 (cf. **140c**).

g. MS 14819: list 1666 of householders of *46, 54, 92,* with claims for burnt properties.

311. St. Edmund Lombard Street (*56*)
Estate before 1548: *56, 62, 119*. PRO, E135/4/55 is part of the original return to the chantry inquiry.

a. MS 4286: leases, 17C to 19C (*56*). MS 20437: 18C extracts from will, 1593 (*56*). MS 4281: 19C papers incl. copy will, chantry certificate, 16C (*56*); also copy letters patent, 1549, 1608 (*9, 36, 44, 45, 56, 61, 93, 98, 100, 108, 141, 145, 149*). MS 20390: Fire Ct. decrees (*56*).

b. MS 4268: Register Bk. of parish estates; lists endowments, benefactions, 1788.

c. MS 20391: papers, 1672–6, with notes of arrears of par. rents since Fire.

d. MS 20388–9: papers, *c.* 1670–1, rel. to rebuilding of church, incl. viewers' report on site.

312. St. Ethelburga (*58*)
Estate before 1548: *58*.

a. MS 4241/1, churchwardens' a/cs 1569–1681; incl. rents, repairs (*58*); assessment most years, arranged by street.

313. St. Faith (*59*)
No estate recorded 1548.

a. MS 1339: lease 1613 to this and other pars. of Puddle Dock (*18*).

314. St. Gabriel Fenchurch (*60*)
Estate before 1548: *60*.

315. St. George Botolph Lane (*61*)
Estate before 1548: *61, 90, 108*.

a. MS 11020: Fire Ct. decree 1671 (*44*).

b. MS 4791: register of BMB 1546–1617; also incl. memorandum of laystall at Billingsgate 1592–3, notes of burials in church and yard *c.* 1390–1597; odd vestry mins., 1590s.

c. MS 951/1, churchwardens' a/cs, 1589–1695: incl. rents, repairs (*44, 61*); some vestry mins. incl. business relating to par. houses.

d. MS 952/1, vestry min. bk. 1600–85: principally elections.

316. St. Giles Cripplegate (*62*)
Estate before 1548: *15, 62*, Swan Alley.

a. MS 6085: vol. cont. register of wills and leases, *c.* 1500–1651 (*62, 144*, Watling Street); also incl. a/cs for John Sworder's charity (see **b**, below). MS 11828: bk. of abs. of title deeds to par. estates from 1323, comp. mid 18C and later (*23, 62, 87, 144, 155*, Bread Street, Philip Lane, Thames Street). MS 6086: bk. of wills extracts, *c.* 1500–1788, much faded, and MS 6087, 19C copy of same, made when more legible (*62, 144, 155*, Fetter

Lane, Watling Street). MS 9354: churchwardens' remembrancer of charitable bequests, 16C to 18C, comp. late 18C (*62*, Fetter Lane, Holborn, Philip Lane, Whitechapel, unidentified).

b. BL, Add. MS 12222, churchwardens' a/cs, 1570–80, 1596–1607: rents repairs (*62*, unidentified); also incl. some vestry mins. 1575–6 about letting Quest House. GL, MS 6047/1, churchwardens' a/cs, 1648–69: rents (*62, 144, 155*, Aldgate, Philip Lane, unidentified). Cf. MS 6085, incl. a/c for John Sworder's charity lands 1581–1618; rents, repairs (*62*).

c. MS 6048/1, vestry min. bk. 1659–1808: incl. business relating to par. houses, leases (*23, 62*, Mile End, unidentified).

317. St. Gregory (*63*)
Estate before 1548: *9, 42*.

a. MS 12190: petition *c.* 1686 with 2 plans relating to apportionment of St. Paul's churchyard.

b. MS 1336/1, vestry min. bk. 1642–1701: incl. details of repairs to church 1642–6; lease of rectory, 1663.

c. MS 25652: rate bk., 17C.

318. St. Helen (*64*)
No estate recorded 1548.

a. MS 10914: deeds and papers, 1599–1761 (*42, 64, 73, 141*, Houndsditch).

b. MS 3516: Benefactors' Bk. comp. *c.* 1784–1800; memoranda of benefactions (*64, 73, 141*); list of deeds (*64, 73, 141*). Bodl, MS Rawl. D 1480, ff. 402–5: 18C extracts of grants to par., 1599–1696 (*64, 73, 141*).

c. MS 6836, churchwardens' a/cs 1565–1654: rents; also (from f. 262) copy leases, extracts from wills (*64, 73, 141*); (ff. 282, 305 et seqq.) tithe assessments 1589, 1653, and related case. MS 6844/1, churchwardens' a/cs 1655–1715: rents.

319. Holy Trinity the Less (*67*)
Estate before 1548: *67, 152*, Old Fish Street.

a. MS 7299: misc. 18C papers incl. copy notes relating to case, with abs. will 1375 (*114*).

b. MSS 4835/1, 2, churchwardens' a/cs 1582–1725: rents, repairs (incl. rebuilding of church 1606); at end of MS 4835/1, vestry orders, memoranda of leases.

320. St. James Garlickhithe (*71*)
Estate before 1548: *9, 10, 13, 54, 67, 71, 74, 81, 93, 96, 114, 127, 152*.

a. MSS 4843, 7043, 7047: deeds, 1550–1671 (*71*). MS 4844: deeds, 1446–1500 (*152*). MS 4838: 17C copies of chantry certificate (*9, 10, 13, 67, 71,*

74, 81, 93, 96, 114, 127, 152). MS 7299: 17C to 18C papers incl. case 1664 (*114*).

b. MS 4820: vol. comp. 1750–1817, cont. copy wills and abs. titles to par. estate from 1375 (*9, 67, 71, 74, 93, 96, 114, 152*); abs. of gifts or annuities (*71*, Addle Hill, Black Swan Alley, Wood Street).

c. MS 4810/1, churchwardens' a/cs 1555–1627: rents, fines, repairs (*67, 71, 74, 93, 96, 114, 152*): (pp. 254–5) list of former chantries and lands (*10, 67, 71, 74, 93, 96, 114, 127, 152*, Fleet Street, Gracechurch Street); (p. 256) copy will 1572 (*71*). MS 4839, churchwardens' rent rolls *c.* 1625, 1626, 1629, 1648 (estate as in MS 4810/1, above). MS 4810/2, churchwardens' a/cs, 1627–99: rents, fines, etc. (as in MS 4810/1); (p. 144) memorandum 1653 of delivery of writings, listed. MS 4824: a/c of annual distributions to poor, 1598–1630; incl. at end, note of costs of building vestry house, 1598.

d. MS 4813/1, vestry min. bk. 1615–93: business relating to par. houses, copy wills and leases, extract from chantry certificate (as MS 4838). MS 4813/2, 'Vestry Book' 1643–86: record of elections of officers; at end, list of leases *c.* 1666–71.

321. St. John the Evangelist (*73*)
Estate before 1548: *73, 83*.

322. St. John Walbrook (*74*)
Estate before 1548: *43, 74, 118, 124*, nr. London Wall.

a. MSS 4881/1, 2: deeds, 1644–1850, with plans 1674 (*74*). MS 579: Fire Ct. decree 1671 (*74*).

b. MS 580: list of par. rents and annuities, 1673 (*74*, Finch Lane, unidentified). MS 581/1: vol. comp. *c.* 1720; (ff. 5–14) copy deeds, wills, Fire Ct. decree, from 1403 (*74, 124*); (ff. 15–16) list of annuities (*67, 74*); (ff. 23–33) list of par. bks. incl. contents of a lost register of deeds begun *c.* 1615 (*67, 74*); (f. 34) schedule of deeds; (f. 47ᵛ) plan of plot near churchyard 1751. MS 581/2: bk. of copy inventories of deeds, bks., etc., as in MS 581/1, signed by succeeding churchwardens. MS 455: memoranda incl. copy deeds relating to Lawrence Campe's charity, 1610–1887 (*74*); also incl. a/cs for rent from same, 1614–1853.

c. MS 577/1, churchwardens' a/cs 1595–1679: rents, quit-rents, fines; at end, list of goods bought, ? from departing tenant, 1644.

323. St. John Zachary (*75*)
Extracts relating to the parish from the following and other records are printed in W. McMurray, *The Records of Two City Parishes . . . SS. Anne and Agnes, Aldersgate, and St. John Zachary, London* (1925).
No estate recorded 1548.

a. MS 9516: view 1565 of tenement in dispute with Wax Chandlers' Company (*75*).

b. MS 1619: schedule of annuities etc., comp. *c.* 1730–1822, listing wills etc. from 1430 (*75, 159*).

324. ST. KATHARINE COLEMAN (*77*)
No estate recorded 1548.

a. MS 7728: deeds, leases, etc. 1626–75 (*77*). MS 7743: misc. par. papers 1616–1846, incl. receipts and bonds, probably associated with leases. MS 7742: copy wills etc. 1607–1729 (unidentified and outside London).

b. MS 1131: bk. of memoranda of par. bequests, comp. 1658 and later, incl. abs. wills, deeds from 1596 (*77*).

c. MS 1124/1, churchwardens' a/cs 1609–71: rents, annuities; numerous assessments, mostly arranged by street; (f. 113) copy lease 1630 (*77*); (ff. 249ᵛ–254ᵛ) abs. wills etc. from 1569 (*77*).

d. MS 1125/1, 'Choice of Par. Officers 1626–1751': incl. vestry mins., business relating to par. houses; assessment, *c.* 1653, arranged by street. MS 1123/1, vestry min. bk. 1659–1727: incl. business relating to church and burials; names of signatories to oath of allegiance 1663.

325. ST. KATHARINE CREE (*78*)
Estate before 1548: *94.*

a. MS 1213: deeds, leases (incl. leases of rectory) 1612–1777 (*78*).

b. MS 7896, 'Benefactors' Bk.', begun 1728: memoranda of wills, gifts etc., from *c.* 1605 (*43, 78*).

c. MS 1198/1, churchwardens' a/cs 1650–91: rents, fines (*43, 78*); tithe receipts; payments incl. rent for rectory; inventory 1650 of deeds and evidences (*43, 78*). MS 7706: leaves from overseers' a/c bk. 1638–42; assessments, receipt of annuities.

d. MS 1196/1, vestry min. bk. 1639–1718: incl. mins. and copy agreements relating to par. houses.

326. ST. LAWRENCE CANDLEWICK STREET (POUNTNEY) (*80*)
The parish church became the college of Corpus Christi and St. John the Baptist, with endowments given by Sir John de Pulteney and others, *c.* 1332. The college was dissolved in 1548 and the church became purely parochial again. See H. B. Wilson, *A History of the Parish of St. Laurence Pountney* (1831); incl. extracts from par. and other records.
Estate before 1548: *12* (rectory and property), *80, 98* (rectory).

a. MS 3936: copy will 1549 (*80*). MS 3933: 'Sundry papers 1599–1834', incl. bond 1599 (*80*), petition 1671 (*85*).

b. MS 3907/1, churchwardens' a/cs 1529–1681 (not paginated): rents, fines, payments incl. lease of rectory; assessments most years from 1584, arranged by street from *c.* 1647; copy will, 1549 (*80*); schedules of fixtures in house let to minister, *c.* 1582, 1594.

c. MS 3908/1, vestry min. bk. 1614–73, incl. some business relating to par. houses (*80, 85*).

327. St. Lawrence Jewry (*81*)
Estate before 1548: *62, 81, 104, 116, 127, 145*, Aldermanbury. In the later 16th and 17th centuries the parish held property in: *44, 62, 67, 80, 81, 116, 127, 145*, and a quit-rent (from 1637) in Cheapside.

a. MS 2593/1, churchwardens' a/cs 1579–1649: rents, fines, repairs, quit-rent payments (estate above); also incl. inventory of lands, 1580–1; contributions to and repairs of church, 1587–8; memorandum of purchase of house, 1606–7 (*145*); remembrance of writings, 1614–15; memorandum of leases 1616–17 (*80, 81*); signed receipts for lease of rectory, most years. MS 2593/2, churchwardens' a/cs 1640–97: rents, fines, repairs, quit-rent payments (as above).

b. MS 2590/1, vestry min. bk. 1556–1669; incl. business relating to par. houses (estate above); (p. 1) note of gift of land in *67*; (p. 8) rental 1559; (pp. 118–19) ref. to view of ten. at Puddle Wharf, 1598; (p. 426) schedule of goods in vicarage house, 1653; (pp. 432–7) settlement of vicar's stipend, charged on par. lands, 1652–3; (p. 611) Fire Ct. decree (Cheapside); inverted at end, schedule of wainscot in vicarage house, 1614. MS 2590/2, vestry min. bk. 1669–1720, incl. grants of post-Fire leases.

c. PRO, E101/675/44: tithe list, 1586. GL, MS 6974: register of BMB 1538–1605, incl. assessment 1643, arranged by street.

328. St. Leonard Eastcheap (*83*)
Estate before 1548: *10, 12, 44, 83, 87*.

a. MS 9372: 19C bk. of extracts from vestry mins. 1664–1790 (original apparently now lost) relating to par. estates (*83, 87*, Gracechurch Street).

329. St. Leonard Foster Lane (*84*)
Estate before 1548: *42, 46, 62, 84, 100, 128, 134, 148*.

330. St. Magnus (*85*)
Estate before 1548: *85, 87, 131, 157*, Gracechurch Street.

a. MS 1184, lease bk. 1668–1885: copy leases (*85, 87*); 18C plans.

b. MS 1179/1, churchwardens' a/cs, 1638–1734: rents (annual rental), fines, repairs, quit-rent payments; at end, plans (late 17C), note of par. bounds 1663, inventory of leases 1664, copy Fire Ct. decree 1667 (*85*), petitions about rebuilding church, memoranda of areas cut off par. lands before rebuilding.

c. MS 2791/1, vestry min. bk. 1667–1782: incl. business relating to rebuilding of par. houses, with plans.

331. St. Margaret Bridge Street (*87*)
Estate before 1548: *21, 56, 82, 87, 125*, unspec.

a. MS 1174, parish cartulary comp. *c.* 1477–84 with additions (Davis, no. 628; A. G. Dyson, 'A Calendar of the Cartulary of the Parish Church of St. Margaret, Bridge Street . . .', *Guildhall Studies in London History*, vol. 1, no. 3 (1974), 163–91): copy and abs. wills and deeds 1220–1484 (*4, 21, 44, 56, 61, 85, 87*, Mark Lane; also refs. to *15, 83, 131, 135*); (ff. 95ᵛ–97ᵛ) abs. wills 1625–39 (Anchor Lane).

b. MS 1176/1, churchwardens' a/cs, 1576–1678: rents, fines, repairs, payment of quit-rent (*87*, unspecified); assessment 1599.

c. MS 1175/2, vestry min. bk, 1578–1789; business relating to par. houses; note, *c.* 1581, of sittings in church; at end, 18C memorandum of some legacies and gifts.

332. Sᴛ. Mᴀʀɢᴀʀᴇᴛ Lᴏᴛʜʙᴜʀʏ (*88*)
Estate before 1548: *88, 92, 155*.

a. MS 8871: leases etc. 1607–60 (*88, 155*).

b. MS 4352/1, vestry min. bk. 1571–1677 (*The Vestry Minute Book of St. Margaret Lothbury*, ed. E. Freshfield, 1887): incl. business relating to par. houses (*88*); assessments.

c. MS 8861: misc. churchwardens' papers, 1577–1684, incl. memorandum of par. bounds, 1657.

333. Sᴛ. Mᴀʀɢᴀʀᴇᴛ Mᴏsᴇs (*89*)
Estate before 1548: *43, 46, 51, 89, 131, 138*, Distaff Lane.

a. MS 10137: 16C copy chantry certificate (*89*).

334. Sᴛ. Mᴀʀɢᴀʀᴇᴛ Pᴀᴛᴛᴇɴs (*90*)
Estate before 1548: *53, 90*, unspec.

a. MS 4569: vol. of inventories etc., 15C and 16C (fragmentary), incl. memoranda of par. estates, comp. *c.* 1470, with copy deeds (*53, 90, 93*). MS 4572: churchwardens' remembrancer, comp. *c.* 1704–40: inventory of deeds, late 17C (*53, 90*). MS 4573: similar vol. comp. *c.* 1772, incl. abs. lease 1645 (*53*).

b. MSS 4570/1–3, churchwardens' a/cs 1506–1760: rents, fines, repairs (*53, 90*, unspecified); MS 4570/2 also incl. a vol. with vestry mins., early 17C, with business relating to par. houses.

c. MS 4571/1, vestry min. bk. 1640–83; incl. copies of earlier mins., probably from MS 4570/2; business relating to par. houses (*53, 90*); abs. wills, copy agreements; at end, copy legal proceedings, 16C (*53*); memorandum of leases 1565–1662.

d. MS 4579: legal papers 1543–1762, relating to property disputes, incl. copy wills and leases, Fire Ct. decree (*90*). MS 4575: copy Exchequer judgment, 1554 (*53*, tenants listed).

335. St. Martin Ludgate (*92*)
Estate before 1548: *46, 49, 53, 92*.

a. MS 1311/1 (Davis, no. 629): ff. 13–66, record bk., comp. 15C, of copy wills, deeds, pleas, from 13C (*92*; also (ff. 31ᵛ, 56–58) *46*; (f. 33) *49*; (f. 45) *137*; (ff. 51ᵛ–55ᵛ) *104, 127, 141*); ff. 1–12, 68-end, 16C–18C memoranda, vestry mins. 1576–1715, incl. business relating to par. houses, pew rents, assessments. MS 1334: 18C bk. of memoranda of gifts and rents, 1594–1739 (*10, 43, 85, 92, 152*). MS 1512: 18C bk., material similar to preceding, incl. extracts from wills, abs. title (to *10*).

b. MS 1313/1, churchwardens' a/cs, 1649–90: rents (not located), repairs to parsonage house, memoranda of arrears on rates; inventory of furniture etc. in parsonage and vestry house, 1650.

c. For vestry mins. 1576–1715, see **a**, above.

d. MS 14819: list 1666 of householders of *46, 54, 92*, with claims for burnt properties.

336. St. Martin Orgar (*93*)
Estate before 1548: *10, 49, 62, 93, 98, 125, 141, 157*.

a. MS 968, 'Abstract Memorandum book, 1862': incl. copy and abs. wills from 1431 (*93, 96, 141, 152, 157*); lists of expired leases from 1658 (*152, 157*).

b. MS 959/1, churchwardens' a/cs and vestry mins.: (ff. 1–15ᵛ) rental and a/cs, *c*. 1469–71, rents, quit-rents, repairs (*21, 49, 51, 62, 93, 96*); (ff. 17ᵛ et seqq.) concurrent a/cs 1557–1707 and vestry mins., 1557–1631, rents, fines, business relating to par. houses (*93, 141, 152, 157*); (ff. 381ᵛ–382) signatures to 'Vow and Covenant', 1643; (ff. 388–396) copy deeds, wills etc. from 1547 (unspecified, *152*, Lambeth Hill); (f. 396ᵛ) copy order of masses, 1240; (f. 397–9) inventory 1629 of writings from 1240 (*49, 62, 93, 125, 141, 152, 157*); (ff. 400ᵛ–401) signatures to 'Protestation', 1641. Lambeth, CM ix/14, churchwardens' a/cs 1517–1637: rents, repairs (*49, 62, 93, 98, 125, 141, 157*, Cock Alley, Raven Alley).

c. MS 959/2, vestry min. bk. 1644–95: principally elections, some business relating to par. houses; inverted in centre, notes of collections on briefs, 1644–81, sometimes listing contributors; notes of distribution of Cotton's gift to poor.

337. St. Martin Outwich (*94*)
Estate before 1548: *85*, Watling Street.

a. MS 11405: deeds 1589–1707 (*94*).

b. MS 11396, 'Abstract of Charities', comp. 1735, 1771: 2 similar vols. of abs. deeds and wills from 1538 (*14, 94*).

c. MS 6842, churchwardens' a/cs 1508–28, 1537–46: rent or quit-rent (probably *94*); assessment 1545, some locations; at end, copy deed and wills, 1536, 1543 (*85*). MS 11394/1, churchwardens' a/cs 1632–1743: no rent income, some legacies; *c.* 1640, notes of evidence (incl. *14*); refs. 1645, 1664 to burials in Papey churchyard (*14*).

338. St. Martin Pomary (*95*)
Estate before 1548: *43, 95*, Bishopsgate Street, ward of Farringdon within.

339. St. Martin Vintry (*96*)
Estate before 1548: *124*.

340. St. Mary Abchurch (*98*)
Estate before 1548: *98*, unspec.

a. MS 9450: vol. comp. *c.* 1732, incl. inventory of leases from 1647 (*96, 98*).

b. MS 3891/1, churchwardens' a/cs 1629–92: rents, fines, quit-rent payments (*96, 98*).

c. MS 3892/1, vestry min. bk. 1667–1749: incl. letting of tofts, 1668, 1671 (*96, 98*).

341. St. Mary Aldermanbury (*99*)
Estate before 1548: *99, 100, 151*.

a. MSS 3598/1–2: 19C papers incl. copy deeds from 1580 (*99*), copy letters patent 1606 (rectory).

b. MSS 3556/1–2, churchwardens' a/cs 1570–92, 1631–77: rents, fines, annual tithe receipt, payments for quit-rents, farm of rectory, repairs (*99*).

c. MSS 3570/1–2, vestry min. bks. 1569–1763: incl. business relating to par. houses; assessments.

d. MSS 2500A/1–6: 6 assessments 1577–96 (no topographical detail).

342. St. Mary Aldermary (*100*)
Estate before 1548: *5, 10, 15, 44, 62, 100, 126*.

a. MS 9048: misc. papers 1605–1861, incl. bond 1605 for repairs; lease 1672 (*100*); plan, late 17C (Bow Lane).

b. MS 4865: vol. comp. early 17C of abs. wills, deeds, memoranda relating to par. estate, 1569–1635 (*43, 100, 131*). MS 10991: papers incl. abs. comp. 1742 of leases from 1629 (*100*).

c. MS 6574, churchwardens' a/cs, 1597–1665: rents, fines, quit-rent payments (no details of locations). MS 4863/1, churchwardens' a/cs for poor, 1630–1708: income from gifts; assessments 1634.

343. St. Mary Axe (*101*)
The parish was united with St. Andrew Undershaft (*19*) in 1562; the records listed for that parish also include material relating to this.

344. St. Mary Bothaw (*103*)
Estate before 1548: *74, 93, 100, 103, ?124, 155*.

a. GL, Add. MSS 492–505: leases 1594–1696, incl. plan 1680 (*89*).

345. St. Mary le Bow (*104*)
Estate before 1548: *26, 46, 104, 129, 145, 155, 156*.

a. MS 7811: papers, 18C and 19C, incl. copy and abs. deeds and leases from 1538 (*104*).

b. MS 5006/1, vestry min. bk. 1675–1763: incl. (f. 339 et seqq.) abs. leases from 1668 (*104*).

c. MS 10917, 'Annals of St. Mary le Bow' by Thomas Lott: 19C MS history of church and parish, with notes on vaults and excavations.

346. St. Mary Colechurch (*105*)
Estate before 1548: *100, 105*.

a. MS 66, churchwardens' a/cs 1612–1700: no rent income; rent and repairs paid for house for rector (*105*); numerous assessments.

b. MS 64, vestry min. bk. 1612–1701: principally elections; business relating to par. houses (*105*); assessments and collections; at end, lists of sittings in church, 1613–58.

c. Mercers' Company, Reg. of Writings ii: incl. (ff. 11–14ᵛ) tithe and other assessments for this par., 1558–1602.

347. St. Mary at Hill (*108*)
Estate before 1548: *4, 21, 48, 61, 83, 84, 108*.
See H. Littlehales, *The Medieval Records of a London City Church, 1420–1559* (EETS 1904–5, 2 pts.) for transcripts of much of MSS 1239/1–2.

a. MS 4809/1: deeds 1637–1737, relating to rectory and advowson.

b. MS 1239/2: vol. of wills and a/cs, begun 1486; (ff. 2–23ᵛ, 78–80, 106ᵛ, 113ᵛ–114ᵛ) wills, deeds, leases, memoranda 1323–1577 (*21, 43, 48, 61, 83, 84, 108*); (f. 24) inventory of goods in house, 1485 (Botolph Lane); (ff. 29–105, 112ᵛ) rental 1485 and a/cs 1485–1537, mostly summary of rents, repairs, quit-rent payments (*21, 43, 48, 61, 83, 84, 108*); at end, names of (some) parishioners, 1486.

c. MS 1239/1, churchwardens' a/cs, 1420–31, 1477–1526, 1537–40, 1549–59: rents, repairs, quit-rent payments (as in MS 1239/2); (ff. 125–40) inventory of goods in house, after 1525 (Billingsgate).

d. MS 1240/1, vestry min. bk. 1609–1752: incl. business relating to par. houses; 1635 (not paginated), note of leases, followed by inventory of writings, 1629 (*83, 108*, Eastcheap, St. Katharine's and East Smithfield); (ff. 40–1) rental 1637; (ff. 41ᵛ–42), list of gifts and annuities (*44, 108*, unspecified); at end, similar list of gifts and annuities, 1635–6; terrier of glebe, 1637.

348. St. Mary Magdalen Milk Street (*111*)
Estate before 1548: *81, 104, 111, 123*.

a. MS 2596/1, churchwardens' a/cs 1518–1606: rents, fines, repairs, quit-rent payments (*11, 81, 104, 111, 123*); (f. 1) copy will 1375 (*111*); also incl. some vestry mins., later 16C, relating to par. houses; assessments. MS 2596/2, churchwardens' a/cs 1606–67: rents, fines, quit-rent payments; (f. 1) copy will 1375 (*111*); some vestry mins. to 1619; assessments.

b. MS 2597/1, vestry min. bk. 1619–68: business relating to par. houses; (ff. 59, 67, 68–73) signatures to 'Protestation' and 'Solemn League and Covenant'; assessments incl. rate 1639 with topographical notes. GL, Add. MS 301 is an index to MS 2597/1.

349. St. Mary Magdalen Old Fish Street (*112*)
Estate before 1548: *10, 15, 112, 135*.

a. MS 1339: copy lease 1613 to this and other pars. of Puddle Dock (*18*). MS 1346: leases 1644–1810 (*112*).

b. MS 1342, 'Account of gifts and legacies', comp. 1764–1835: copy deeds, leases from 1448 (*18, 112*); list of benefactions (*112*).

c. MS 1341/1, churchwardens' a/cs, 1648–1721: rents, fines.

350. St. Mary Somerset (*116*)
Estate before 1548: *53, 116*.

a. MS 5714/1, churchwardens' a/cs, 1614–1701: rents, fines (properties not identified).

351. St. Mary Staining (*117*)
No estate recorded 1548.

a. MS 1542/2, churchwardens' a/cs 1644–1718: rents 1646–55 (probably *117*).

352. St. Mary Woolchurch (*118*)
Estate before 1548: *105, 118, 119, 124, 132*.

a. MS 1013/1, churchwardens' a/cs: rents, repairs, (*118*, Bearbinder Lane). MS 1012/1, vestry mins. 1647–72: leases, repairs (*118*).

353. St. Mary Woolnoth (*119*)
Estate before 1548: *119*, Sherborne Lane.

a. BL, MS Harl. 877 (Davis, no. 630): register, comp. 15C to 16C, of deeds and wills from 14C (*98, 119, 124*). GL, MS 1005/1: register, comp. 16C to 19C, of deeds and wills from 14C (*98, 119, 124*; also refs. to *51, 96, 148*, Fleet Street, unspecified).

b. MSS 1002/1A, 1B, churchwardens' a/cs 1539–1641: rents, quit-rents (*119, 134*, unspecified); some vestry orders; assessments.

354. St. Matthew Friday Street (*120*)
Estate before 1548: *120*.

a. MS 1016/1, churchwardens' a/cs 1547–1678: rents, fines (*120*, unidentified); tithe assessment 1650; some vestry mins.; (f. 9ᵛ) list of deeds (Bread Street).

b. MS 3579, vestry min. bk. 1576–1743: incl. business relating to par. houses (*120*); abs. and copy leases of vestry and other rooms; assessments 1624, 1634.

355. St. Michael Bassishaw (*123*)
Estate before 1548: *43, 74, 123*, ?unspec. See also PRO, E301/89: original certificate, 1546.

a. MS 2496: papers, copy deeds, leases, 1589–1816, and abs. or memoranda of deeds, 14C and later (*123*, possibly some unidentified).

b. MS 3505: 'Record and Assessment Bk.' cont. notes and abs. relating to par. and ward, *c.* 1610–63, incl. copy wills, leases (*123*); assessments by street; certificate of strangers, 1618; valuation of living, 1638.

c. MS 2601/1, churchwardens' a/cs 1617–1716: rents, quit-rents (*123*); repairs and paving, vestry and churchyard; assessment 1625. MS 1731/1, a/cs of Lady Bainton's charity, 1618–63: rents, also copy deeds from 1575 (*123*).

356. St. Michael Cornhill (*124*)
Estate before 1548: *9, 45, 108, 124, 151*, Gracechurch Street.

a. MSS 392–405, 4091: deeds and leases from 1623 (*124*).

b. MS 4083: 'Ancient' bk., comp. 1693, of abs. and copy wills, deeds, and leases, 16C and 17C (*32, 45, 124, 144*). MS 4084: 19C copy of MS 4083. MS 4082: 19C vol. of copy papers, cases etc. relating to par. property from 16C (*45*).

c. MS 4070/1, churchwardens' a/cs 1455–76, 1547–1608 (see *The accounts of the churchwardens of the parish of St. Michael, Cornhill, . . . from 1456 to 1608*, ed. W. H. Overall, *c.* 1869–71): no early rents, some repairs to church; rents, quit-rents, 1547–1608 (*45, 124*, Cannon Street, Finch Lane); at end, memoranda incl. abs. wills, notes of deeds (*32*, Gracechurch Street); notes on site of Royal Exchange (*32, 48, 124*), list of obits; (f. 196) drawing of steeple, ?1421.

d. MS 4072/1, vestry min. bk. 1563–1697: business relating to par. houses, churchyard (*32, 45, 124, 144*); assessment by street 1624; extracts printed in Overall, *Accounts*.

357. St. Michael Crooked Lane (*125*)
Estate before 1548: *10, 80, 83, 85, 125, 149*, unspec.

a. MSS 830, 832, 834: leases 1654–69 (*125*).

b. MS 2767: bk. of par. estates and donations, incl. copy wills, leases, vestry decisions, 16C to 17C (*44, 98, 125*, Westcheap); wills relating to quit-rents payable by Fishmongers' Company (*85, 93, 112*, Black Raven Alley).

c. MS 1188/1, churchwardens' a/cs 1617–93: rents, fines (*98*; unidentified, probably *125*).

358. St. Michael Paternoster (*126*) with Whittington College
The parish church of *126* became a college of priests, with an almshouse attached, under the will of Richard Whittington (d. 1424). The endowment of the college was administered by the Mercers' Company, and the records relating to it are at Mercers' Hall (**47**). See J. Imray, *The Charity of Richard Whittington* (1968).
Estate (other than Whittington College) before 1548: *83, 96, 126, 136*.

a. MS 5142, register of BMB 1558–1653: on flyleaf, note of gift 1620 (*155*).

359. St. Michael Queenhithe (*127*)
Estate before 1548: *81, 127*.

a. PRO, E101/675/43: a/c of Hatherley's lands, 1482–3 (*123*, Baynards Castle, unidentified). PRO, E315/406, ff. 33–5, and PRO, E315/402, f. 35: a/c and rental of Hatherley's chantry in church of St. Michael Queenhithe, 1525–6 (*123, 127*, Baynards Castle). GL, MS 4825/1, churchwardens' a/cs 1625–1706: rents, repairs (*127*, unidentified); collections or assessments, 1642.

b. MS 4827/1, vestry min. bk. 1667–1808: business relating to par. houses, incl. leases (*116, 127*).

360. St. Michael le Querne (*128*)
Estate before 1548: *123, 126, 128*, Leadenhall.

a. MS 805: register of deeds, leases etc. 1570–1837 (*128, 131, 158*).

b. MS 2895/1, churchwardens' a/cs 1514–1604: rents, fines, repairs (*128, 131, 158*); copy leases (*128*). MS 2895/2, churchwardens' a/cs 1605–1718: rents, fines (*128, 131, 158*); at end, memorandum of lease (?*131*).

361. St. Michael Wood Street (*129*)
Estate before 1548: *81, 129*. See also PRO, SC12/11/44: certificate, 1546×48.

a. MS 1575: will 1422 (*129*). MSS 520–522: deeds relating to advowson, 17C.

b. Bodl, MS Rawl. B 377, f. 179r-v: 18C translation of deed 1392 (*129*).

c. MS 524/1, churchwardens' a/cs 1619–1718: rents, fines, payment of quit-rents (*129*, unidentified); collection for church repair, 1620–1. MS 525/1, poor rate a/c bk. 1644–1702: assessments; memoranda of leases 1654–5 (unidentified).

362. St. Mildred Bread Street (*131*)
Estate before 1548: *81, 127, 131*, Smithfield.

a. MS 3470/1A, churchwardens' a/cs 1648–93: rents, fines, payment of quit-rents (*112, 131*, Golden Lane, Queenhithe, Stew Lane); annual lists of evidences (mostly unidentified).

363. St. Mildred Poultry (*132*)
Estate before 1548: *98, 105, 132*.

a. MS 4429: register of BMB 1538–1724; between 1557–8, notes on par. lands (*58, 132*).

b. MS 62/1, vestry min. bk. 1641–1713: business relating to par. houses, incl. leases (*132*, unidentified).

364. St. Nicholas Acon (*134*)
Estate before 1548: *134*, Abchurch Lane, Lombard Street.

a. MS 4060/1, vestry min. bk. 1619–1738: business relating to par. houses (*134*, Abchurch Lane); memorandum of dispute, 1636 (*56, 134*).

b. MS 4296: plan bk. 1761 incl. plans of par. estate and churchyard.

365. St. Nicholas Cole Abbey (*135*)
Estate before 1548: *114, 135*.

a. MS 1533: fragmentary list of inhabitants of jurymen of par., 16C.

366. St. Nicholas Olave (*136*)
Estate before 1548: *127*.

367. St. Nicholas Shambles (*137*)
Taken into Christ Church Newgate Street (*47*) in 1547.

a. St. Bartholomew's Hospital, SBL 9/2, churchwardens' a/cs 1453–1526: rents, payment of quit-rents (*137*, unidentified). Ibid., Minutes of Board of Governors, vol. 1, churchwardens' a/cs 1526–46: rents (*137*, Aldersgate Street, Cheke Lane, Pentecost Lane); assessments.

368. St. Olave Hart Street (*141*)
Estate before 1548: *141*.

a. MS 861: register bk. comp. 1739 of wills, deeds, leases etc. from 16C (*13, 58, 141, 155*).

b. MSS 872/1–14: poor rate bks. 1647–78; assessments. MS 863: bk. of communion collections 1642–1707. MS 875: assessment 1661 for church repair.

369. St. Olave Old Jewry (*142*)
Estate before 1548: *77, 81, 132, 142*.

a. MS 3057: register bk. comp. 1649 of abs. wills etc, 17C (*2, 43, 157*).

b. MS 4409/1, 2, churchwardens' a/cs 1586–1705: rents, fines, payment of quit-rents, repairs (*142, 157*, unidentified); lists of evidences (*2, 80, 98, 157*).

c. MS 4415/1, vestry minute bk. 1574–1680: business relating to par. houses (*142, 157*); agreement 1614 with *88, 155*, over ward responsibilities; collections and assessments; signatures to 'Solemn League and Covenant', 1643.

370. St. Olave Silver Street (*144*)
Estate before 1548: *144*.

a. MS 1257/1, churchwardens' a/cs 1630–82: rents, some repairs (*144*, Pope Lane, St. Anne's Lane).

371. St. Pancras Soper Lane (*145*)
Estate before 1548: *26, 38, 54, 71, 85, 126, 128, 132, 145*.

a. MS 5020 (Davis, no. 631): 'Evidence Bk.', comp. early 16C to 19C, of wills, deeds, leases, etc. (*26, 38, 53, 62, 105, 126, 132, 145*; (ff. 51–74) refs. to *20, 45, 54, 62, 67, 85, 88, 89, 90, 92, 95, 104, 116, 118, 120, 126, 128,135,156*); (ff. 8–9) list of obits (*105, 132, 145*, Vintry); (f. 101) plan 1811 (*145*). MS 8656A: 19C extracts and translations from MS 5020.

b. MS 5018/1, churchwardens' a/cs 1616–1740: rents, repairs (*62, 145*, Houndsditch (possibly in *62*), unidentified).

c. MS 5019/1, vestry min. bk. 1626–99: business relating to par. houses (*62, 145*, Houndsditch); assessments.

d. MS 7350: 18C bk. of rules relating to burials in churchyard, with plan.

e. PRO, E135/19/35: draft licence, 1534, to sell house in *126*.

372. St. Peter Broad Street (le Poor) (*148*)
Estate before 1548: *148*, unspec.

373. St. Peter Cornhill (*149*)
Estate before 1548: *14, 21, 58, 94, 149, 151*, 'St. Albert', Leadenhall.

a. MS 4194, deeds and leases 1603–1879 (*149*). MS 10994A, copy deeds and papers, 17C to 19C (*149*).

b. MS 4158 (Davis, no. 632): cartulary comp. 15C, of wills, deeds (*21, 61, 85, 94, 105, 118, 124, 149, 151, 155*); (f. 249 et seqq.) copy proceedings relating to tithes, par. boundaries, etc. MS 70/1: vol. begun 16C, of lists and transcripts of deeds and wills, 14C to 17C (*21, 61, 85, 94, 105, ?118, 149, 151*, Bishopsgate ward); also (ff. 122–70) extracts from Cornhill ward bk., 1653–1733 (see **416**, below). MS 70/2: 18C vol. incl. copy leases, transcripts, 17C to 18C (*87, 88, 149, 155*), and 18C plans. MSS 4210/1–2: 19C schedules of par. records and deeds.

c. Bodl, MS Rawl. D 897 (GL, Microfilm 426), churchwardens' a/cs

1664–90: rents and fines (props. not always identified but incl. *85* or *87, 149, 155*).

d. MS 4165/1, vestry min. bk. 1574–1717; business relating to par. houses, incl. copy wills, views (*85* or *87, 149, 155*); assessments.

374. St. Peter Paul's Wharf (*150*)
Estate before 1548: *53, 62, 150*. See also **17**.

375. St. Peter Westcheap (*151*)
Estate before 1548: *151*, unspec.

a. MS 645/1, churchwardens' a/cs 1435–45, 1535–6, 1555–1601: rents, payment of quit-rents, repairs (*80, 151*; possibly *53*); (f. 161ᵛ) list of rents and charges, *c.* 1450; (f. 252 et seqq.) abs. and memoranda of wills, deeds etc. from 14C (*53, 80, 151*); 16C assessments by precinct. MS 645/2, churchwardens' a/cs 1601–1702: rents, fines (unidentified, probably *151*); (f. 9ᵛ) memoranda about former par. land (*80*).

b. MSS 642/1, 2, vestry min. bks. 1619–1787: business relating to par. houses (probably *151*); list of fittings in parsonage house, 1653; assessments, some by precinct or street. Bodl, MS Rawl. D 148, ff. 474–5: extracts from vestry bks. 1623–97.

376. St. Sepulchre (*152*)
Estate before 1548: *20, 42, 88, 152*. See also PRO, SC12/11/47: certificate, 1548, with copy wills and rental (*42, 88, 152*).

a. MS 3281/1: deeds, 16C to 17C (*152*). MS 3183: deeds 1674–97 (incl. earlier refs.), Reeve's bequest (Threadneedle Street). MS 8928: deeds 1634–1877, Dickinson's charity (*77*).

b. MSS 7227, 7228 (copy): churchwardens' remembrancer, comp. 17C, noting endowments, leases, etc., 16C to 17C (*9, 152*, Blackfriars, Watling Street). MS 3209: record of donations to par., 1780–6, continuation of MS 7228 with refs. to it. MS 3215: 19C schedule of 17C deeds and leases (*152*).

c. MSS 3146/1, 2, churchwardens' a/cs, 1648–64, 1664–83: rent receipts, repairs (*9, 152*); ref. to annuity from Watling Street.

d. MSS 3149/1, 2, vestry min. bks. 1653–61, 1662–83; business relating to par. houses, incl. views (*9, 152*, Watling Street).

e. MSS 3121/1–3: tithe rate assessments 1657–72, arranged by precincts.

377. St. Stephen Coleman Street (*155*)
Estate before 1548: *155*, unspec.
See E. Freshfield, 'Some remarks upon the Book of Records and History of the parish of St. Stephen, Coleman Street, in the City of London', *Archaeologia* 50 (1887), 17–57.

a. MS 4456 (Davis, no. 633): record bk. 1466–1832, incl. copy wills, 15C and later (*46, 81, 155*); also (p. 150), 15C note of par. boundaries; (pp. 1–18) 15C and 16C inventories of church goods; (pp. 52–3) list, 1719, of par. rents (*155*, Old Fish Street). MS 4499: 18C schedule of par. deeds and documents, 17C to 19C (*45, 155*).

b. MS 4457/1, churchwardens' a/cs, 1486–1509: rents, quit-rents, repairs (*81, ?123, 155*). MS 4457/2, churchwardens' a/cs, 1586–1640: rents (properties usually not specified); payment for purchase of rectory 1590; tithe assessments, some arranged by alleys, from 1592. MS 4457/3, churchwardens' a/cs, 1656–85: rents (*155*, Old Fish Street).

c. MS 4458/1, vestry min. bk. 1622–1726: business relating to par. houses, incl. views, sales, purchases (*155*, Old Fish Street).

378. St. Stephen Walbrook (*156*)
Estate before 1548: *87, 88, 118, 145, 156, 158*.

a. GL, Add. MSS 181, 214, 215, 222, 244, 251, 261, 279, 289: deeds, 15C to 17C (*156*). GL, Add. MSS 161, 163, 172, 206, 263: deeds etc., 16C to 17C (*38, 74, 93, 103, 127, 156*). GL, Add. MS 308: deed, 17C (*38*). GL, Add. MS 245: extracts from will and evidences, 15C (*13, 74, 156*). GL, MS 3611: papers, 16C, incl. receipts for quit-rents, bill for repairs (*145*). GL, Add. MS 237: agreement 1484 (*118, 156*).

b. MS 3103: 16C vol. of copy deeds and leases, incl. rental (*38, 74, 93, 103, 127, 156*). MS 596: 18C schedule and abs. of deeds and leases, 16C and later (*38, 74, 77, 93, 103, 127, 156*, Duke's Place).

c. MS 593/1, churchwardens' a/cs, 1471–85, 1507–8, 1510–11, 1518–38 (odd years missing): rent receipts, repairs (*88, 118, 145, 156, 158*, Bucklersbury, Walbrook). MS 593/2, churchwardens' a/cs 1548–1637: rent receipts, 1548–9 (*88, 145, 158*, Walbrook); rent receipts, fines, repairs, 1549–1637 (*38, 74, 93, 103, 127, 156*); (ff. 1–4) vestry mins., 1570s–80s, with view (*74*); also incl. list of furniture in parsonage house, 1636–7. MS 593/3, churchwardens' a/cs 1578–81: rents (*127, 156*, London Stone); a/c for church repair, 1600. GL, Add. MS 292, churchwardens' a/c and rental, 1586–7 (*38, 74, 93, 103, 127, 156*). GL, Add. MS 207, churchwardens' a/c 1592–3: rents, but properties not located. MS 593/4, churchwardens' a/cs 1637–1748: rents, fines (properties not usually located); assessments. GL, Add. MS 240: a/c for repairs 1607 (*38*).

d. MS 594/1, vestry min. bk. 1587–1614: business relating to par. houses, incl. views (mostly unspecified, but incl. *93*, Walbrook). MS 594/2, vestry min. bk. 1648–99: business relating to par. houses; views 1653, and later (*38, 93*, Cannon Street, unspecified).

e. MS 3106: assessment 1483–8. GL, Add. MSS 243, 260: assessments, 1664, 1679. GL, Add. MSS 175, 210, 225, 241, 248, 252, 254, 256, 262: misc. par. papers incl. bonds.

379. St. Swithin (*157*)
Estate before 1548: *49, 98, 104, 125, 157*.

a. GL, Add. MSS 419–91: deeds and leases, 13C–18C (*30, 49, 67, 98, 104, 125, 157*; list in box).

b. MS 3349: 18C to 19C vol. of copy and abs. deeds from 1668, incl. refs. to pre-Fire leases (*125, 157*).

c. MS 559/1, churchwardens' a/cs 1602–1725: rents, fines, quit-rents received and paid (properties not usually located, but some in *157*, Eastcheap).

d. MS 560/1, vestry min. bk. 1647–1729: business relating to par. houses, but not usually located; at end, inventory of goods in parsonage house *c.* 1647.

380. St. Thomas the Apostle (*158*)
Estate before 1548: *158*, Old Fish Street, unspec.

a. MSS 675–683: deeds 1574–1671 (*158*; MS 675 also ref. to *152*). MSS 760–1: papers incl. copy will and deeds 1536–76 (*158*). MS 764: par. papers incl. copy and abs. wills 16C and 17C (*62, 158*). MS 745: Fire Ct. decree 1671 (*158*).

b. MS 664/1: bk. of inventories and views of par. property, 1628–66 (*158*, Old Fish Street, Silver Street).

c. MS 662/1, churchwardens' a/cs 1612–1725: rents, payment of quit-rents, repairs (*158*, Old Fish Street, Silver Street).

d. MS 663/1, vestry min. bk. 1659–1738: business relating to par. houses (*158*, Silver Street, unspec.).

381. St. Vedast (*159*)
Estate before 1548: *84, 123, 128, 159*.

382. London parochial charities
GL. Deeds, late 13C to 17C, deposited by trustees of London parochial charities: *2, 4, 9, 11, 13, 15, 18, 19, 23, 30, 36, 38, 39, 42, 43, 44, 45, 47, 49, 51, 53, 54, 56, 62, 64, 71, 74, 75, 78, 80, 81, 84, 85, 87, 90, 93, 94, 96, 98, 99, 101, 103, 104, 111, 112, 116, 118, 123, 124, 125, 127, 128, 129, 131, 136, 141, 145, 148, 149, 151, 152, 155, 156, 157, 158, 159*. The deeds are arranged according to the parishes which owned the properties and there is a TS calendar with full index. The collection includes later deeds, some relating to other parishes.

383. London, non-parochial chapels and fraternities
The chantries in St. Paul's, and the chapels and fraternities of the guilds or companies, are not listed here: for these see above, **16–69** and **70–7**; also Kitching, *Chantry Certificate*, 108–113, 191–224. See also **438**, below.

a. Guildhall Chapel (St. Mary, St. Mary Magdalen, and All Saints). Built late 13C; college of priests founded 1356. Estate before 1548: *21, 62, 81, 159*. See C. M. Barron, *The Medieval Guildhall of London* (1974).

b. Fraternity of Jesus 'in the Crowds' or 'under St Paul's'. Fd. 1453. Estate before 1548: unspec., but probably not London. For statutes, deeds, a/cs, see Bodl, MS Tanner 221, described and part printed in *Registrum Statutorum et Consuetudinum Ecclesie Cathedralis Sancti Pauli Londinensis*, ed. W. S. Simpson (1873), pp. 435–62, 483–4; f. 14, memorandum of sale of Bull Head Tavern, St. Martin's Lane.

c. Fraternity of Sixty Priests. Estate before 1548: *144, 158*.

384. CHURCHES AND CHAPELS OUTSIDE LONDON
A number of churches and chapels outside London held property in the city, usually chantry endowments lost in 1548. There is no systematic way of identifying all of these, but the following sources provide some guide. Collegiate churches are treated under 'Religious houses' (**70–274**).

a. *Calendar of Wills proved and enrolled in the Court of Husting, London, 1258–1688*, ed. R. R. Sharpe (1889–90).
Endowments in perpetuity are recorded for the following churches and chantries: Ash, Kent (*125*); Biddenham, Beds. (*53, 123*); Boylestone, Derbys. (Cheap, Vintry); Bromley, Kent (*137*); Chinnor, Oxon. (unspec.); Coventry, fraternity of Holy Trinity, St. Mary, and St. John the Baptist (Smithfield); Farthinghoe, Northants. (*81*); Finedon ('Thyngden'), Northants. (*92*); chapel of 'Grenge' Manor, nr. Gillingham, Kent (unspec.); Hellesdon, Norf. (*9*); Hitchin, Herts. (*12*); Hornchurch, Essex (*58*); Sevenoaks, Kent (*4*); Shottesbrook, Berks. (*56*); St. Olave's, Southwark, Surrey (*51*); Standon, Herts. (*36, 88*, Broad Street); Strood, Kent (*93, 125*).

b. Survey of ecclesiastical property in the city of London, 1392, in *The Church in London 1375–1392*, ed. A. K. McHardy (LRS 13, 1977).
The following held city property: Colney chapel, Shenley, Herts. (*93*); vicarage of Fulham, Middx. (Langbourn ward); chapel of Watton, Herts. (Walbrook ward); rector of Widmerpool, Notts. (Castle Baynard ward).

c. Chantry certificates. Published editions are listed in *Texts and Calendars*, ed. E. L. C. Mullins, (RHS: vol. 1, 1958, reprinted with corrections 1978; vol. 2, 1983). These editions are of varying value, and not all are indexed. Neither they nor PRO originals for churches outside London have been searched systematically, but there are London references in: *Kent Chantries*, ed. A. Hussey (Kent Arch. Soc. Records Branch, 1936); *London and Middlesex Chantry Certificate*, ed. C. J. Kitching (LRS 16, 1980); *Sussex Chantry Records*, ed. John E. Ray (Sussex Rec. Soc., 1930).

d. PRO, SC12/37/13: survey of collegiate chantry lands in London and Middlesex, *c.* 1548; refers to colleges of Fotheringhay and Irthlyngborough (**157, 169**) and chantries of Farthinghoe and Finedon, Northants. (see **a**, above).

COLLEGES AND SCHOOLS

CAMBRIDGE COLLEGE ARCHIVES

Unless otherwise stated, the records are kept by the individual colleges. See A. N. L. Munby, *Cambridge College Libraries* (2nd edition 1962). PRO, E315/440, is a survey of the possessions of the Cambridge colleges, 1545–6, noting London properties for Michael House (Trinity), Jesus, Pembroke, Magdalene, St. John's and King's; other colleges held property then or later.

385. CAMBRIDGE: CORPUS CHRISTI COLLEGE
Fd. 1352. The college held the rectory of *98* and property in the parish.

a. XLB 1–11: deeds, leases and copies, 16C and 17C (*98*; also ref. to *80*).

386. CAMBRIDGE: EMMANUEL COLLEGE
Fd. 1584. The London estate lay in *9, 53, 58, 94, 152.*

a. Deeds (15C and later) and papers relating to London properties are in DBX 1 (*53*), DBX 25 (*9, 152*, also *46*), DBX 26–7 (*58, 94*), BUR 0.9 (*152*). These are listed in BUR 2.6, 'Catalogue of Deeds, 1887' (which also lists deeds in *152* and Old Bailey (Whichcott Exhibition) no longer surviving), and in catalogues of 'Bishopsgate Street and Threadneedle Street', and 'Properties no longer owned' (under Gracechurch Street).

b. COL 8.1: register of deeds 1583–9 (*9, 58, 152*, London unspecified).

c. BUR 2.1A: rental 1585 with additions (*9, 58, 152*). BUR 2.1B: rental 1588, as BUR 2.1A. BUR 2.1(3): rental 1632 with copious later annotations (*9, 53, 58, 94, 152*). BUR 11.1: rental 1585 (*9, 58*) and rent a/cs 1585–1652 (properties identified by tenants' names, London rents grouped together). BUR 0.9 (misc. papers) incl. a/cs (rent receipts, quit-rent payments, rough notes) for *9* (1631–8; also correspondence about leases, 1629–30) and *94* (1627–31). BUR 8.1, 'Long Book': expenses 1591–1621, incl. some quit-rent payments from unspecified properties.

387. CAMBRIDGE: GONVILLE AND CAIUS COLLEGE
Fd. 1348. The London estate lay in *99.*

a. Drawer 34, nos. 1–37, 39–40: deeds, leases etc., 1491–1595. Ibid. no. 38: will 1586 (*99, 159*, Barbican). Ibid. no. 42: 19C memorandum on value, rent, fines, etc.

b. 'Registrum Magnum': catalogue of deeds etc., begun 17C (London property indexed under Philip Lane); incl. abs. will 1586 (*99*).

c. 'Liber Evidentiarum': lease bk. 1551–1655, indexed. 'Leases, wills, etc.': lease bk. 1659–1769, indexed.

d. 'Liber Bursarii', 3 vols.: quarterly rent a/cs, 1609–87, incl. fines for leases.

388. CAMBRIDGE: JESUS COLLEGE
Fd. 1496. The estate lay in: *32, 46, 88, 99.* See TS account of 'Jesus College London Estates' by Mrs. F. Jones, former archivist. Volumes are described in Muniment Room Catalogue, 'Books'.

a. Deeds, listed in Muniment Room Catalogue, 'Documents K-Q, estates outside Cambridge', under London. Boxes 1, 2, 8–10: deeds, leases, post-Fire plans, *c.* 1550– *c.* 1800. Steel press, documents relating to Dr. Reston's foundation: 16C deeds and copy will (*46, 99*).

b. EST. 1.1, 'Jesus College leases 1578': lease bk., copy leases from 1543, indexed by county and parish; miscellanea at end incl. memorandum of London rents, list of evidences *c.* 1604. EST. 1.2, 'Leases etc. 1618–75': copy leases, with list of tenants, indexed; at end, notes on some leases, survey of house in *99*, note of land cut off 1676 (*46*). EST. 1.3, 'Jesus College Lease Book 1675–1718': copy leases indexed by tenants; incl. surveys and valuations of London property, 1713, 1726.

c. A/C.1.1, 'Foundationes Collegii Jesu': a/cs 1557–9, rent receipts, quit-rent payments. A/C.1.2–4, Audit Bks.: a/cs 1560–1676, rents (usually totalled for London), quit-rent payments, rent-collectors' fees; fines not included.

d. COL.1.1, Register I 1618–89: incl. brief memoranda of leases granted, not indexed.

e. ANT.2.1: vol. of papers and copies, incl. 17C memoranda of conveyances (*99*); list of tenants, 1702. Table of contents, catalogued in card catalogue.

389. CAMBRIDGE: KING'S COLLEGE
Fd. 1441. The London estate ('Duke Humphrey's wardrobe') lay in *18.* There is a 19C catalogue of deeds.

a. T1–9: deeds, leases and correspondence, 13C to 18C, incl. 18C plan. A22: royal grant, 1447.

b. 'The Oak Cartulary' (Davis, no. 146): 15C cartulary; (f. 29) grant of property in *18*; (f. 68) copy inquisition 1324 into lands of alien houses, incl. Ogbourne (*18*, Billingsgate ward), Fécamp (Castle Baynard ward), Lewes (Walbrook ward), St. Valéry (Cripplegate ward), Bermondsey (unspec.).

c. 'Ledger Books', 1451–1681, 6 vols.: lease bks., with rough contemp. indexes in each.

d. Shelf S9.3: two 16C–17C paper bks. with memoranda of estates, incl. valuations, notes of fines and leases, tables of rents. 'Mundum Books', from 1447: incl. foreign receipts, with some arrears and fines; no general series of rentals or rent a/cs exists.

390. CAMBRIDGE: MAGDALENE COLLEGE
Fd. 1542. The London estate lay in *43, 78*. There is a TS list of the archives in CUL; cf. HMC (4) *5th Report*, 481–4.

a. Box A27, nos. 1–18: deeds, copy will, leases, papers, 1533–1677.

b. B411, 'The Old Book': register of deeds and leases from 1574; also incl. (f. 17ᵛ) list of evidences 1595.

c. B421, 'Register I' 1575–1695: incl. rent a/cs 1575–1680.

d. B422, 'Register II 1644–76: incl. (reversed at end) minutes of sealing of leases 1644–70.

391. CAMBRIDGE: PEMBROKE COLLEGE
Fd. 1347. The London estate lay in: *26, 30, 87, 125*. The deeds are listed in a 19C MS catalogue; see also HMC (1) *First Report*, Appendix pp. 69–72.

a. Bundles A, B: deeds, leases, papers, incl. surveys, Fire Ct. papers, 1533–1697 (*87, 125*); bundles D, E, listed in catalogue, included counter-part leases, 17C and later, to same properties, handed over to London Bridge Committee on compulsory purchase, 1830. Bundle F: leases, 1555–1840 (*26*). Bundle C, listed in catalogue, included survey and rebuilding agreement for same property, now missing. Bundles H, I: deeds, leases, 16C and later (*30*); some listed were sold 1854.

b. 'Great Register' (Davis, no. 153): cartulary, *c.* 1390–1400; (ff. 65 et seqq.) 14C deeds, wills, probably all included in Husting Rolls (*5, 100*). Leases, vols. 1, 2: lease bks., 1619–1710, indexed.

c. Treasury a/cs, vols. I, II: annual rent a/cs, 1550–1641, 1648–99. It is not clear where income from fines was recorded.

d. Registers, vols. 2, 4: minute bks., 1616–54, 1660–67, incl. notes of grants of leases; vol. 2 indexed (under 'leases'), vol. 4 not indexed but may incl. London leases.

e. 'Surveys': late 18C vol., incl. (f. 25) plan, 1780 (*87, 125*).

392. CAMBRIDGE: ST. JOHN'S COLLEGE
Fd. 1511. The London estate lay in *4, 38, 129*, and *152* (Middlesex): see A. F. Torry, *Founders and Benefactors of St. John's College Cambridge* (1888). The contents of the former drawer sequence D1–110 (deeds, rentals) are calendared in typescript and listed and indexed on computer print-out.

a. Deeds and leases, 13C to 20C (estate above; also refs to *71, 125*, London unspec.): listed as above.

b. 'Thin Red Book', 'Thick Black Book', 'Thin Black Book', 'White Vellum Book': registers of leases, misc. other contents, *c.* 1513–1609;

briefly calendared in T. Baker, *History of the College of St. John the Evangelist, Cambridge* (1869). Lease Bks. 1609–69, 3 vols., indexed by tenants' names, some place-names.

c. D106.11, 14: rough a/cs, *c.* 1520–37, incl. refs to London rents. Rentals 1555–1684, 7 vols.: rent a/cs, incl. arrears, quit-rents paid, repairs (estate above, also quit-rents received from Fleet Street). ˢB6.1, 'Old Dividend and Fine Book', 1613–1770: chronological memoranda of leases and fines, possibly not comprehensive.

d. D94.426: correspondence about lease, 1617 (*4*).

393. CAMBRIDGE: TRINITY COLLEGE
Fd. 1546 incorporating King's Hall (fd. 1337) and Michael House (fd. 1324). The London estate lay in *81, 92* (latter also known as Blackfriars).

a. Deeds, leases, etc. relating to the London properties from 1539 are kept mostly in Box 43; these, and similar MSS stored elsewhere, are listed in the Bird card-catalogue under Box 43.

b. Registers, 9 vols. 1545–1672: registers of deeds and leases, indexed.

c. Lease bks., 3 vols. 1608–55, 1662–1754: chronological memoranda of leases, extensions and assignments, with fines. 'Rents A': bk. cont. brief notes of leases, begun mid 17C, arranged by location, indexed. 'Notitia B', 'C', and 'F', 'Leases E', 'Dr. Barrow G': 5 small bks., possibly bursars' memorandum bks., cont. similar and duplicate material to 'Rents A'. 'Mr. Castry D', similar to above, cont. rough notes on properties, incl. (p. 8) ref. to *92*.

d. Senior Bursars' a/c bks., 6 vols. 1545–1674, cont. a/cs for individual years subsequently bound up (1621–37 and odd years mising): rent receipts totalled, fines noted by location or lessee; some a/cs incl. details of arrears. Arrears bks., 4 vols. 1545–1677, cont. a/cs for individual years (some missing) subsequently bound up: details of rent arrears, tenant and location usually named.

394. CAMBRIDGE: TRINITY HALL
Fd. 1350. The college leased property in *38* (Doctors' Commons) from St. Paul's Cathedral.

a. In the chest: unnumbered bundle of counterpart leases, 1650 to 18C.

b. Lease Book 1671–1765: copy leases incl. plans.

c. 'Accounts 1587–1795': incl. rent receipts and payments, tithes, unspecified repairs.

d. 'Miscellaneous Papers' vol. iv: collection of loose papers, 16C and 17C, now bound up and numbered; incl. *passim* suits for leases; no. 27, list of evidences and leases, 1593; no. 38, memoranda of repairs; no. 134, notes on legal proceedings, 1599; no. 145, proposals for post-Fire rebuilding. In the chest, 2 bundles of papers: 1, concerning suit 1656, rebuilding 1666, etc.; 2, copy legal papers, 1599.

OXFORD COLLEGES AND THE
UNIVERSITY

Unless otherwise stated, the records are kept by the individual colleges. The best introduction to the archives and their current location is P. Morgan, *Oxford Libraries outside the Bodleian* (2nd. ed., 1980). PRO, E315/441 is a survey of college estates, 1545–6, noting London properties for Balliol, Brasenose, Magdalen, and Merton.

395. OXFORD: UNIVERSITY OF OXFORD
During the first half of the 17C the university successively acquired tenements in *30* (towards the maintenance of the library: see W. D. Macray, *Annals of the Bodleian Library* (2nd. ed., 1890), 15n., 37); an annuity in *54* (towards the teaching of divinity); and tenements in *81* (for the maintenance of 3 fellows from Jersey and Guernsey). The tenements remained in the possession of the university, but the annuity may have been lost by *c.* 1675 for it is not entered in the rental of that date (see **c**, below).
The archives (Arch. Univ. Oxon.) are produced for consultation at the Bodleian Library in Duke Humphrey's reading room, where a copy of a manuscript list is available. See T. H. Aston and D. G. Vaisey, 'University Archives' in P. Morgan, *Oxford Libraries outside the Bodleian* (2nd. ed., 1980), 200–5.

a. Deeds and papers. W. P. α 4: leases and counterparts, 1669 onwards (*30*). N.W. 3, 1ᵇ: letter of attorney for receipt of rents, 1613 (*30*). N.E.P. Pyx E, 7ᵃ⁻ᵈ and 8: deeds and papers, 1584–1649 (*54*). S.E.P. K.I: leases, deed, and Fire Court decree, 1620 onwards (*81*). Bodl, MS Top. Oxon. c. 27: binding is part of late 17C lease (*81*).

b. N.E.P. Supra and Subtus: Registers of Convocation, incl. records of university decisions and fines concerning all the London properties and copies of leases.

c. W.P. R 16: general rental, *c.* 1675 (*30, 81*). London rent receipts are not itemized in the surviving series of accounts.

396. OXFORD: BALLIOL COLLEGE
Fd. 1260–6. The London estate was in *81* and *90*. See also **272**.

a. Deeds and leases, 12C to 20C. There is a 19C list and index (not always reliable); a new guide is being prepared. 12C and 13C deeds concerning *81* also refer to property in Cheapside and Fink Lane.

b. Lease books 1 and 2, copies of leases and Fire Court decrees, 1588–1762.

c. Bursars' a/cs, 4 vols. 1568–1677 (extracts made *c.* 1910 from the now lost vol. for 1544–64 are in Bodl, MS Top. Oxon. e. 124/9): brief records of rents and tenants.

d. Latin register 1, 1514–1682: ordinances of the governing body incl.

records of the London property. Lease log book or fine book (entitled 'Balliol College Estates'), comp. *c.* 1675 and later: abs. of leases noting fines, 1588–1850, arranged by properties. Bursars' book IJ: private notebook comp. *c.* 1655 incl. notes on London rents and tenants.

397. OXFORD: BRASENOSE COLLEGE
Fd. 1260. Unless otherwise stated, the estate comprised: houses in *42*; rents from *81* and from the Skinners' Company (charged on property in Gracechurch Street); rents from *95* and Old Fish Street as part of the endowment of the grammar school at Middleton, Lancs. See A. J. Butler, 'An Account of the Benefactions Bestowed upon the College' and 'The College Estates and the Advowsons held by the College' in *Brasenose College quatercentenary monographs* i (Oxf. Hist. Soc. 52, 1909).
See 'Calendar of Muniments' (comp. by H. Hurst, 1900–4) and 'List of Archives not calendared by Hurst' (HMC typescript, 1966).

a. Deeds and leases, 16C–17C (*42*): see 'Calendar of Muniments', s.n. London.

b. B1c/1, 'Liber Col: Ænei Nasi': comp. 16C–18C, incl. copies of deeds and wills. A3/19, 'Principal Yate's Book': comp. 1668 and later, incl. copies of deeds and evidences and a table of abs. of leases of college properties from 1485. B1d/35: late 17C 'Copies of evidences'. 'BNC Ledger no. 1': copies of leases granted 1596–1717, incl. 18C list of contents.

c. Bursars' a/c rolls (now bound in volumes), 1516 onwards incl. receipts of rents. A2/41–8, senior bursars' a/cs, various years from 1631–2 on: bks. cont. daily record of receipts and payments incl. rents and fines.

d. A1, 'Vice-Principals' Registers': Registrum A, 1539–94 incl. grants of leases (cf. above, **b**), which may be identified from the 19C MS slips pasted in the vol. 'Extracts from the Principals' Registers, 1539/40–1896'. B1d/36, 'Principals' Fine Book': grants of leases and fines, 1650–1705.

e. B.1.4.1, folder of estate maps and plans: incl. plans 1674 and later for *42*, and late 17C/early 18C map of *113* parish (Brasenose acquired the advowson in 1721).

398. OXFORD: CHRIST CHURCH
Fd. 1546. The London estate was in *152*. The main series of archives is at Christ Church; in 1927 some items were deposited in Bodl (described in *Cartulary of the Medieval Archives of Christ Church*, ed. N. Denholm-Young, Oxf. Hist. Soc. 92, 1931). Unless otherwise stated the records are in the Christ Church Archives.

a. Deeds A. London, St. Sepulchres: deeds, leases, papers, 16C and 17C. See also Bodl, MS Christ Church MM. 10.

b. 1. b. 5: register of estates *c.* 1665. 1. c. 2–3, 'Book of Evidences' comp. *c.* 1667: abs. of title and notes of deeds and leases. D. P. i. b. 11, 'Liber Ecclesiae Christi Oxon.': a draft for the 'Book of Evidences'. XX. c. 1–5,

'Estates Ledgers', 1553–1675: copies of acts of dean and chapter incl. leases (no London refs in vols. 1 and 2; contents of vol. 5 onwards are indexed in 1. c. 4, 'Index to Register of Leases vol. 1', comp. 18C and 19C). See also 1. b. 2 and 1. b. 4: registers of leases comp. *c*. 1660 and *c*. 1664, respectively.

c. lvi. c. 1–85, bailiffs' a/cs, 1548–1633: receipts of rent from London, but tenants not named. Similar information appears in 'Receipt Books' (42 vols. 1592–1667: xi. b. 1, 2, 3, 6, 7, 9, etc.) and in annual 'Treasurers' Statements' (rolls for 1549–1624 are in iii. c. 5–9 and Bodl, MSS Christ Church MM Rolls 4–14, Oxon. Rolls 18, Top. Oxon. c. 23). See also iii. c. 1 (vol. of draft a/cs, 1527–1630) and iii. c. 4 (a/c for 1546–7).

d. MS Estates 45: 17C Fire Court papers and a plan of 1610 by Ralph Treswell (a 17C copy of the plan is filed among the deeds, cf. above, **a**).

399. OXFORD: MAGDALEN COLLEGE
Fd. 1448, 1458. The college's only property in the city before 1666 was an annuity in Little Wood Street acquired in the 17C, for which few records survive. It had extensive holdings in Southwark and in Middlesex in the parishes of St. Clement Danes and *54*.
The archive is divided into three main sections: 'Macray Deeds' (see below, **a**); 'Estate Records' (recently numbered and indexed; TS list available in Bodl); 'Records' (concerning central and domestic administration).

a. Deeds and some other papers are identifiable in a TS calendar compiled by W. D. Macray and arranged principally by counties. For Little Wood Street, see Macray Deeds, Kent, London, and Somerset, no. 144 (now lost). See also **186** and **198**.

b. The Little Wood Street rent is mentioned in two late 17C and 18C books of rentals (Records, CP 3/6, 7). It is probably included in the various totals for London recorded in the following: bursars' a/c rolls (annual series, 1480–1667: Estate Records 186/1 to 214/13); 'Libri Computi' (annual series from 1490: not numbered).

400. OXFORD: MERTON COLLEGE
Fd. 1264, 1266. Unless otherwise stated, the London estate lay in *5, 37, 38, 46, 123*.

a. Deeds, leases, wills, and other papers, 13C to 17C, identifiable from vol. 9 of the catalogue compiled by W. H. Stevenson: estate as above, also refs. to *104, 127, 134, 137* (in items 143, 1203, 2977).

b. Registers of leases, 3 vols. 1578–1682, each with a contemp. list of contents ('Records' 6. 1–3). Late 17C terrier listing tenants, dates of leases, and fines from late 16C ('Records' 5.19A). These 4 vols. concern estate as above, except for *37*.

c. Rentals, 1638 and mid 17C ('Records' 2.9, 5.36): estate as above. Bursars' rolls for most years 1277–1638 (three separate bursars rendered a/cs for successive parts of each year; the rolls are listed in vol. 1b of Stevenson's catalogue): incl. receipts of rent, but not always possible to identify London totals; more detail on London rents appears in the 17C rolls. 'Liber Rationarius Bursarium', 3 vols. 1585–1677 ('Records' 3.1–3) incl. bursars' a/cs followed by a general a/c for whole year: information as in bursars' rolls. Walter de Merton held a house in Maiden Lane and his executors paid rent for a house in Ivy Lane: *The Early Rolls of Merton College, Oxford*, ed. J. R. L. Highfield (Oxf. Hist. Soc. n.s. 18, 1964 for 1963), 32, 110.

d. College Registers, 2 vols. 1482–1731 ('Records' 1.2,3): business of the governing body, incl. granting of leases; the text to 1603 has been edited as *Registrum Annalium Collegii Mertonensis* by H. E. Salter (Oxf. Hist. Soc. 76, 1933) and John M. Fletcher (Oxf. Hist. Soc. n.s. 23–4, 1974 and 1976); there is a MS index to the later contents of the registers ('Records' 1.5 S).

401. OXFORD: NEW COLLEGE

Fd. 1379. In 1391 the college acquired former properties of Hornchurch Priory (**166**) in *77* and *78*, and of Takeley Priory (**233**) in *144*; property in *33* was acquired in the later 16C. For the records, which are identified by means of a single sequence of numbers, see F. W. Steer, *The Archives of New College, Oxford* (1974). This book (cited as Steer) contains detailed descriptions of many items, but also conceals much and should be used with caution.

a. Deeds and Leases. For deeds up to 1391, see **166** and **233**. Loose deeds, leases, papers, surveys, and plans of a later date are described by Steer in a series of artificial groups as follows:

33 (pp. 319–20), 16C–17C deeds, 17C leases, 17C particulars and plans, 18C abs. of title (14C–16C) concerning adjacent property in *42*;
77 and *78* (p. 321), 17C–18C leases and plans;
144 (pp. 322–4), 15C–17C leases, 17C particulars and plans, Fire Ct. decree, 17C receipts for quit-rents.

b. Registers of deeds: 9744 ('Liber Niger'; Davis, no. 746), 16C register cont. (f. 154), copy deed of acquisition for *77* and *78*; 9791 ('Registrum Evidentiarum' vol. 5; cf. Davis, no. 748), mid 17C register cont. (pp. 333–7, 343–6, 353–81) copies of 13C–17C deeds and Fire Ct. decrees and surveys. Registers of leases: 9654 ('Registrum Primum' or White Book; Davis, no. 747), cont. (ff. 57, 146ᵛ, 153, 181) copies of 15C leases (*77, 78, 144*); 9757–66 ('Registra Dimissiones ad Firmam', nos. 2–12), cont. copies of leases 1480–1668. Registers of fines, cont. summaries of leases and specifying fines for London properties from mid 17C onwards: 39, 967, 9793.

c. Valors and rentals: Steer, p. 73, lists valors and rentals from late 15C onwards, most of which incl. totals of rent due from the London properties; for 3578, incl. in this list, see below, **d.** Accounts: 6589–6649 (Steer, pp. 34–5) are separate a/cs for the London properties listing receipts and expenditure, 1395–1495 (with gaps); many similar London a/cs are to be found in the series of bailiffs' a/cs running from 1466 to 1596, and totals received from London are incl. in the bursars' a/cs from the late 14C onwards (these two series are described and listed in Steer, pp. 16–30).

d. Surveys and plans: for loose items, see above, **a**; 3578 is a 17C volume cont. both drawn and written surveys (details of London properties on pp. 179–80, 343, 347); 11917 is another 17C description of the property in *144*.

402. OXFORD: ST. JOHN'S COLLEGE
Fd. 1557. The London estates were as follows:
   A. Properties acquired under the founder's will of 1566 and disposed of by 1590: *18, 36, 39, 46, 81, 87, 93, 100, 104, 123, 126, 137, 158* (see H. E. Salter, 'Particulars of properties in the city of London belonging to St. John's College, Oxford', *LTR* 15 (1931), 92–108, and W. H. Stevenson and H. E. Salter, *The early history of St. John's College Oxford* (Oxf. Hist. Soc. n.s. 1, 1939) esp. 273–4, 396–405.
   B. Properties acquired after 1590: *9* (acq. 1757–88), *54* and Whitefriars precinct (acq. 1657); *152* (acq. 1632).
See TS 'Summary Guide' to the records by H. M. Colvin.

a. 'Muniments', i.e. deeds, wills, inquisitions, memoranda, and other papers, 16C and 17C (there is a card calendar of each item): estate A, as above, (sections I, XXI); estate B, as above, and also refs. to *37, 141* (sections XXX, XXXIII, LXIII, LXVI).

b. 'Computus Annuus', annual series of bursars' a/cs beginning 1568–9, but London rents not entered until 1657 (cf. estate B, above).

c. 'Registers', 3 vols. 1557–1667, records of college meetings incl. decisions on estate management and copies of leases (contemp. indexes of names can be used to identify London refs.): estates A and B, as above.

403. CHARTERHOUSE (SUTTON'S HOSPITAL AND SCHOOL), LONDON
Hospital and free school fd. 1611 on site and adjacent lands of former Carthusian priory, just outside the N.W. limits of the city in the liberties of Charterhouse and Glasshouse Yard and the parishes of St. Sepulchre (*152*) and Clerkenwell. The records relate to this area. The school moved to Godalming, Surrey, in 1872.
The records are at Charterhouse, London EC1. There is a card index, arranged by class, listing individual deeds etc. in some detail.

a. G1/1–6: foundation deeds and charters from 1611. D1/1–26: deeds, leases, etc., 1371, 1538–1661 (Charterhouse site). D1/693–700: deeds, 1604–56 (Charterhouse churchyard). D1/179 et seqq.: deeds, leases, etc. from 1548 (Pardon churchyard).

b. AR5/2: list and survey of lands and leases with abstracts, 1633. D1/A/2: survey and rental of Pardon churchyard, 1654.

c. G7/1'A': reg. of leases, patents, etc., 1611–22 indexed by tenants; table at end identifies properties. G7/2'B': similar vol., 1630–70.

d. AR3/2–35, 'Quarter Books' 1621–67: rough bks. of quarterly rent receipts, arranged by place; also payments, incl. to workmen for repairs and building. AR1/1–66, receivers' a/c rolls, 1614–70 (with duplicates and some other a/cs: see card index): total receipts from each manor or estate, incl. Charterhouse area.

e. G2/1–3, 'Assembly Orders', 1613–98: minutes of governing body, incl. notes of leases granted, indexed by personal names and (some) subjects; microfilm to be deposited in GL.

f. Plan chest, 'London' drawer: plan of tenements to N. of Charterhouse, ? 1677.

404. CHRIST'S HOSPITAL, LONDON (NOW HORSHAM, SURREY)
Fd. 1553, on the site of the former Franciscan (Grey) Friars' precinct (*47*). The school moved to Horsham in 1902.
The London estate, which included short-term leases and annuities as well as freeholds, increased steadily in extent from 1553 to the late 17C. Unless otherwise stated, the records cover properties in: *9, 20, 21, 23, 26, 36, 38, 42, 43, 45, 46, 47, 51, 53, 54, 56, 59, 60, 62, 67, 75, 81, 83, 85, 87, 89, 92, 93, 94, 99, 104, 111, 112, 113, 119, 120, 123, 124, 125, 128, 131, 132, 134, 137, 139, 141, 144, 145, 148, 149, 150, 151, 152, 155,* Bucklersbury, Distaff Lane, Fenchurch Street, Friday Street, Lothbury, Old Fish Street, Philip Lane; the records also concern interests in Blackwell Hall (in *123*) and Leadenhall (in *149*).
The records, not all of which have been catalogued (November 1983), are in GL.

a. Deeds, leases, papers, and loose plans, 14C to 19C, arranged by 'gifts' (i.e. names of donors). MSS 12886–13816 incl. refs. to London properties, the locations of which can be identified from the catalogue entries. Of the uncatalogued boxes of deeds and papers the following incl. refs. to London properties up to 1666: 'Wale, Warren, Webb' (*149*); 'Weld' (*89*); 'West (*26, 56, 60, 112, 148*); 'Wilcox' (*155*); 'Woodward' (*46*); 'Wood' (*152*); 'Papers re Wills' (*38, 45, 46, 93, 134, 145*); 'Purchase: Holborn' (*20*); 'Purchases and properties outside London' (*128*); 'Purchase: Pudding Lane and New Fish Street' (*36, 87, 94*); 'Purchase: Spring Gardens; Friday Street' (*89*); 'Purchase: 63–5 Friday Street' (*120*); 'London Properties' (*20, 23, 42, 46, 89, 119, 131, 137, 152*); 'Properties exchanged with St. Bartholomew's Hospital, 1819' (*42, 152*); 'Deeds and Papers for Various Gifts' (*131*); 'Blackwell Hall' (*123*).

b. MS 12815/1: register of wills, gifts, and grants, comp. *c.* 1552–1702; incl. refs. to Bridewell (**409**) and mid 16C rentals for Bethlem, Savoy, and St. Thomas's, Southwark, hospitals (**102, 105, 226**); also (f. 219 et seqq.) refs. to *9, 73, 105*, Birchin Lane. MS 12805: register of lands, leases, and annuities, incl. late 16C list of gifts and properties (details of tenants and rents); 17C plans of London properties. MS 12879/1: register of leases (dated 1660 but comp. 1665–6 and later), with details of leases and annuities in tabular form. MS 12812/1: register of benefactions (cash gifts and legacies only), 1552–1820.

c. MSS 12819/1–10, treasurers' a/c books. 1552–78: particulars of rents (arranged by 'gifts', but few locations named), fines, and expenditure on maintenance (principally at the hospital); MS 12819/1 also incl. a/cs for Savoy and St. Thomas's hospitals. MS 12826/1: rough a/c, 1653–4. MSS 12820/1–4, treasurers' cash bks., and MSS 12821/1–3, treasurers' day bks., 1624–57: 2 sets of bks. forming single series (for 17C) recording daily receipts and expenditure. MS 12848: a/c for rebuilding Blackwell Hall (*123*), 1612–15. MS 12849: a/cs and other papers concerning Blackwell Hall. Uncatalogued box 'Blackwell Hall Building Accts. 17/18ᵗʰC': a/cs concerning Blackwell Hall (incl. plan, 1681), and building at the hospital. MS 12825/1: incl. a/c for repairs to church of *47*, 1605–8.

d. MSS 12806/1–6, court min. bks., 1556–1677 (contemp. indexes, most reliable for names): much detail on estate management; MSS 12806/1–2 incl. circumstantial and topographical information on children admitted, incl. parentage. MS 12806A: rough court mins., 1611–32. MSS 12811/1–3, committee bks., 1654–69 (contemp. indexes to vols. 1 and 2): mins. of delegated court business. MS 12828/1: letter bk. 1579–85, 1624–38, incl. some letters concerning property.

e. MSS 12834/1–2, view bks. 1622–1722: detailed reports on structures, dimensions, valuations (contemp. indexes; best guide to contents via personal names indexed). MS 12862: memorandum and a/c bk., Aldworth's charity, 1646–58; incl. inventory of house (*111*). MS 12864: as preceding, 1660–3; incl. expenditure on fabric of hospital.

f. For plans of properties, see above, **a-c**. The uncatalogued box 'Precincts of the Hospital' incl. 17C–18C plans of properties near the hospital, incl. city wall and ditch.

405. DULWICH COLLEGE, LONDON SE21
The college, fd. 1619, had property in *45* and in *62* outside the liberty. The records are described in G. F. Warner, *Catalogue of Manuscripts and Muniments of Alleyn's College of God's Gift at Dulwich* (1881), and F. B. Bickley, *Catalogue of Manuscripts and Muniments . . . Second Series* (1903). Some account of and transcripts from the records are given in W. Young, *The History of Dulwich College* (1889). The records are in the library at the college.

a. Muniments: deeds, leases, etc. from 1537 (*45*, *62*, also *25*), calendared and indexed in Warner, *Catalogue*. MSS (2nd series) 100/1–323: incl. deeds, leases, etc. from 1604 (*45*, *62*), calendared and indexed in Bickley, *Catalogue*. Further muniments, 17C and later (*45*, *62*), stored in numbered boxes; MS index available.

b. MSS (2nd series) 27, 28, Register Bks. of a/cs, 1626–78: yearly a/cs of rents, fines, expenditure, with minutes (incl. leasing decisions) of Audit meetings; extracts in Bickley, *Catalogue*, and Young, *History*. MSS (2nd series) 35–8, Rent Bks. I–IV: tabular rent a/cs, with notes of payment.

c. MS IX, Edward Alleyn's diary and a/c bk., 1617–22, transcribed in full in Young, *History*, and extracts in Warner, *Catalogue*: incl. notes of rents, legal costs, repairs (*25, 45, 62*); MS index available. MSS I–VII, vols. of letters and papers, calendared/listed and indexed in Warner, *Catalogue*: refs. to *25, 45, 62*. MS VIII, Alleyn's memorandum bk., 1594–1616: incl. notes on purchase of properties, lists of evidences.

KING EDWARD'S SCHOOL, WITLEY, SURREY, see **102** and **409**.

406. ETON COLLEGE, ETON, BERKS.
Fd. 1440. Property in *5* and *111, 96*, and *152*, and quit-rents (several of which were lost or in arrears by the mid 16th century) in *5, 14, 38, 42, 54, 85, 123, 137*, Carter Lane, Distaff Lane, Holborn Bridge, Whitefriars. Some of this estate derived from St. James's Hospital, Westminster (**255**), placed in the custody of the college in 1449.
The records (ECR) are at the college. A series of TS lists and calendars, of which further volumes are in preparation, is available on request in PRO. London deeds are listed principally in vols. 16 and 49; vol. 39 calendars letters patent, 1440–1686, incl. some London references. Vol. 54 (Misc.) also contains some London references.

a. Deeds, leases, etc., 15C to 18C. ECR 16/White Bear/1–52 (*5, 111*). ECR 16/St. Botolph Aldersgate/1–4 (*42*). ECR 16/Vintry/3–10, ECR 49/247–9 (*96*). ECR 16/The Ball in Holborn/1–30 (*152*). ECR 16/ London Miscellaneous/1–6, 13C–17C (*2, 81, 123*, Distaff Lane).

b. ECR 60/LB/1–6: lease bks. or registers, 1445–1670, contemp. indexes (*5* and *111, 96; 152* from *c.* 1600).

c. ECR 60/RB/1: bk. cont. 16C rentals (estate above), survey 1617 (*5, 111*; cf. **f**, below).

d. Rentals, etc. ECR 60/VR/A/1 (formerly ECR 49/294): valor 1441–2 (*42*). ECR 60/VR/E/5: extent 1538 (*96*). ECR 49/312: rental *c.* 1574 (most of estate above). ECR 63/ as yet unnumbered: rental *c.* 1584, similar to preceding.

e. Accounts: see ECR calendars vols. 61 (completed), 62 (in preparation 1983). Rent receipts are recorded in rent rolls (ECR 61/RR), *c.* 1445–1542 (*96; 5, 111* from *c.* 1530); bursars' rolls (ECR 61/BR), 1549–1642 (estate as above); and audit bks. (ECR 62) thereafter (estate as above). Final a/cs (rent totals) are in audit rolls (ECR 61/AR), 1445–1505 (*96*); see also bursars' draft a/cs (ECR 61/BD), 1448–1556. ECR 16/Vintry/1–2, rent a/cs 1446–8 (*96*).

f. ECR 16/White Bear/42–5, 49: plans and survey, 1617, *c.* 1666, 1770 (*5, 111*); see *LTR* 19 (1947), 1–12. ECR 49/250: rough plan, early 18C (*96*). ECR 60/RB/5: plan bk. of 'Eton College Tenements', 1777 (*5, 111, 152*).

407. WINCHESTER COLLEGE, WINCHESTER, HANTS.
Fd. 1382. Property in *67* (from 1470) and probably *114* (for short period in late 14C and early 15C). Unless otherwise stated, the records are at the college, where they are identified in a single sequence of numbers as

W[inchester] C[ollege] M[uniments]. There is a card catalogue/calendar, reproduced by NRA.

a. WCM 12787–817 (described in S. Himsworth, *Winchester College Muniments, a descriptive list* ii, 1984): deeds, leases, bonds, papers, and an inventory, 14C to 17C (*67*, except for WCM 12813). WCM 12813 is a lease of 'Bealknapp's Inn' made in 1412 on behalf of the warden; this was probably the former property of Robert Bealknapp in *114*, acquired by William of Wykeham in 1388 (*Cal. Pat. R. 1385–9*, p. 492; see also New College, Oxford, records 9836), which was probably restored to Bealknapp's heirs *c*. 1415.

b. WCM 22990[b-c], 'Evidentiae Θ' (Davis, no. 1058), ff. 104[v]–112[v]: mid 16C transcripts of deeds as in **a**, above. WCM 22993–23001: registers of leases, 1522–1667; from 22996 onwards they incl. contemporary indexes; the first register in the series (WCM 22992, 'Liber Albus') contains no London material.

c. For rentals covering London, see WCM 22236–7, 22238A (16C and 17C; earlier rentals do not cover London). Rent receipts from the London property are to be found in the a/cs of the 'general collector of rents', of which one separate a/c survives (WCM 2118, for 1545–6); copies of the general collectors' a/cs are to be found in the series of farmers' and collectors' a/cs, WCM 22239–71 (1530 to 1638, with gaps), and in the series of court books, WCM 23039–54 (1556–1667); the general collectors' a/cs usually name tenants for the property in *67*, and by the mid 17C incl. receipts of rent from Petty Wales (perhaps in *33*, where New College had property: see **401**). The bursars' a/cs (WCM 22082–22212, a/c rolls, 1397–1556; WCM 22213–20, a/c bks., 1556–1671) frequently include receipts specifically from London property, and may also incl. expenditure on repairs (e.g. a/cs for 1526–7 and 1629–30).

OTHER INSTITUTIONS

408. LONDON, BANK OF ENGLAND
Established 1694; archive includes title deeds relating to the Bank site
(*32, 48, 88*), 16C to 19C, numbered consecutively and arranged in packets
or bundles according to the property to which they relate. There is a TS
list and index to the deeds.
The following deeds relate also to properties outside the site area. No.
380: grant, 1659 (Grub Street, Huggin Lane). Nos. 407–416: deeds and
will, 1607–56 (*104, 123*). Nos. 907–914: deeds, 1572–1639 (*142*; no. 913
also ref. to *51*). Nos. 932–3: copy charter, 1453, and will, 1551 (*142*). No.
971: lease, 1651 (*94*). The deeds listed as '74 Single Deeds' may in fact be
items from the main series, removed and listed twice.

409. LONDON, BRIDEWELL ROYAL HOSPITAL
Fd. 1553 as house of correction and occupation; prison closed 1855;
hospital reorganised as school, *c.* 1860, now King Edward's School,
Witley, Surrey. Bridewell Hospital was under the authority of the City,
and administered jointly with Bethlem Hospital (**102**, above) from the
later 16C until 1948. The records at Witley include material relating to
Bethlem Hospital. See NRA report, 1962, by A. E. B. Owen.
The estate lay in Bridewell precinct (extraparochial, formerly part of
46).

a. Witley, Box N: leases, 17C–19C (precinct). Ibid., Box 51, bundle 1:
deeds, incl. lease 1654 (*151*).

b. Witley, Muniment Bk. 1554–1732: incl. material relating to other royal
hospitals; (ff. 56^v–170) leases, incl. Bridewell properties, 16C to 18C; (ff.
222^v–224) Fire Ct. decree (Bridewell).

c. Witley, Box 67: rent rolls, 1605–6, 1621–2, 1665–6, and later (Bethlem
and Bridewell). Ibid., Treasurer's Account Bk. 1, 1643–8: incl. total rent
receipt (Bridewell).

d. CLRO, Repertories, mid to late 16C, incl. decisions relating to
Bridewell properties. Witley, Court Minute Bks. 1559–62, 1574–9, 1597–
1610, 1617–59, 1666 to date (microfilms at Bethlem Hospital, Archive
Department; also GL microfilms 510–515, 1559–1659 only): minutes incl.
leasing business (Bethlem and Bridewell; contemp. indexes to personal
names only).

e. At Witley: plans of Bridewell precinct and estate, ?late 17C to 20C. See
also late 18C Bk. of Surveys of precinct.

410. LONDON, COMPANY FOR THE PROPAGATION OF THE GOSPEL IN NEW ENGLAND ('NEW ENGLAND COMPANY')
The company, fd. by ordinance 1649 and royal charter 1662, acquired property in London and elsewhere to finance its work. Most of the records are in GL. See W. Kellaway 'The Archives of the New England Company', *Archives* 2 (1953–6), 175–82; idem, *The New England Company, 1649–1776* (1961).
The London estate lay in: *67, 132, 156.*

a. MS 7971: deeds, leases, etc., 1548–1791, incl. views 1597, 1598, 1619, case depositions 1586–7 (*132, 156*). MS 7972: will 1598 (*156*). MS 7974: deeds, leases, etc., 1572–1779 (*67*). MS 7975: leases, 1640–46 (*95, 98, 119*). MS 8001: inspeximus 1579 of charter 1352 (Blackfriars).

b. MS 7932: list, comp. *c.* 1780, of evidences and writings, 1662–1780.

c. MS 7945, treasurers' 'sundry' a/cs, loose, 1649–1728: some memoranda of property purchases. MS 7944/1, treasurers' a/cs, loose, 1659–72: ref. to house in St. Paul's churchyard, 1658–9. MS 7911/1, treasurers' general and estate a/c bk., 1660–79: rent receipts, estate above. G. P. Winship, *The New England Company of 1649 and John Eliot* (The Prince Society, Boston, Mass., 1920) edits the Company's Minute Book (see **d**, below), and a Treasurer's Ledger, 1650–60, then in the State Library of New Jersey, Trenton, N.J.: summary rent totals, expenses, incl. legal costs for house purchase.

d. Houghton Library, Harvard University, MS Am 1802: Court Min. Bk., 1656–85 (ed. G. P. Winship, *The New England Company*, as above; photocopy in GL, MS 8011); mins., incl. refs. to properties and leasing. GL, MS 7952, loose court and cttee. mins., 1655–1816: incl. refs. to proposed purchases in *67*, Cheapside, Gutter lane.

411. LONDON, DUTCH CHURCH, AUSTIN FRIARS
The congregation was recognised in 1550 and was granted the church and site of the former Austin Friars (in *148*) by charter in 1611. The records are in GL.

a. MS 7418: deeds, *c.* 1611–1874 (*148*); incl. plan of church, probably early 17C. MS 18974: photograph of charter, 1550, with ref. to church. MS. 18948: 20C papers, incl. copy charter 1611 and abs. title from 1611 (*148*).

b. MS 7408: memorandum bk. (Dutch) 1594–1714, incl. some notes on property, rents.

c. MSS 7390/1, 7389/1: a/c bks., 1606–57, 1658–1705 (Dutch), incl. collection lists, repairs to church, few refs. to leases. MSS 7396/1–6: bills, receipts, rough a/cs, collection lists (Dutch and English), 1565–1670.

d. MSS 7428/1–27: 'Archivum' (letters, deeds,memoranda, 1462–1900); calendared and indexed in J. H. Hessels, *Ecclesiae Londino-Batavae Archivum . . . Epistulae et Tractatus*, vol. 3 pt. 1 (1897); see index refs. and esp. no. 2466, viewers' report, 17C.

412. LONDON, EAST INDIA COMPANY
The company, fd. 1600, acquired its city freeholds in the 18C along with many earlier deeds. From *c.* 1600 onwards it occupied several city properties as tenant. The records are at the India Office Library and Records, London.

a. Deeds, leases, and other records of title, mid 16C onwards. These exist in two series (A/1, 'Charters and Deeds'; L/L, 'Legal Advisor's Records') in the process of being investigated, sorted, and collated. In 1984 the best guide was the early 19C 'Register of Charters and Deeds' (Z/L/L), which calendars the deeds chronologically by property; not all those listed remain in this archive. Groups of entries concerning city properties before 1670 begin on pp. 12, 19, 26, 50, 56, 69, 71, 81, 84, 93, 130, 187, 234, 309, 368, 416, 478, 503, 513, 524, 550, 563, 568, 584, 600, 608, 770. The properties lay in *4, 19, 43, 77, 78, 141, 149*; there is also a ref. to *51*.

b. Court Minutes. Those for 1599–1634 are calendared in *Calendar of State Papers, Colonial* ii-iv, vi, viii; and those for 1635–67 in *A calendar of the Court Minutes etc. of the East India Company*, ed. E. B. Sainsbury (6 vols, 1907–25). They include records of the company's tenure of its successive headquarters in Philpot Lane, *64* (Crosby House), and *19* (East India House).

c. Early 19C plans and elevations of the company's headquarters and warehouses, incl. some plans of leasehold boundaries (H/763).

413. LONDON, INNS OF COURT AND CHANCERY
The records of the Inns of Court and Chancery (in the parishes of *20* and *54*, in extraparochial precincts close by, and outside the city) were not searched; they relate directly only to those areas, but may include casual references to other parts of the city. The records are in the libraries of the inns, and in PRO; for sources in print see J. M. Sims, *London and Middlesex Published Records, a handlist* (LRS 1970), 28–9.

a. Inner Temple. See J. Conway Davies, *Catalogue of Manuscripts in the Inner Temple Library* (1972). Many of the administrative records are covered by *A Calendar of the Inner Temple Records* i–iii, *1505–1714*, ed. F. A. Inderwick (1896–1901); for a list of records see vol. 1, pp. vii-viii. The calendared items incl.: 'Acts of Parliament' (minute books) from 1505 onwards, containing assignments of chambers, licences to build, orders for building and repairs, letting of shops, and views, all within the precinct; 'Book of Evidences, 1568–1732', containing deeds (precinct and *54*); Account Bks. 1606 onwards, containing receipts of rent. Deeds and leases are not calendared and may incl. items concerning the precinct before 1666.

b. Middle Temple. The records are listed on pp. ix-x of *A Calendar of the Middle Temple Records*, ed. C. H. Hopwood (1903): incl. extracts from the series of a/cs, which begin in 1637 (details of payments for building and rents). *Minutes of Parliament of the Middle Temple* 4 vols., ed. C. T.

Martin (1904–5): incl. decisions on building, admissions to chambers, notes of leases; rental of chambers and shops s.a. 1567 (within the precinct and in the street at Temple Bar). Uncalendared items incl. 17C deeds and leases, rental bks. (date not given).

c. Other inns. D. S. Bland, *Early records of Furnival's Inn, edited from a Middle Temple Manuscript* (pamphlet, Department of Extramural Studies, King's College, Newcastle upon Tyne, 1957) also incl. notes on the early records of other inns. For Serjeants' Inn, see also **263**.

414. LONDON, ROYAL COLLEGE OF PHYSICIANS
The college, fd. 1518, has pre-Fire records of the properties it occupied in *38, 92*, and *47*, successively, and of other properties in the city. The records, a card catalogue of the later items, and the catalogue noted below are at the college (11, St. Andrew's Place, London NW1).

a. Deeds and leases. See 'A Descriptive Catalogue of the Legal and other documents in the Archives of the Royal College of Physicians of London' (TS, 1924), where 17C and later deeds and leases are listed under the following headings: 'Amen Corner', from 1649 (*92*: site of college, 1614–66); 'King's Head Tavern', from 1614 (*112*: an 18C endowment); 'Oxenbridge', 1637 (*39*: stray deed); 'Warwick Lane', from 1610 (*47*: site of college post-Fire).

b. Annals (minutes of college busines; TS transcript and translation) vols. 1–4, 1518–1677: incl. copy 16C lease (*38*, s.a. 1558), proposal to buy property in Charterhouse (s.a. 1598), 17C business concerning the two college houses pre-Fire (*38, 92*) and the post-Fire premises (*47*). For the dimensions of the house in *38*, see W. Munk, *The Roll of the Royal College of Physicians* (2nd. ed., 1878) iii, 321 n. 2 (citing the MS now identified as SR 2189).

415. LONDON, SION COLLEGE
The college, fd. 1623 as a college and almshouse for the clergy by the Revd. Thomas White, lay in *15*; see W. H. Milman, 'Some account of Sion College . . .', *Trans LMAS* 6 (1890), 53–122. The records are GL. See also **310**.

a. MS 10518: deeds, etc., 1611–1734 (*18*, Blackfriars). MS 10519: deeds, leases, 1650–1739 (*15*). MS 10529: papers, 1631–74, incl. abs. title from 1540, view 1633 (*15*). MS 9252, copy will of founder, 1623.

b. MS 10504/1: loose draft a/cs, 1665–80, noting rent receipts (probably *15*), taxes paid. MS 10526: sundry a/cs, 1664–98, incl. workmens' bills, 1670.

c. MS 10530: papers, 1663–93, incl. list of deeds and leases from 1631; late 17C sketch plans and elevations (*18*); extracts from minutes, 1664; fragment of a/c, 1666.

416. LONDON, WARDS AND LIBERTIES
In most cases ward records do not begin until after 1666. Presentations

and assessment lists can contain topographical detail. For the series of ward presentments in CLRO, beginning in 1668, see card index there; otherwise the records are in GL.

a. Aldersgate. MS 2050/1: wardmote bk., begun *c.* 1584; lists of officers *c.* 1467–1801, some presentments and inquest orders, memoranda of ward goods. MSS 1499–1502; wardmote presentments 1510, 1528, 16C, 1614. MSS 1503/1–10: assessments, various precincts, 1580–1661.

b. Aldgate. MSS 1162/1, 1A, 2–5: precinct bks., listing officers nominated and elected, 1594–1851.

c. Bridge. MSS 3461/1, 2: wardmote bks. 1627–62, 1663–88: lists of officers, a/cs, presentments, lists of ward inhabitants 1634 and frequently thereafter.

d. Candlewick. MS 473: wardmote bk. 1676–1802; (f. 3ʳ·ᵛ) view of ward bounds, agreement with neighbouring wards over some houses.

e. Cheap. MS 60: wardmote bk. 1701–1829; (f. 1) view of ward bounds, with reference to occupants of some houses before the Fire.

f. Cornhill. MSS 4069/1, 2: wardmote bks. 1571–1651, 1652–1733; lists of officers, a/cs, presentments, several assessments. MS 2942 B: list of contributors to 'voluntary gift', ?1661.

g. Farringdon within. MS 9257: subsidy a/c 1628.

h. Farringdon without. MS 3018/1: bk. of presentments and inquest mins., precinct of St. Dunstan West, 1558–1823. MS 3180/1: minute bks. of precinct meetings, incl. lists of officers, inhabitants, Smithfield precinct, 1646–1724.

j. Lime Street. MS 1169/1: wardmote bk. 1654–1779: lists of officers, a/cs; no presentments till after *c.* 1700.

k. Portsoken. CLRO: presentments, 1464–82, 1507. MS 2649/1: wardmote bk. 1684–1798, listing precincts. MS 2636: bk. of John Webster's charity, with copy deed 1639 (*43*), list of recipients 1644–1890. MS 10335: rental of poor's lands, 1666–7 (*43*). See **301**.

l. Queenhithe. MS 4829: wardmote bk. 1667–1746; lists of officers, orders for conduct of inquest.

m. Walbrook. MS 455: bk. of Lawrence Campe's charity, with copy deed 1602, will 1616, a/cs of rent receipt and distribution, 1618–1887, some memoranda on leasing and rebuilding (*74*).

n Liberty of St. Martin le Grand. MS 50: 'Court bk.' 1615–1814; lists of officers, orders for conduct of inquest, inventory of goods.

417. BRISTOL, REVD. THOMAS WHITE'S ALMSHOUSE ('TEMPLE HOSPITAL')
The almshouse, fd. 1615 by the Revd. Thomas White, was endowed with property in *105* and Bristol; the rent from the former made up most of its income for some years. The records are in Bristol RO.

a. MSS 12966/71–82: deeds, copy deeds, leases, bonds, 1544–1644. MS 12966/83, petition to Fire Ct. 1671. MS 12966/150: incl. copy lease 1671.

b. MSS 12966/112–114, a/c bks. 1615–1723: rent receipts.

418. ROCHESTER BRIDGE TRUST, ROCHESTER, KENT

The Trust, fd. 1387 to undertake the upkeep and repair of Rochester Bridge, was endowed with income and estates including a property in *19*. The records, with the exception of a number of deeds and plans deposited in GL, are kept by the Clerk at the Bridge Chamber, 5 Esplanade, Rochester, Kent.

There is a TS catalogue/calendar to the whole archive. See E. S. Scroggs, 'The records of Rochester Bridge and of the New College of Cobham', *Archives* 2 (1953–6), 183–91.

a. GL, MS 8514: deeds and leases, 1546–1906. GL, MS 8522: original petitions for leases, 1633–72.

b. Ad. 1: 15C memorandum bk. of chaplain, listing endowments. Ad. 109, 'The Black Book': compilation *c.* 1595 of evidences, list of founders, etc., from 1399. Ad. 101, 'Inquisitions, Statutes, Elections, Accounts, etc.': vol. comp. 1587 with lists of lands and benefactors, summary a/cs 1576–1732. Ad. 2, 3: copies of letters patent 1398–1702 relating to endowments.

c. E 1, 'Lease Book': (f. 10) detailed survey and rental, *c.* 1575–77, with note of repairs needed; (ff. 15ᵛ, 17) rentals 1624, 1661; (f. 46 et seqq.) copy leases *c.* 1577–1658 (listed on flyleaf). E 2: lease bk. 1662–1723, indexed by tenants' names.

d. RS 1 (roll): valor of estates 1506–7. RS 2 (paper): rental *c.* 1550. Ad. 97: brief memorandum of estates, 1575. RS 3: bk. of surveys of estates, 1575–77, as in E 1, f. 10; photograph of London section in GL, MS 8513. RS 4 (roll): rental 1597. RS 95: survey 1661.

e. Ac. 1–90: incomplete series of a/c rolls and bklets., 1391–1561, incl. some rent a/cs from *c.* 1423–4, with repairs, also Bridge paymasters and repair a/cs; see typescript catalogue. Ac. 91–102: wardens' a/c bks. I–XII, 1576–1675 (series continues), incl. detailed annual rentals.

f. GL, MS 8517: plan 1687. MAPS 1: bk. of estate maps incl. 2 London plans, *c.* 1713, 1717. GL, MS 8516: draft plan, apparently for MAPS 1, *c.* 1713.

419. SHERBORNE ALMSHOUSE, SHERBORNE, DORSET

The almshouse succeeded the hospital of St. John dissolved in 1547. Under a will of 1629 part of the income from leasehold houses in London was assigned for the maintenance of the poor in Sherborne. The Merchant Taylors' Company (see **48**) acted as trustee. The charity expired *c.* 1771 when the leases ran out. MSS relating to the management of the almshouse are in Dorset RO (D204).

The London estate (rarely specified) probably lay in: *34, 63, 99.*

a. D204/CH 719: lease, 1671 (*63*). D204/SC 709–33A: copies of deeds, letters, Fire Ct. papers, 1649 onwards. D204/474A-C: Fire Ct. papers. D204/615: list of writings at Merchant Taylors' Hall. D204/SC 607: extract from will.

b. D204/SC 805B: bk. of abstracts of leases, 1669 onwards (*34, 63, 99*). D204/D 24: register, 1582–1866, incl. extract from will.

c. D204/SC 614, 616: rents and arrears, late 17C.

PRIVATE COLLECTIONS

This section covers family collections still in private hands; collections deposited in record offices and libraries are described under those headings. The collections were identified from references in the HMC *Reports* and additional lists at the NRA. In most cases they are described in relation to the individual or family traditionally associated with them, although the ownership may now be vested in trustees or other bodies, from which permission to consult the records should be sought.

420. MARQUESS OF ANGLESEY, PLAS NEWYDD, ANGLESEY
Not visited. See list at NRA. See also **123**, **458**, **500**.

a. Inventories, 16C (city of London, Charterhouse).

421. MARQUESS OF BATH, LONGLEAT, WILTS.
Not visited.

a. See HMC (58) *Bath IV*, p. 127, receipts for rent, 16C (*151*); ibid. p. 159, ref. to purchase of house, 16C (*25*). See also *Bath V*, for casual refs. to parts of London.

422. DUKE OF BEDFORD
See TS report made in 1948 (NRA 10492), pp. 68–9 and *Guide to Russell Estate Collections for Bedfordshire and Devon* (Bedford, 1966). The records are at the Bedford Office, 29A, Montague Street, London WC1B 5BL.

a. Deeds. F1/1–13, F2/1–46, and A2/1–2 (missing in 1983 but known from earlier lists or abstracts on cards): deeds, 15C–16C (*158*); deeds and a rental, 13C–16C (*53*); deeds 16C–17C (*44*). R1–17: deeds, 16C–17C (*4, 5, 20, 38, 42, 54, 61, 151*). A1/1–12: deeds, 16C–17C (*44*). B/1–13: deeds, 17C (*53*). C/1–13: deeds. 16C–17C (*158*). D/1–11: deeds, 17C (*118*). E/1–10: deeds, 17C (*156*). G/1–7: deeds, 16C–18C (*18*).

423. TRUSTEES OF THE BERKELEY ESTATES, BERKELEY CASTLE, GLOS.
Not visited. See I. H. Jeayes, *Descriptive catalogue of the charters and muniments . . . of Lord Fitzhardinge at Berkeley Castle* (1892).

a. Charter 581 (*Catalogue*, p. 182): grant, 1417, incl. advowson of *18*.

b. Select books 68(1) (*Catalogue*, p. 315): inventory, 16C, of household goods (Shoe Lane).

424. DUKE OF DEVONSHIRE, CHATSWORTH HOUSE, DERBYS.
See NRA Report 20594/4, p. 60: rental, 1527, lands of James Burton
(incl. London, not necessarily city).

425. GOODWYN MSS
See HMC list (NRA 5914). The MSS belong to C. W. Goodwyn, Esq.,
Hinton House, 132 High Street, Amersham, Bucks.

a. Bundles 1 and 8, containing 97 items, form a collection of surveyors'
particulars of houses and leases, with some plans and correspondence,
concerning properties in and near London for the period *c.* 1660–*c.* 1680.
The following parishes and other locations in the city are covered: *18, 22,
25, 45, 46, 62, 64, 101, 105, 108, 142, 148, 158*, Aldersgate Street, Austin
Friars, Bevis Marks, Birchin Lane, Bishopsgate Street, Blackhorse
Alley, Broad Street, Bucklersbury, Coldharbour, Durham Yard, Fen-
church Street, Fish Street Hill, Fleet Street, Foster Lane, Gulley Key,
Lothbury, Lumber Street (probably not Lombard Street), Milk Street,
Mincing Lane, Old Bailey, Old Jewry, Queen Street, Rood Lane, St.
Martin le Grand, St. Martin's Lane, St. Sithe's Lane, Throgmorton
Street, Tower Dock, Tower Hill, Warwick Lane.

426. MSS FORMERLY OF F. W. LEYBORNE-POPHAM
See HMC (51) *Mr F. W. Leyborne-Popham*, 103: ref. to inventory of
house in St. Martin's Lane (possibly *93* or St. Martin le Grand). These
MSS are now in a number of collections and the inventory has not been
traced.

427. J. C. G. MILLAR, ESQ.
15C deed (*112*), in 1982 in care of Mr. Millar, 25 Greenland Avenue,
Derby. Transcript deposited in GL.

428. DUKE OF NORFOLK, ARUNDEL CASTLE, SUSSEX
Archives incl. 17C a/cs for Lothbury House; see *Arundel Castle Archives*,
ed. F. W. Steer (1972) ii, 127.

429. DUKE OF NORTHUMBERLAND
Not visited. For the records, apply in the first instance to the Northumberland Estates Office, Alnwick Castle, Alnwick, Northumberland. The
16C and later records of London property concern holdings outside the
city.

a. Cartulary, 14C (Davis, no. 1306; *The Percy Cartulary*, ed. M. T.
Martin, Surtees Society 117, 1911): incl. 13C–14C deeds (*1*, London
unspec.).

430. DUKE OF RUTLAND, BELVOIR CASTLE, LEICS.
Not visited.

a. See HMC (24) *Twelfth Report, Appendix IV*, pp. 145, 384, 477:

correspondence, 16C–17C (refs. to church(es) of *17* and *20*, and to property by Bishopsgate).

431. SALISBURY (CECIL) MSS, HATFIELD, HERTS.
Not visited. There are microfilms of the calendared MSS in BL (M/485, 1–127). For relevant material, see HMC (3) *Fourth Report*, (4) *Fifth Report*, (6) *Seventh Report*, (9) *Salisbury (Cecil) MSS*, Parts 1–24, to which abbreviated refs. are given below. The material is 16C and early 17C in date. In addition to the items noted here, there are numerous incidental references to localities in the city.

a. Deeds, leases, and copies thereof: *45*, HMC (9) Pt. 19, p. 310; *58*, HMC (9) Pt. 21, pp. 361–2; Austin Friars, HMC (9) Pt. 9, p. 150; Thames Street, HMC (9) Pt. 13, p. 263.

b. Rent receipts: *18*, HMC (9) Pt. 2, p. 149, Pt. 13, p. 178; *19*, HMC (4), p. 216.

c. Misc. refs. to property and tenancies in letters, petitions etc.: *25*, HMC (9) Pt. 12, p. 219, Pt. 15, p. 452; *45*, HMC (9) Pt. 20, p. 191; *47*, HMC (9) Pt. 10, p. 112; *64*, HMC (9) Pt. 11, p. 88; *99*, HMC (9) Pt. 4, p. 73; benefices of *13, 19, 99, 101*, HMC (9) Pt. 7, p. 112, Pt. 13, p. 243, Pt. 14, p. 328; Bishopsgate, HMC (9) Pt. 8, p. 361, Pt. 13, p. 47; Fleet Street, HMC (9) Pt. 14, p. 279; brewhouse called Hartshorn, HMC (9) Pt. 14, p. 72; Holborn, HMC (9) Pt. 23, p. 90; Moorfields, HMC (9) Pt. 7, p. 298; Newgate Market, HMC (9) Pt. 24, pp. 102–3, 208; New Inn, Clements Inn, Lyons Inn, HMC (9) Pt. 4, p. 73; Old Jewry, HMC (4), p. 217; Custom House Quay, Queen's Wharf, HMC (9) Pt. 2, p. 520, Pt. 5, p. 145; St. Martin's Lane (possibly *93* or St. Martin le Grand), HMC (9) Pt. 22, pp. 278, 384, 392; St. Martin (cf. above), HMC (9) Pt. 24, p. 216; St. Paul's churchyard, HMC (9) Pt. 1, p. 138; Steelyard, HMC (9) Pt. 8, p. 268, Pt. 24, pp. 102–3, 208; Tower Hill, HMC (9) Pt. 3, p. 428; London (unspec.), HMC (9) Pt. 14, p. 124.

d. Inventories: *25*, HMC (5), p. 262, (9) Pt. 1, p. 318, (9) Pt. 6, p. 199; Fleet Street, HMC (9) Pt. 13, p. 267; Holborn, HMC (9) Pt. 8, p. 544.

e. Plans: Duke's Place (site of Holy Trinity Priory), HMC (5), p. 192, (9) Pt. 14, p. 48; Royal Exchange, HMC (9) Pt. 14, p. 338.

f. Lists of inhabitants: Blackfriars (*25*), St. Katharine's precinct, and St. Martin le Grand, HMC (4), p. 222, (9) Pt. 2, p. 105, Pt. 13, pp. 219–27, 240.

432. SALWEY FAMILY MSS, LUDLOW, SALOP
Not visited.

a. See HMC (13) *Tenth Report, Appendix IV*, p. 409: letters patent, 16C (*44*), apparently not among the Salwey MSS deposited in Shropshire RO.

433. H. V. SHEBBEARE, ESQ.
See HMC list (NRA 5774): deed, 17C (*62*).

434. Uppark, Sussex
The Meade-Fetherstonhaugh deeds (NRA 2576), formerly at West Sussex Record Office, incl. (nos. 373–534) 16C and 17C records of property in *19, 20, 42, 75, 87, 101, 152*, Cheapside.

435. Verney family, Claydon, Bucks.
Not visited. See HMC list comp. 1978.

a. Deeds, 1599–1626 (London, incl. St. John's Street and possibly all outside the city).

PUBLIC RECORD OFFICE, LONDON

Material relating to property-holding in London is to be found in PRO in the records concerning lands in the Crown's hands (Crown estate and Duchy of Lancaster, lands of dissolved religious houses, and escheats and forfeitures); in records, mostly judicial, relating to the properties of private citizens (enrolled deeds, fines, recoveries, Chancery decrees, eyres, inquisitions, and judicial proceedings); in records, such as Chancery Rolls and State Papers, that cover both categories; and in some of the records of taxation. All these are at present (1983) in Chancery Lane. Not all the classes noted below as containing, or likely to contain, relevant material could be fully searched, nor was it feasible to search other classes that might possibly contain such material. This survey does not supersede the PRO *Guide to the contents of the Public Record Office*, vols. i–ii (1963), but it directs attention to the most important classes or groups containing London material, and in some cases supplements existing PRO indexes to these. The varied nature of PRO records, and in particular the existence of the valuable but artificial Special Collections classes, means that description by strict categories is not possible. PRO records relating to the estates of dissolved religious houses are described partly in this section (**438**, **441**) and partly under the headings of individual houses (**70–274**); occasional or stray records relating to other archives or institutions are described under those headings. The classes described here are explained in further detail in PRO *Guide*, and in most cases are listed and/or indexed in search room class lists and List and Index Society volumes: see HMSO *Sectional List* 24.

For wills and inventories now kept at PRO, see **529–30**.

436. PRO: ROYAL PROPERTIES IN LONDON
At various times the king or queen and other members of the royal family held properties in London for use as residences or wardrobes, but there was no extensive long-term Crown holding within the city. The Tower and its liberty lay outside: for these see *History of the King's Works*, ed. H. M. Colvin, ii (1963), iv (1982), and **439** below.

A few accounts survive for specific properties; the entries in *History of the King's Works* noted below refer to further building and repair accounts not listed in detail here. It was not possible to search all likely records for references to royal holdings. There are references in the main series of Household and Wardrobe accounts (single accounts (E101), listed in PRO Handbook 7, *List of documents relating to the Household and Wardrobe, John to Edward I* (1964), and PRO *Lists and Indexes* XXXV, *List of Exchequer Accounts Various*; enrolled accounts (E361), 1258–1547, listed in PRO *Lists and Indexes* XI, *List of foreign accounts enrolled on the Great Rolls of the Exchequer*), but these classes were not searched. More distant members of the royal family also held London properties, often granted by the Crown from forfeited lands, but accounts relating to these do not usually survive in the public records; some may however be included in **437**. For Duchy of Lancaster properties, incl. the queens' jointures in the 15C, see **440**.

a. King's wardrobe. This was in Lombard Street in the early 14C: E101/388/4, a/c of repairs 1338. In the 1360s a new wardrobe was built in *18: History of the King's Works* ii (1963), 980–1.

b. Prince's wardrobe, Old Jewry (*95, 142*; used by the Prince of Wales, 14C and 15C). See *Register of Edward, the Black Prince* (1930–3); SC6/815/7, a/c of repairs, 1433–4; E101/474/2, a/c of repairs, 1469–70; *History of the King's Works* ii (1963), 981–2. See also Social and Economic Study of Medieval London, Gazetteer 95/8–12 (TS, available in IHR, Museum of London, etc.).

c. Exchange, Lombard Street. The exchange was kept there in at least the late 14C– early 15C: E101/292/29, E101/293/4, E101/300/14, 16, and possibly other mint a/cs (listed in PRO *Lists and Indexes* XXXV).

d. Baynards Castle (*38*; held by the Crown from 1461). See E101/474/16, E101/544/26, a/cs of works, 1547, 1549; *History of the King's Works* iv (1982), 50–2.

e. Bridewell Palace (*46* or extraparochial; built 1515–23). See *History of the King's Works* iv (1982), 53–8; D. Gadd and T. Dyson, 'Bridewell Palace: Excavations . . . 1978', *Post-Medieval Archaeology* 15 (1981). Cf. **409**.

f. Coldharbour (*12*; in the Crown's hands at intervals in the 15C, occupied by Lady Margaret, countess of Richmond, 1485–1509). E101/474/3, a/c of repairs, 1485; printed in C. L. Kingsford, 'Some London houses of the early Tudor period', *Archaeologia* 71 (1921), 43–50. See also St. John's College, Cambridge, MS D 91.22: a/c bk. of Lady Margaret's clerk of works, 1505–7, incl. (ff. 201–10) repairs to Coldharbour.

g. Works for tournaments at (West) Smithfield. E101/473/16: a/c, 1408–9, of works at Smithfield. E101/44/1: similar a/c, 1467–8.

437. PRO: ESCHEATS, FORFEITURES, ETC., PRIVATE ESTATES
At various times the Crown acquired the city properties of private individuals, as a result of escheat or forfeiture, temporary or permanent. Properties were not usually kept for long, but were returned to the original holder or his heirs or were granted to a third party. In addition, inquisitions and returns were made concerning properties which might have been liable to escheat or forfeiture but which did not in the event pass to the Crown. Not all the records relating to these subjects were fully searched, but those that were, and other areas of interest, are outlined below. Rentals, surveys, and accounts relating to alien priories, religious houses, and vacant sees are noted under those headings, **70–274**.

a. Deeds. Title deeds retained in PRO relating to forfeited properties are included in the index to PRO deeds, **441**.

b. Inquisitions (post mortem, ad quod damnum, miscellaneous). These relate both to feudal tenures and to forfeitures, and survive in Chancery (C132–145) and Exchequer (E149–50) classes: see PRO *Guide* i, 27–8, 59–60, and class lists. A substantial part of these classes is calendared and printed: see HMSO *Sectional List* 24 for details of HMSO etc. publications, also *Abstracts of inquisitions post mortem relating to the city of London 1485–1603*, ed. G. S. Fry, S. J. Madge, and E. A. Fry (British Record Soc. 15, 26, 36, 1896–1908).
Escheators' Files (E153; not searched) contain some similar inquisitions: see PRO *Guide* i, 58. See also CLRO, Escheat Rolls (**5**).

c. Rentals and accounts. The earliest surviving accounts for escheats are recorded by county in the Pipe Rolls (E372), from the mid 12C. Most of the relevant rolls (to 1219) have been published by Record Commission and Pipe Roll Society; see also *The great roll of the pipe for the 26th year of King Henry III, A.D. 1242*, ed. H. L. Cannon (New Haven, Conn., 1918). Some extracts relating to London debts, 1244–53, are printed in *London Eyre 1244*, pp. xxvii–xxxii. From the mid 13C escheats were accounted for separately by escheators (PRO *Guide* i, 77). The main series of Escheators' Accounts (E136), mid 13C to 17C, is arranged by county; London a/cs form a separate group from 1348. The bundles are listed in PRO class list. The accounts contain information about estates currently in the escheators' hands, and the London a/cs relate closely to CLRO Escheat Rolls (**5**). The class as a whole was not searched, nor were the escheators' enrolled a/cs (listed in PRO, *Lists and Indexes* XI: *List of foreign accounts enrolled on the Great Rolls of the Exchequer*, 282–4), but both contain valuable material.
In addition to these accounts a large number of individual rentals and a/cs were made by receivers and others, for the estates of individuals (often of nobles) temporarily held by the Crown. Rentals are in E142, E164, E315, LR2/262, SC11 and SC12 (listed in PRO, *Lists and Indexes* XXV: *List of Rentals and Surveys*); a/cs are in SC6 (listed in PRO, *Lists and Indexes* V, VIII, XXXIV, and *Supplementary* II: *Lists of Ministers' Accounts*). These classes were searched and the following index compiled: reference to the appropriate *List* will identify the person in question and the approximate date. Included in the index are a/cs for the estates of unidentified persons or bodies, some of which may relate to religious houses. Also included in the index are references to enrolled Ministers' Accounts, Territorial, and Sheriffs' Seizures, taken from PRO, *Lists and Indexes* XI: *List of foreign accounts enrolled on the Great Rolls of the Exchequer*, 172–3, 247–9; the rolls were not searched.

Parishes

4: *L&I* XI, pp. 247–9	10: SC12/36/32
5: SC12/11/37; SC6/917/13(m. 1); *L&I* XI, pp. 247–9	10 or 12: SC11/797
8: SC12/1/21	12: SC6/1123/8–9; SC6/Hen 8/6852–63; *L&I* XI, pp. 247–9
9: *L&I* XI, pp. 247–9	13: SC12/40/62; *L&I* XI, pp. 172–3

18: SC6/Phil & Mary/277
19: SC11/1025; SC12/40/62
20: LR2/262, f. 20ᵛ; SC12/11/37; SC6/ Edw 6/292; *L&I* XI, pp. 247–9
21: SC12/1/21
22: *L&I* XI, pp. 247–9
26: *L&I* XI, pp. 247–9
30: SC11/797
32: E142/83/1; SC6/1123/7; SC6/Hen 8/ 5972–5; *L&I* XI, pp. 247–9
36: E142/83/1
38: SC12/40/62; *L&I* XI, pp. 247–9
39: *L&I* XI, pp. 172–3, 247–9
41: SC12/40/62; *L&I* XI, pp. 247–9
42: SC6/1116/1; *L&I* XI, pp. 247–9
43: SC12/1/21; SC12/26/61; SC12/36/33
44: SC6/1276/7
45: SC11/797, 1025; SC12/1/21
46: SC12/11/37
47: SC12/40/62
51: SC6/917/2
52: SC6/917/2, 6
53: LR2/262, f. 20ᵛ; SC12/36/32; SC12/40/ 62; SC6/917/13 (m. 4); SC6/1276/7; *L&I* XI, pp. 247–9
54: SC12/11/37
59: SC12/40/62; cf. Lovell's Inn, below
62: SC12/40/62; SC6/917/20, 22; *L&I* XI, pp. 172–3
64: SC12/36/33; SC6/1117/11
65: *L&I* XI, pp. 172–3, 247–9
66: SC6/1276/7
67: SC11/797
71: SC12/11/37; SC12/40/62; *L&I* XI, pp. 247–9
74: SC11/797
77: SC12/40/62; SC6/Hen 7/1242
78: SC12/26/61
79: SC6/917/6
80: E315/12/9; E315/13/296; SC12/11/37; SC6/Hen 8/5841–76; SC6/Edw 6/292
81: SC12/1/21; SC6/1116/11; *L&I* XI, pp. 247–9
85: SC12/11/37; SC6/917/2; *L&I* XI, pp. 247–9
87: *L&I* XI, pp. 247–9
88: E142/83/1
89: SC12/11/37

90: *L&I* XI, pp. 247–9
92: SC12/11/37; SC12/40/62
93: SC12/40/62
94: SC12/11/37
96: SC12/11/37; SC6/1123/8–9
98: SC12/11/37
101: SC12/36/33
103: SC11/797; SC12/11/34
104: SC11/797; SC6/Hen 8/6146–7
106: *L&I* XI, pp. 247–9
111: SC12/1/21; *L&I* XI, pp. 247–9
112: SC12/40/62
113: LR2/262, f. 12ᵛ
116: SC11/797; SC12/40/62
117: SC6/917/13 (m. 2), 14, 17, 19; *L&I* XI, pp. 172–3, 247–9
118: SC6/917/10; *L&I* XI, pp. 247–9
119: SC12/40/62
123: SC12/11/37
124: *L&I* XI, pp. 247–9
125: *L&I* XI, pp. 172–3
126: SC12/36/32
127: SC6/1123/7–9; *L&I* XI, pp. 247–9
128: SC6/917/3 (mm. 5–6)
131: SC12/11/37
135: SC12/11/37
135 or *136*: SC6/917/13 (m. 2), 14
137: SC11/1025; SC12/1/21; SC12/11/37; SC12/36/33; SC6/917/13 (m. 2), 14; SC6/1148/14
138: *L&I* XI, pp. 247–9
144: SC12/11/37; SC6/1124/1
145: SC6/917/2; *L&I* XI, pp. 247–9
146: SC12/11/37
148: SC12/40/62; SC6/Hen 8/5971
149: SC12/40/62; *L&I* XI, pp. 247–9
150: SC12/40/62
151: SC11/797
152: E164/45; SC12/11/37, 49; SC12/40/62; SC6/Hen 8/6882, 6892; *L&I* XI, pp. 247–9
155: SC6/Hen 8/5972–5
156: SC12/11/37
157: SC12/40/62; *L&I* XI, pp. 247–9
158: SC6/Hen 8/5972–5
159: SC12/11/37; SC6/917/13 (m. 2), 14
162: SC6/917/2

Other localities

London: E142/83/1; SC6/915/1; SC6/917/8, 9, 13; SC6/1116/11; SC6/1119/12; SC6/ 1120/7; SC6/1148/1; SC6/1245/16, 17; SC6/Hen 8/345 (m. 7), 2082–6, 6217; SC6/Edw 6/295, 461; *L&I* XI, pp. 172– 3, 247–9
Abchurch Lane: SC12/40/62–3
Addle Street: SC12/36/33
Aldersgate: *L&I* XI, pp. 247–9

Aldersgate Street: SC12/36/33
Aldgate: *L&I* XI, pp. 247–9
Aldgate Street: SC12/11/31
Austin Friars: SC12/36/33
Bailey, the: *L&I* XI, pp. 247–9
Barbican: SC12/40/62
Bartholomew Lane: SC12/36/33
Basing Lane: SC12/36/33; SC6/Hen 8/6128; *L&I* XI, pp. 247–9

171

Bassishaw: SC12/1/1 (m. 12); SC12/40/63
Baynards Castle: SC12/40/62; SC6/1148/14
Bearbinder Lane: SC12/1/21; SC12/36/33
Bevis Marks: SC12/36/33
Billingsgate: SC12/1/21; SC12/40/62; SC6/
    1116/11; *L&I* XI, pp. 247–9
Billingsgate ward: SC6/1146/7
Billiter Lane: SC12/36/33; SC12/40/62
Bishopsgate Street: SC12/36/33; SC12/40/
    62; *L&I* XI, pp. 247–9
Bishopsgate, within: SC12/1/21
Blanchappleton: SC6/1094/8–10; SC6/1117/
    3–4; SC6/1121/12–17; SC6/1148/14
Bordhawe Lane:*L&I* XI, pp. 247–9
Botolph Lane: SC11/797
Bread Street: SC12/36/33; SC6/1116/11;
    L&I XI, pp. 247–9
Bread Street ward: *L&I* XI, pp. 247–9
Bridge Street: SC11/1025; SC6/1148/14
Broad Street: SC12/36/33
Broad Street ward: E142/83/1
Broken Wharf: *L&I* XI, pp. 172–3
Budge Row: SC12/1/1 (m. 12)
Bush Lane: SC12/11/34; SC6/1123/6
Candlewick Street: SC11/1025; SC6/917/4,
    7
Carter Lane: SC12/11/34; SC6/Hen 7/401;
    SC6/Hen 8/1793, 2081–6, 6867
Castle Baynard ward: *L&I* XI, pp. 247–9
Chancery Lane: SC12/36/33
Charterhouse   Lane: SC12/40/62;
    SC6/Eliz/1554
Cheapside: SC12/36/33; SC12/40/62; SC6/
    917/3–7
le Cheker, tenement called: SC6/1123/6;
    SC6/Hen 8/6867
Chick Lane: SC12/36/33
Coleman Street: SC12/36/33
Cordwainer Street: SC12/1/1 (m. 12)
Cornhill: SC11/1025; SC12/1/21; SC12/11/
    33; SC12/36/33
Cowcross: SC12/40/63
Creed Lane: SC12/36/33
Cripplegate, outside: SC12/1/1 (m. 12)
Crooked Lane: *L&I* XI, pp. 247–9
Crutched Friars: SC12/36/33
Dowgate ward: *L&I* XI, pp. 247–9
Duck Lane: SC12/36/33
Eastcheap: SC12/36/33; SC6/Hen 8/6128
Fenchurch Street: SC11/1025; SC12/36/33
Fetter Lane: SC12/36/33
Finch Lane: SC12/36/33
Fleet Alley: SC11/11
Fleet Street: SC12/1/21; SC12/36/33; SC12/
    40/62; *L&I* XI, pp. 247–9
'Franchelane': SC12/1/21
Friday Street: SC12/1/21; SC12/36/33; *L&I*
    XI, pp. 247–9
'Gofairlane': SC6/1148/14
Golden Lane: SC12/36/33

Goswell Street: SC12/36/33
Gracechurch Street: SC11/1025; SC12/36/
    32–3
Grub Street: SC12/1/21
le Herber, tenement called: SC6/1123/6;
    SC6/Hen 8/2082–6
Holborn: SC11/1025; SC12/11/23, 30; SC12/
    36/33; SC12/40/64
Houndsditch: SC12/36/33
Huggin Lane: SC12/36/33
Ivy Lane: SC12/36/33
Lad Lane: SC12/36/33
Leadenhall Street: SC12/36/33
Lime Street: SC12/36/33
Lombard Street: SC11/1025; SC12/11/33;
    SC12/36/33
London Bridge: SC12/11/33
London Wall: SC12/36/33
Long Lane: SC12/36/33
Lothbury: SC12/36/33; SC12/40/63
Lovell's Inn (in *59*): SC6/Hen 8/5879–80;
    SC6/Edw 6/740, 750–1
Ludgate: *L&I* XI, pp. 247–9
Ludgate Hill: SC12/36/33
Maiden Lane: SC12/36/33
Mark Lane: SC11/1025; SC12/1/21; SC12/
    36/33; *L&I* XI, pp. 172–3, 247–9
Milk Street: SC12/36/33; SC12/40/62; SC6/
    Hen 8/5972–5; SC6/Edw 6/292
Mincing Lane: SC12/36/33; *L&I* XI, pp.
    247–9
Monkwell Street: SC12/36/33
'New Inn': *L&I* XI, pp. 172–3
Nicholas Lane: *L&I* XI, pp. 247–9
Noble Street: SC12/36/33
Old Bailey: SC12/36/33
Old Change: SC11/1025
Old Fish Street: SC11/11, 1025; SC12/
    40/63
Old Jewry: SC12/40/62
Ormonds Inn: SC6/1094/5, 8–10
Oystergate: SC6/917/2
Paternoster Row: SC11/1025; SC12/36/33;
    SC6/1148/14
Paul's wharf: *L&I* XI, pp. 247–9
Philpot Lane: SC12/40/62
Poor Jewry Lane: SC12/36/33
Poultry: SC12/1/21; SC12/36/33
Queenhithe: SC12/1/21; SC6/1094/13; SC6/
    1095/1
Queenhithe ward: SC12/11/37
Red Cross Street: SC12/36/33
Rood Lane: SC12/36/33
'Rynged hall': SC12/40/62
St. John's Street: SC12/36/33
St. Lawrence Lane: SC11/1025; SC12/
    1/21
St. Martin le Grand: SC12/36/33
St. Nicholas Lane: SC12/36/33
St. Peter's Hill: SC6/1246/19

St. Sithe's Lane: SC12/40/62
Seacoal Lane: SC12/1/21; *L&I* XI, pp. 247–9
Seething Lane: SC12/36/33
Sherborne Lane: SC12/36/33
Shoe Lane: SC12/36/33
Smithfield: SC12/1/21; SC6/917/13 (m. 3); *L&I* XI, pp. 172–3, 247–9
Smithfield Bars: SC12/40/63
Soper Lane: SC12/36/33
Stocks, the: SC11/1025
Temple Bar: SC12/36/33
Thames Street: LR2/262, f. 20ᵛ; SC6/1117/11; SC6/1148/14; SC6/Hen 8/5879–80; SC6/Edw 6/740, 750–1
Threadneedle Street: SC12/36/33
Timberhithe: SC6/917/4, 7

Tower Street: SC11/1025; SC12/36/33
Tower ward: *L&I* XI, pp. 247–9
Tower Wharf: *L&I* XI, pp. 172–3
Turnmill Street: SC12/36/33
Vintry ward: SC6/1116/11; *L&I* XI, pp. 247–9
Walbrook: *L&I* XI, pp. 247–9
Wardrobe Lane: SC6/Hen 7/401; SC6/Hen 8/1793, 2081
Warwick Inn: SC12/11/49; SC6/Hen 8/6882
Warwick Lane: SC12/36/33; SC6/1148/14
Watling Street: SC11/11, 1025; *L&I* XI, pp. 172–3, 247–9
Whitechapel field: SC12/11/31
Whitecross Street: SC12/36/33
Whitefriars: SC12/36/33
Wood Street: SC12/36/33

438. PRO: FORMER MONASTIC AND CHANTRY PROPERTIES

For a period in the mid 16C the Crown held a large number of properties in London, the result of the dissolution of religious houses and chantry foundations. The great majority of these properties had been sold by 1570, but income was still received from a few until the mid 17C. During the Interregnum the remaining lands and rents were surveyed and sold. They were resumed at the Restoration. Records of these estates include title deeds, rentals and accounts for revenues, particulars for Crown grants and leases, some deeds of grants and leases. There are parliamentary surveys of the mid 17C (**439**). The title deeds for these estates, and from some other sources, are described and indexed under **441**. Rentals and accounts for the estates of dissolved religious houses up to 1547, and leases granted by those houses (E303), are listed under individual houses, **70–274**.

The properties and parishes covered in this section can be identified by reference to the descriptions of the estates of religious houses (**70–274**) and of chantry estates of London parish churches (**275–381**). The accounts continued to be arranged under the headings of individual houses or chantries; the particulars for and deeds of grants and leases are arranged by grantee, but with reference to the former holder. The guides, calendars, lists, and indexes referred to are PRO class lists, etc., available in the search room, identifiable by reference to the class card-catalogue.

Several 16C and 17C MSS relating to surveys and sales of Crown lands are now in CUL and Bodl: they are described in this section (below, **f, g**) since some at least may be strays from official records in the 17C.

a. Grants and leases: particulars. London lands were often granted in large parcels, comprising properties in many different parishes from the estates of many religious houses or chantries. The particulars for each grant provide valuable details (location, tenant, rent, term, net value p.a., etc.) of the properties to be sold or leased. Most of the groups of particulars are listed or indexed in some way.

E318: particulars for grants, Henry VIII to James I, arranged alphabetically by grantee by reign; calendars and indexes (numerous

London refs.). E310: particulars for leases, arranged by county in 2 groups, Henry VIII to Philip and Mary and Elizabeth to James I; lists and indexes (numerous London refs.). E315/67–8: books of particulars for sale of college and chantry lands in London, 1548; list of contents, no index. E147: particulars for grants and leases, 16C to 17C; bundles 2–4, 17C, calendared but not indexed (East Smithfield, Watling Street, Westcheap); bundles 5–7, 16C and 17C, not calendared but see 5/1 (*25, 152*), 5/2 (*20, 62*), 5/9 (*42*), 6/4 (*47, 51, 54, 90, 152*). E320: particulars for sale of lands, Commonwealth; calendar and index, under Middlesex (refs. to *43, 112, 113, 125, 147* and nr. Tower). E308/3/20: particulars for sale of fee farm rents in London, Interregnum; calendar and index (numerous London refs.).

b. Grants. Crown grants were enrolled on the Patent Rolls (C66) and are calendared and printed in *Letters and Papers of Henry VIII* and *Calendar of Patent Rolls* from 1547; the surviving deeds noted here have a much more limited coverage. See also **449a**.

E305: deeds of purchase and exchange, *c.* 1536–53; indexed calendar for *temp.* Henry VIII (refs. to *64, 78, 81, 95, 105, 142, 155, 156*); indexed calendar for *temp.* Edward VI (refs. to *13, 43, 54, 59, 62, 71, 92, 112*, St. Katharine's precinct, Whitefriars precinct). E307: deeds for sale of fee farm rents, Interregnum, arranged alphabetically by grantee; calendar and index (numerous London refs.).

c. Leases. In general, Crown leases are less fully listed than grants; where the calendars or indexes to particulars for leases (E310 and E147, described under **a**, above) indicate that property in a particular parish or area was leased, it may be worth searching the unlisted classes for further information. Leases granted by religious houses before the Dissolution (E303) are noted under individual houses, **70–274**.

E311: transcripts of Crown leases, Henry VIII to James I; no guide to bundles 1–3, Henry VIII to Philip and Mary; bundles 4–51, Elizabeth and James I, indexed (refs. to *4, 10, 14, 18, 38, 43, 47, 59, 62, 64, 67, 71, 74, 77, 80, 83, 87, 93, 94, 100, 111, 112, 114, 116, 118, 119, 123, 125, 126, 127, 128, 131, 132, 135, 145, 149, 151, 152, 155, 157, 159*, Adling Street, Bow Lane (*126*), Crutched Friars, Distaff Lane, Gutter Lane, Holborn, Knightrider Street, Philip Lane, East Smithfield, Thames Street, Tower Hill, Wood Street). E315/209–29: enrolments of Crown leases, Henry VIII to James I; name index to all vols. in *49th Report of the Deputy Keeper of the Public Records* (1888); vols. 209–217 (1536–47) briefly calendared in *Letters and Papers of Henry VIII*, x–xxi. E315/231: repertory of Crown leases, 1566–8, 1582–98, arranged chronologically; no guide. E309: enrolments of Crown leases, 1560–89; indexed under London (*2, 4, 10, 12, 43, 62, 74, 77, 80, 83, 93, 125, 127, 152, 155, 157*, Crutched Friars, Holborn, Knightrider Street, Old Change, Paternoster Row,Tower Hill, Wood Street). E312: surrendered leases, Henry VIII to Edward VI; no guide.

d. Accounts from 1547. In the reign of Edward VI the Crown received rent from a large number of unsold monastic and chantry properties, and also 'fee-farm rents' or rents reserved on properties already sold. The number of rents diminished as further properties were sold, mostly without any rents reserved; by the 17C the number of properties from which any kind of rent was due was much smaller. The accounts are listed in PRO *Lists and Indexes Supplementary* II; the relevant ones are SC6/Edw 6/290–99; SC6/Phil & Mary/181–6, 489; SC6/Eliz/1370–1413; SC6/Jas 1/622–43; SC6/Chas 1/596–610.Cf. SC12/38/57–9: a/cs of collectors of chantry rents, *c.* 1550, arranged by parishes owning the rents; little topographical detail. E351/1484–1520, declared accounts of fee farm rents, *temp*. Charles II, may include London refs.; class not searched.

e. Rentals and Surveys after 1547. SP14/106: memorandum of former chantry rents, 1619, arranged by parishes owning the rents; little information, often outdated. SC11/957: rental of quit-rents and reserved rents due from former monastic and chantry properties, 1664, arranged by former owner; some valuable detail, not always up to date.

f. MSS in CUL. Ee. 3. 6: rental or particular for grant, *c.* 1631 (*56*, Hart Street, The Burse). Ee. 3. 14: part 1, particulars for grant, *c.* 1632 (*53*); part 2, ff. 50–57ᵛ, rental of Crown revenues in London, 1638, arranged by religious house or chantry (numerous refs. but pars. not named in every case). Ee. 3. 28, 29: a/cs of receipts for Elector Palatine, 1645–7 (Tower Hill). Ee. 3. 42: note of current leases of Crown lands, ?1649; f. 20ᵛ (Tower ditch). Dd. 13. 20: tabular note of Crown lands sold 1650–55; nos. 13 (*125*), 416 (Tower ditch).

g. MSS in Bodl. MS Rawl. B 309: 17C vol. 'Entries of grants, transfers of lands etc.', with brief notes of particulars, grants, leases, *temp*. Elizabeth and James I; London refs. on ff. 89–92ᵛ, 202–205ᵛ. MS Rawl. B 253: 17C vol. of particular of Crown lands sold 1609–11, 1618; London refs. on ff. 73ᵛ–74 (*10, 112*, Minories), ff. 58ᵛ–59 (*51*).

439. PRO: parliamentary surveys, Crown lands
These surveys, 1649–54, cover both original crown lands (*147*, Tower liberty) and some former monastic or chantry properties still in Crown hands. All are in E317/Middlesex file.
    Nos. 1–2, 94 (*43*); 9, 77 (*152*); 14 (*78*); 15, 23 (*54*); 21 (*112*); 37 (*20*); 60 (*125*); 89 (Thames Street); 91–4 (*147*, Tower liberty).

440. PRO: Duchy of Lancaster
Several properties in the city were, at various times, in the possession of the duchy, although the bulk of its London holdings lay in the Strand outside the city. London properties were a minute part of the whole estate, and references to them in the unindexed series of duchy records are difficult to identify. In general, duchy records of the 13C and 14C refer to properties in *20, 59, 88, 99, 137*, New Temple; those of the 15C to properties in *67, 141*, Blanchappleton; those of the 16C to properties in *51*; and those of the 17C to properties in *51, 141*, Blanchappleton, although by this time the duchy seems to have had property only in *51*. There are references throughout to the duchy house in St. Paul's

churchyard and to properties hired for the use of the duchy. In the 16C and 17C several pleas in the duchy court concern matters in the city (see **f**).

From the 16C onwards numerous abstracts from, and guides to, the records have been compiled, although most of them are partial or selective in character; see the TS 'Guide to Lists etc. of Duchy of Lancaster records' in PRO. The principal guide to the records is *Lists and Indexes* XIV and *Supplementary Lists and Indexes* V, vol. 1. For some of the London properties, including short-term interests in wardrobes, and the honour court held in Walbrook, see R. Somerville, *History of the Duchy of Lancaster* i, *1265–1603* (1953). Only records known or suspected to contain information on city properties are mentioned below.

a. For original deeds, see PRO Deeds Index (**441**). Royal charters (DL10) are listed in *Supplementary Lists and Indexes* V, vol. 2. DL15/1–50: counterparts of leases, 16C–17C; IND/18647 calendars DL15/50, but incl. no London leases. DL14/1–96: draft leases and particulars, 16C–17C; IND/17596 calendars 17C bundles, but incl. no London property apart from the Strand.

b. Registers and enrolments: for a survey of this topic, see TS statement on 'Duchy of Lancaster enrolments' in PRO. DL41/1/38 (cf. Davis, no. 1266): 14C roll incl. copies of 13C London deeds (*59, 99, 137*, New Temple). DL42/11 (Davis, no. 1265; abs. in IND/17594): 14C register incl. copies of 13C London deeds (as preceding). DL42/1 and 2 ('The Great Cowcher'; Davis, nos. 1268–9; calendar in IND/17591; see *EHR* 51 (1936), 598–615): 15C register incl. copies of 13C–14C London deeds (*88*; 'Sholand', presumably in *20*; Temple). DL42/18 (abs. in IND/17593): 15C register, incl. lease (Stewards Inn in *141*). DL42/19: 15C register, incl. grant on f. 2ᵛ (*141*, Blanchappleton). DL42/24: 17C register, incl. grant (Blanchappleton, Stewards Inn, 'St. Olive': the latter two in *141*). IND/17599: 17C summary particulars of grants in fee farm (incl. one in *51*: Liber A, f. 19); this summary seems to relate to warrants under the duchy privy seal, of which the surviving bundles covering 16C–17C are DL12/1–39; grants in fee are listed in the 18C 'Index to Grants in Fee' (IND/17598, available in Round Room), which in addition refers to grants in some of the registers in the DL42 series. DL37/1–62: 14C–15C rolls of patents (principally concerning appointments), warrants, and leases; rolls 1–7 contain no London leases, but there is no list of leases entered on later rolls; a 20C transcript of the old calendar of decrees and orders of the duchy known as 'Great Ayloffe' (available in Round Room) refers to DL37/20 (allowance for repairs on the duchy house in St. Paul's churchyard). Patents (principally concerning appointments) entered in the 16C registers, DL42/22–3, and in the 16C–17C bundles of drafts and particulars for patents, DL13/3–37, are indexed in the 'Duchy of Lancaster: Index to Patents Henry VIII to 1835' available in the Round Room (DL13/1–3, of mid 16C date, are not covered); this index does not refer to any properties in the city but does mention leases of holdings in the Strand (in DL42/22), so that the unindexed patents may incl. some city material. DL42/28–33, 35–37B: books of enrolments of leases, 15C–17C;

DL42/34 is a 16C name index; IND/17596 incl. calendars of DL42/30–3, 35–37B (London entries principally concern the Strand, but there are leases for *51*). DL42/73–89: 'South Auditors' Books for Leases' or entry bks. for patents and leases, 16C–17C; DL41/36/2 is a 17C index to places in DL42/82, 84–5, 87–8 (incl. *51*). DL41/35/18: 'Mr. Tusser's Book of Leases', a useful 16C summary of leases (incl. *51*).

c. Accounts.
DL29: local receivers and auditors' a/cs in the duchy records. Those to 1485 are listed in *Lists and Indexes* V, *Ministers Accounts*: DL29/1/2, incl. a/c for earl of Lincoln's establishment in *20*, 1304–5; DL29/1/3, a/c for earl of Lancaster's lands, 1313–14, incl. under heading 'Essex, Middlesex and London' rents in the Strand, unspecified rents (perhaps London), and rents of houses 'de Vienna' (perhaps *59*); in the 15C receivers' and auditors' a/cs receipts from duchy holdings in the city, which for much of the time formed part of the queens' jointures, were generally entered in the a/cs for 'Essex, Surrey, Kent, and London', 'Essex and Herts.' or variants of these (specific refs. to Blanchappleton, Stewards Inn in *141*, Ormonds Inn in *67*); a/cs concerning the Savoy do not incl. receipts from the city. The London a/cs for the period 1485–1547 listed in *Lists and Indexes* XXXIV, *Ministers Accounts*, do not cover duchy property in city, receipts from which, if there were any, may appear in the receivers a/cs for Essex etc. in DL29/bundles 60–3/1129–83. Later a/cs are listed only in Appendix I of the *45th annual report of the Deputy Keeper of the Public Records* (1884): London receipts (possibly concerning only the estate outside the city) are to be found in the a/cs with the headings 'Essex, Herts., Middlesex, and Surrey', or variants, described on pp. 14–19 of the Appendix (DL29, bundles 42–74); receipts from a London property formerly belonging to the College of Newark, Leicester (see **176**), appear in the series of 16C–17C accounts under that heading (DL29, bundles 224–38); receipts from a property (in *51*) of Knolles College, Pontefract (**203**), may be entered in the 16C–17C a/cs for chantries and colleges in Yorkshire in DL29, bundles 564–70; 16C a/cs under the heading 'South Parts Chantries, Kent' (DL29, bundle 723) incl. refs. to the Lancaster chantry in St. Paul's.
   DL28, bundles 3–4: receiver general's a/cs, 14C–17C; London rents appear as part of a single total with those from Essex and elsewhere; expenses incl. payments for repairs and hire of houses in London.
   DL28/78: box of late 17C–18C papers, incl. rent vouchers for *51*, which seems by then to have been the only duchy property in the city.

d. Administration of estate. DL42/95–100: bks. of commissions and orders, 16C–18C, many concerning estate administration; DL42/95–6 and 98 are briefly calendared in a 17C MS available in the Round Room which may help to identify London material.

e. Miscellaneous. DL41/3/4: extract from court roll, 16C (*53*).

f. Equity jurisdiction in lands held in right of the duchy. DL1: pleadings, late 15C onwards; those to 1603 are calendared in *Ducatus Lancastriae*, 3 vols. (Rec. Com. 1823–34) and incl. cases concerning payment of toll in

London and tenements in the city (*51, 152*); for MS indexes of plaintiffs after 1603, see IND/16918–20. DL3: depositions and examinations, 1485–1548; calendared in *Ducatus Lancastriae* vols. 1 and 2 (Rec. Com. 1823–7). DL4: depositions and examinations, 1558 onwards, listed in MS calendar available in Round Room; DL4/39/53, 41/61, 43/83, 43/91, 89/44 concern properties in the city (*20, 51, 141, 152*, Blanchappleton). DL5, entry bks. of decrees and orders, 15C onwards, and DL6, bundles of draft decrees, 16C onwards: refs. to both these series are given in the transcript of 'Great Ayloffe' (see above, **b**) and incl. orders concerning wharfage in London and a property boundary (*51*); for MS indexes of plaintiffs in DL5, see IND/16923–31. DL41/16/6: abs. of 17C depositions concerning tolls at Billingsgate and elsewhere.

441. PRO: DEEDS
There are in PRO many thousands of medieval and early modern deeds, in a large number of classes. The aim here is to provide a single index to London deeds (to *c.* 1670) in the various classes. The index is based on the lists and shelf guides (including some List and Index Society volumes) in PRO, and on searches in a limited number of unlisted or partly listed classes (a few classes which were extensive but unlisted could not be searched). References taken from this index should be checked against the lists, where they exist, for dates and any further details. The deeds fall into three main groups, with some miscellanea:

Ancient deeds (11C/12C to 16C), including Chancery, Exchequer, Pipe Office, and Duchy of Lancaster: C146–8, DL25–7, E40–3, E210–13, E326–9, E354–5, and LR14–15. Mostly title deeds etc. from the archives of dissolved religious houses, retained by the Crown after the lands in question were disposed of. In few cases, if any, were original deeds handed over to the purchaser or grantee. This class relates closely to the records of individual religious houses described under **70–274**, but since the original archive groups have mostly been broken up through rearrangement it can only be described and indexed as a whole. The divisions (by government departments, etc.) of the Ancient Deeds are explained in PRO *Guide* i, 14, 57, 73, 82–3, 91, 111, 185. Parts of the principal classes are calendared and printed in *Catalogue of Ancient Deeds* (6 vols., 1890–1915), covering C146/1–8060, E40/1–13672, E210/1–1330, and E326/1–4232. The remaining deeds are listed in shelf guides.

Modern Deeds (17C and later): E44, E214, E330, LR16. Apparently from various sources, including forfeited lands; only E214 is adequately listed. C149, a similar class (63 boxes, unlisted) was not searched.

Exhibits from Court of Chancery, Six Clerks Office, Court of Wards and Liveries (mostly 16C and later): C103–11, C113–15, C171, WARD 2. Unclaimed deeds deposited as exhibits in court. The bundles are listed in shelf guides: all with London refs. were then searched for details.

The index also covers: Cartae Antiquae and Miscellaneae, medieval deeds now bound into volumes (DL36, E315/29–54); Chancery miscellanea, transcripts of deeds and evidences (C47/9); conventual leases

(E118). E303, a larger class of conventual leases, is not indexed here, as it retained sufficient order to be described under the headings of individual religious houses (**70–274**).

Parishes

1: E40/1515, 1530, 1870, 1983, 10412; E42/353; E210/5349, 8059, 9074; E326/2007–8, 2011

2: C146/44; E40/2450–9, 2484, 2486, 2490, 2501–2, 2506, 2705, 2707–9, 2717, 2719–21, 2728; E42/429; E210/8714, 9839; E211/457; E315/38/235; E326/1993–4, 4369, 11798; E329/447

4: C146/1295, 6990, 9287, 9301, 9320, 9323; C147/131, 133; C148/58; E40/1613, 1628, 1640, 1648–50, 1653, 1844, 1847, 1858, 1889, 1925, 5521, 7155, 14311–13; E210/1056, 9869, 11117, 11120; E211/16, 313; E214/928; E326/2020, 2074, 2076, 11324, 11512; E355/2/44, E355/3/118–19; LR14/15, 92, 480, 486, 560, 574, 578, 1101; LR15/1/1

5: C106/167–8; C107/70–1; C111/31; C146/6077, 10518; E40/1631, 1634, 1683, 1852, 1856, 1861, 2186, 2625; E42/11; E210/1043, 6762; E326/1961–91, 2305, 4366, 4371–6, 5735, 5737–8, 6666, 6701, 6871, 6890, 7020, 7233, 8219–20, 9928, 12209, 12222; E329/59, 179; WARD 2/14/52/1

6: C146/6857; E40/1495, 1616, 1632, 1883–4, 1897, 1913, 1916, 1920, 1989, 1994, 2000, 2007, 2010, 2013, 2017, 2026–7, 2042, 2048, 2058, 2064, 2069, 2075, 2135, 2141–3, 2264–5, 2712, 7350, 11559; E42/445

7: E40/2122, 7288

8: E40/2172, 2178, 2184, 5262; E42/428; E315/47/17; E326/10352

9: C146/1610; DL26/18–19; E40/2124. 2213, 2215–16, 2219, 2223, 2226, 2228; E210/4123, 4135, 11293; E211/411; E212/1; E326/1995–2006, 2013–19, 6660, 9927, 9929, 11208, 11919, 11922–3, 12178, 12643, 12650, 12655; E327/343; LR15/4/117/9, 16(i), 40(i)

10: C146/6591, 8240, 9206; C147/103, 126, 144, 175; E40/1638, 1683, 1707,1709, 1716, 1789–93, 1852, 1861, 2186, 2410, 2532, 2625, 2677, 2723, 12629; E41/98; E326/6493, 11209, 12210, 12220; E329/482; LR14/37, 537

11: E40/1985, 7302; E214/1101; LR14/202, 1092; LR15/6/156

12: E210/1126–7, 10926; LR15/6/156

13: C147/214; E40/2172, 2406, 2569; E210/415, 2211; E211/372; E326/2012, 2030, 4368, 10681

14: E40/2013; E212/8

15: E40/1497, 1505, 1583, 1591, 1593, 1979, 2066, 2626, 2727, 7926–7, 11858–9; E213/293; E326/11798; ER14/94, 110, 113, 120, 341, 343, 476, 487, 527, 1151

17: E40/1982, 7284

18: C111/46; E40/1592, 1899, 2063; E326/5710; LR14/693

19: E40/1470, 1636, 1981, 7285; E326/12947

20: C107/70–1; C110/184; C113/202/2, C113/203/1–2; DL25/131–45, 148; DL27/59; E210/4098, 8149, 9951, 9966, 9970; E214/446; E315/39/199; E315/43/11; E326/2190–4, 2197, 2333, 2337, 2340, 2363–4, 2388, 2399–401, 5861, 6646, 10046, 10611–14, 11453, 11896, 11899, 12644, 12646, 12648; E327/245; E329/8, 366, 482; LR15/4/117/1

21: C103/157; C146/6563; E40/1696, 1723, 1970, 2117, 2119, 2303, 7256; E210/2389; E326/4370, 10348; E355/2/44

24: E214/1074

25: C105/32 (Part 2); C107/187 (25); E214/1089

26: C146/47, 286, 319, 376, 406, 413, 466, 850, 1027, 1049, 1367, 1630, 1656, 1722, 2407, 2549, 2861, 3014, 3055, 3978, 5043, 5111, 6140, 6871, 8188, 9519, 9528, 9631; C147/138; E210/2767, 4577, 9217, 9855; E326/2042, 2285, 10349; LR14/534

27: C106/155

28: C146/408, 2953; C148/33, 44; E40/1510; LR14/592

29: E40/1974

30: C106/135–7; C146/35, 829, 992, 1722, 3055, 3426, 6175; E40/1605, 1966, 10953; LR14/9, 474, 502

31: C146/8528

32: E40/1625, 1678, 1905, 1914, 1985, 2513; E210/1710, 1712, 2252, 2322, 2581, 5498, 8412, 9573, 9388; E315/31/176; E326/4277, 9969, 9971–2; LR14/1075

33: C107/71, 184(12), 185 (15), 186 (18), 187 (25); C171/18; E210/10436; E211/277; E214/4–7, 20, 23–4, 29–34, 36–7, 40, 55–7, 59–61, 68–73, 75–90, 92, 111–19, 141, 143–6, 148–51, 153, 194–5, 199, 230–8, 240–1, 278, 284, 305,

7294, 7824; E41/212; E210/9609; E315/30/33; E326/2077, 4315; E329/155; WARD 2/23/82/1, 3

60: E326/12197; LR15/4/117/20, 29(i)

61: C146/414, 2390; E40/1686, 1723, 1744, 1806, 2089, 2103; E326/2020, 2074–6

62: C47/9/10; C105/13; C106/146–7; C107/70, 186(21); C110/162(Part 2); C146/9549, 9605; C147/138, 298; DL26/78; DL36/3/52–3; E40/2119, 2263, 7930, 7932, 11854–7, 11860–6, 12276, 14797, 14808; E41/188; E42/92; E210/9951; E211/171, 403, 418, 559, 643; E315/38/37; E326/11600, 12222; E329/59; LR14/40, 195–6, 343, 699; LR15/4/115; LR15/8/186

63: C103/197, 203(Part 2); C107/184(13), 187(22); C108/110; E40/14689; E211/686; E214/692, 1167; E326/4283, 11909

64: E40/1488, 1642, 2649; E42/95; LR15/8/186; WARD 2/28/94D/10

65: E40/2098

66: E40/1495, 1516–17, 1895, 1971, 2047, 6397, 14804

67: C146/189, 1052, 2734, 2780, 2795, 2890, 5022, 6372, 9589; C148/20, 46; E40/2513, 2531

68: C107/80; C146/9323; E214/404

69: E40/2122

71: C107/71; E40/1644, 1852, 1861, 2125, 2625, 6457, 7824; E211/347; LR15/8/186

74: C146/10, 47, 319, 406, 413, 586, 971, 1027, 1049, 1367, 1656, 2407, 2549, 8188, 9519, 9589, 9625; E40/2462, 2492, 2500, 7296

75: C108/110; E40/1570, 1998, 2037, 2061, 2136, 2218, 2224, 2240–1, 2485, 7818, 7834, 7843–6, 10798, 11681; E355/4/184

76: E326/4314

77: C107/78; DL25/154–8; DL27/69; E40/2239, 12313; E315/30/42; LR15/1/27

78: C106/169; C107/187(25); C108/305; E40/1508, 1588, 1607–8, 1619, 1941, 2054, 2086–7, 2229, 2232, 2246–7, 2273, 5280, 5769, 6398–9, 12326, 12365, 12369–70, 12388, 12763, 12765, 13111, 13116, 13848; E41/12, 35; E210/2671, 6796, 8631, 9594; E326/2072, 10681; LR15/8/186

79: E326/2071

80: C146/257, 2521, 2802, 3588, 4076, 9207; C148/14; DL25/3365; E40/1609–10, 1618, 1629, 1633, 1898, 2018, 2050–3, 2068, 2076, 2286, 2364, 7360; E41/280; E210/805, 2543, 5888, 10097; E326/9928, 11649; E329/179;

LR14/1055; LR15/8/186; WARD 2/23/81M/20

81: C106/120–1; C110/61; C146/2260, 3719, 4115, 5198, 7534, 7542, 9178, 9184, 10356; DL25/3318; DL36/3/53; E40/1477, 1492, 1787–8, 1852, 1861, 1985, 2186, 2385, 2625, 14688; E41/328; E42/50; E132/3/43; E210/11108; E214/1613; E315/30/18; E326/12226; LR14/484, 700, 1154, 1157, 1159, 1164–6, 1170; LR15/8/186; LR16/13

82: E40/6684

83: E40/1691, 1719, 1731–4, 1742–4, 1810, 2036, 2132, 2274, 2305, 2323, 7315, 7827, 7837, 11610; E42/450; E315/31/87; E326/1997, 2014–16, 2018, 4313; E355/2/44

85: C107/71; C146/504, 508, 1295, 1690, 1813–15, 2178, 2202, 6990; C148/58; E40/644, 2329, 2440, 7309, 7361, 12276; E41/188; E211/347; E326/2063–8, 4312–13, 9939, 12213; LR14/20, 500–1, 564, 705; LR15/8/186

86: C146/65

87: C146/262, 414, 1258, 1295, 2390, 2588, 2757, 3583, 6990; C148/50; E40/1615, 1859, 1893, 1909, 2433, 2468; E41/63, 367; E44/8; E210/733, 1096; E213/43; E315/34/44; E315/46/153; E315/52/69; E326/2034–5, 2037–51, 2064, 2074, 2076, 4290–1, 7992, 8004, 8106, 9940, 9943, 9979–82, 11596, 12227; E329/34, 41, 184; LR15/8/186

88: E40/1472–3, 1500, 1518, 1584, 1606, 2251–2, 2260–2, 2343, 2347, 2356, 2359–61, 2363, 7355, 7817, 7825, 9163, 10390–2, 12349, 12942; E42/6, 32; E210/3806, 8599; E214/512; E315/41/226; E326/2053–9, 2061, 2211–12, 4281, 4286–7, 6749, 8511, 9373, 9748–51, 9757, 9762–4, 9944–5, 11910, 12146, 12221; E328/68; LR14/797, 1075; WARD 2/29/96A/87

89: E40/2182–3; E210/5838, 6320, 7387, 7952, 9371, 10304; E212/55; E326/2036, 2052, 2060, 4281, 4288–9

90: E40/2303; E41/293; E326/997, 2014–16, 2018

92: E40/5280, 12793, 13520; E210/597, 6110; LR15/8/186

93: C107/116, 164; C146/1292–3, 2900, 6990, 9207, 9625; C148/58; E40/1898, 2002, 2025, 5280, 7294; E326/2036; LR15/8/186

94: C103/194; E40/2002, 2258–9, 2393, 2394, 2649, 2658, 2665, 2667–8, 2680–1, 2683, 2698; E44/3; E210/10437; E326/4283, 11909

95: C146/596; DL25/146, 3345; DL36/1/221

96: C107/71; C146/9169; E40/1476, 1647, 2330, 2341, 2487; E210/4603
97: E326/11322
98: C146/414, 2390, 2588; E40/1511, 1514, 1614, 1786, 1871, 1874, 1876, 1930–32, 1943–5, 1954–7, 1961, 1964, 1980, 2101, 2464–7, 2469–78, 2542, 7349; E42/396, 438; E210/7799; E326/ 2096–105, 6560, 8005, 9983–93, 12165; E328/268; E329/74; LR14/ 1174; LR15/6/156; LR15/8/186
99: C146/5198, 7534, 9178, 9184, 10356; C147/201; E40/1477, 1489, 1490, 1492, 1644, 1881, 1882, 1885, 1904, 1975–6, 15044; E213/293; E315/52/ 206; E326/4369; E329/155; LR14/94, 111, 113, 120, 124, 141–2, 146, 190, 341, 357, 471, 479, 487, 523–5, 527–9, 541, 551, 600,1047, 1151, 1153, 1155, 1163, 1167
100: C146/21, 28, 123, 257, 2098, 2394, 2802, 3541, 3719, 7940, 10625, 10686; C147/138; E40/1877; E210/11119; E326/2095, 9255; LR14/16–17, 42, 89, 203, 292, 475, 484, 559, 563, 575, 604, 812; LR15/1/7–8
101: E40/1517, 1863, 1938, 1939, 2416, 2420, 2425–6, 2431–2, 2438–9, 2443, 2447, 2662–4, 7307, 7368
103: C103/186; C146/9625; E40/1786, 2629, 7351; E327/340
104: C103/39; C146/2134, 6121; E40/1474, 1513, 1614, 1644, 1667, 1942, 1960, 2024, 2156, 2415, 2509, 2542, 2604, 14778, 15625; E211/209; E326/9751, 9753–6, 9976–7; LR14/16–17, 93, 122, 139, 220, 230, 280, 285, 318, 326, 386, 481, 519, 549–50, 556, 567, 569, 605, 904, 1063, 1088, 1140, 1149–50; LR15/ 8/186; WARD 2/29/96A/2, 4, 11, 13, 89, 91–3; WARD 2/29/96B/1–3, 14– 16, 19, 24–26
105: C146/529, 596, 3414, 8778, 9605; DL25/1404; E40/1646, 1672–3, 1915, 1984, 1986, 1988, 1991, 1995–6, 2004– 5, 2007, 2019, 2022, 2041, 2049, 2057, 2065, 2067, 2072–4, 2077, 2116, 2236, 2495, 6869, 7356, 7373, 7593–5, 7819, 7833, 9761, 11938–47, 13126; E42/88; E210/10705; LR14/125, 534
106: E40/1683, 1861, 2174–5, 2186; E326/ 2111, 2113–22, 4321, 11598, 12231
108: E40/1604, 2303, 2412–14, 2418, 2421– 2, 2424, 2427–8, 2435–6, 2441–2, 2445–6, 7444, 11332, 13608; E42/294; E210/2389, 8149, 9880; E326/4370, 10348, 12226
109: C146/1079; E326/4283
110: E40/2417, 6884
111: C103/203/2; C146/246, 410, 2387,

2762, 3538, 4139, 9641; C148/15, 21; E40/2430, 2444, 2449, 15625; E214/1362
112: C146/257, 582, 2802, 3588; C148/14; DL36/3/53; E40/2173, 2507, 10355, 12793, 13520; E210/1086; E213/431; E326/2021, 2085–94, 2106, 2181, 2245, 6383, 9941–2, 9946–7, 9964, 11909; E329/93
113: C103/157; C109/82; C110/61, 114; C146/284, 373, 482, 549, 569, 892, 1099, 2842, 2869, 4610, 4713, 5089; E40/1507, 2610; LR14/18, 489; LR16/13
116: E40/1803, 2346, 2362, 2561–2, 2576, 2584, 2586, 2603, 2606, 2613, 2615, 2624, 2676, 2684, 7314, 10402, 11609; E211/557; E314/44/32; E326/2083–4, 4316, 9955; E328/150; E329/1, 5, 22, 47, 57, 60; LR14/608; LR15/4/117/18
117: E326/2082
118: E40/1683, 1958, 2274, 2631, 13650; E315/35/224; E315/45/333; E326/ 2078, 2080–1, 2107, 2110, 2112, 2123– 31, 4317–19, 4324–5, 8129, 9949, 9951, 9969, 9972, 12223, 12226; E329/ 31, 33; LR15/1/1; LR15/8/186
119: C47/9/6; C149/1092; E40/2248, 2461, 2491, 2661, 12276; E42/5; E210/7730; E214/834; E326/2078, 2123, 2127, 4317, 8002, 9949, 12947; LR14/121, 213, 608
120: C146/5062; C148/97; E40/2179; E329/482
121: E40/2448
122: E40/1476, 1946, 2434, 10791
123: C110/123; C146/1040, 1570, 2325, 3612, 10045; E40/1501–2, 1611, 1637, 1651–2, 1658, 1857, 1860, 1910, 1918– 19, 1921, 1923, 1926, 1951–2, 2012, 2060, 2081, 2084, 2507, 2726, 5758, 6684, 7822, 10369; E42/38, 440; E210/ 4718; E328/125
124: C47/9/6; C108/412; C146/4115; E40/ 1622, 1630, 1917, 1992, 1997, 2055, 2126, 2134, 2248, 2337, 2448, 2661; E42/5, 354; E210/4447, 7730; E211/ 499; E326/2108–9, 2127–8, 4323, 9951, 9969, 9972, 12341; E329/33
125: E40/2001, 2009, 2023, 2028, 2045, 2059, 2062, 2129, 5771, 6677, 12773, 12805, 13199, 13241; E210/6974, 7836, 8598, 9877; E315/30/42; E326/ 2247–50, 9950; E327/202; E355/6/263; LR14/206; LR15/8/186
126: E40/1572, 2250, 2387–8, 7823–4, 9048; E211/347; E326/125; LR14/8, 35, 49, 58, 473, 496, 520–2, 538, 926, 1090; LR15/8/186
127: C146/257, 1910, 2802, 3588, 3950;

C148/14; DL36/3/67; E40/1852, 1861, 2186, 2429, 2437, 2513, 2625, 2684, 6684; E42/468; E210/1108, 1192; E213/431; E315/35/90; E315/44/78; E315/48/275; E315/49/210, 227; E315/50/244; E315/51/97; E326/6015, 6845, 7229, 8078, 11654, 12602; E329/161; LR14/696, 840; LR15/4/117/6–7, 39

128: E40/13611, 14666; E210/6413, 8121; E326/4322, 5599, 9277; LR14/142, 190, 600

129: E40/2124, 2460, 2718; E42/358; E315/30/18; E326/2244–6, 6724, 12208, 12221

131: C110/114; C146/257, 2802; E40/1605, 1655

132: C146/2853; E44/11; LR14/369; LR15/8/186; WARD 2/10/34

133: E40/1695, 1973, 2332, 2335, 2410, 2480–1, 2493–4, 2496, 2510, 2588, 2722, 2724–5, 7294, 7824

134: C146/9625; E315/30/42

135: C146/372, 435, 3542, 9589; C148/82; E40/2288, 2488, 7326; E210/1044; E315/48/96; E315/49/94; E326/2083–4, 2238, 2240–3, 2279, 4284, 4316, 10003–5; E328/150; E329/22, 57, 60; LR14/702; LR15/4/117/18

136: E40/2340, 2390, 2563–4, 2654, 2659, 2691–4, 5778, 7291, 7327, 7816, 7847–9; E42/146

137: DL25/150–1; DL36/3/53; E40/2507; E210/11125; E211/325, 347, 409; E315/31/107; E315/39/36; E315/50/213; E326/2215–37, 4278, 4282, 4285, 5857, 6997, 8798, 9994–10002, 12217, 12252; E327/336, 712; LR14/546, 714; LR15/4/117/5, 16(i)

138: E40/2701; E210/9323; E326/2198–203

140: C146/410; E40/1612

141: C110/155; E40/1627, 2392, 2395, 2399–2405, 2497–9, 2651–3, 2655, 2666, 2669, 2673–5, 2679, 2682, 2686–7, 2696, 2700, 7155, 7274, 7303, 7354, 7820, 7840, 12598; E210/4570; E326/1997, 2014–16, 2018–19, 2196, 2205, 2210, 2213–14, 4275, 9952, 11895, 11913, 12394; E355/2/44

142: C107/187(22); E40/2343, 12349; E41/292; E326/2053–4, 2059, 2061, 2211–12, 4281, 4287, 6749, 8511, 9751, 12057, 12146; LR15/6/156.

144: E40/1494, 2409, 5754, 6001, 7933; E315/30/42; E326/2206–9, 2304, 4274, 4279–80, 4283, 11909, 11917; E329/452; LR15/4/117/17

145: C111/31; E40/2448, 2697, 9656, 11640; E214/140; E315/30/18; LR14/5, 381,1084; LR15/6/156

147: E214/928, 1350

148: C107/71, 78(Part 2); E41/300; LR14/85; LR15/11/321

149: C106/40–1; C146/9455, 9532; C147/29; DL25/152; DL36/1/6; E40/1903, 1985, 7294

150: C107/78; C146/2728, 3171, 9488; E40/1656, 2383–4, 2485, 2504, 7364, 13600; E210/1973, 2539; E326/4283, 6058, 9930, 11909; LR15/4/117/19

151: E40/1641, 1683, 1851–2, 1861, 2186, 2625, 2704, 12464; E326/10682; LR14/1047

152: C103/170, 198; C106/146–7; C107/70–2, 113, 181(2), 184(12, 13), 185(14), 186(16, 17, 20), 187(24–5); C110/123; C146/3601, 9589; DL25/1565; DL26/20; DL36/2/176; E40/1865, 1965, 2328, 2331, 2333, 2336, 2391, 2397, 2568, 2572, 2578, 2581, 2585, 2594, 2604–5, 2608, 2616–17, 2619, 2621, 2628, 2630, 2637, 2678, 2685, 2688–9, 2699, 5814, 7499, 7829, 7842, 12793, 13520; E42/259, 437, 475; E118/17; E210/808, 1060, 1086, 4118, 5793, 5871, 5873, 5896, 9966; E213/431; E214/847–60, 862–6, 918, 1100, 1107, 1185–93, 1195, 1197–9, 1201; E315/40/97; E315/47/30; E315/49/27; E315/50/206; E315/51/66, 111, 169; E326/2021, 2132–64, 2170–83, 2185, 2204, 4267, 4271, 4302, 5628, 5700, 6721, 6750, 8004, 8550, 10610, 10698, 11756, 11903, 12059, 12166, 12209, 12589, 12642, 12905; E328/125; E329/2, 15, 93, 141; E355/7/unnumbered; LR14/17, 723, 844; LR15/1/36; LR15/4/117/10–11, 28, 35, 43; LR15/6/154(i), 158

154: WARD 2/29/96A/87

155: C108/409; DL36/2/189; E40/1662, 1669, 1676, 1837–9, 1891, 1901–2,1987, 1990, 1999, 2043, 2070–1, 2078–80, 2083, 2090–1, 2343, 6684, 9808, 12349, 12774; E315/44/86, 268; E326/6945, 12943; LR14/276; LR15/6/156; LR15/8/186; LR15/9/228

156: C106/149–50; C146/87; E40/1683, 15351; E326/2181; LR14/36

157: C106/167–8; C146/9625; E40/1670, 2006, 2016, 2030, 2410, 2491, 2627, 2641, 2657; E326/6380, 11148; LR14/496; LR15/8/186

158: E40/1936, 2279, 2295, 2511, 2518–19, 2521–2, 2526, 2539–40, 2546, 2550, 7824, 15625; E315/52/52; LR14/388; LR15/1/11

159: C111/31; E40/1852; E212/97; E315/32/69; E315/38/237; E315/53/84, 96; E315/54/208; E326/2069, 2085, 2088–9, 2092, 2094, 2106, 2181, 2245, 4320

162: E40/10402; E42/448

Holborn: DL27/62, 64–6; E315/33/200; E315/38/7; E326/10608
Holborn Bridge, by: E210/2950
Holy Innocents, Savoy: DL25/2342, 2344
Holy Trinity Priory: E42/447
Holy Trinity Priory, soke of: E40/7279, 7353, 7358, 7367, 7369, 7374
Houndsditch: E315/42/42
Huggin Lane: E315/48/282
Ivy Lane: E315/32/10
Jewry, Saint — in: E40/1645
Katherine Wheel, Bridge ward: LR14/351
Knightrider Street: E210/9979: E329/431
Langbourn: E315/31/171; E315/35/224
Langbourn ward: E326/4318, 6676
Leadenhall: DL25/153; DL27/68; DL36/1/179
Leadenhall Street: C107/70
Lime Street: E40/2249, 2355, 2358, 2590, 2977, 5934, 7035, 7370, 7826, 11559; E42/28, 79
Lombard Street: C146/9550; E40/644; E41/188; E42/19; LR14/555, 690, 695, 703
London Bridge, *see* Bridge
Lothbury: E315/35/26; E315/44/86; E326/2283
Ludgate Hill: E214/706
Mark Lane: E315/33/90
Milk Street: C146/1028, 6137, 9855, 9859
Mincing Lane: C146/6161; E40/5929
Minories: E326/12096, 12131, 12133–4, 12776; E328/122, 399, 400; E329/415–16
Monkwell Street: LR15/11/295
New Fish Street Hill: E40/12959
Newgate: LR14/842, 872
Newgate Market: C106/155
Old Change: C147/138; DL26/21; E210/1585; E315/34/219; E326/2289, 9948, 9963, 9965; LR14/706
Old Dean's Lane: DL25/1566
Old Fish Street: E40/1677, 13179; E315/38/74; E329/47
Oystergate: LR14/241
Paternoster Row: C110/65; E315/54/90; WARD 2/3/14A/26
Pentecost Lane: E315/38/218; E315/48/78
Philip Lane: LR14/30, 1152, 1161–2
Philpot Lane: C103/190
Portsoken: LR14/107, 152, 194
Poultry: C146/9323
Poultry Compter: E40/1683
Pudding Lane: E210/4959, 11025
Riole Street, la: LR14/379
Roper Street: E40/10402
St. Clement's Street: C146/9550

St. Katharine by the Tower: E40/2541, 11970
St. Katharine by the Tower (precinct): C146/7584
St. Lawrence Lane: LR14/1156, 1160
St. Mark's Alley off St. Clement's Lane: C146/1058
St. Martin's Lane: E40/13866
St. Mary Graces: DL25/1032(i); E326/12493
St. Nicholas Lane: E315/48/78
St. Paul's churchyard: C115/E17, F9
St. Paul's, houses near: DL27/60
St. Paul's (precinct): E326/11906
St. Petronilla, parish of, in Fleet Street: C146/2983
St. Swithin's Lane: E40/14670
Savoy, houses of or near: DL25/3600, 3604, 3611–12
Seacoal Lane: C146/3580
Shambles: E315/39/36; E315/41/226
Sherborne Lane: C146/9486; LR14/704
Shoe Lane: E40/2362
Silver Street: E40/2607
Smithfield: E40/15399; E211/125; E315/45/282; LR15/4/117/28, 43
Smithfield, East: C114/134; C146/7630, 7685, 8660; E40/2212, 2639, 2703, 6683, 13348; E210/1661, 1692, 3437, 5731, 5843, 6778, 8920, 9089, E211/160; E315/47/110; E326/2313–28, 4404, 6730, 11597, 11599; E328/255
Smithfield, West: C146/9641; E210/10167; E315/41/226; E326/7985, 9954; LR15/6/147
Soper Lane: C148/29; E40/1509, 2560, 2565, 2609
Staining Lane: E40/2124
Temple, New: DL25/2343; E40/1469
Thames Street: C108/110; C148/58; E40/2547; E42/30, 62; E210/8264; E326/7167–8
Thavie's Inn: E315/42/192
Tower Hill: E40/2536, 2645–7; E210/6811, 7824, 9368; E214/702; E326/2313–14, 7083, 8508, 9933–4, 11599
Tower Wharf: C107/80; E214/702; E326/11212
Trinity Lane: E315/52/181
Vintry: E40/2133
Warwick Lane: C107/184(13), 185(15)
Watling Street: LR15/4/117/41
Whitechapel: E40/2559
Whitefriars: E328/274
Wood Street: E40/2122, 2549; E42/13, 43; E315/34/249; E315/35/16; E326/2082

442. PRO: MAPS AND PLANS
See *Maps and Plans in the Public Record Office* i, *British Isles*, c. *1410–*

1860 (1967), nos. 126–8, 174–6, 267–70 (*10, 20*, Chancery Lane, Cornhill, near St. Katharine's Hospital, St. Mary Graces, St. Paul's, Tower Liberty).

443. PRO: CHANCERY ROLLS
There are several series of Chancery rolls, representing the main administrative output of central government up to the 16C, and an important part of it thereafter. These include contemporary enrolments of charters and inspeximuses (Charter Rolls, C53), letters patent (C66) and close (C54), and writs relating to expenditure (Liberate Rolls, C62), all issued under the Great Seal; enrolments of earlier charters of varying dates and authenticity (Cartae Antiquae Rolls, C52); and enrolled records of payments for grants and privileges (Fine Rolls, C60). These contain much valuable material for London property-holding. All are published for most of the period of their existence or for most of the period covered by this survey, in transcripts or calendars, with indexes. From the 16C they are supplemented by the State Papers series (**444**). See PRO *Guide* i, 14–26; HMSO *Sectional List* 24. For Cartae Antiquae see also *Regesta*. For other kinds of enrolment on the Close Rolls see **449a**.

444. PRO: STATE PAPERS
From the 16C much business formerly executed by the Chancellor came to be handled by the King's Secretary or Secretary of State. The result of this was the formation of the class of State Papers, of which the State Papers, Domestic (SPI, SP10–18, 25–27, 29–30, etc.; published in calendar form), contain a substantial amount of material relating to London property-holding. See PRO *Guide* ii, 1–6; HMSO *Sectional List* 24.

445. PRO: EYRES AND CROWN PLEAS
The records of the principal London eyres do not survive in PRO, but are described here as being of public origin.

a. Eyre of 1244. CLRO, Misc. Roll AA, printed as *The London Eyre of 1244*, ed. H. M. Chew and M. Weinbaum (LRS 6, 1970): copy of lost rolls for crown pleas, 1244, and inquest into purprestures, 1246, with much topographical information.

b. Eyre of 1276. BL, Add. Ch. 5153 (plea roll), and CLRO, Misc. Roll BB (estreat) printed together as *The London Eyre of 1276*, ed. M. Weinbaum (LRS 12, 1976): plea roll and list of fines and amercements relating to it, with some topographical information.

c. Eyre of 1321. *The Eyre of London, A.D. 1321*, ed. H. M. Cam (Selden Soc., Year Books of Edward II, vol. 26, 1968–9) is compiled principally from law reports in 8 MSS (listed by Cam) with extracts from the plea rolls, PRO, JUST 1/546–7. Limited topographical information, usually as references to location of crimes.

d. Later pleas, etc. (see PRO, *Lists and Indexes* IV). PRO, JUST 1/548: crown pleas, 1329; information as in preceding. PRO, JUST 1/549: pleas,

1341; incl. disseisins as well as felonies (disseisins in *10, 42, 45, 54, 85, 156*). PRO, JUST 1/556: roll of extracts from Husting Rolls of lands conveyed in mortmain, 1278–9 to 1364. PRO, JUST 1/557/1–10: collection of misc. pleas, 13C to 14C, incl. record of pleadings in Husting Court; 557/2 concerns building (St. Paul's churchyard); 557/3, disseisin (*42, 123*); 557/4, disseisin (*81*); 557/5, trespass (*162*); 557/6, plea of service (*90*); 557/9, disseisin (*137*).

446. PRO: OTHER JUDICIAL PROCEEDINGS
Cases concerning London lands could be heard in, or transferred to, the royal courts of Chancery, Exchequer, King's Bench and Common Pleas. For the equity jurisdiction of the Duchy of Lancaster, see **440**; for judicial eyres and assizes, see **445**. For private deeds enrolled on the rolls of these courts, see **449**.

a. Chancery. See PRO *Guide* i, 29–35. Chancery Proceedings (C1–3) are calendared and in part indexed (London refs. otherwise identifiable by scanning): PRO *Guide* i, 32–4. For Chancery Decrees (C78), see **447**.

b. Exchequer. See PRO *Guide* i, 92–4. Plea Rolls (E13) not searched; Jews' Plea Rolls (E9) contain useful information: *Calendar of the Plea Rolls of the Jewish Exchequer, 1218–1277* i-iv (Jewish Historical Soc. 1905–29, 1972).

c. King's Bench, Curia Regis Rolls (KB26) and Coram Rege Rolls (KB27). Some London material; for calendars, transcripts, etc. see PRO *Guide* i, 117–18.

d. Common Pleas. See PRO *Guide* i, 137. Plea rolls (CP40), *Posteas* (CP41), etc., not searched; for fines and recoveries in Common Pleas see **448**.

447. PRO: CHANCERY DECREE ROLLS
These rolls (C78) contain the enrolled decrees of the court, *c.* 1534 to early 18C, settling cases (genuine or otherwise) concerning land and other matters. SSRC project no. HG. 113/19/1 listed and indexed contents of rolls 1–45, and listed samples from rolls 46–1250 (of 2257 rolls). The lists are available in PRO, IHR, ESRC office, and through BL (Lending Division). The procedure, and some of the results, of the listing are described by M. W. Beresford 'The Decree Rolls of Chancery as a source for economic history, 1547–*c.* 1700', *EconHR* 32 (1979), pp. 1–10.

a. Rolls 1–14, London refs. from index: *15, 18, 19, 30, 33* or *34, 43, 46, 53, 60, 62, 71, 77, 81, 100, 108, 120, 123, 125, 126, 137*, Billingsgate, Bishopsgate Street, Grey Friars, St. Martin le Grand, St. Paul's churchyard, Westcheap, unspec.

b. Rolls 15–45, London refs. from index: *12, 21, 30, 36, 38, 43, 46, 47, 51, 56, 80, 87, 96, 108, 111, 118, 120, 123, 134, 141, 149, 152, 157*, Bread Street, Budge Row, Friday Street, Milk Street, St. Paul's churchyard, Wood Street.

c. Rolls 46–1250. These were sampled and listed, but not indexed. The following is an index to London refs. to 1685 identified from reading through the lists.

Parishes

2: C78/264/2, 4
4: C78/154/10; 285/4; 446/1; 555/14
10: C78/530/1
12: C78/295/9; 743/5
13: C78/105/5; 621/16
15: C78/203/8
18: C78/676/14
20: C78/110/13; 581/4, 12; 582/9; 583/13; 653/1; 1212/1
21: C78/201/15
25: C78/205/1; 228/4; 231/6; 502/1; 604/6; 644/20
26: C78/659/3
31: C78/528/12
33: C78/127/10
36: C78/1206/8
38: C78/371/8; 746/1
42: C78/175/15; 230/12; 291/7; 407/11; 485/10; 545/12, 548/18; 695/8
43: C78/151/9; 625/18; 695/5; 1212/8
44: C78/305/10; 390/2
45: C78/133/4; 163/12; 604/9; 664/5; 670/8
46: C78/568/2; 601/8; 700/9; 1223/7, 8
47: C78/444/11; 508/12; 739/18
48: C78/696/6
54: C78/195/8; 970/9
59: C78/90/6; 133/24; 422/8; 638/3
61: C78/95/7
62: C78/407/11; 417/17; 425/8; 548/18; 574/2; 607/13; 695/8
63: C78/524/6
64: C78/413/9; 1220/10
67: C78/422/8; 910/1
70: C78/575/3
71: C78/168/11; 276/5; 380/5; 659/3; 910/1
75: C78/149/3; 180/9

77: C78/260/4
80: C78/460/3
81: C78/60/3; 269/10; 488/25
83: C78/492/6
85: C78/242/4; 259/1
87: C78/727/3
91: C78/511/2
92: C78/129/14
93: C78/1206/13
96: C78/133/13
99: C78/479/14; 703/8; 875/3; 1212/10
100: C78/693/1
108: C78/390/2; 435/5
116: C78/726/2
118: C78/700/16
123: C78/149/10; 356/4
124: C78/630/14
127: C78/950/8
128: C78/583/9
132: C78/242/11
137: C78/399/40
138: C78/413/3; 503/12
138: (? Southwark): C78/700/20
144: C78/459/10; 1206/12
145: C78/271/5; 489/19; 694/6
148: C78/1206/8
149: C78/478/19
150: C78/371/8
151: C78/594/12
152: C78/144/12; 381/1; 430/1; 583/13; 1050/3
155: C78/402/10; 435/8; 490/28–9; 499/13; 671/17; 1206/11, 15
156: C78/151/3; 222/2
157: C78/413/3
158: C78/331/10; 422/8

Other localities

London: C78/100/7, 14; 144/5; 171/16; 264/3; 315/8; 339/4; 455/11; 489/1; 533/12; 580/8; 582/9; 583/17; 657/11; 665/18; 726/16, 19; 727/13
Addle Street: C78/693/16
Aldermanbury: C78/536/1
Aldersgate: C78/286/8
Aldersgate Street, near: C78/256/5
Aldgate: C78/503/12
Billingsgate: C78/696/6
Bishopsgate: C78/579/4; 1212/1
Bishopsgate, near: C78/563/16
Bishopsgate Street: C78/604/2; 747/11
Blackhorse Alley: C78/258/10
Bow Lane: C78/145/16
Bread Street: C78/1010/8; 1206/7

Broad Street: C78/285/5; 720/22
Candlewick Street: C78/409/10
Carter Lane: C78/562/1
Chancery Lane: C78/144/9; 499/13
Cheapside: C78/145/16; 173/11; 207/5; 271/5; 418/1; 721/2; 740/10; 1010/8
'Clampton Court': C78/630/19
Cordwainer Street: C78/700/2
Cornhill: C78/195/3; 545/5
Creed Lane: C78/413/5
Crooked Lane: C78/156/4
Eastcheap: C78/299/5; 541/1; 573/5
Fenchurch Street: C78/447/5; 547/14; 640/10; 671/17
Fetter Lane: C78/299/6; 516/5; 583/10; 670/6; 749/9

Finch Lane: C78/241/5
Fish Street Hill, see New Fish Street
Fleet Bridge: C78/381/2
Fleet Street: C78/174/17; 231/5; 258/10; 283/9; 340/7, 17; 445/4; 489/16; 503/12; 705/12; 738/15; 1220/4
Fleet Street, near; C78/241/6; 648/3
Foster Lane: C78/207/5
Friday Street: C78/217/11; 242/1; 274/2
Golden Lane: C78/741/7
Gracechurch Street: C78/379/8; 409/11; 597/12
Greyfriars: C78/749/4
Holborn: C78/168/16; 267/2; 354/3; 524/3; 666/21; 725/17
Knightrider Street: C78/530/17
Leadenhall, near: C78/334/16
Leadenhall Street: C78/695/13; 721/7
Little Britain: C78/230/12
Lombard Street: C78/545/5; 561/8
Long Lane: C78/574/2
Ludgate, outside: C78/738/4
Milk Street: C78/281/11; 412/12, 13
Mill Street: C78/581/11
Mincing Lane: C78/275/3
New Fish Street, Fish Street Hill: C78/133/16; 339/3
Newgate: C78/508/12
Newgate Market: C78/637/20; 666/21; 711/13
Old Change: C78/433/7; 475/1; 619/5; 675/16
Old Fish Street: C78/727/11; 732/12

Paternoster Row: C78/238/4; 606/12
Philip Lane: C78/391/9
Philpot Lane: C78/600/1
Pudding Lane: C78/880/1
St. Agnes' Lane: C78/276/8
St. Clement's Lane: C78/258/10
St. Katharine near the Tower: C78/217/6
St. Lawrence Lane: C78/659/4
St. Martin le Grand: C78/555/9; 607/7
St. Martin's Lane: C78/433/7; 638/1; 644/9
St. Paul's churchyard: C78/152/14; 203/6; 276/8; 485/9; 558/3; 741/14; 950/8
St. Paul's, near: C78/629/4
St. Peter's Hill: C78/270/7; 468/2
St. Swithin's Lane: C78/729/4
School Lane: C78/557/13
Shoe Lane: C78/354/3; 637/10
Silver Street: C78/367/3
Smithfield (West): C78/299/6; 389/14; 550/6
Temple Gate, by: C78/458/4
Thames Street: C78/171/16; 289/7; 352/4; 409/11; 605/1; 670/11
Thomas Street: C78/1220/8
Throgmorton Street: C78/950/8
Tower, lands near: C78/286/9
Tower Ditch, tenements on: C78/617/5
Tower Street: C78/482/21; 721/15; 1208/5
Tower Wharf: C78/431/12
Walbrook: C78/695/6
Watling Street: C78/583/8
Whitefriars: C78/503/12; 672/7
Wood Street, Little: C78/309/3

448. PRO: FINES AND RECOVERIES

See PRO *Guide* i, 135–8

Property conveyance by means of a final concord in the Court of Common Pleas was not a common practice for London holdings before the 16C. For feet of fines (CP25), 1196–1569, see *A calendar of feet of fines for London and Middlesex*, ed. W. J. Hardy and W. Page (1892–3). For later feet of fines, see PRO class lists and calendars. The corresponding concords (CP24) and notes of fines (CP26) add little further information.

The city had its own procedure for common recovery in the Court of Husting (**2c**); recoveries in the royal Court of Common Pleas (enrolled in CP40 to 1582; CP43 thereafter) are therefore not very frequent. These classes were not searched; recoveries are indexed by term, by parties' names with a note of property and county, from 1515, in IND/17180–9. For enrolments of other deeds in CP40, 43, see **449f, g**.

449. PRO: ENROLLED DEEDS

Enrolment of private deeds on the great rolls of Chancery, Exchequer, King's Bench and Common Pleas began in the 13C (PRO *Guide* i, 16). It may never have been very common for private London deeds up to the 16C, owing to the simplicity of land tenure in London and the popularity of enrolment in the Court of Husting. During the early modern period, and always for some kinds of deeds, such enrolment seems to have been more popular. The availability of other means of securing title, however, means that there is probably only a limited amount of London material in the enrolments, some of which is accessible only with great difficulty. Access to the information in the enrolments is through various guides, lists, catalogues, and indexes, some nearly contemporary with the enrolments. Some of these guides etc. are available in the search rooms (identification numbers not given because liable to change: see class card-catalogue); others, all with IND-numbers, have to be called up (see TS Catalogue of Index Volumes). These guides were not fully searched, nor was any of the unlisted material; the following descriptions indicate the means of access, where available, to the enrolled deeds in each class, and, where possible, the kind or amount of information likely to be yielded.

a. Chancery, Close Rolls (C54). See PRO *Guide* i, 16–18. For royal letters close, see **443**. The dorse of the Close Rolls was probably the most popular place, among those listed in this section, for enrolment of private deeds: such enrolments are numerous, but identification of deeds relating to specific places is difficult. In general they are listed or calendared, in chronological groups, and not indexed: for guides etc. to these and other enrolments (Crown grants, sales during the Interregnum, trust deeds, etc.), see TS Catalogue of Index Volumes.

b. Exchequer, King's Remembrancer, Memoranda Rolls (E159). See PRO *Guide* i, 61. Lists in repertory rolls and agenda books: IND/7031–72. There is an index to enrolled deeds, 1272–1307 (*5, ?10, 12, 43, 46, 75, ?96, 111, 129, 150, 151,* unspec.).

c. Exchequer, Lord Treasurer's Remembrancer, Memoranda Rolls (E368). See PRO *Guide* i, 75. Lists in repertory rolls, 1327–1653: IND/6935. Index to charters and grants, to 1558: IND/17043.

d. Exchequer of Pleas, Plea Rolls (E13). See PRO *Guide* i, 94. 'Selective calendar', arranged alphabetically by place, 1293–1820 (*4, 9, 10, ?12, 14, 15, 18, 19, 20, 23, 25, 26, 30,34, 35, 36, 39, 42, 43, 44, 45, 46, 47, 51, 53, 54, 56, 59, 62, 63, 65, 71, 73, 78, 80, 81, 84, 85, 90, 92, 96, 100, 104, 108, 112, 117, 118, 119, 120, 126, 128, 129, 134, 135, 136, 137, 141, 145, 147, 148, 149, 150, 152, 155, 157, 158,* Ebbgate, Gracechurch Street, Old Change, St. Katharine's by the Tower, Warwick Lane).

e. King's Bench, Coram Rege Rolls (KB27). See PRO *Guide* i, 117. Enrolled deeds, Edward I to Edward II, listed, indexed by place (*20, 36, 105*). Deeds enrolled 1390–1655, listed chronologically in docket rolls and remembrance rolls: IND 1322–52, 1378–87, not searched. Deeds enrolled 1652–1750 listed by party by term, county not always given (some London unspec. refs. to 1666).

f. Common Pleas, Plea Rolls (CP40). See PRO *Guide* i, 137–8. Enrolled deeds, mid 13C to 1344, calendared and indexed by place (several London refs., particularly extramural parishes). Deeds enrolled 1539–47 calendared but not indexed: (refs., identifiable from marginal notes, to

53, 62, 93, 111, 126, 131, Crooked Lane, Tower Street). Deeds enrolled 1547–55 calendared but not indexed (refs., as above, to *20, 45, 54, 78, 96, 128, 132, 141*). Deeds enrolled 1555–1629, calendared (IND/16943) and indexed by place (several London refs.).

g. Common Pleas, Recovery Rolls (CP43). See PRO *Guide* i, 137–8. Enrolled deeds 1555–69, 1630–1717, calendared but not indexed: IND/ 16943–4, not searched. For recoveries, see **448**.

450. PRO: PRIVATE CARTULARIES
This section covers private cartularies (apart from Duchy of Lancaster: see **440**) in PRO that appeared from Davis's descriptions (nos. 1186– 1344) to contain, or to be likely to contain, London material.

a. Beauchamp. E315/58 (Davis, no. 1191; *Two Registers . . . of Beauchamp of Hatch*, ed. H. C. Maxwell Lyte, Somerset Rec. Soc. 35, 1920): 14C register, incl. ? early 13C deeds (*42*, nr. Fleet Bridge, Seacoal Lane).

b. Bohun, Humphrey earl of, 1276–1322. DL41/10/12 (Davis, no. 1199): 14C inventory of charters (incl. Aldermanbury, Old Deans Lane).

c. Despenser. E101/332/27, E101/333/6 (Davis, no. 1234): memoranda of deeds delivered, 1327, 1331 (*20, 28, 152, 162*, Lime Street).

451. PRO: PRIVATE ESTATES, LIBERTY OF ST. BARTHOLOMEW, SMITHFIELD
This estate, the site of the former priory, lay in *33*, and included St. Bartholomew's Fair.

a. Deeds: numerous 17C leases etc. of the site, then belonging to the earls of Holland, are in PRO, E214/4–1073 (see PRO deeds index, **441**, above).

b. PRO: SC12/11/39, detailed rental 1616; SC12/1/22, particular of leases, 1622: SC12/11/48, rental of St. Bartholomew's Fair, 1624; SC12/40/65, SC12/11/40, similar rentals 1627, 1629; SC12/40/66, rental of liberty, 1631; SC12/1/23, 24, surveys of liberty, 1641; SC12/40/67, rental of liberty, 1671.

c. Bodl, MS Rawl. C 182: an 18C collection of copies of proceedings, letters patent, etc. concerning the fair and the site of the priory, principally 16C–17C, but some 14C. PRO, E192/13–18: papers of Robert, Earl Holland, *c.* 1650– *c.* 1700, incl. papers rel. to property in Smithfield.

452. PRO: TAXATION AND OTHER RETURNS
E179 (subsidy rolls, etc.) includes returns for lay and clerical subsidies, the poll tax (1377–81), and the hearth tax (1662–74), and subsidies and censuses of aliens. The most valuable of these returns for this study are those with a wide incidence and topographical arrangement; the hearth tax of 1666 is particularly useful. For a list of printed texts see J. M. Sims, *London and Middlesex Published Records, a handlist* (LRS 1970), 7–9;

also *Two Tudor Lay Subsidies* (1541, 1582), ed. R. G. Lang (LRS, forthcoming). For the valuable tithe assessment of 1638, see **462c**; for other assessments, see **275–381**, **416**, and the GL handlist, *London rate assessments and inhabitants' lists in GL and CLRO* (2nd edn. 1968).

453. PRO: DOMESDAY BOOK
In 1086 several manors in Essex and Surrey included houses or rents in London: *VCH Essex* i, 446b, 448, 513b; *VCH Surrey* i, 296b, 299b, 303, 312a-b, 314b, 316b, 325b. The locations are not usually identifiable, but cf. **108**, **133**, **151**.

LIBRARIES AND RECORD OFFICES
IN THE UNITED KINGDOM

This section covers libraries and record offices known to hold material relating to London before *c.* 1670. In general such material is derived from family collections and deposits; sometimes the source of a deposit is not known. In some cases access to, or use of, deposited family material is restricted. Records in these repositories forming part of the archives of institutions which held property in the city are covered elsewhere in this survey by the entries for such institutions, and are not referred to again here.

London material in these locations was identified in three ways:
- i. by means of the topographical index at the National Register of Archives, which identifies only collections described in lists deposited at the Register and deemed to contain a 'substantial' body of material on a particular place;
- ii. by visiting libraries and record offices in London and the Home Counties and major collections of MSS elsewhere in England, and using lists and indexes available there;
- iii. by writing to all other county record offices and major libraries in the United Kingdom.[1]

It was not possible to visit many record offices and libraries holding material on London before *c.* 1670, but it is always stated when this was the case. The accounts of those not visited are based on information provided by the archivists and librarians, and on lists available in London. Some of the material in these unvisited locations said to relate simply to 'London' may not, in fact, concern the city; in other instances such material may relate to specific localities in the city which are not mentioned in the available lists and indexes.

Descriptions of the collections are arranged as follows: London libraries and record offices (CLRO and PRO form separate sections, **1–15** and **436–453**, because of their very different character); other libraries and record offices in England (arranged under the name of the place for libraries and the name of the county for CROs); libraries and record offices in Wales; Scotland; Northern Ireland. For collections in USA see **518–528**.

454. LONDON, BISHOPSGATE INSTITUTE
The institute was founded in 1894 and endowed with properties formerly belonging to the parish of St. Botolph Bishopsgate. The reference library has a large collection of deeds, 16C to 19C, mostly uncatalogued and

1. No replies were received from: North Yorkshire County Record Office, North-allerton; Shakespeare Birthplace Trust Records Office, Stratford-upon-Avon.

193

mostly relating to the Bishopsgate area, which probably include the title deeds to the site and endowment (*45* and elsewhere). The catalogued collections are as follows:

a. Crosby Hall Deeds, 16C (*64*), transcribed in C. W. F. Goss, *Crosby Hall* (1908): in same box, papers, incl. view, transcripts, 17C to 19C (*152*).

b. Deeds 1–172, with card catalogue, 16C to 19C. Deeds before *c.* 1670 relate to the following parishes and areas:

2: 120, 122–3, 166	*81*: 94
11: 73	*87*: 132
14: 64–6, 93	*94*: 5, 7
19: 6, 30, 35, 138–43	*101*: see *19*
32: 83–91, 94, 145	*105*: 94
36: 146	*119*: 126
44: 147	*128*: 94
49: 104–111	Bishopsgate Street: 2, 4, 6
53: 165	Mark Lane: 129
64: 26–7, 72–3	St. Mary without Bishopsgate, hospital of
78: 138–43	(St. Mary Spital): 75–6

c. Document 3 in Deeds sequence 1–172: rental, prob. 17C, estate in *67*, *158*, Bishopsgate Street, Bread Street, Broken Wharf, Five Foot Lane, Jelly Alley, Long Lane, Old Fish Street, Pudding Lane, Somers Key.

455. London, British Library, Department of Manuscripts (indexed collections)

Many items in this collection deriving from the archives of religious houses and other institutions are described in other entries of this survey. In addition, there are many records derived from a wide variety of sources which are of value for the topographical study of most parts of the city before the Great Fire. These include deeds, rentals, surveys, inventories, petitions, diaries, miscellaneous papers, plans and drawings, and antiquarian or historical collections. The most convenient form of access is via the Amalgamated Index on cards kept in the corridor leading to the Students' Room. This index is made up from the indexes in the printed catalogues of collections (for which see M. A. E. Nickson, *The British Library: Guide to the catalogues and indexes of the Department of Manuscripts*, 1982), but does not include items from the indexes to additions made between 1756 and 1782 and from 1946 onwards, for which reference should be made to the individual catalogues. London items will be found in the Amalgamated Index under the general heading 'London: City and County' and with reference to more specific locations under the general heading 'London parishes'. It should be noted that the printed indexes, and hence the Amalgamated Index, are often less specific as to locations than the catalogue entries to which they refer, so that many references to particular parishes in the catalogues will simply be covered by the heading 'London' in the index. A detailed index to charters and rolls acquired up to the end of 1900 will be found in *Index to the Charters and Rolls in the Department of Manuscripts, British Museum* 2 vols., ed.

H. J. Ellis and F. B. Bickley (1900, 1912), which is incorporated in the Amalgamated Index. Several religious houses near London appear in the Amalgamated Index under what may be unexpected headings. Thus, for Clerkenwell Priory, see Finsbury; for Haliwell Priory, see Shoreditch; for St. Giles's Hospital, see Holborn; and for Stratford-at-Bow, see Poplar.

456. LONDON, BRITISH LIBRARY, DEPARTMENT OF MANUSCRIPTS (PRIVATE CARTULARIES)
This section covers private cartularies etc. in BL that appeared from Davis's descriptions (nos. 1186–1344) to contain, or to be likely to contain, London material. Other cartularies were not examined.

a. Badlesmere. Egerton Roll 8724 (Davis, no. 1293): 14C inventory of muniments of lords Mortimer, incl. refs. (box J) to acquisitions of Bartholomew de Badlesmere (*43, 77*). MS Harley 1240 ('Liber Niger de Wigmore'; Davis, no. 1292): late 14C cartulary, incl. (f. 111) ref. to possessions of Giles de Badelesmere (inn in Aldgate).

b. Braybrooke. MS Sloane 986 (Davis, no. 1206): late 13C cartulary, incl. (ff. 47$^{r\text{-}v}$, 66^v, 74^v) London refs. (*13, 51*, unspec.).

c. Darell. MS Harl. 1623 (Davis, no. 1232): 15C cartulary, incl. (ff. 7^v–8) rental, 1427 (*118*, Bishopsgate, Clement's Lane, Milk Street).

d. Macclesfield, John de. MS Cotton Cleop. D vi (Davis, no. 1282): 15C cartulary, incl. refs. (ff. 92$^{r\text{-}v}$, 97^v, 98, 121^v–122) to advowson of *36*.

457. LONDON, COLLEGE OF ARMS

a. MS Arundel 33 incl.: f. 162^v, receipts, 16C (Warwick Inn); ff. 244–6, valor, 16C (*116*); ff. 305–10, 312^v, inventory, 16C (Carter Lane); f. 313^v, lease, 16C (*38*).

b. MS Vincent 64: late 14C-early 15C private cartulary (not in Davis), incl. (ff. 1–17^v) deeds for London properties puchased by Adam Fraunceys and John Pyel (*4, 5, 49, 62, 64, 111, 128, 132*, Mincing Lane).

c. Combwell Charters: 258–60, deeds, 12C–13C (*94*); 310/1, 312/4, 326/ 186, letters of attorney and bond, 14C–15C (London).

d. Muniment Room MSS: E.8, rental, 16C (incl. London); L.30A, lease, 17C (*71*); N.87, copy lease, 17C (*144*).

458. LONDON, GREATER LONDON RECORD OFFICE
Formed from the former London County RO and Middlesex RO. The reference and index systems of the 2 original repositories have been retained. More details are to be found in separate files on individual accessions. The archive of St. Thomas's Hospital (described under **226**) is listed and indexed separately. For probate records see **529, 530**.

a. London County RO (Index Card list 3). Refs., mostly 17C, to properties in *2, 18, 19, 23, 43, 46, 53, 62, 145, 152, 156*, St. Katharine by the Tower, St. Martin le Grand (incl. alleys), Fenchurch Street, Fleet

Street, Gunpowder Alley, Houndsditch, Newgate Market, Old Street, (West) Smithfield, Watling Street. See also E/HOD (Hodson) and E/TD (Tyrwhitt-Drake): unindexed refs. to *20*.

b. Middlesex RO (Index Card Lists 1, 'Parish Index . . . City of London', and 2, 'Metropolitan parishes and Westminster.' Some material may be indexed in both. Both also include refs. to 'Extra-mural collections' (EMC) in other record offices, and to Sessions Rolls (SR), but these and other refs. not relating to property are not noted here). Indexed refs., mostly 17C, to *42, 43, 45, 152*. See also files on Acc. 349, Radcliffe of Hitchin (deeds, etc., 16C to 17C, concerning *42, 45, 85, 87*, Old Fish Street, Trinity Lane) and Acc. 446, Paget/Anglesey Collection (deeds, etc., 16C to 17C, concerning *30, 54, 155*; also notes on deeds, etc., 14C to 17C, concerning *25, 152*, not deposited).

459. LONDON, GUILDHALL LIBRARY, MANUSCRIPTS DEPARTMENT (MAIN MS SERIES)
GL holds several complete or nearly complete archives relating to the city of London, and numerous single documents or small groups, in many cases deposited by B.R.A. but otherwise of undiscoverable origin. The main MS series, numbered for the most part in accession order, is described in the Numerical Catalogue and the Card Catalogue; both contain the same information but the latter is arranged according to the library's London subject classification. The most recent accessions at any time may be uncatalogued, or listed in the Numerical Catalogue only. There is also a series of Additional MSS, consisting chiefly of deeds, listed in a separate catalogue in GL: see **460**, below. The contents of the principal deposited archives with material relevant to this enquiry are described elsewhere in this survey: they comprise the records of St. Paul's Cathedral (**70–77**), the bishop of London's estate (**78**), livery companies (**16–69**), city parish, ward, and charity records (**275–382, 416**), and several hospitals, trusts, and smaller bodies. For probate records see **529, 530**.
See P. E. Jones and R. Smith, *A Guide to the Records in the Corporation of London Record Office and the Guildhall Library Muniment Room* (1950).

a. Deeds.
The deeds in the main MS series, including deeds in the archives listed above, are indexed in the Card Catalogue under L 86 by street, or, when the street is unknown, by parish. That index does not cover the London parochial charities deeds (**382**), the Additional MSS series (**460**), most deeds from the early part of the numerical sequence (MSS 1–7137), and any uncatalogued accessions. The following indexes are intended to supplement the GL index, for deeds and similar material dating from before *c.* 1670 that do not belong to archives or groups described elsewhere in this survey. The first is arranged by parish, and covers all such deeds catalogued by 30 September 1983 (MSS 1–20578). The second, arranged by streets and other localities, covers all such deeds in MSS 1–7137 which cannot be indexed by parish, since some at least of

these are not covered under L 86. The L 86 street-index should also be used, therefore, for deeds among MSS 7138–20578 which cannot be indexed by parish.

Parishes

2: MSS 10334, 20530
4: MSS 6187, 7052, 8486, 11476, 14786, 15604, 15606, 19969, 20094, 20181
5: MS 10368
9: MSS 1781, 7871, 8956, 9260, 20544, 20572
10: MSS 15747, 20090, 20547, 20552
11: MSS 10957, 11488
12: MSS 19960, 20534
13: MSS 9577, 10890, 17874, 19962, 20098
14: MSS 10299/1, 10375, 10827, 20093, 20159
15: MS 19949
18: MSS 10327, 20099
19: MSS 1843–4, 2231, 10827, 14773, 19531–40
20: MSS 1846, 1870, 6046, 18441, 19764, 19959, 20070, 20099, 20541, 20562
21: MSS 6827–8, 10589
23: MSS 2228, 3717
25: MSS 7130, 14570, 16957
26: MSS 2907, 3754 (inventory), 14580, 20558–9
32: MSS 10956–7
34: MS 2829
37: MSS 10854, 20573
38: MSS 10327, 10627, 11145, 16953
39: MS 19944
42: MSS 7066, 10957, 14806, 20092, 20171, 20545, 20578
43: MSS 1873, 9411, 10818, 11482, 19945, 19950, 20093, 20521–2
44: MSS 2828, 14001–14010, 19963, 20565
45: MSS 19959, 20073–4, 20098, 20538, 20578
46: MSS 1848, 1856, 1859–60, 1908, 7851, 9841, 11479, 19951, 19957, 20095, 20184, 20537, 20551, 20563
47: MSS 18666, 19942, 19946, 20068, 20077, 20529, 20542–3
48: MSS 385–7, 10956–7, 15747, 20527
49: MSS 20518, 20536
51: MSS 1871, 8489, 8491A
53: MSS 6187, 8486, 11431, 11438, 14772, 14788, 18662, 19962
54: MSS 1854, 1975, 3673, 6367, 8959, 11897, 15747, 18667, 19948, 19952, 19957, 19966, 19968, 20069, 20095, 20098, 20340, 20550
56: MSS 2120–1, 20098
59: MSS 10371, 11970, 20173, 20532, 20535, 20551
60: MSS 15609, 20098

61: MS 20553
62: MSS 829, 14762–3, 15747, 20182, 20519
63: MSS 15610, 20535
64: MSS 828, 15609, 20526, 20569
67: MSS 825, 14574
70: MSS 7845, 10970
71: MSS 7085, 20090
73: MSS 20176, 20531
74: MSS 9849, 14297, 14580
77: MS 7048
78: MSS 7048, 7329/1, 7845, 10970
80: MS 20520
81: MSS 8490A, 8770–1, 8780, 9855, 11106/1, 15608, 20518, 20533, 20539
83: MSS 1858, 16261
85: MSS 10957, 14002, 14007, 14277
87: MSS 9376, 11490, 14009, 19947, 19965
88: MS 20072
90: MS 14772
92: MSS 1857, 7134, 7867, 19955, 19959, 20562
93: MSS 2907, 9645, 20180
95: MSS 7062, 7072, 8490, 8490A, 20071, 20090, 20505
98: MSS 3798, 11332
99: MS 20528
100: MS 20516
101: MS 19961
103: MSS 10320, 20172
104: MSS 7132–3, 7877, 14155, 18872, 20503, 20506, 20507, 20517
105: MSS 11488, 19956, 20071, 20504
106: MS 1871
108: MSS 388–391, 5211, 11437
111: MS 19964
112: MSS 9835, 19953
113: MSS 11432, 20098
119: MSS 7077, 11491, 16905, 20174, 20544
120: MSS 10088A, 10958, 20096
123: MSS 11489, 20100
124: MSS 11478, 11487, 20523, 20555–6
125: MSS 19958, 20091, 20562
126: MSS 7085, 16839
128: MSS 20097, 20179
129: MSS 7069, 20551
131: MS 7880
132: MSS 2907, 8962, 19956
134: MSS 7849, 8963, 9838, 19958
141: MSS 14787, 19943, 19967, 20075, 20178, 20549
142: MS 12163
144: MSS 1864, 20540, 20570

145: MS 8187

148: MSS 7061, 10299/1, 10319, 20076, 20093, 20159, 20183

149: MSS 7871, 11487, 20175, 20177, 20554, 20560–2, 20571–2

151: MS 19964

152: MSS 1872, 2828, 9840, 10370, 10635, 11330, 11897, 15747, 20078, 20483, 20524–5, 20541, 20557, 20566–8

155: MSS 8491, 20072

156: MSS 411, 412, 2476, 3069, 3620, 7587, 7587A, 11143, 19954

157: MS 20160

159: MS 20564

Other localities

Abchurch Lane: MS 3798
Aldersgate Street: MS 2919
Blackfriars: MSS 3738–9
Bucklersbury: MS 1529
Budge Row: MS 377
Cheapside (Westcheap): MS 376
Cornhill: MS 5677
Creed Lane: MS 89
Exchange Alley: MS 6373
Fenchurch Street: MS 2741
Fetter Lane: MSS 1842, 1863
Fleet Street: MS 1851

Friday Street: MS 376
Huggin Lane: MSS 518–19
King Street: MS 3108
Lombard Street: MSS 2825, 6373
Ludgate Street: MS 89
Old Bailey: MS 1852
Old Jewry: MSS 406–7
St. Martin le Grand: MS 826
Shoe Lane: MS 2181
Tennis Court Lane: MS 1720
Thames Street: MS 1720
Tower, precinct or liberty of: MS 20507

b. Transcripts of deeds: records of the partnership of Sir Robert Clayton and John Morris, bankers and scriveners, dating mostly from 1669, incl. copy and abstract deeds from before 1666.

MSS 5286/1, 2: bundles of 17C particulars, rentals, memoranda (*46, 71, 77, 104, 142, 156*, Abchurch Lane, Austin Friars, Bishopsgate Street, Broad Street, Fleet Street, Gracechurch Street). MS 5386: 17C papers, copy deeds, abstracts of title, 15C–17C; Box 1 (*18, 20, 46, 56, 64, 77, 104, 114, 124, 141*, Austin Friars, Lombard Street); Box 2 (*18, 19, 32, 43, 45, 56, 77, 80, 83, 88, 98, 105, 123, 124, 134, 141, 148, 149, 152*, Austin Friars, Broad Street, Lime Street, Lombard Street, St. Katharine by the Tower, East Smithfield).

c. Miscellaneous accounts: a few private a/cs or a/c bks. relating to property are deposited in GL.

MS 2931: a/c bk. of Robert Abbot, scrivener, 1646–52, incl. rents (unspec.). MS 4159: record and a/c bk. of Nicholas Geffe, *c.* 1593 (*26, 152*, Cheapside). MS 6238: (part) rental, 1628 (Austin Friars). MS 6437: administrator's a/c of intestate's estate 1623 (*156*). MS 9277: a/c of executors of Sir Thomas Kneseworth, 1515–23, incl. building of Bishopsgate conduit.

460. London, Guildhall Library, Manuscripts Department (Additional Manuscripts)

This series comprises some 1187 documents (chiefly deeds, 13C to 19C) deposited in GL and CLRO from various sources before 1948. They are described in a numerically-arranged catalogue but are not indexed. The series includes major parts of the archives of the parishes of St. Andrew Hubbard, St. Benet Paul's Wharf, St. Botolph Aldersgate, St. Mary Bothaw, St. Stephen Walbrook, and St. Swithin, and a few documents that are clearly from other parish archives. Where such a provenance can be ascertained the documents are described in this survey under the archive to which they belong. The series also contains documents which may have belonged to the same or other archives, but which cannot be so ascribed with certainty: these are indexed below, with the rest of the series, which has no known provenance. The following index, based on the descriptions in the catalogue of Additional Manuscripts, is to deeds and similar material before *c.* 1670. The documents are known as GL, Add. MS 1, etc.

Parishes
2: 631, 635–7, 685
3: 727
4: 42, 377–83, 700, 731
5: 825
10: 56, 703, 714–15
11: 1111
12: 1137, 1144–7
13: 598, 623, 853, 1011
14: 662, 836
15: 891, 1136
18: 898–905
19: 646, 827, 870, 1123–35
21: 143–7, 599, 977–9
33: 399, 960–1
34: 1140
36: 873, 878–881
37: 700
38: 198, 202, 208, 239
39: 759
41: 361
42: 374, 375, 724, 761–2
43: 6, 8, 12–13, 20–1, 24–30, 35, 37, 39, 41, 47, ?49–50, 366–9, 722, 764–5, 768, 770–1, 888, 960–1
44: 174, 1033–7
45: 350, 629
46: 360, 629, 723, 730, 860, 1079–82, 1142
47: 373, 375, 721, 871, 1112
48: 601
49: 158, 164, 179, 557, 719
51: 851, 876, 1143, 1151, 1153
53: 1, 4, 42, 629, 643, 692–3, 825, 851, 941–52, 970
54: 388, 751
56: 319
59: 640, 709, 711, 924
60: 1139
61: 40, 42
62: 585, 632, 690, 704, 738–47, 749–50, 752–3, 760, 763, 766, 828, 960–1
63: 707, 1141
64: 630, 658, 667, 687, 826
67: 648, ?656, 664,681
70: 227, 231, 250, 287
71: 345
74: 200–1, 219, 235, 255, 257, 266, 268, 271–3, 290
77: 698, 712, 856
78: 969, 1011

80: 725
81: 639, 647, 651–2, 663, 679, ?683, 686, 702
83: 40, 638, 668
85: 173, 597, 1028–33
87: 40
89: 626
92: 1076–8, 1083–5
93: 178, 1094
94: 882
95: 694, 782, 784–91, 801–3, 805–10, 812–18, 820–2
96: 32, 45
98: 600, 634, 666, 678, 825
101: 830
103: 200–1, 203, 255, 257, 266, 268, 271–3, 290, 894, 907
104: 660, 689
105: 99, 825, 1043–60
108: 576–7, 831–42, 844–50
113: 9, 22
114: 48–50, 960
118: 313, 1103
119: 676, ?677, 684, 777, 825, 1070
123: 872, 894
124: 716–18, 824–5, 1138
125: 726, 729
127: 836
129: 735–7, 755–6
131: 626, 645–6, 825
132: 375, 688, 696, 710, 875, 1043–60
134: 654, 675, 708, 960–1
135: 584
136: 160, 162, 167, 180, 606
141: 590, 977–80, 983
142: 38, 710, 1055, 1088–90, 1102
144: 346, 579–80, 811
145: 139, 362–5, 592
148: 641–2, 662, 665, 669–71, 680, 698–9, 781, 783, 792–9, 819, 825
149: 116–17, 825, 895–905, 909–11, 926–9
151: 587, 650, 673, 701, 757, 825, 1087
152: 370–2, 374–6, 655, 674, 691, 705–6, 767, 829, 865–6, 869, 884, 1011, 1118, 1120
155: 139, 653, 854, 1152
156: 232, 713
157: 544, 659, 823, 955–61
158: 825
159: 778

Other localities

London: 36, 81, 82, 90, 91, 161, 169, ?603, 628
Abchurch Lane: 347
Aldgate: 1011
Basing Lane: 825
Bread Street: 624
Broad Street: 627
Bush Lane: 697
Candlewick Street: 836
Chick Lane: 625
Cock Lane: 234
Crooked Lane: 836
Distaff Lane: 989
Fenchurch Street: 157, 960, 1011
Fetter Lane: 1019
Fleet Bridge: 310

Friday Street: 331
Mark Lane: 165, 976, 1011
Old Jewry: 159, 400
'Roplane': 576
St. Katharine's Hospital: 155
St. Martin le Grand: 354, 862
Serjeants' Inn: 384
Shoe Lane: 728
Smithfield, East: 618
Staining Lane: 736
Steelyard: 1011
Thames Street: 230, 358
Trinity Lane: 656
Walbrook: 204, 244
Whitefriars: 386–98, 511–33, 560

Other records

Wills (unspecified): 195, 196, 267, 282, 582, 720, 869a

Bonds (unspecified): 286, 291, 316, 602, 605, 607, 610, 682, 800, 858, 877

461. LONDON, HOUSE OF LORDS

The calendars in HMC (2–7) *Third* to *Eighth Reports* contain numerous references to properties and parish churches in the city, 17C. For the small quantity of additional material, see M. F. Bond, *Guide to the Records of Parliament* (1971).

462. LONDON, LAMBETH PALACE LIBRARY

Records concerning the London properties of religious bodies are dealt with in the entries concerning those bodies. For references with the prefix CM, see D. M. Owen, *A catalogue of Lambeth Manuscripts 889 to 901 (Carte Antique et Miscellanee)* (1968). Other relevant catalogues are noted below. See also **529f**.

a. Deeds etc: CM II/4: deed, 16C (*20*). CM VI/95: copy of sentence in tithe dispute, 16C (*53*). CM 27/3: assignment, 17C (Bell Alley). COMM XIb/12: lease, 1609 (*114*).

b. Records of church estates during the Interregnum. For the records of the administration of the former lands and impropriate tithes of bishops and of deans and chapters over the period *c.* 1650–1660, see J. Houston, *Catalogue of the Ecclesiastical Records of the Commonwealth, 1643–1660, in the Lambeth Palace Library* (1968), 66–87. These include minute books and day books recording decisions to grant leases; 'Augmentation Order Books' (records of orders classified according to the committees which issued them); a schedule and abstract of leases; particulars of rents and revenues. There appear to be no counterparts of leases for London properties granted in this period, but for a lease of 1609 catalogued in this series, see above, **a**. Where appropriate the contents of these records are arranged by counties and most are indexed with reference to place or county (incl. London). Parliamentary surveys at Lambeth which concern London (all valuations of benefices) are indexed in the catalogue. The following item, formerly in the St. Paul's Cathedral archive (WD 51), is not covered by the printed catalogue: Add. Comm. 1, transcript of minute book of persons appointed to deal with bishops' lands, 1647–55 (*47, 54, 59, 63*, bishop of London's palace, Holborn, Whitefriars).

c. Lists and assessments. MS 272: lists of house valuations and tithe assessments for most city parishes, 1638; substantially printed as *The Inhabitants of London in 1638*, 2 vols., ed. T. C. Dale (Society of Genealogists, London, 1931). CM VIII/18 and 25: lists of tithe valuations and numbers of communicants for most city parishes, early 17C and 1634. CM VIII/16 and CM IX/54: tithe valuations and names of inhabitants, 1634, and 1638 (*93*).

d. Papers concerning the London tithe cause, 1634–9. In addition to the specific items noted in **c**, above, a number of more general items concerning this matter are described in the catalogue entries for CM VIII/1–50 and CM IX/1–89.

e. Other collections. *A calendar of the Shrewsbury papers in Lambeth Palace Library*, ed. E. G. W. Bill (Derbyshire Archaeological Society Record Series 1, 1966 for 1965; HMC, joint publications 6): MSS 695, 709, 697, 699 incl. refs. to sale, and lease of, and repairs to Coldharbour, late 16C (*12*). *Index to the papers of Anthony Bacon (1558–1601) in Lambeth Palace Library (MSS 647–662)* (1974): MSS 659–60 incl. refs to lease and finance of Fleet Prison, 16C.

463. LONDON, MUSEUM OF LONDON
The museum contains a number of relevant items. In 1983 they were kept in a number of locations within the museum, but there is no guide or list and some items may not have been discovered. The numbers given below are accession numbers.

a. Deeds and similar material. 33.107/1–2: deed and bills, 14C (*108*, London). A.15611: inquest, early 16C (Soper Lane). 265, A.4254: deeds, 16C (*81*, Paternoster Row). A.16035–6, 16038–9: will and deeds, 16C–17C (*27*). Z.526/2 and two unnumbered items: deeds, 16C–17C (*92*). 70.81/1, 70.81/3, 70.81/82, 2525/3, 2525/8, 27534, A.15607, A.15615: deeds, 17C (*25, 78, 99, 124, 135*, Fleet Street, St. Paul's churchyard). 42.39: letters and memoranda at time of Great Fire.

464. UNIVERSITY OF LONDON, SENATE HOUSE LIBRARY, PALAEOGRAPHY ROOM (FULLER COLLECTION)
Private collection of misc. deeds from many sources, deposited in Library 1965; only partially listed.

a. 33 boxes, catalogued and indexed by location: Box 4/9, lease 1413 (*109*); Box 30/15, deed 1502 (*9*); Box 31/18, deed 1584 (*101*).

b. 7 cabinets (III, IV, and VI contain seals only). Cabinet I (rough list): I/5/7, deed 1551 (*44*); I/15/5, deed 1656 (*152*); I/16/5, extract from Husting Roll, 1477 (*19, 32, 39*). Cabinet II (list and index): II/13/7, lease 1653 (? *4*); II/16/31, deed 1440 (*144*); II/16/38, deed 1596 (*12*); II/18/34, receipt

1511 (*42*); II/19/18, deed 1440 (*144*). Cabinet VII (rough list): VII/9, deed 1591 (*152*); VII/10, 12, deeds 1642, 1660 (*20*); VII/11, fine 1651 (*46, 92*). VII/15, inventory, *c.* 1660 (unspec., possibly one of preceding); VII/36, deed 1669 (*93*).

465. BEDFORDSHIRE RECORD OFFICE
Not visited.

a. Miscellaneous. AD 1099: deed, 17C (*33*). FN 596–600, 601–4, 606, 608–12: deeds, 17C (*14, 67, 112, 135, 148*). L 75–6 and 24/700–17: lease and paper, 16C–17C (Barbican). L 21/80: deed, 16C (Billingsgate ward). L 24/13, 410: valor, 16C (incl. London). LK 229–47 (calendar in GL, MS 14923): deeds, 17C–19C (*45*). M 1/13/1–26: deeds, 17C–18C (*20, 43*). M 1/14/1: deed, 17C (behind mansion of earl of Oxford, probably in *157*). M 1/14/2: deed, 17C (Candlewick Street). PO 77–81: deeds, 17C (*59, 63*). RO 5/255–9: deeds, 16C–17C (*5, 54*). TW 238: deed, 16C (Aldersgate Street). TW 643: deed, 16C (Chancery Lane). W 3194, 3196: deeds, 17C (*18, 59*).

b. The *Guide to the Bedfordshire Record Office* (1957 and supplement to 1962) also mentions the following collections as including London material, some of which may be relevant: St. John (deeds n.d., a/cs from 1652); Stuart (deeds from 1666); Williamson (deeds from 1623); Larken & Co. (deeds from 1663); Preston and Redman (deeds, 13C–17C); Miscellaneous deposits (London deeds, 16C–19C).

466. BERKSHIRE RECORD OFFICE, SHIRE HALL, SHINFIELD, READING

a. Hunter Papers. D/EHr/T26–9: deeds, 17C (*81, 157*).

b. Stapleton MSS. D/Est/T16, 57: deeds, 16C–17C (*25*). D/Est/T17: deeds, 16C–18C (*127*).

c. Other collections. D/EHe/T2–4: deeds, 17C (*20*). D/EL1/T28–9: deeds, 17C (*34, 105*).

d. Bouverie-Pusey MSS should incl. 13C deed (*8*) mentioned in HMC (6) *Seventh Report* i, 681a.

467. BIRMINGHAM, CITY REFERENCE LIBRARY
Not visited.

a. Baker collection (5573L). Incl. deeds, 16C–17C (*4, 54, 108, 144*, Gatehorseprison (*sic*), London).

b. Licences of alienation, 1624–40, found in papers of Thomas Coventry, Lord Keeper of the Great Seal (597244). Each licence has a number and they are arranged topographically as follows: *19* (no. 1113), *151* (nos. 1029, 1179), *152* (nos. 1063, 1095), Aldermanbury (nos. 45, 204), Aldersgate (no. 880), Bishopsgate (no. 876), Charterhouse (no. 42), Cheapside (no. 1173), Cornhill (nos. 189, 362), Cripplegate (nos. 45, 204), Ludgate hill (no. 947), city of London (nos. 206, 261, 286, 362, 382, 215, 319, 441, 457, 587–8, 612, 631, 646, 707, 887).

468. Buckinghamshire Record Office, Aylesbury
Not visited.

a. Drake Deeds. AR 112/81: deeds, 15C–17C (*19, 152*, Broad Street ward, Bucklersbury, Leadenhall Street, Lime Street).

b. Other collections. D/GA/1: grant and valor, 16C (London). D/X/671: grant, 16C (*75*). D/U/3/4 and D/X/171/36: grants, 17C (*68*). D/LE/9/16, 17: receipts, 17C (Fresh Wharf).

469. Cambridge, University Library, Department of Manuscripts
CUL MSS concerning the London properties of institutions whose archives are covered by entries in this survey are described in those entries. This entry covers the miscellaneous items. See *Catalogue of the manuscripts preserved in the library of the University of Cambridge* (6 vols., 1856–67).

a. Dd. 9. 60: memorandum bk. of Robert Chambers of London, *c.* 1630–2; incl. (f. 18) note of lands bought (Birchin Lane).

b. Ee. 3. 27: bailiff's a/c, 1640, for manors and London (*33*); tenants named.

470. Cambridge County Record Office, Cambridge

a. Parish records of Caxton. P 37/25/33–6 incl. copies and recitations of 16C–17C deeds and leases, and a 17C covenant (*88*).

b. Miscellaneous. TR 324/8: photograph of 15C will (*108*). 279/T14: lease, 17C (*127*).

471. Cambridge County Record Office, Huntingdon
Not visited.

a. Manchester collection. DDM 69/3–5, 7, 8: deeds, 17C (*20*). DDM 24A/2, DDM 47B/9: deeds, 17C (*42*). DDM 20B/5: deed, 16C (St. Bartholomew's Close: probably *33*).

b. Heathcote collection. No. 4: deed, 17C (*62*).

472. Canterbury, Kent, Cathedral Library
For records of Christ Church priory, and subsequently the dean and chapter of Canterbury, in this library, see **127–32**.

a. Bothamley deeds, 17C (*85*).

473. Cheshire Record Office
Not visited.

a. Cholmondeley collection. 13C–16C deeds concerning site of Crutched Friars (*53, 141*; see also **93**). 17C inventory (*141*).

474. Cornwall County Record Office, Truro
Not visited.

a. Miscellaneous. Buller 203, 203B: deeds (*59, 128*) and leases (*15*), 17C. GR 773–9: deeds and leases, 17C (London). DS 25: recital of title, 17C (London). DDT 2034A: letter describing Great Fire.

475. DEVON RECORD OFFICE, EXETER

a. Sidmouth papers. 152M/SO/2, 3: 17C deeds (*5*, Walbrook).

b. Miscellaneous. DD 30003, 30382–3, 30391, 30495: 15C deeds (*89; 30003* also refs. to *24, 62, 157*). 96M/92/4: deeds and letters, 16C (*152* rectory). DD 30022, 30373: deeds, 17C (*54*). 2530M/B1/29–30: bonds, 16C (Bishopsgate). 152M/Box 57/2: leases, 17C–19C (Bow Lane). 2530M/L6/5/1, 2530M/E1/1: assignment and valuation, 16C (Old Bailey). 872A/P2 205: mortgage, 16C (London).

c. References to Exeter city collections. 58/3/7/1: 17C deed (city of London). Pearse Boxes 197, Box 1: 17C deeds (Middlesex incl. London).

476. DORSET RECORD OFFICE
See also **416.**

a. Earl of Ilchester's MSS. D 124 (uncatalogued): p. 10 of rough list refers to 15C deed (*150*).

b. Weld deposits. D 16/T61: quitclaim, 14C (London). D 10/L1: extracts of pleas, 14C (London properties to which Elsing Spital had a claim).

c. Other collections. D 86/T523: incl. 16C and 17C deeds and leases used as covers (*14, 132*, London). D 10/213: royal order for demolition of houses to prevent spread of Great Fire from Aldersgate, 1666.

d. Crichel Estates MSS, formerly deposited at Dorset Record Office (D 84) but not now (1982–3) accessible: London deeds 15C–19C (*3, 31, 36, 37, 41, 46, 49, 52, 59, 62, 74, 77, 78, 81, 83, 90, 95, 99, 152, 155*).

477. DURHAM COUNTY RECORD OFFICE
Not visited.

a. Londonderry Papers. See *Catalogue of the documents deposited in the Durham County Record Office by the 9th Marquess of Londonderry*, ed. S. C. Newton (Durham, 1969), 70 (D/Lo F 298): release, 17C (*145*).

b. Strathmore Papers (uncatalogued): incl. some post-17C London deeds and possibly some of earlier date (letter from County Archivist).

478. ESSEX RECORD OFFICE, CHELMSFORD

a. Petre family (D/DP). F238: will 1571 (*34*). F252/9, 10: will 1583 (*42*). T271, T286–7, F29, F50, F57: deeds, 1545–1826 (*42*). T283: deed, 1376 (*126*). T284: bond, 1474 (*62*). T285: lease, 1550 (*46*). E29: register of deeds, 1506–*c.* 1586 (*42*). E188: similar register, comp. *c.* 1620 (*42*). E24: lease bk., 1554–68 (*42*). E5: valuation 1567 (*42*). E6: schedule and valuation *c.* 1595 (*42, 96*). E9: valuation *c.* 1640 (*33, 42*). E22/2: rental 1645 (*33, 42*). A1: rent a/cs, 1539–44 (*?42*). A83–6: rent a/cs, 1563–5,

1569–71 (*42*). A2–9: a/cs of household in London (*42*), 1544–7, incl. (A7) payment for conveying water to house. A41: a/c of household in London (*42*), 1651–60. A169: building a/cs, 1608 (*?33* or *42*). F205: vol. of inventories of household stuff, 1562–71 (*42*). F224: file of inventories, with typed transcript, 1638–9 (*42*).

b. Other collections. D/DAy T59, 60: deeds, 1599–1635 (*100*). D/DMs T7/1, 6: deeds, 16C (*92, 125, 146*). D/DRc T28A: deeds, 1652–1710 (*98*). D/DRc T29A: deeds, 1529–1716 (*80*). D/DRc T32: deed, 1668 (*93*). D/DRo T6: deeds, 1633–1809 (*74, 156*). D/DRo 78: deed, 1641 (*74, 105, 142, 156*). D/DRu T18: leases, 1642–89 (*99*). D/DRu T20: deed, 1591 (*53*). D/DSo T28: deeds, 1590–1719 (*151*). D/DSo T29: deed, 1669 (*46*). D/DSp T117: deeds, incl. view, 1602–29 (*51*). D/DSp T118: deeds, 1661–84 (*105*). D/DTW T26: deeds, 1622–1801 (*77*, Eastcheap, New Fish Street). D/DU 161/312: deeds, 1651–83 (*51*). D/DU 161/353: deeds, 1661–1724 (*56, 119*). D/DU 414/12–13: copy deeds, 1636–8 (*152, 158*). D/DU 450/1: probate of will 1576 (London).

479. GLOUCESTERSHIRE RECORD OFFICE
See also **159**.

a. Batsford Park muniments. D1447 (uncatalogued): 17C deeds (*11, 53, 54, 62*).

b. Duke of Beaufort's records. D2700 Acc 3702/111.3.1: deed, 15C (*71*).

c. Earl of Ducie's MSS. D340a/T190–1: deeds, 17C (*32, 123*).

d. Hicks family papers. D1866/T66–9, F1, L1: deeds, papers, and rentals, 16C–17C (*19, 43, 62, 116, 148, 150*).

e. Stephens and related family papers (D547a). 17C deeds, as follows: T76 (*152*), T77 (*20, 46*), T4/9 (*4*), T4/10–16 (*62*, Coleman Street, Crooked Lane, Bishopsgate Street, Wood Street), T4/17 (*46*).

f. Other collections. D225/Z8: list of tenants in Royal Exchange *c.* 1600 (photostat in GL, MS 6433). D1305: incl. 16C–17C deeds (*152*). D1406: incl. 16C deed (*20*). D1460: incl. 16C deed (*45, 119*). D1637/T53: deeds, 17C (*123*). D2025/Box 111: deeds, 17C (*46*). D3549/Deeds/Box 7a: assignment, 17C (*157*).

480. HAMPSHIRE RECORD OFFICE, WINCHESTER
See also **257**.

a. Basingstoke borough records. 148M71/7/3/1: deeds, 17C (*80*). 148M71/9/2: deeds, 14C to 17C (principally concerning *71*; also refs. to *12, 26, 67, 127*).

b. Mildmay papers. 15M50/1396, 1558, 1561: return, inquisition, and settlement (*152*: apparently former property of bishopric of Oxford, see above, **197**). 15M50/1604: assignment, 17C (*32*). 15M50/1613: lease, 17C (*54*). 16M48/367: deed 16C (*46*). 16M48/378: deed, 14C (*73*); 5M58/78: copy of letters patent, 16C (*43, 53*).

c. Wriothesley family documents (5M53). From 1545 the estate included the advowsons of *20* and *151*: see 5M53/230, 272, 1008, (15C–17C grants and an agreement). The extensive property in *20* lay outside the city. The following items also concern London property: 5M53/151–2, will, 16C (*13*; also refs. to *43, 74, 156*); 5M53/214, covenant, 16C (*13*); 4M62/38, letters patent, 16C (*150*); 5M53/1543, lease, 16C (*63*).

d. Other collections. 43M48/316–17, 361–3, 374–5: deeds, wills, Chancery decree, 17C (*4*). 43M48/117: will, 16C (*150*). 18M61/Box 30/8: copy deed, 16C (*46*).

481. HEREFORD AND WORCESTER RECORD OFFICE, WORCESTER
Not visited. See also **261**.

a. Norbury family archive. 705: 484 BA 5025/1–10: deeds, 16C–19C (Poultry).

b. Other collections. 705: 99 BA 3375/15 (iii): deeds, 14C–16C (Eastcheap). 009: 1 BA 5401: deeds, 17C (Whitefriars). The following collections incl. 17C deeds concerning London property, but whether this was in the city or not remains uncertain: 705: 260 BA 4000/570; 705: 27 BA 385/27; 705: 580 BA 1628/2.

482. HERTFORDSHIRE RECORD OFFICE

a. Garrard (separate catalogue, indexed). 27030, 27143: deeds, 17C (*10*). 27423: inventory of goods, 1571.

b. Halsey (separate catalogue, indexed). Deeds, leases wills, 16C to 17C (principally *67, 112, 135*; also *19, 42, 54, 62, 92, 111*).

c. Lawes-Wittewronge (D/ELw). T98–101, E70–2; deeds, papers, etc., 17C (*10, 54, 141, 151*, Smart's Key).

d. Panshanger, Earls Cowper (D/EP). T4054–4099: deeds, etc., 16C to 17C (*124*). T4341–62: deeds, 17C to 18C (*19, 64, 156*). T4363: deed, 1661 (*159*).T4365–72: deeds, late 17C (*4*).T4373–82: papers, incl. plan, concerning rebuilding, 1671–99 (*155*). D/EP F1: inventory of goods, 1609.

e. Sebright. 15728: deed, 1567 (*62*). 17309: fine, 1589 (*108*).

f. Other collections. 5001: fine, 1666 (*74, 105, 142, 156*). 19720: case depositions, 1565–6 (Thames Street). 75039–41, 75052, 75057, 75059: deeds, 17C to 18C (*62*). D/EB 1622, T34: deeds, 1591–1670 (*78*). D/EDp, T86: deeds, late 17C to 18C (*26*).

483. HUMBERSIDE COUNTY RECORD OFFICE, BEVERLEY
Not visited.

a. Miscellaneous collections. DDHV 80/1: quitclaim, 17C (*54*). DDCC 111/25: covenant, 17C (*64, 148*). DDKP 15/3b: letter patent, 16C (*46*). DDKP 15/6: covenant, 17C (*112, 152, 155*).

484. KEELE, STAFFS., UNIVERSITY LIBRARY
Not visited.

a. Hatton Wood MSS. M72/25/1–28 incl. deeds relating to *20* (17C), *21* (16C), *32* (14C–16C), *44* (15C–16C), *49* (17C), *53* (14C, 17C), *74* (16C), *78* (16C), *81* (17C), *87* (13C), *103* (16C), *152* (17C), and Walbrook; also part of a subsidy list, 1590.

b. Raymond Richards collection III. 53/4: incl. quitclaim, 13C–14C (*158*). 49/4: deeds, 17C (Bishopsgate). 43: incl. deed, 17C (St. Paul's churchyard).

485. KENT COUNTY ARCHIVES OFFICE, MAIDSTONE
See also **210–11**.

a. Sackville of Knole (U269): see HMC (3) *Fourth Report* (Earl de la Warr, Knole MSS) and HMC (6) *Seventh Report* (Lord Sackville, Knole MSS). Deeds, 17C: T70/1–2 (*46, 116*); T70/6–7 (*46, 54*); T90/6, T98/1–4 (*54*); T98/5 (*18*). Estate papers: E53, abs. title, *c.* 1564–1704, and rental with dimensions, *c.* 1704 (*46, 54*); E61/2, receipt 1544 (*116*). L4, Fire Ct. petition, 1667 (*46*). Accounts: A1/1–6, rent a/cs, 1607–21 (*46, 54, 116*).

b. Cranfield, with Sackville (U269). Deeds, 17C: T100/3 (*2*); T102/2 (*33*). Estate papers: E264, inventories, 1626–32 (*33*); E265/5–6, E266, quit-claims, rent receipts, 1625–52 (*33*). Accounts: A389/1–2, A402/1–2, A403, A454/1–8, A508/1, repair and household a/cs, vouchers, *c.* 1630–40 (*33*); A509, bills etc., 1605–41 (incl. *60*); cf. A526, household a/cs, Bourchier family (London).

c. De L'Isle (U1475): see HMC (77) *De L'Isle* and (more recent) list in Kent C.A.O. T257: deeds, 14C (*10*). T189: deed, 17C (*25*). M57: extent, 14C (*10*). A4/3: a/c, 1571–2, incl. repairs to *10*. A33/3: a/c, 1573–4, incl. ref. to rent in 'St. Anthony' (?*26*). 27/4: household a/c bk. at Baynards Castle, 1600–1. References to properties in correspondence, 16C–17C (Aldersgate Street, Baynards Castle, Broad Street, Holborn, Little Britain): see HMC (77) *De L'Isle* II, pp. 157, 293–4; VI, pp. 133, 528. Petition, 17C (advowson of *18*): see HMC (77) *De L'Isle* VI, p. 7.

d. Denton Court (U805). T15: deeds, 1652–1832 (*89*). T16: deeds, 1661–1820 (*59*). T26: deeds 1569–1880 (Whitechapel).

e. Fane (U282); cf. Stapleton MSS, Berks. RO (**466**). T81: lease 1576 (*4*). T129: deed 1633 (*127*). E32: abs. title, 1667–83 (*25*).

f. Faunce-Delaune (U145). T2, T61/1–3, T71/3, T101/1, E24–5, E26/1, L14: deeds, leases, will, Fire Ct. decree, etc., 1659–1734 (*25*). T71/1–2, deeds, will administration, 1621–38 (*128*).

g. Lambarde: U962/T84–5, U1823/37/T41–2, deeds etc., 1571–1635 (*10*).

h. Pratt (U840). T142: deeds, 1616–1786 (*4, 19, 49*, outside London). T189–191: deeds, 1616–1784 (*19*). T205: deeds, 1621–1740 (*4*).

j. Smith-Marriott (U513). T1, 15, 16: deeds, 1586–1767 (*37*).

k. Tufton (U455). T132: deeds 1538–1746 (*42*). T133, L7: deeds, valuation, 1543–1617, 1631 (*152*).

l. Warde (U678). T14: deeds, 1661–70 (*59*). T16: deeds, 1539–1748 (*80*). T19, deeds, 1659–1687 (*119*).

m. Other collections. 17C deeds etc.: U1823/1/T46 (*63, 75*); U1823/1/T47 (*124*); U2065/T32 (*42*); U2113/T51 (*62*).

486. LANCASHIRE RECORD OFFICE, PRESTON
Not visited.

a. Earl of Derby (DDK). 1/20 and 5/4: deed and letters patent, 15C–16C (*150*). 2/8: deed, 15C (*43*). 6/11 and 9/4: settlements, 16C–17C (*20*).

b. Other collections. DD1b (unlisted): incl. copy deeds, 14C (*112*). DDX 444: lease, 17C (*81*). DDPt (unlisted): incl. deeds, 14C (London). DDM: inventories, 17C (London: property of Viscount Molyneux).

487. LEICESTERSHIRE RECORD OFFICE
Not visited.

a. Herrick MSS DG9/2337: assignment, 17C (Cheapside: possibly *159*). DG9/2407–22: will and papers, 16C–17C (*159*).

488. LINCOLNSHIRE ARCHIVES OFFICE
Not visited.

a. Ancaster. 2 Anc 1/43: deeds, 14C–17C (Barbican: probably *62*).

b. Massingberd. 14/1–14: deeds, 16C (*58, 131*, Trinity Lane).

c. Cragg. 5/2/2/10–12, 16, 17, deeds and leases as follows: 10, 15C (*49*); 11, 17C (St. Paul's churchyard); 12, 17C (*152*); 16, 17C (*128*); 17, 17C (*113*).

d. Other collections. Aswardby 1B/25: lease, 17C (Paternoster Row). Nelthorpe 3/18 and 7/7: deeds, 16C–17C (*83* and St. Katharine's precinct).

489. MANCHESTER CENTRAL LIBRARY, ARCHIVES DEPARTMENT
Not visited.

a. Farrer papers. L1/28/5/1, 6, 7: deeds and inquisition, 16C (*92*). L1/28/12/3: deed, 17C (*20, 23*).

490. MANCHESTER, JOHN RYLANDS UNIVERSITY LIBRARY
Not visited.

a. Bromley Davenport Muniments: incl. 18 deeds, 15C–19C (London).

b. Other collections, see M. Tyson and F. Taylor, *Hand-list of Charters, Deeds and similar documents* . . . ii (1935) and iii (1975), nos. 277, 3261–77, 3762, 3774, 4668: deeds, leases, and particulars, 16C–17C (*20, 61*, Bucklersbury, London).

491. NORFOLK RECORD OFFICE

a. Beauchamp-Proctor papers. BEA 112–256: deeds, 13C–17C (*62*). BEA 257–9: deeds, 17C (*152*).

b. Norfolk Record Society deeds and papers. NRS 9457–63 (22 C 4), 8069 (24 B 3), 8092 (24 B 4), 8112 (24 B 5), 8133 (24 B 6): deeds 14C–18C (*9*). NRS 8063 (24 B 3), 8083 (24 B 4), 8122 (24 B 6): deeds, 17C (*58*). NRS 11188 (26 A 1), 18132 (33 A 2): deed and receipt, 15C–16C (*104*). NRS 8481 (21 B 3): deed, 16C (*111*). NRS 8168 (24 C 1): deed, 16C (*149*).

c. Other collections. KNY 401 (371 × 7): deed, 16C (*155*). MS 12628 (30 E 4): deed, 17C (*19*).

492. NORTHAMPTONSHIRE RECORD OFFICE
See also **200–201**.

a. Bateman-Hanbury. Deeds, leases, 16C to 17C: BH (K) 407, 502–3 (*53*); 799–849, 894–928 (*104, 132*); 929–52 (*80*); 953–74 (*93*); 975–1014 (*141*); 1181 (*77*); 1235–8 (*19*); 1254 (*20, 46*).

b. Bouverie (Delapré). B(D) 187–316: deeds, etc., 16C to 18C (*4*).

c. Cecil. 27/2: list of deeds, 16C ('Barkley's inn'). 89/3, 5/38, 92/9: deeds, rental, 16C (*63*). 96/56: grant, 1547 (Fleet Street, Friday Street).

d. Fermor-Hesketh. Boxes AMC 74–5: deeds, 16C–19C (*2*, unspec.). MTD/D/18/9, MTD/F/28/3: deed, valuation, 16C (London).

e. Finch-Hatton (FH): see catalogue for details. Deeds, etc. 16C to 17C (*45, 152*, Haberdashers' Hall, Hatton Garden); assessment, 1642 (*47*); refs. to St. Paul's 1643–6.

f. Gompertz (Glendon). Acc. no. 32: misc. early deeds, incl. grant of rent, 1297 (London).

g. Isham: see catalogue for details. Property in *26, 95*; see *John Isham, Mercer and Merchant Adventurer, Two Account Books . . .*, ed. G. D. Ramsay (Northants. Rec. Soc. 21, 1961), comprising 2 account books and inventory, 1558–72.

h. Papillon. P(L) 241: notebk., 1656–60, with notes of inhabitants (*77*, Aldgate). P(L) 3: dispute, 1646 (Moorfields).

j. Thornton (uncatalogued). Copy deed, 1634 (*26, 74*).

k. For 16C–17C material in other collections, see index under 'London' (*25, 34, 46, 80, 84, 93, 104, 148, 159*, Bridge, Broad Street, Fenchurch Street, Fleet Street, East Smithfield, (West) Smithfield, Thames Street).

l. Buccleuch MSS. For 17C refs. to lease and rent of house in Little Britain, see HMC (45), *Fifteenth Report, Appendix VIII, Buccleuch I*, p. 214 and *Buccleuch III*, p. 315.

493. UNIVERSITY OF NOTTINGHAM, DEPARTMENT OF MANUSCRIPTS (MIDDLETON MSS)
Not visited. See list and HMC (69) *Lord Middleton*.

a. Deeds and leases, 13C–17C (*4, 157*, London).

b. Rentals and a/cs, 16C (*20*).

c. Inventory, 16C (*59*); letters, 16C (Whitefriars).

494. NOTTINGHAMSHIRE RECORD OFFICE
Not visited.

a. Portland papers. DD. 4P/18/11–24: will, deeds, and papers, 17C (*152*, St. Martin le Grand, Wood Street).

b. Savile MSS. DD. SR5: 9A, 10P: leases and papers, 17C, plans, 19C (London).

495. OXFORD, BODLEIAN LIBRARY, DEPARTMENT OF WESTERN MANUSCRIPTS
Bodleian MSS concerning the London properties of institutions whose archives are covered by entries in this survey are described in those entries. This entry covers miscellaneous items, principally deeds, concerning London properties which are to be found in the library.

a. Principal collections of deeds for which there are unified searching aids.
For deeds acquired up to 1878, see W. H. Turner and H. O. Coxe, *Calendar of Charters and Rolls preserved in the Bodleian Library* (1878): deeds, plans, and inventories, 13C and 15C–17C (*26, 51, 62, 104, 124, 150*, la Riole (*126, 158*), Fleet Prison, London). The principal guide to deeds acquired since 1878 takes the form of a topographically-arranged slip catalogue kept in a cubicle near the Selden end: decision on parochial rights, 12C (Smithfield, probably *152*); deeds, abstracts of title, wills, inventories, 14C–17C (*25, 30, 33, 44, 45, 46, 47, 55, 58, 62, 63, 64, 77, 79, 81, 84, 88, 92, 104, 112, 119, 128, 135, 144, 145, 152*, Aldermanbury, Foster Lane, Gutter Lane, Kyron Lane, St. Paul's churchyard, Watling Street, London).

b. Deeds etc. in collections not covered by the guides cited in **a** above.
MS Ashmole 1544: deed, 17C (*116*). MS Hatton 97, in flyleaf: lease, 16C (St. Paul's churchyard). Rawlinson MSS: B 66, f. 76, copies of 15C grants (*38*); C 182, ff. 1–38, copies of grants, settlements, pleas and inquiries, 14C–17C (*33*); D 548, f. 6, notes of leases, 17C (London Wall near Bishopsgate); D 699, f. 48, copy assignment, 16C (*77*).

c. Miscellaneous. MS Douce 280: bk. of treatises, 17C, incl. (f. 115) list of artificers and their addresses in the city. MS Add. c. 94: inventories, mid 16C, described in HMC (2) *Second Report, Appendix*, 101–2 (Ely House in *20*).

d. Plans. Gough Maps 21, f. 28: survey of houses, 1670 (*53*). Ibid, f. 41^v: elevation of Newgate, ? pre-Fire. Gough Drawings a. 4, f. 41: plans of property in city ditch. See also **a**, above, for plans attached to leases.

496. OXFORDSHIRE COUNTY RECORD OFFICE

a. Bly. I/iv/3: schedule of properties, 17C (incl. London). Clayton III/2: brief a/c of rents due to Brasenose College, 1669 (incl. London). Hey. X/

ix/2: will 1670 citing earlier settlement (Aldersgate Street, Old Jewry). Misc. B. I/1: will, 17C (Cheapside). Misc. Essex. IV/1: royal warrant for livery, 17C (*104, 111, 157*). PL. VIII/2, 4: deeds, 16C (*81, 124*).

497. SHEFFIELD CITY LIBRARIES, ARCHIVES DIVISION
Not visited.

a. Miscellaneous. B. D. 143: Chancery decree, 17C (*30*). MD 945: deed, 17C (*132*).

498. SHROPSHIRE RECORD OFFICE, SHREWSBURY
Not visited.

a. Ludford Park. 11/12: deed, 16C (*152*). 11/68: inquisition, 17C (*37, 51, 60*).

b. Other collections. BO/1/2/17–18: settlement, 16C (London). 81/288–9: will, 17C (*54*).

499. SOMERSET RECORD OFFICE, TAUNTON
Not visited.

a. Privately deposited documents (DD). POt 149 and BR/su 21: valuation and deed, 17C (*37, 51, 106*). PH 177, 205, 216, 219: deeds, 17C (*25*). AH 57/6: deed, 17C (*39, 78*). SE 38: inquisition, 17C (Aldersgate Street, Cripplegate).

500. STAFFORDSHIRE RECORD OFFICE AND WILLIAM SALT LIBRARY
The two collections are adjacent and administered jointly. Not visited. Unless otherwise stated, references are to collections in the record office.

a. Cavanagh-Mainwaring papers. D(W) 1743/3, T 384, T 387–96: deeds, leases, and papers, 16C–17C (*31, 76*, London).

b. Paget papers. D(W) 1734/1/4/144, 150: deeds, n.d. (*54*). D(W) 1734/1056–62: deeds, 13C, 14C, and 16C (*152*: a Burton Abbey property, see **123**).

c. Stafford papers. For the residence in London, see C. Rawcliffe, *The Staffords, Earls of Stafford and Dukes of Buckingham, 1394–1521* (1979), 60, 191. D 641/1/2/4, 5, 260–1: 14C–15C a/cs, incl. receipts of rents, payments to Sawtry Abbey (see **218**), repairs (Bread Street: probably *136*). William Salt Library, M. 558: valor, 15C (incl. London). D641/1/3/3: debts to London tradesmen, *c.* 1445.

d. Sutherland papers (incl. Leveson-Gower property). D 593/B/2/7/7, D 593/I/4/5/1–6, D 593/C/6/2–23/11: deeds and leases, 16C–19C (London). D 593/A/1/18/15: deed, 14C (*141*). D 593/B/11: assignment, 17C (*25*). D 593/A/1/30/14: deed, 16C (Queenhithe and Bread Street ward). D 593/A/1/34/6: rent receipt, 15C (probably *141*). D 868/1/67: list of Sir John Leveson's property, 16C. D 593/R/1/1/2–5/1: household a/cs, 17C–19C (incl. London).

e. Other collections. D 682/18: assignment, 17C (*149*). D(W) 1733/1–6: deed, 16C (*81*).

501. SUFFOLK RECORD OFFICE, BURY ST. EDMUNDS
Not visited.

a. 449/2/727–39: deeds and leases, 14C–16C (*4, 51, 89, 111, 138, 155*). 1341/2/27–8: deeds, 16C–17C (*124, 144*). 1674/7: deed, 17C (*14, 58*).

502. SUFFOLK RECORD OFFICE, IPSWICH
Not visited.

a. Barne collection. HA 53: incl. deeds, 16C–17C (Fleet Street, Ludgate Hill).

b. Saumarez collection. HA 93: deeds, 14C–17C (various parts of London, described in a slip catalogue).

c. Vernon-Wentworth collection. HA 34: 50/21/12.1–3: deeds, 16C–17C (*81, 124, 152*).

d. Other collections. S1/1/22.12: deed, 17C (Aldersgate Street). S1/14/7.2: final concord, 17C (*64, 148*). HA 24: 50/19/1.3: lease, 17C (Cursitors' Alley). HA 30: 50/22/1.32: deeds, 17C (London).

503. SURREY RECORD OFFICE, GUILDFORD MUNIMENT ROOM

a. Loseley MSS (LM). There is a detailed list of the records, which incl.: deeds, 14C–15C (*62*); deeds and leases, 16C–17C (*25, 43, 45, 62,* Ludgate, London); papers, 16C (*25,* Whitefriars precinct); receipts, 16C (*25, 71*); rentals and a/cs, 16C (*18, 25*); wills, 15C–17C (parishioners of *25, 32, 157*); lay and ecclesiastical subsidy lists, 16C. For the other part of the Loseley collection, see **528.** For the whole collection see HMC (6) *Seventh Report.*

b. Onslow MSS (97). Detailed list comp. 1817: deeds, 17C, lost since 1817 (*48, 158*); surviving deeds, 17C (*20, 54, 85, 88, 138, 152*).

c. Other collections. 6/1/9, 10, 28 (1), 29: deeds, 16C (*93, 104, 123,* Aldersgate). 6/2/85–7: deeds, 17C (*93*). 20/2/15: schedule of deeds, 17C (Nicholas Lane: probably *134*). 21/3/4: deed, 16C (*158*). 101/1/15, 51, 58, 63, 83: deeds and particulars, 17C (*19, 42, 45, 78, 155*). 101/2/6 (2): deed, 15C (*159*).

d. Lists 28: ref. to 16C deed formerly (1950) in possession of H. M. Philipson-Stow (*19, 104, 152, 156*).

504. SURREY RECORD OFFICE, KINGSTON UPON THAMES

a. Lee Steere. 43/58/285–98, 43/50/1–4: deeds, etc. 1647–1716 (*18*).

b. Leveson-Gower. 2186/30/25–32, 63, 72: deeds, rental, etc., 1550–1637 (*15, 62, 81, 155*).

c. Other collections. 26/13/2: 18C notebk. with ref. to title and deeds from *c.* 1616 (St. Clement's Lane).

505. EAST SUSSEX RECORD OFFICE, LEWES
Not visited.

a. Danny Archives. See *The Danny Archives: a Catalogue*, ed. J. A. Wooldridge (1966), 99–102, 116–17: deeds, leases, wills, 16C–17C (*45, 54*).

b. Frewen Archives. See *A Catalogue of the Frewen Archives*, ed. H. M. Warne (1972), p. 12, nos. 491–518: deeds, 16C–17C (London).

c. Glynde Place Archives. See *Catalogue of the Glynde Place Archives*, ed. R. F. Dell (1964), pp. 131–2, MSS 1342–5: deeds, 1329–1408 (*9, 19*, unspec.).

d. Sussex Archaeological Society Collections. CO 638–708: deeds, 16C–18C (*45, 78*). CO c/18, 93–104: deeds, 16C–17C (*45, 78, 138*, Gracechurch Street). G 21/18, 19: deeds, 16C (*92*, Lambeth Hill). M 750–2: deeds, 17C (*85*). OR 327: assessment, 17C (Candlewick Ward). RF 12/ 31, 34–6: deeds, 17C (*46, 54*). A 220, 279: deeds, 17C (*155*). B 805: deeds, 17C (*152*).

506. WEST SUSSEX RECORD OFFICE, CHICHESTER
See also **139–40** and **434**.

a. Goodwood MSS. E 304: 17C deed (*42*); see *The Goodwood Estate Archives* i, ed. F. W. Steer and J. E. A. Venables (1970), 45.

b. West Dean MSS. 16C and 17C deeds (*20, 53, 71, 78, 104, 134, 148, 152*); see K. J. Wallace, 'A Calendar of part of the West Dean Estate Collection' (submitted in part requirement for University of London Diploma in Archive Administration, 1966).

c. Wiston MSS. 16C and 17C deeds (*12*; also refs. to *10, 62*, Tower Street); see *The Wiston Archives: a catalogue*, ed. J. M. L. Booker (1975).

507. WARWICK COUNTY RECORD OFFICE
Not visited.

a. Miscellaneous. CR 26: deeds, 16C–19C (London). CR 114/1: deed, not dated in list (London). CR 162: deeds, 17C–18C (London). CR 764: deeds, 16C–18C (*68*, Gracechurch Street).

508. WILTSHIRE RECORD OFFICE, TROWBRIDGE
See also **216–17**.

a. Archive of earl of Radnor. 490/71: deeds, 16C–18C (*54*, Whitefriars). 490/558–62: deeds, 16C–17C, and a plan, 17C (Whitefriars). 490/627: deed, 16C (*152*).

b. Other collections. 56/9: deed, 17C (*36*). 283/159: lease, 17C (*63*). 515/ 93: lease, 17C (New Fish Street). 753/1: commonplace bk. incl. copy deeds, 16C–17C (Fetter Lane). 332/207: deeds, 17C (*45*). 490/63/3: deed, 17C (*152*).

509. York, City Archives Department
Not visited.

a. A 14C quitclaim (*63*) is entered in the city's memorandum book: *York Memorandum Book* iii, ed. J. W. Percy (Surtees Society 186, 1969), p. 19. There may be similar entries in unpublished records, but there are no index refs. to them.

510. Yorkshire Archaeological Society, Leeds
Administered from the West Yorkshire Record Office.

a. Papers of duke of Leeds. DD5/9 (Box 3, in process of being listed): incl. deeds, 16C–17C (*37, 38, 39, 51, 87, 90, 93, 98, 125, 126, 150*).

b. Akeroid/Thomlinson papers. MS 149: incl. deeds, 17C (*116*).

511. Aberystwyth, National Library of Wales
Not visited.

a. Deeds and leases. Badminton Deeds and Documents (permission needed to consult), 1192–3: deeds, 15C (*71*). Chirk Castle MSS and Documents (Group F), 273, 1053, 1666, 5542: deeds and leases, 16C–17C (*18, 38, 141*). Downing Deeds, 70: will, 16C (*152*). Llangibby Castle Deeds and Documents, B1848, C873: letters patent, 16C (*62*), and lawsuit 17C (*53*). A. R. Llewellin-Taylour Deeds and Documents, 78–9, 81: deeds, 16C (*32, 46*). Milborne Papers and Documents, 2078, 2083: lease and will, 17C (*18, 62*). Wynnstay Deeds and Documents, L112: deed, 17C (*51*).

b. Other material. Chirk Castle MSS and Documents (Group F), 1253: assessment list of subscribers to Welsh expedition, 1643–4 (numerous London parishes). *Calendar of Wynn (of Gwydir) papers 1515–1690 in National Library of Wales and elsewhere* (1926): principally letters incl. many refs. to business and localities in the city.

512. Clwyd Record Office, Hawarden
Not visited.

a. Trevor-Roper muniments. D/PT/694–5: deeds, 17C (*123*). D/PT/696–725: deeds, 14C–18C (*26, 30*). D/PT/726: deed, 15C (*11*).

b. Other collections. D/E/2262: deed, 17C ('Lady Lane', perhaps for Lad Lane). D/E/2198–211: deeds, 16C–18C (incl. Mark Lane, Thames Street, and perhaps also Blackfriars and Queen Street).

513. Dyfed Archives: Pembrokeshire Record Office,
Haverfordwest
Not visited.

a. Miscellaneous. D/LP/658: deed, 17C (*44*).

514. EDINBURGH, NATIONAL LIBRARY OF SCOTLAND
Not visited.

a. Ch. 1245–6 (Neilson collection): 2 deeds, 17C (*23, 105*); noted in *Catalogue of MSS acquired since 1925* (1938–82), vol. 2. Ch. 5771: inspeximus, 1539, concerning lands of St. Paul's; noted in *Catalogue*, vol. 4.

515. EDINBURGH, SCOTTISH RECORD OFFICE
Not visited. See 'Material in Scottish RO relating to London' (typescript list, 1981; for exhibition purposes, not exhaustive). The following references are taken from this list.

a. GD 18 (Clerk of Penicuik muniments): incl. letters and papers, *c*. 1630–70, to and from John Clerk, merchant, in London.

b. RH 15/22/10 (Register House Series, misc. papers): household bk. of Dame Barbara Cob, York and London, 1662–99.

c. RH 9/6/11 (Register House Series, bills and legal): indenture, 1627, ? concerning London property.

d. Wills: references to London/Londoners, taken from Scottish Rec. Soc. *Indexes to Registers of testaments in General Register House*, are noted in 'Material . . . relating to London', 55–6. Some of these may be Westminster; the only specific locality mentioned is Blackfriars.

516. EDINBURGH UNIVERSITY LIBRARY, DEPARTMENT OF MANUSCRIPTS
Not visited. See HMC (72) *Laing MSS . . . in the University of Edinburgh* i, p. 156: 17C deed (*54*).

517. PUBLIC RECORD OFFICE OF NORTHERN IRELAND, BELFAST
Not visited.

a. Ker family papers. D. 892, B, C, D: deeds and leases, 17C (*94, 145, 156*).

b. D. 1556/20: deeds, survey, a/cs, 17C (New Fish Street).

COLLECTIONS IN THE
UNITED STATES OF AMERICA

Several American collections contain London material, principally miscellaneous items of 16C and 17C date. We have not visited the collections, and the following entries are based on: *Library of Congress Catalogs: National Union Catalog of Manuscript Collections* (1959 onwards); S. De Ricci with W. J. Wilson, *Census of Medieval and Renaissance Manuscripts in the United States and Canada* (3 vols., New York, 1935–40), with a *Supplement* by C. V. Faye and W. H. Bond (New York, 1962); notes compiled by Dr. Caroline M. Barron in the U.S.A. during 1981.

The entries are arranged alphabetically by place.

518. CAMBRIDGE, HARVARD LAW SCHOOL LIBRARY
Laugdell Hall, Cambridge, MA 02138.

a. Deeds etc. 3.345.7: deed, 14C (*108*). 2.394.xii: deeds, 14C (*53, 108*). 3.462.11: deed, 15C (*112*). 8.457: deed, 15C (*144*). 2.418.3: deed, 15C (*157*). 728/4.590: deed, 16C (*54*). 6.629: lease, 17C (*71*). Misc. doc. 1.656: recovery, 17C (*156*).

519. CHARLOTTESVILLE, UNIVERSITY OF VIRGINIA LIBRARY
Manuscripts Department, University of Virginia Library, Charlottesville, VA 22901.

a. Hench Collection. 6435a, no. 7: deed, 15C (*4*). 6435a, no. 16: 17C copy of 16C letters patent (*43, 127*, Charterhouse, East Smithfield).

520. CHICAGO, UNIVERSITY OF CHICAGO LIBRARY
Chicago, IL 60637. The following items are all from the collection of Bacon papers, and the reference numbers should be cited with the preface BACON. Photocopies of these items are available for consultation at the Social and Economic Study of Medieval London, c/o Museum of London.

a. Deeds etc. (16C, unless otherwise stated). 2435: copy deed (*23*). 2436: agreement on purchase price (*45*). 2599: sale (*62*). 2451: sale (*123*). 2452 and 2463–4: deeds (*149*). 2688: agreement, 17C (probably West Smithfield).

b. Rentals etc. (all 16C). 881: rental (*14, 43, 62, 76, 83, 103, 123, 144, 149*, Bishopsgate Street, Paternoster Row, Seething Lane). 884: rental (*42*). 883: particulars for grant (*14, 20, 43, 45, 49, 62, 74, 83, 89, 93, 98, 103, 104, 116, 128, 135, 144, 149, 151, 152, 159*).

c. Receipts for purchase money (all 16C): 3237 (*64*, Paternoster Row); 3245–6 (London, probably *45*); 3431 (Foster Lane).

d. Receipts for rent (all 16C): 3070, 3214, 3260, and 3262 (*53*, Breges Quay); 3340, 3348, 3356, and 3363 (*92*); 3233 (West Smithfield, but includes wharves); 3297, 3442, 3449, 3453, and 3640 (Holborn).

521. NEW HAVEN, YALE UNIVERSITY, BEINECKE RARE BOOK AND MANU-SCRIPT LIBRARY
Wall and High Streets, New Haven, CT 06520.

a. Osborn Collection, Box 50, no. 11: deeds, 16C (*83*).

522. NEW YORK, PIERPONT MORGAN LIBRARY
29 East 36th Street, New York, NY 10016.

a. RE, Box 1, no. 55: deed, 16C, concerning endowment of chapel in church of *37*. RE, Mary I: incl. deed, 16C (London). RE, Whittington: deed, 14C (London).

523. NEW YORK UNIVERSITY LAW SCHOOL
New York University Libraries, Washington Square South, New York, NY 10012.

a. Frederick Brown Collection: incl. deeds, 16C (*60, 141*).

524. PHILADELPHIA, BIDDLE LAW LIBRARY
University of Pennsylvania Libraries, 3420 Walnut Street, Philadelphia, PA 19104.

a. Document no. 04: deed, 16C (*32*). Doc. no. 08: deed, 16C (*155*).

525. PHILADELPHIA, FREE LIBRARY
Logan Square, Philadelphia, PA 19103.

a. J. F. Lewis Collection, English Documents: Folder 4 (doc. 1) acknow-ledgement of debt to a mercer, 14C; Folder 5 (no doc. number), deed, 15C (*46*).

526. PRINCETON UNIVERSITY LIBRARY
Harvey S. Firestone Memorial Library, Princeton, NJ 08540.

a. Deed Collection of W. T. Scheilde, Box 209, no. 7140 (formerly Phillipps MS 31191): deed, 16C (*108*).

527. SAN MARINO, HENRY E. HUNTINGTON LIBRARY
1151 Oxford Road, San Marino, CA 91108.

a. Hastings Manuscripts. Deeds and leases, 14C–15C (*32, 38, 63, 118, 152*). Some items are briefly mentioned in *The Huntington Library Bulletin* 5 (1934), 23; for a fuller description of the collection in its former location, see HMC (*78*) *Mr. Reginald Rawdon Hastings*, 212–14.

528. WASHINGTON, FOLGER SHAKESPEARE LIBRARY
201, East Capitol Street, Washington, DC 20003.

a. Loseley Collection: MSS concerning the Office of Revels and the Blackfriars area, incl. deeds, leases, a/cs, rentals, receipts, lists of inhabitants, and a plan, 16C and early 17C (*25*). For a list, see NRA 8125; there is a microfilm of the MSS in BL (M/437). For the other part of the Loseley Collection, see **503**.

b. Other items. 93.4–5: deeds, 16C–17C (London). 432.1: deed, 16C (Chancery Lane). 449.1: deed, 17C (*25*). 484.2: deed, 16C (*60*). 495.3: deed, 16C (*49* or St. Clement Danes). 495.4: deed, 16C (*148*). 651.7: deed, 16C (*138*). 663.1: rent receipt, 16C (St. Mary Spital). 940.3: deed, 17C (*23*). 1036.1: deed, 17C (near St. Paul's). 1096.2: deed, 16C (Hart Street). 1291.1: inventory, 17C (London). 1742.1: deed, 16C (*43*). 4693.7: deed and inventory, 17C (Aldermanbury). There is probably other London material later than 1600 and therefore not included in De Ricci's *Census*.

528A. WASHINGTON, LIBRARY OF CONGRESS MANUSCRIPT DIVISION
Washington, DC 20540.

a. Wakefield Collection, Box 44: deeds, 17C (Cheapside); see N. W. Alcock, 'English Archives at the Library of Congress', *Archives* 16 (1984), 273–7.

WILLS AND INVENTORIES

529. WILLS AND TESTAMENTARY RECORDS
Londoners' wills could be enrolled or registered in one or more of several courts, the choice being determined principally by the nature and extent of the testator's estate and by his place of residence. Disposition of freehold estates was normal in wills enrolled in the Husting Court and fairly frequent in PCC wills; other PCC wills, and wills registered in other courts, usually concern personal estate, sometimes including leasehold interests. See A. J. Camp, *Wills and their whereabouts* (1974) for an introduction to testamentary records and fuller lists of records, calendars, and indexes. Although the jurisdictions of the London courts and peculiars (**d-j**) usually dictated where the wills of persons living in particular parishes were registered, such wills may also contain references to property in other areas. For wills registered in Scotland, see **515**.

In the following descriptions, reference is made to printed indexes etc.; the other indexes noted are MS or TS, available in the record office concerned.

a. City of London Court of Husting (CLRO). Enrolled wills (or parts of wills dealing with real property), principally of citizens, from 1258; calendared and indexed in *Calendar of wills proved and enrolled in the Court of Husting, London, 1258–1688*, ed. R. R. Sharpe (1889–90); the calendar entries sometimes omit properties when many are mentioned in a will. See **2a**.

b. Prerogative Court of Canterbury (PRO). Registers from 1393, original wills from late 15C; indexed by name and places mentioned: *Index of wills proved in the Prerogative Court of Canterbury* (British Rec. Soc. Index Library, vols. 10, 11, 18, 25, 43, 44, 54, 61, 67). During vacancies of the see of Canterbury some wills were proved in the court of the prior of Christ Church, Canterbury, and subsequently of the dean and chapter (at Canterbury); indexed 1278–1559 in C. E. Woodruff, *Sede vacante wills* (Kent Archaeological Society Records Branch 3, 1914).

c. Consistory Court of London (GLRO). Registers from 1492, original wills from 1508; first register ('Palmer', 1492–1520) and some wills printed as *London Consistory Court wills 1492–1547*, ed. I. Darlington (LRS 3, 1967). Name indexes to later registers and wills.

d. Archdeaconry of London Court (GL). Registers from 1393, original wills from 1524; calendars; printed indexes to 1649: *Index to testamentary records in the Archdeaconry Court of London* (British Rec. Soc. Index Library, vol. 89).

219

e. Commissary Court of London, London division (GL). Registers from 1374, original wills from 1523; calendars; printed indexes to 1570: *Index to testamentary records in the Commissary Court of London* (British Rec. Soc. Index Library, vols. 82, 86). Name and place index to 1629; name index to 1669.

f. Court of Arches (Lambeth). Covers deanery of Arches (*5, 9, 51, 53, 73, 83, 100, 103, 104, 125, 126, 145, 159*).Original wills from 1620, registers from 1684; place and name index.

g. Peculiar of dean and chapter of St. Paul's (GL). Covers part of *20* and *59, 62, 63, 64*. Registers from 1534, original wills from 1660; name index.

h. Royal peculiar of dean and chapter of Westminster (Westminster City Library Archives Department, 160 Buckingham Palace Road, London SW1). Covers precinct of St. Martin le Grand and parts of *23, 84*. Registers from 1504, original wills from 1591; name index.

j. Peculiar and exempt jurisdiction of St. Peter *ad Vincula* in the Tower of London (*147*): Bodl, MS Rawl. C 121 is MS register of probates, 1586–1614, 1660–5.

k. A few wills, including some London wills, were registered in episcopal and archiepiscopal registers: see Camp, *Wills*, 86, 90–1; J. H. Bloom, 'List of wills and administrations registered in episcopal registers of the bishop of London, 1313–1548' (TS, 1927), available in GL; *Index to wills recorded in the archiepiscopal registers at Lambeth Palace* (1919), reprinted from *The Genealogist*, n.s. 34–5.

530. INVENTORIES
Inventories of personal estate are found principally in the records of courts granting probate, and are usually associated with surviving or registered wills proved in that court (see **529**); indexing is usually by name of testator only. CLRO, Mayor's Court original bills contain numerous schedules of goods, 16C to 18C (**4**); Court of Orphans records also include household and stock inventories, 17C and later (**7**). There are also stray inventories in PRO and GL (see **f, g**, below) and in other record offices (treated under individual headings).

a. PRO, Prerogative Court of Canterbury. PROB 2/1–824: inventories, from 1417; name index, parish not usually given. PROB 5: original paper inventories, from 1660, mostly related to wills in PROB 11 (registers); name index.

b. GLRO, Consistory Court of London. Few if any probate inventories for 16C/17C; name index.

c. GL, Archdeaconry Court of London. MS 9898: inventories, 1662–1705 (boxes 1–2 cover to 1666), arranged alphabetically by year; name index.

d. GL, Commissary Court of London. MS 9174: inventories and declarations, 1660–1741 (boxes 1–17 cover to 1666; a few earlier inventories exhibited 1660 and later), arranged alphabetically by year and month;

name index, including parish ref. if given in original. MS 9174A/1: another box of inventories, 1664–6, arranged alphabetically, not indexed.

e. GL, Dean and Chapter of St. Paul's. MS 19504: inventories, 1660–1725, in annual bundles; not indexed at present.

f. PRO, other inventories. E154: odd inventories, incl. some probate, 13C to 18C, incl. several for Londoners; listed by name, usually without location: see search room list. Places named are: *34* (E154/3/13); *152* (6/35); Cripplegate (1/12); Fetter Lane (7/12); St. Nicholas Lane (3/40); Soper Lane (1/18a); Wood Street (3/37).

g. GL, other inventories. Loose inventories (probably some probate) and inventories in archives (livery company records, parish records, etc.) kept in GL all indexed in class card catalogue L57.5.

ADDENDA

531. LONDON BOROUGH LIBRARIES
The archives departments of several boroughs hold large, and sometimes uncatalogued, collections of deeds, etc. for the Greater London area. It was possible to identify the following relevant material.

a. Barnet Public Libraries, Local History Library: Box 9131 incl. 17C schedule of 16C–17C deeds (*15, 43, 46, 64, 78, 92, 104, 152*).

b. Lambeth Archives Department, Minet Library. Surrey Deeds (calendared, but imperfectly indexed), 6236, 12933: 17C deeds (*62*, Seething Lane).

c. Lewisham Archives and Local History Department: A81/66, 7/2 Box B incl. 17C lease (Thames Street).

532. PORT OF LONDON AUTHORITY
PLA Library and Archives, Cannon Workshops, West India Dock, London E14. The archive incl. 17C deeds and papers (*43*, East Smithfield) and a 19C copy of a 17C drawn survey (East Smithfield).

533. LAUNCESTON, CORNWALL, PRIORY OF ST. STEPHEN
Fd. 1127; diss. 1539.

a. Lambeth, MS 719 (Davis, no. 542); 15C cartulary; (f. 99v) 12C deed (*148, gildhalla tannorum*).

TOPOGRAPHICAL INDEX

This index covers the locations of properties to which the records described in the survey refer. Where possible a location is defined as the parish in which the property lay; only where this is not possible are street or other place-names used (see above, p. xv). References denote the **bold** entry numbers in the survey; a locality may occur more than once in a single entry, but this is not noted in the index. For the coverage of the survey, which includes some parishes partly or wholly outside the city, see pp. xii–xiii, above.

The index is in three parts: i., references to sources covering the whole of the city; ii., references to properties in particular parishes (identified by name, with principal variants, and by the *italic* code numbers listed on pp. xviii–xix, above); iii., references to properties in the city identified in the sources not by parish but by street- or other place-names, incorporating the few references to properties outside the city.

Parish names are arranged alphabetically by dedication (ignoring 'Saint', but observing 'All' and 'Holy') and principal surname (see p. xvii), ignoring all prefixes (at, de, in, le, etc.), with cross-references to the main index entry from alternative surname forms. Where a parish had more than one dedication, either at one time or successively, there are index entries for each dedication with references to the sources in which it occurs, and cross-references to the index entries for other dedications of the same church. The index also includes the following rare, possibly erroneous, parish or church names: St. Albert, St. Anthony, St. Peter *Reineri*, St. Petronilla in Fleet Street, St. Sexburga. Several ambiguous names or dedications are deal with by cross-references.

In the parish index, the phrase 'rights in church' denotes references in the text which specifically concern rights in that church; if the sources which the text describes relate both to rights in the church and to other property in the same parish, without always making a clear distinction, then there will be no specific reference in the text, or hence in the index, to the former.

Parish surnames not covered in the index are noted and explained in Harben, where identifications for street- and locality-names are also given.

i. ALL LOCALITIES WITHIN LONDON

Sources covering all or many parishes and places in London, for many of which indexes are available elsewhere: 1–12, 436–8, 443–6, 448–9, 452, 455, 461–2, 511, 529–30; ecclesiastical matters, all churches, 462; for surveys of ecclesiastical property in 1392 and 1535, *see* p. 37

Taxation and assessment lists covering all or specific parts of London: 12, 275–381 (see introduction to this section), 416, 431, 452–3, 462, 484, 492, 503, 511, 528

Tradesmen, lists of (usually practitioners of one particular trade, in many localities): 23–5, 38, 51, 65–6, 495c

ii. CITY PARISHES

St. — in Jewry (St. Lawrence or St. Olave), 441 (under Jewry)

St. Agnes (*1*), 70–1, 80, 83, 88, 115, 213, 247–51, 271, 429, 441; rights in church, 248; *identical with* St. Anne & St. Agnes, St. Anne Aldersgate, *qq.v.*

St. Alban Wood Street (*2*), 13–14, 22, 26, 32, 38–9, 45, 48, 50, 53–4, 58, 70, 73–4, 79–81, 87, 89, 100, 103, 108, 149, 177, 188, 203, 213, 225, 230, 247–51, 254, 275, 284, 369, 382, 406, 438, 441, 447, 454, 458–60, 485, 492; rights in church, 248; *see also* St. Albert

St. Albert (uncertain, probably identical with St. Alban), 103, 373

All Hallows unspecified (*3*), 247–9, 460, 476

All Hallows Barking, by the Tower (*4*), 1, 13–14, 17, 21, 26, 28, 32, 47–8, 61, 70–1, 73–4, 79, 87, 89, 93, 96, 100–101, 103–4, 115, 165, 203, 226, 241, 247–51, 254, 276, 307, 309, 331, 347, 382, 384, 392, 412, 422, 437–8, 441, 447, 449, 457, 459–60, 464, 467, 479–80, 482, 485, 492–3, 501, 519; rights in church, 108, 128, 210; *identical with* Berkyng-church, *q.v.*, St. Mary de Berkyng-cherch; *see also* All Hallows unspec., St. Mary unspec.

All Hallows Bread Street, Watling Street (*5*), 26, 31, 38, 41, 47–8, 59, 61, 68, 70–1, 73–4, 79–80, 85, 87, 89, 100, 103, 108, 127–130, 133, 165, 171, 186, 248–51, 255, 277, 305, 342, 391, 400, 406, 422, 437, 441, 449, 457, 459–60, 465, 475; rights in church, 128–9, 131–2; *see also* All Hallows unspec., Bread Street parish

All Hallows on the Cellars, *see* All Hallows the Less

All Hallows Colemanchurch (*6*), 79, 83, 115, 225, 247, 441; rights in church, 83; *identical with* Colemanchurch, St. Katharine Coleman, *qq.v; see also* All Hallows unspec.

All Hallows Cornhill (*7*), 441; *probably identical with* All Hallows Grace-church, *q.v.; see also* All Hallows unspec.

All Hallows Fenchurch (*8*), 79–80, 89, 103, 111, 115, 300, 437, 441, 466; rights in church, 79; *identical with* St. Gabriel Fenchurch, St. Mary Fenchurch, St. Mary & St. Gabriel Fenchurch, *qq.v.; see also* All Hallows unspec.

All Hallows *ad fenum, see* All Hallows the Great

All Hallows Gracechurch, Lombard Street (*9*), 14, 17, 32, 34, 39, 41, 47–8, 57, 61, 66, 70–1, 73, 79–80, 87, 90, 103–4, 115, 127–32, 152, 203, 210, 225, 278, 294, 297, 306, 311, 317, 320, 356, 376, 382, 384, 386, 402, 404, 437, 441, 449, 459, 464, 491, 505; rights in church, 128–9, 131–2; *probably identical with* All Hallows Cornhill, *q.v.; see also* All Hallows unspec., Gracechurch parish

All Hallows the Great, *ad fenum*, at the Hay Wharf, in the Ropery, earlier *Seman-nescyrce* (*10*), 6, 13–14, 26, 29, 32, 38, 41, 44, 47–8, 56, 61, 70–1, 73–4, 79–81, 84, 89–91, 93, 96, 100, 103–4, 112, 115, 137, 144, 165, 171, 207, 213, 225, 234, 249, 254, 257, 279, 289, 291, 302, 309, 320, 328, 335–6, 342, 349, 357, 437–8, 441–2, 445, 447, 449, 459–60, 482, 485, 506; rights in church, 234; *see also* All Hallows unspec., 'Other localities' s.n. '*Germani, vicus*'

All Hallows Honey Lane (*11*), 13–14, 17, 32, 38–9, 47, 61, 70–1, 79–81, 89–90, 97, 103–5, 186, 196, 206, 225–6, 247, 258, 280, 306, 348, 382, 441, 454, 459–60, 479, 512; *see also* All Hallows unspec.

All Hallows the Less, on the Cellars, on the Solars (*12*), 13–14, 26, 29, 33, 47–8, 52, 66, 70, 85, 89–90, 100, 115, 149, 152–3, 225–6, 257, 265, 281, 305, 326, 328, 384, 436–8, 441, 447, 449, 459–60, 462, 464, 480, 506; *see also* All Hallows unspec., 'Other localities' s.n. 'Coldharbour'

All Hallows Lombard Street, *see* All Hallows Gracechurch

All Hallows London Wall, *see* All Hallows on the Wall

All Hallows in the Ropery, *see* All Hallows the Great

All Hallows on the Solars, *see* All Hallows the Less

All Hallows Staining (*13*), 13–14, 21, 24, 26, 28, 32, 34, 38, 43, 57, 70, 73, 79, 84, 100, 103, 115, 226, 255A, 282, 309, 320, 368, 378, 382, 437–8, 441, 447, 456, 459–60, 480; rights in church, 73, 431; *see also* All Hallows unspec., church of *Stanengah', Stanyngchurch*

All Hallows Thames Street, *identical with either* All Hallows the Great *or* All Hallows the Less, *qq.v.*

488, 491, 495, 503–4, 506, 511, 520, 531; rights in church, 71, 73

Gracechurch parish (All Hallows or St. Benet), 73

St. Gregory by St. Paul's (*63*), 17, 32, 47–8, 61, 70–6, 78–80, 87, 100, 165, 200–201, 226, 305, 317, 419, 441, 447, 449, 459–60, 462, 465, 480, 485, 492, 495, 508–9, 527; rights in church, 71, 73

St. Helen Bishopsgate (*64*), 4, 15, 24, 32, 41, 45, 47–8, 56, 61, 70–1, 73, 81, 111, 178, 318, 382, 412, 425, 431, 437–8, 441, 447, 454, 457, 459–60, 482–3, 495, 502, 520, 531; rights in church, 71, 73; *see also* 'Other localities' s.n. 'Crosby Hall'

Holy Innocents (Middx.), *see under* 'Other localities'

Holy Trinity unspecified (*65*), 73, 103, 247, 437, 441, 449

Holy Trinity Aldgate (*66*; absorbed by St. Katharine Cree parish or precinct of Holy Trinity Priory), 73, 79, 124, 154, 247, 437, 441; *see also* Holy Trinity unspec.

Holy Trinity the Less (*67*), 13, 48–9, 61, 66, 70–1, 73, 79–80, 100, 115, 129, 131, 186, 188, 213, 225, 247–51, 254, 261, 319–20, 322, 327, 371, 379, 404, 407, 410, 437–8, 440–1, 447, 454, 459–60, 465, 480, 482; rights in church, 129, 131–2; *see also* Holy Trinity unspec., 'Other localities' s.n. 'Ormond's Inn'

Holy Trinity Minories (*68*; in Middx.; created after the Dissolution from the Minoresses' precinct), 32, 48, 96, 111, 278, 286, 441, 468, 507; *see also* Holy Trinity unspec.

St. James unspecified (*69*), 441

St. James Duke's Place (*70*; created 17C from former precinct of Holy Trinity Priory), 13, 447, 459–60; *see also* St. James unspec.

St. James Garlickhithe, Vintry (*71*), 14, 21, 26, 28, 32–3, 47–8, 51, 66, 70, 73–4, 79–80, 85, 88–9, 103, 115, 225, 247–8, 250–1, 254, 258, 280, 282, 285, 320, 371, 382, 392, 437–8, 441, 447, 449, 457, 459–60, 479–80, 503, 506, 511, 518; rights in church, 248–9, 253; *see also* St. James unspec.

St. James in the Wall, *see under* 'Other localities'

St. John unspecified (*72*), 14, 71

St. John the Baptist, *see* St. John Walbrook, St. John Zachary

St. John the Evangelist, Watling Street (*73*), 14, 31, 59, 70–5, 78, 88, 127–9,

131–2, 247–51, 293, 318, 321, 404, 449, 459, 480; rights in church, 128–9, 131–2; *identical with* St. Werburga, *q.v.; see also* St. John unspec.

St. John (the Baptist) Walbrook (*74*), 13–14, 19, 26, 31–33, 38, 41, 47–8, 61, 63, 66, 70–6, 79, 81, 85, 88–9, 96, 100, 103, 115, 165, 171, 174, 189, 211, 225–6, 240, 247–51, 254, 263, 300, 320, 322, 344, 355, 378, 382, 416, 437–8, 441, 459–60, 476, 478, 480, 482, 484, 492, 520; rights in church, 71, 73; *see also* St. John unspec.

St. John (the Baptist) Zachary (*75*), 14, 38, 61, 67, 70–6, 79–80, 88–9, 100, 102–3, 115, 165, 171, 186, 194, 210–11, 213, 226, 240, 242, 247–51, 260, 300, 305, 323, 382, 404, 434, 441, 447, 449, 468, 485; rights in church, 71, 73; *see also* St. John unspec.

St. Katharine unspecified (*76*), 441, 500, 520

St. Katharine Christ Church, *see* St. Katharine Cree

St. Katharine Coleman (*77*), 13, 24, 26, 29, 34, 36, 66, 70, 72–3, 75, 79–80, 89, 166, 247–51, 254, 301, 324, 369, 376, 378, 401, 412, 437–8, 441, 447, 456, 459–60, 476, 478, 492, 495; *identical with* All Hallows Colemanchurch, Colemanchurch, *qq.v.; see also* St. Katharine unspec.

St. Katharine Cree, Christ Church (*78*), 6, 13–14, 17, 21, 24, 26, 32, 34, 41, 48, 58, 61, 65–6, 70–1, 79, 124, 149, 154, 166, 177, 226, 249, 301, 304, 325, 382, 390, 401, 412, 437–9, 441, 449, 454, 459–60, 463, 476, 482, 484, 499, 503, 505–6, 531; rights in church, 79; *see also* St. Katharine unspec.

St. Katharine's Hospital by the Tower, *see under* 'Other localities'

St. Lawrence unspecified (*79*), 248–9, 437, 441, 495

St. Lawrence Candlewick Street, Pountney (*80*), 6, 13–14, 32, 34, 47–8, 61, 70–6, 79, 81, 85, 87–9, 100–101, 103, 115, 127–132, 145, 164, 186, 207, 225–6, 247–51, 257, 306, 326–7, 357, 369, 375, 382, 385, 437–8, 441, 447, 449, 459–60, 478, 480, 485, 492, 496; rights in church, 249, 253; *see also* St. Lawrence unspec.

St. Lawrence Jewry (*81*), 4, 13, 26, 32, 47, 61, 70–5, 79–81, 85, 89–91, 96, 100, 103–4, 108, 127–32, 165, 196, 247–51, 254, 258, 272, 306, 320, 327, 348, 359, 361–2, 369, 377, 382–4, 393, 395–7, 402, 404, 406, 437–8, 441, 445, 447,

229

iii. OTHER LOCALITIES

236

238

INDEX TO PROPERTY- AND
ARCHIVE-HOLDERS

This index provides a guide to the main headings of the survey (holders of property, and libraries and record offices with collections relating to London), arranged alphabetically by name or place. Several group- and subject-headings are also included. The index does not cover subheadings within entries, except for **265**, **383–4**, **416**, where the subheadings relate to different entities. It therefore does not include those private property holders whose present or former records are described in entries for libraries and record offices. Nor does it cover individual MSS and their locations. References denote the **bold** entry numbers in the survey.

Institutions, including religious houses, in London are indexed by name, other institutions by place, county record offices and libraries by name. The London entries cover references to groups of records, and the city's own records.

LONDON RECORD SOCIETY

The London Record Society was founded in December 1964 to publish transcripts, abstracts and lists of the primary sources for the history of London, and generally to stimulate interest in archives relating to London. Membership is open to any individual or institution; the annual subscription is £7 ($15) for individuals and £10 ($23) for institutions, which entitles a member to receive one copy of each volume published during the year and to attend and vote at meetings of the Society. Prospective members should apply to the Hon. Secretary, Miss Heather Creaton, c/o Institute of Historical Research, Senate House, London, WC1E 7HU.

The following volumes have already been published:
1. *London Possessory Assizes: a calendar*, edited by Helena M. Chew (1965)
2. *London Inhabitants within the Walls, 1695*, with an introduction by D. V. Glass (1966)
3. *London Consistory Court Wills, 1492–1547*, edited by Ida Darling-ton (1967)
4. *Scriveners' Company Common Paper, 1357–1628, with a continuation to 1678*, edited by Francis W. Steer (1968)
5. *London Radicalism, 1830–1843: a selection from the papers of Francis Place*, edited by D. J. Rowe (1970)
6. *The London Eyre of 1244*, edited by Helena M. Chew and Martin Weinbaum (1970)
7. *The Cartulary of Holy Trinity Aldgate*, edited by Gerald A. J. Hodgett (1971)
8. *The Port and Trade of Early Elizabethan London: documents*, edited by Brian Dietz (1972)
9. *The Spanish Company*, by Pauline Croft (1973)
10. *London Assize of Nuisance, 1301–1431: a calendar*, edited by Helena M. Chew and William Kellaway (1973)
11. *Two Calvinistic Methodist Chapels, 1743–1811: the London Tabernacle and Spa Fields Chapel*, edited by Edwin Welch (1975)
12. *The London Eyre of 1276*, edited by Martin Weinbaum (1976)
13. *The Church in London, 1375–1392*, edited by A. K. McHardy (1977)
14. *Committees for Repeal of the Test and Corporation Acts: Minutes, 1786–90 and 1827–8*, edited by Thomas W. Davis (1978)
15. *Joshua Johnson's Letterbook, 1771–4: letters from a merchant in London to his partners in Maryland*, edited by Jacob M. Price (1979)
16. *London and Middlesex Chantry Certificate, 1548*, edited by C. J. Kitching (1980)

All volumes are still in print; apply to Hon. Secretary. Price to individual members £7 ($15) each; to institutional members £10 ($23) each; and to non-members £12 ($28) each.